Popular Politics and Political Culture in Upper Canada, 1800–1850

In *Popular Politics and Political Culture in Upper Canada, 1800–1850* Carol Wilton shows us that ordinary Canadians were much more involved in the political process than previous accounts have lead us to believe. They demonstrated their interest in politics, and their commitment to a particular viewpoint, by active participation in the petitioning movements that were an important element of provincial political culture.

Wilton demonstrates that by the 1830s the political energies of Upper Canadians were far more likely to be channelled through petitioning movements than election campaigns. Petitioning movements, which were connected not only with public meetings but with demonstrations and parades, were also increasingly associated with political violence. The resulting assaults, riots, and effigy-burnings – prominent features of Tory governance – not only contributed to the striking political polarization of the population but also helped provoke the Rebellion of 1837.

Wilton provides new insights into the careers of leading figures, explores the developing ethnic and religious conflicts in the context of the petitioning movements, and illuminates the question of officially sponsored political violence. Through a thorough examination of primary resources, including a wide range of newspapers, Colonial Office records, published records of the Upper Canadian government, pamphlet literature, and private correspondence, Wilton demonstrates how the province's dissidents challenged established patterns of paternalism, subverted official notions of hierarchy, and promoted the development of an expanded public sphere in ways that had a lasting influence on the province's political culture.

CAROL WILTON has published widely in Upper Canadian and legal history and received the 1994 Riddell Award from the Ontario Historical Society for her article on the Durham Meetings.

Popular Politics and Political Culture in Upper Canada, 1800–1850

CAROL WILTON

McGill-Queen's University Press
Montreal & Kingston · London · Ithaca

ISBN 0-7735-2053-8 (cloth)
ISBN 0-7735-2054-6 (paper)

Legal deposit third quarter 2000
Bibliothèque nationale du Québec

Printed in Canada on acid-free paper

This book has been published with the help of a grant from the Humanities and Social Sciences Federation of Canada, using funds provided by the Social Sciences and Humanities Research Council of Canada.

McGill-Queen's University Press acknowledges the financial support of the Government of Canada through the Book Publishing Industry Development Program (BPIDP) for its publishing activities. It also acknowledges the support of the Canada Council for the Arts for its publishing program.

Canadian Cataloguing in Publication Data

Wilton, Carol
Popular politics and political culture in Upper Canada, 1800–1850
Includes bibliographical references and index.
ISBN 0-7735-2053-8 (bnd)
ISBN 0-7735-2054-6 (pbk)
1. Ontario – Politics and government – 19th century.
2. Political culture – Ontario – History – 19th century.
3. Political participation – Ontario – History – 19th century.
I. Title.
FC3071.2.W54 2000 320.9713'09'034
C00-900059-3 F1058.W54 2000

This book was typeset by Typo Litho Composition Inc. in 10/12 Baskerville.

For my daughter, Margaret

Contents

Acknowledgments ix

Abbreviations xi

Illustrations and maps xii

Introduction 3

1 Early Upper Canadian Petitioners, 1800–1831 21

2 The Petitioning Movement of 1831 55

3 The Expulsion Crisis and the Oppositionist Response 85

4 Pro-Government Popular Politics, 1832 115

5 Political Unions and Electoral Organization, 1832–36 144

6 Popular Politics and the Rebellion of 1837 in Upper Canada 168

7 The Durham Meetings and Popular Politics in Upper Canada 194

Conclusion 221

Appendices 235

Notes 245

Bibliography 291

Index 305

Acknowledgments

Popular politics has been a source of endless fascination to me since, as a second-year undergraduate, I was introduced to the subject in Professor John Beattie's course on eighteenth-century England at the University of Toronto. Since then, I have focused my interest on the relationship between popular politics and the emergence of party systems in the context of parliamentary government.

My doctoral work on political parties in Ontario in the 1840s suggested that there was an important story to be told about popular politics in the Upper Canadian period. The party organizers of the 1840s, it became clear, were working in the context of a province-wide political culture whose existence could not logically be explained simply as the product of infrequent general elections. Moreover, the deep political divisions within the province seemed to antedate the Rebellions of 1837. How had this political culture emerged, and what were the sources of the divisions?

My efforts to answer these questions have taken me far longer than I ever imagined. The subject, however, has sustained my interest through the production of three other books, innumerable life crises, and my return to school to study law.

Many institutions and individuals have contributed to the completion of this book. I am particularly grateful to the Canada Council for a generous Arts Grant in 1996 that allowed me to complete a first draft of the manuscript. In addition, this book has been published with the help of a grant from the Humanities and Social Sciences Federation of Canada, using funds provided by the Social Sciences and Humanities

Research Council of Canada. I am also grateful to Dean Ronald J. Daniels of the Faculty of Law, University of Toronto, who provided a grant to assist in the completion of the manuscript. The anonymous readers for the HSSFC and McGill-Queen's University Press provided extremely helpful comments. I would also like to thank the University of Toronto Press for allowing me to include, in chapter 7, material that appeared in the *Canadian Historical Review.*

My thanks are also due to the many archivists who assisted me over the years, including Patricia Kennedy at the National Archives, Leon Warmski at the Archives of Ontario, and Christine Mosser and the rest of the staff at the Baldwin Room, Toronto Reference Library. I would also like to thank the staff of the United Church Archives, the Thomas Fisher Rare Book Library, and the University of Toronto Archives. Christine Bourolias at the Ontario Archives, Catherine Elliot Shaw at the McIntosh Gallery, University of Western Ontario, and Dorothy Kealey at the Anglican Archdiocese of Toronto were especially helpful in locating photographs. My research assistants, Janice Boneham and David Olivier, ably and enthusiastically collected some of the materials for the book.

A number of individuals have provided timely advice on particular matters relating to popular politics, including Carl Benn of Fort York and Professor Nick Rogers of York University. I enjoyed a lively exchange of information on the subject of John Brown of Port Hope with Susan Lewthwaite, now of the Archives of the Law Society of Upper Canada. Both she and Philip Sworden were kind enough to read and comment on early drafts of two chapters of this book. I am also grateful to Professor Jim Phillips of the Faculty of Law, University of Toronto, for encouraging me to present my ideas to his legal history and early Canadian history seminars.

I would like to thank John Zucchi and Philip Cercone, both editors at McGill-Queen's University Press, for their assistance. Joanne Pisano has kept me posted on new developments, and Joan McGilvray has been unfailingly helpful in smoothing the production of the manuscript. Claude Lalumière has been an extremely helpful copy-editor.

The encouragement of many friends has sustained me during the writing of this manuscript. Heather MacDougall, Margaret Johnstone, and Nancy Iadeluca have been pillars of moral support. My thanks are also due to Ann Wilton and Brian Morgan, Margaret and Keith Pilley, Nancy Falconer and Lance McIntosh, Nancy Miles, Pat Grady, Trish Morley and Ben Forster, and Maria Rocha. Margaret Ann Fitzpatrick Hanly has helped me steer a steady course more often than she knows. My greatest debt is to my daughter, Margaret, for the pleasure of her company and for making me laugh.

Abbreviations

BC *British Colonist*
BG *Bytown Gazette*
BR *Brockville Recorder*
CA *Colonial Advocate*
C&A *Correspondent and Advocate*
CG *Christian Guardian*
CHR *Canadian Historical Review*
CO42 National Archives, Colonial Office
DCB *Dictionary of Canadian Biography*
HP Canadian Historical Association, *Historical Papers*
JCS *Journal of Canadian Studies*
JLUAC *Journals of the Legislative Assembly of Upper Canada*
KC *Kingston Chronicle*
NA National Archives
NC *Niagara Chronicle*
NG *Niagara Gleaner*
OA Ontario Archives
OH *Ontario History*
PACR *Public Archives of Canada, Report*
SCJ *St Catharine's Journal*
Sundries R.G. 5, Civil Secretary's Correspondence, Upper Canada Sundries
TRL Toronto Reference Library, Toronto Public Library, Baldwin Room

The Rival Candidates, 1828 (Toronto Reference Library (TRL)T14481)

Robert Gourlay in his seventies
(TRL J. Ross Robertson Collection T16969)

William Lyon Mackenzie
(Ontario Archives S2123)

Jesse Ketchum, photo probably taken in the 1860s
(TRL T13721)

Portrait of W.W. Baldwin by Theophile Hamel, ca 1850
(TRL J. Ross Robertson Collection T31037)

Egerton Ryerson, 1838
(TRL J. Ross Robertson Collection T16286)

John Strachan
(Anglican Church Diocese of Toronto P7565-122)

Portrait of the Most Reverend Alexander McDonell, 1823–24, oil on canvas by Martin Archer Shee (National Archives of Canada, Negative no. C-140071)

Portrait of Sir John Colborne, first Baron Seaton (1778–1863),
engraved by James Scott; published 1864
(TRL J. Ross Robertson Collection 14945)

Portrait of John Willson
(TRL T13836)

Sir Allan MacNab, by Theophile Hamel, 1853
(TRL T13738)

Colonel Thomas Talbot, *Portrait of Colonel Thomas Talbot*, nd, by James B. Wandesford (Collection of McIntosh Gallery, the University of Western Ontario, watercolour on card, 67.3 × 49.5 cm., gift of Judge Talbot MacBeth, 1941)

Sun Tavern, York (Toronto), 1830s (TRL J. Ross Robertson Collection T11086)

Red Lion Hotel, York (Toronto) (TRL T11064)

Court House, York (Toronto), 1827–53 (TRL J. Ross Robertson Collection T11810)

Government House, York (Toronto), 1815–60 (TRL T11867)

Sir Francis Bond Head, lieutenant-governor of Upper Canada. Detail from mezzotint engraved by Charles Turner in 1837 after a painting by Nelson Cook
(National Archives of Canada, Negative no. C-041467)

William Botsford Jarvis (left) with his sons in the 1860s (?)
(TRL T13717)

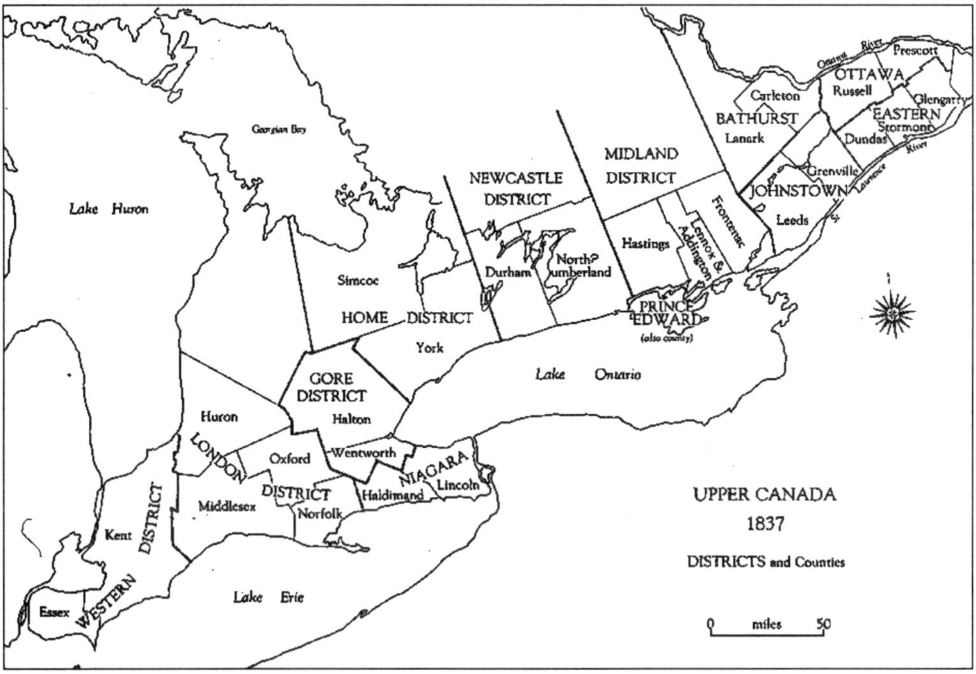

Map 1 Districts and Counties in Upper Canada, 1837
(Colin Read and Ronald J. Stagg, *The Rebellion of 1837 in Upper Canada*
[Canada: The Champlain Society jointly with Carleton University Press, 1985], xviii)

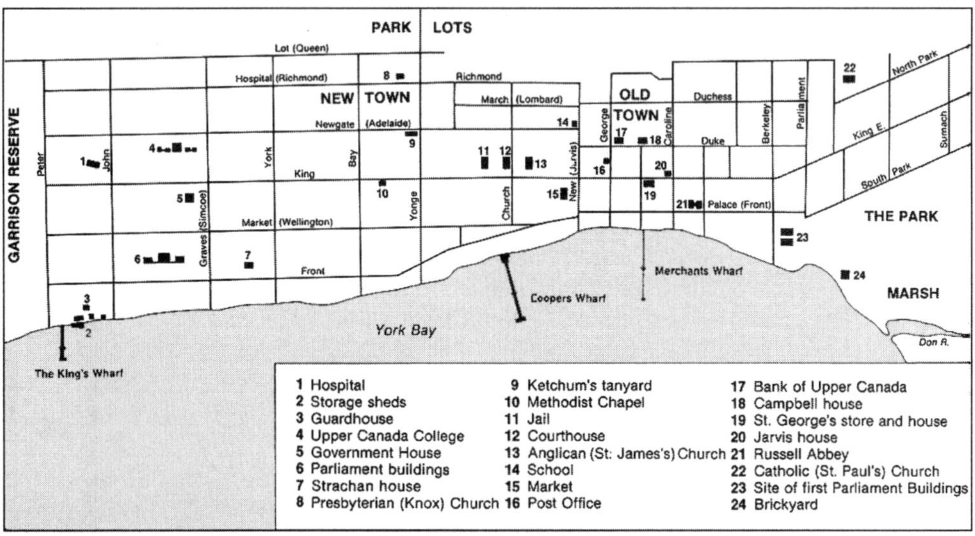

Map 2 York (Toronto) to 1830. (J.M.S. Careless, *Toronto to 1918: An Illustrated History.*
[Toronto: James Lorimer & Company, 1984], 38)

Popular Politics and Political Culture in Upper Canada, 1800–1850

Introduction

In early 1832, the entire province of Upper Canada was in turmoil. William Lyon Mackenzie, whose vitriolic journalism had long made him a scourge of the Family Compact, had once again incurred official ire. This time he had offended by launching a petitioning campaign in the summer of 1831, hoping to convince the British government to endorse a series of political reforms in Upper Canada. For his pains, Mackenzie was punished by expulsion from the Assembly – not once but twice. His constituents, however, promptly re-elected him, and his well-wishers elsewhere blanketed the province with public meetings to petition the British government on his behalf. In the resulting uproar, members of the public who supported the Assembly majority retaliated with political meetings of their own to condemn Mackenzie and endorse the status quo in counter-petitions. More dramatically, they disrupted pro-Mackenzie meetings, physically assaulted Mackenzie and his followers, and burned the Scottish gadfly in effigy. The tumult died down only after Mackenzie left for England in April 1832 to present provincial grievances to the British authorities.

These events were part of the most important focus of popular politics in Upper Canada prior to its union with Lower Canada in 1841: a series of petitioning movements and attempts to institutionalize them by establishing political unions.[1] "Movements" can be distinguished both from political parties and from interest groups. The objective of political parties is to exercise power, while movements attempt to influence how power is exercised. The petitioning movements of Upper Canada were primarily directed towards influencing the policies of the

British government, rather than towards the achievement of political power. Movements may attract the support of pressure groups but they generally have broader goals and are less formally structured.[2]

This book examines the development and activities of two petitioning movements of the different camps: the oppositionists and the government supporters. Though petitioning was only one of the strategies employed by opponents of the Upper Canadian government in the first decade of the nineteenth century, within a generation it had become their method of choice. Emerging after the War of 1812, the Upper Canadian oppositionist petitioning movement drew inspiration from contemporary movements which, after the end of the Napoleonic Wars, favoured political change in Britain. Indeed, the best-known petitioner in Upper Canadian history, Robert Gourlay, himself an experienced petitioner in Great Britain, transferred his skills and interests to Upper Canada in 1817–18. His example was followed by a number of others in the late 1820s and 1830s who remembered his example and that of his predecessors. These later petitioners protested government policies, like the Alien Bill[3] of 1827; they launched crusades against the established church in 1827 and 1830; and they mobilized public support against the judicial system and the existing constitution in 1828–29. After Mackenzie's success in 1831–32, activists attempted to institutionalize the oppositional petitioning movement in 1833 and again in 1836–37 by establishing political unions to promote ongoing pressure for governmental change in the province. Oppositionist petitioning, however, did not end with the Rebellion of 1837. As late as 1839, at the very end of the Upper Canadian period, political activists organized so-called "Durham meetings" throughout the province in support of Lord Durham's recommendations for the union of the Canadas and the introduction of responsible government.[4]

The oppositionist petitioning movement did not go unchallenged. In 1832, and again in 1836, government supporters embarked on highly successful counter-attacks in support of the status quo. Even after the Rebellion, supporters of the old status quo, like their opponents, mobilized to petition against Lord Durham's principal recommendations.

These petitioning movements offer a revealing perspective on the neglected subject of popular politics in Upper Canada. "Popular politics" is the manifestation of public opinion on political questions by those not engaged in the "high politics" of the elite decision-makers at the capital of a state or colony.[5] British historians use the term broadly to cover a wide range of behaviours, including the activities of the press, extraparliamentary organization, parades, and petitioning, as well as rioting and other criminal offences. The term "popular politics" is useful because it does not imply assumptions about the class, ethnicity, voting status, leadership, or motivation of participants; it thus encourages the examination of popular participation in politics from the widest possible angle.[6]

The petitioning movements have hitherto been overlooked by Upper Canadian historians concerned with other aspects of popular politics. The attitudes of the popular press to a number of political questions have been examined by David Mills, Hartwell Bowsfield, and Jane Errington.[7] The petitioning movements, however, expressed the views of a far wider spectrum of Upper Canadian opinion than that offered by newspaper editors. Episodes of political violence have also attracted the attention of many scholars, including Michael Cross, Donald Akenson, Fred Armstrong, Gregory Kealey, and Paul Romney.[8] These episodes, however, must be understood in more than a purely local context.[9] Further, historians of extraparliamentary organization, such as Eric Jackson and Graeme Patterson, have fixed their sights, for the most part, on electoral politics,[10] thereby missing the significance of the petitioning movements, which were not primarily electorally oriented.

Historians who have considered the careers of Robert Gourlay and William Lyon Mackenzie, the best-known of the oppositionist petitioners, have often ignored or minimized the significance of their efforts to mobilize public opinion through petitioning. For example, *The Peoples of Canada* and *Origins* – two recent textbooks on Canadian history – make no mention in their accounts of Gourlay that petitioning was the major focus of his activity in Upper Canada and the cause of his "persecution" at the hands of the authorities.[11] Standard works on Upper Canadian politics have demonstrated a similarly cavalier attitude towards Mackenzie's attempts to stir public awareness of abuses in government. Aileen Dunham's classic, *Political Unrest in Upper Canada*, devoted only three sentences to the petitioning movement of 1831.[12] Gerald Craig's *Upper Canada* considered petitioning primarily in the context of developments in high politics.[13] Meanwhile, the significance of the counteroffensives launched by government supporters has essentially been overlooked by all commentators.

There are several explanations for this lacuna in studies of Upper Canadian history. One lies in the nature of the documentation. The petitioning movements, like other aspects of popular politics, are a problematic subject for historical research. Information on the movements is widely scattered through sources as various as newspapers, manuscripts, Colonial Office records, books, pamphlets, and broadsides. The best material on a riot at one end of the province may be found in a newspaper published at the other end. These materials, moreover, must be tracked over a period of more than forty years. The fragmented nature of the primary sources helps account for historians' neglect of this important aspect of Upper Canadian history.

Certain widespread assumptions may well have discouraged research on the petitioning movements. It is a favoured myth of Upper Canadian history, for example, that participation in politics was restricted to a relatively small percentage of the population. This misconception is fostered by the belief that the only significant form of extraparliamentary activity – apart from newspaper reporting – was electoral organization, and that some form of political party was the primary vehicle of political activism.[14] In addition, the tendency to see Upper Canada as a self-contained political unit has distracted attention from movements that were, like petitioning, primarily directed at influencing British authorities. Petitioning has been considered a "blind alley," a tactic that – in the words of S.F. Wise – "short-circuited reform."[15] For this reason also, its significance has never received serious attention from historians.

The following examination of the petitioning movements, however, firmly overturns these supposed truisms of Upper Canadian history. Contrary to the common wisdom about Upper Canadian politics, the movements repeatedly channelled the energies of thousands of ordinary Upper Canadians into the political process. Some fourteen thousand people, for example, signed the anti-Alien Bill petition in 1827. In a population of less than two hundred thousand, this was a remarkably high number. It would soon be repeatedly exceeded by the number of signatures on petitions for other causes, particularly during the early to mid 1830s. Indeed, a much higher percentage of the population signed petitions than voted in provincial elections. Thus it was not political parties but petitioning that was the most important form of political activism for Upper Canadians.

These numbers, evidence of widespread public engagement in the political process, are all the more remarkable because they emanated from a relatively select element of the population: adult males. The right of petitioning was available to any British subject,[16] and individual women frequently petitioned the government, especially on matters related to land. Many women also petitioned the lieutenant-governor on behalf of their male relatives who had been arrested in the aftermath of the 1837 Rebellion. As we shall see, however, it was generally considered inappropriate for women to sign petitions for or against political reform. Politics in Upper Canada was a male preserve, and women remained unenfranchised until the twentieth century. Accordingly, those who circulated the petitions solicited only the signatures of men. Though women were evidently present at some of the public meetings, they were rarely among the signatories to the petitions.[17]

Petitioners and their opponents employed a wide range of strategies in their efforts to stir up public opinion for their causes. They staged public meetings to draw up addresses and petitions. They held further meetings to publicize their cause in far-flung locations. Banners, flags, bands, and parades often enhanced the drama of these occasions and committees were usually created to circulate documents by whatever means came to hand. Sometimes, for example, petitions were left for signature in local stores and taverns. Opponents of the government also found that Methodist preachers, itinerants by profession, made ideal couriers.

Petitioners fully exploited the media of the day, notwithstanding the difficulties of communication in this pre-railway, pre-telegraph age. They advertised their meetings beforehand in handbills and newspapers, hopeful that their opponents would not counter with advertisements publicizing their intentions of disrupting the process. They circulated the proceedings and resolutions arising from these meetings in pamphlets and in other forms. Sympathetic newspapers triumphantly tracked the progress of collecting signatures. Partisan newspapers lost no opportunity to denigrate the tactics of those whose petitions they disliked and to assassinate the characters of their promoters. All too frequently, abuse took a more tangible form, as petitioners became common targets of effigy burnings, riots, and beatings. The manifestations of popular politics surrounding the petitioning movements were wide-ranging and multi-faceted.

Petitioning was clearly not, as nineteenth-century commentators would have put it, "a hole and corner" affair. For the most part, it was a very public process. The visibility of these movements ensured that they would attract the attention of the highest authorities in the province. They were the subject of comment and sometimes action by the Assembly and Legislative Council and a favourite topic of lieutenant-governors in correspondence with the Colonial Office. Moreover, petitioners and their opponents frequently became entangled in the toils of the legal system. The movements were a central element in Upper Canadian politics.

The petitioning movements occurred in a context that has been clarified by the work of numerous historians of Upper Canada. As they have shown, the major centre of political power in the province did not lie, as in the present day, with a cabinet (executive) dependent for its tenure in office on a majority in the Assembly. Instead, within the province, political power was held by an elite body of officials: essentially a pre-industrial combination of professional, commercial, and administrative elements that governed a rapidly expanding population of farmers and lumberers. Usually residing at the provincial capital of York (called Toronto after 1834), these officials, appointed by the British lieutenant-governor, are known to posterity, somewhat misleadingly, as the "Family Compact."[18] Their numbers included the Anglican prelate John Strachan, his protégé John Beverley Robinson, and members of the Boulton family, as well as their political friends and allies across the province. Among such allies, as S.J.R. Noel has argued, were a variety of "grand patrons," such as Colonel Thomas Talbot, Bishop Alexander McDonell, and William "Tiger" Dunlop. These men acted as "the dominant agents of development" in their respective areas of the province and exerted considerable political influence.[19] Important supporters of the government sometimes engaged in spirited struggles among themselves,[20] and no single figure exerted pre-eminent influence throughout the period from 1815 to 1841. Much of the political history of Upper Canada can be written in terms of relations between members of this elite and their counterparts elsewhere in the province without much reference to developments in the Assembly.

The ties between officials in York and the local elite were based not on party but on friendship, patronage, and ideology. Ties of patronage were important because virtually every subordinate office in the colony – including the judiciary, the magistracy, commissions in the militia, and county and district offices – was at the disposal of the executive. Those who aspired to fill the posts of distinction in this society, therefore, did well to cultivate the authorities in the capital.[21]

The ties of ideology were more complex. Essentially, the authority of the provincial elite and their supporters rested on the twin pillars of loyalty and paternalism. The loyalty of government supporters, according to historian S.F. Wise, went beyond "adherence to the Crown and the Empire" to mean "adherence to those beliefs and institutions the conservative considered essential in the preservation of a form of life different from, and superior to, the manners, politics and social arrangements of the United States."[22] The Constitutional Act of 1791, Upper Canada's constitution, essentially enshrined the basic ingredients of this "form of life" including a monarchical form of government, a "balanced constitution" on the British model, and support for an established church. Together, these features helped guarantee the all-important goal of maintaining the tie to Great Britain.[23] Any apparent threat to official values was routinely denounced as republican, democratic, seditious, and likely to sever the colonial link with Great Britain.

Paternalism was the basis of the elite's ideology of social relations, which sought to replicate the hierarchical social structure of an idealized version of Great Britain in the eighteenth century. To oversimplify, paternalism was a system that conferred significant benefits on those at the lower end of the social scale, such as the provisions offered to the often destitute early Loyalists in the 1780s. In return, those at the higher end demanded deference to their supposedly superior wisdom and political judgment. Upper Canadian paternalism was not utterly rigid, allowing considerable room for negotiation at various levels for those who offered no fundamental threat to the regime. Those who challenged the established hierarchy, however, did so at the risk of invoking the not-inconsiderable wrath of the authorities.[24]

Members of the elite found that preserving stability in Upper Canada was no easy task. It is true that, unlike Britain, Upper Canada was not undergoing the stresses of an industrial revolution or the rise of new social strata whose wealth was based on large-scale industry: until the mid-nineteenth century, it remained a predominantly agricultural economy whose expanding craft sector (carpentry, shoemaking) and industries (milling, distilling, tanneries) were for the most part closely related to the soil. The province, however, was primed for agricultural growth, and rapidly attracted settlers. The provincial population of 20,000 or so in the 1790s had quintupled to over 100,000 by 1820 and quadrupled again to 400,000 by 1840. By 1841, nearly half of the population of Upper Canada had been born in Britain.[25] This growth, however, was not achieved without considerable social and political stress. Among the chief sources of destabilization were massive immigration and the growth of dissenting evangelical Protestant denominations.

Those who possessed the hardihood to oppose the established order in politics were considerably less united than supporters of the government. They voiced their opposition at different times, beginning in the first decade of the nineteenth century, re-emerging after the end of the Napoleonic Wars, and engaging in almost continuous agitation from the late 1820s to the end of the Upper Canadian period in 1841. Their opposition took different forms: addresses to grand juries, petitioning, forming political unions, agitation in the Assembly, and even rebellion. Oppositionist leaders were a heterogeneous crew. Their numbers included Irishmen (Robert Thorpe and W.W. Baldwin), Scots (Robert Gourlay and William Lyon Mackenzie), English-born (John Rolph), and Americans (Jesse Ketchum and Marshall Spring Bidwell). Most, at one time or another, were elected to the Assembly, though some, notably Robert Gourlay, were not. They drew on different ideologies, including country-party rhetoric and Whig constitutionalism.

They espoused different causes, including financial reform, religious disestablishment, changes in land-granting policies, greater rights for the American-born, judicial reform, and responsible government.

Traditional accounts of the development of opposition in Upper Canada portray political conflict as moving from the personal opposition of the first decade of the nineteenth century to more formal, but still relatively haphazard, party activity by the 1820s. The issue of party politics in Upper Canada has never, however, received very systematic attention. As a result, historians have not fully addressed the issues of the weakness of political parties, the absence of a party system, and the significance of antipartyism. These subjects must be understood if the importance of the petitioning movements is to be appreciated.

During the entire Upper Canadian period, political parties were weak both in and outside the legislature. To be sure, the Assembly was an important arena of conflict between supporters of the status quo and their opponents. It would, however, be anachronistic to view the political divisions represented there as "parties" in any sense that would be recognizable today. For one thing, control of the Assembly did not result in the capture of executive power, the major objective of political parties in twentieth-century parliamentary democracies. For another, though government supporters could usually be distinguished from their opponents, neither side was united on anything like a reliable basis. It is true that the government was relatively successful in dominating the membership of the Assembly – with the exception of years 1824–28 and 1834–36, when forces opposed to the government enjoyed a majority there. Yet, though John Beverley Robinson as attorney general from 1818–29 proved adept at marshalling support for the government in the Assembly, he found that government supporters "could not be relied on consistently to support government bills." Governor General Charles Poulett Thomson also found this to be true a decade later.[26] Members of the opposition – despite brief bouts of effectiveness – were more commonly divided amongst themselves.[27] United neither by the goal of determining public policy nor by the binding tie of control of patronage distribution, such groups as did exist in the legislature after the early 1820s were badly divided and poorly organized.

Outside the Assembly, electoral organization during the Upper Canadian period was also generally weak. To some degree, no doubt, this was a reflection of the scattered distribution of the population and the rudimentary nature of communications. Beyond this, however, the relative powerlessness of the Assembly, along with the fragmented character of both government and opposition forces, meant that there was generally little incentive to engage in sustained efforts to capture a majority. The game of electoral organization was not worth the candle of a majority in the Assembly. As a result, extraparliamentary electoral organization throughout the Upper Canadian period was generally uneven and impermanent.

An additional explanation for party weakness in Upper Canada lies in the prevailing climate of antipartyism. Among members of the ruling elite, antipartyism was an aspect of their notorious hostility to any evidence of dissent or opposition. They controlled the levers of political power within Upper Canada, but they did so with no real sense of security. Instead, they were tormented by the never ending and laborious task, as Wise put it, of "attempt[ing] to maintain a counter-revolutionary society on the borders of a revolutionary state."[28] Moreover, memories of the War of 1812, and fears that another conflict with the United States lay just around the corner, produced a permanent siege mentality. As J.K. Johnson has pointed out, "The possibility that the War of 1812 might be the last to be fought on Upper Canadian soil does not appear to have occurred to prominent Upper Canadians at all ... Upper Canadians lived with war, or the rumour of war, or the expectation of war."[29] Like most governments in wartime situations, the Upper Canadian authorities were highly intolerant of internal critics. In fact, government supporters refused to recognize the legitimacy of opposition, from whatever source. "Dissent," as David Mills put it, "was not to be tolerated in Upper Canada."[30] This applied to political parties no less than to other forms of oppositional agitation.

Though petitioning was an important form of oppositional activity, its anti-government proponents never regarded it as an element of party politics. They, just as strongly as government supporters, subscribed to the prevailing doctrine of antipartyism, which had deep roots in the British political tradition. Well into the nineteenth century, as Richard Hofstadter has recorded, parties in Britain were widely condemned as divisive, conducive to tyranny, and contrary to the public good.[31] Under these circumstances, few in Upper Canada were willing to openly proclaim their allegiance to party. Robert Gourlay, for example, according to David Mills, "did not accept the idea of political parties."[32] Like Gourlay, most opponents of the government thought of themselves as speaking not for a political party but for the people of the province against a corrupt administration. Similarly, government supporters portrayed themselves as articulating the views of the community as a whole (or at least the most respectable and influential part) when they denounced the supposed revolutionaries who were, in their view, deluding the ignorant and the unwary. Rather than accepting peaceful competition between opposing views of politics through the vehicle of political parties, which is the defining characteristic of a party system, each side claimed to enjoy a monopoly of concern for the common good. They denounced their opponents as factious, malicious, and motivated chiefly by a desire for personal gain.

Political terminology reflected the shadowy role of parties in colonial politics. For most of the Upper Canadian period, participants in politics did not use party labels. Oppositionists crusaded not against "tories" but against "the executive faction," "the government and its officers," or "the administration." Government supporters, meanwhile, denounced their opponents not as "reformers" but as "rebels" and "revolutionaries," or as members of "the saddlebag faction" (a derogatory reference to their Methodist supporters). It was not until 1832 that the terms "tory" and "reformer" came into common usage, and then primarily in oppositionist newspapers; government supporters continued to refer to their opponents as "rebels" and "revolutionaries" throughout the Upper Canadian period.

Official intolerance of opposition is closely related to another little-understood aspect of Upper Canadian politics, the extent to which the established authorities attempted to control access to the public sphere.[33] The governmental apparatus established when Upper Canada was founded was not designed to seek or encourage public participation in political life. In fact, the authorities went to lengths that are almost unimaginable today to minimize opportunities for the expression of public opinion. Recent publications have thrown some light on this question. Mark Francis has stressed the extent to which ceremonial functions in the British colonies were designed to display gubernatorial authority and dignity rather than to appeal for or demonstrate popular support. More particularly, parliamentary ceremonies were intended to take place before a tiny audience made up mostly of participants.[34] In addition, there was considerable official support for restricted access to information about parliamentary proceedings.[35] Electoral contests were an exception to the aura of government secrecy. They involved public appeals, both written and verbal, by the candidates to electors. But, at least until the late 1820s, electoral contests seem to have been relatively lacking in the ceremony and spectacle that might appeal to the general public. Rowdyism there might be, to be sure, but little in the way of music, processions, or banners.[36]

When Upper Canadian oppositionists failed to follow the official example and appealed for public support, the authorities acted decisively to limit public discussion through the legal system, as Barry Wright has demonstrated.[37] The Sedition Act of 1804, which remained in force until 1829, allowed the government to banish the politically suspect from the province; if they refused to go, the Act provided the penalty of execution. In the wake of Robert Gourlay's petitioning campaign, the Assembly passed the Seditious Meetings Act, in force from 1818–20, prohibiting public meetings. In addition, until the 1820s, libel law could silence the press. The Assembly majority also used its power to expel opponents – notably William Lyon Mackenzie – from their midst. Less formal means to control access to public space, such as denying permission to meet in public buildings like courthouses, were additional weapons in the government's arsenal.

By the late 1820s, formal, legal means of controlling public participation in politics were no longer readily available to the government. The Seditious Meetings Act and the Sedition Act were no longer in force, and public opinion made libel laws all but unenforceable. Under these circumstances, government supporters resorted to violence in order to suppress expressions of hostile public opinion. The Orange Order is frequently associated in the historical literature with violence in Upper Canada, but the aristocratic pretensions of government supporters in Upper Canada were also entirely consistent with a propensity to take the law into their own hands. The historical literature documents apparently isolated incidents of political violence committed by supporters of the Upper Canadian government during the 1820s and 1830s. When these incidents are put in the context of the petitioning campaigns, they are revealed as part of a persistent jihad against the expression of oppositionist public opinion. This crusade was endorsed in the private correspondence of government supporters and in the press. Moreover, such political violence was condoned at the highest levels of the provincial administration and treated with extreme leniency at all levels of the legal system.

At first glance, this resort to naked force seems hard to understand. For one thing, given the extensive control of the Upper Canadian government by supporters of the status quo, it appears almost redundant. For another, the works of social historians more commonly point to violence as a form of plebeian protest against the evils of paternalism, rather than a key weapon of political control by the elite.[38] Moreover, the Rebellion of 1837 has created a lasting association between reformers and political violence. The strategic deployment of force for political purposes by government supporters was nonetheless widespread, particularly after 1830. It was the product of a number of factors, including the British example of the generation after 1790, the rapid spread of the Orange Order from Ireland in the 1830s, and the practical reality of government control of the levers of justice. The systematic use of force by government supporters had important consequences, helping both to undermine the legitimacy of the Upper Canadian state and to shape the character of party development in the province.

This exploration of the general context of the oppositionist petitioning movements helps explain why it was that such an apparently innocuous activity as petitioning should have attracted such strenuous attempts at suppression. After all, as we shall see in chapter 1, petitioning was very much in the British tradition and was a time-honoured method of communication between the people and their government. Indeed, personal petitioning – requests for land grants and other favours – continued to occur throughout the Upper Canadian period without incurring official suspicion or suppression. The regime also tolerated some political petitioning from the Loyalists in the days before the establishment of an Assembly.[39] In the hands of a Thorpe, a Gourlay, or a Mackenzie, however, petitioning assumed threatening dimensions from the perspective of the authorities. This was because, in the course of organizing petitioning campaigns, Gourlay and his successors evaded established mechanisms of political control and, more generally, challenged the hierarchical and patriarchal values of the authorities.

Moreover, it was not just the "respectable" public who were welcomed at oppositionist meetings but all who were anxious to participate. Oppositionists pioneered the process of reaching out to a wider public through the use of speeches and processions (complete with music and banners), making their message accessible even to the illiterate.[40] The implications were that all Upper Canadians – not just members of the political elite – were entitled to inclusion in the political process and that the days of the hierarchical political order were over. Oppositionists also violated established social norms in their lack of deference to authority figures such as the lieutenant-governor and members of the Assembly, challenging paternalistic values in a manner similar to the Methodist threat to traditional authority in religion.[41] It was not petitioning as such but the way in which it was conducted and the messages it conveyed that made oppositionist petitioning objectionable to Upper Canadian authorities.

A close examination of the petitioning movements illuminates not only the significance of efforts to control access to the public sphere and the prevalence of antipartyism but also the central importance of the role of the British government in provincial affairs. Indeed, it was the British government that possessed the final authority on Upper Canadian affairs, be they constitutional, religious, judicial, or economic. The necessity of gaining the sympathetic ear of British officials was not lost on members of the Upper Canadian political and administrative elite. To be sure, they could generally rely on the lieutenant-governor, whoever he might be, to endorse their viewpoint in his communications with the Colonial Office. There were times, however, when only personal representations would do. Accordingly, government supporters trooped to Britain in a seemingly unending parade through the 1820s. Early in the decade, for example, John Beverley Robinson, on leave from his position as solicitor general, negotiated with the Colonial Office on a number of questions including trade, union with Lower Canada, and the post office. He was back again in 1825 for discussions on provincial legislation relating to aliens. Meanwhile, Robinson's mentor, the leading Anglican minister John Strachan, visited Britain in 1824 and in 1826–27 on various matters related to church establishment. Between these two journeys, the Colonial Office also consulted Robinson's brother Peter and H.J. Boulton, Robinson's successor as solicitor general, on a variety of matters.[42] Moreover, Assemblies dominated by government supporters, as well as the reliably like-minded Legislative Council, routinely offered addresses to the lieutenant-governor for transmission to the Colonial Office.

Opponents of the provincial administration were no less aware than their antagonists that the true fount of power lay overseas. After the end of the War of 1812, those who wanted change in the Upper Canadian political, judicial, and religious establishments believed that only the British government could offer them satisfaction. As we have seen, political office in Upper Canada was essentially the preserve of those who identified fully with the prevailing view of the state, from the lieutenant-governorship to the humblest magistrate. Oppositionists realized early on that they could expect no sympathy for change from provincial authorities. Even when they captured a majority in the Assembly, as they did in 1828 and 1834, their best-laid plans could easily be overthrown by highly placed officials within the province itself. They hoped, however, that the British government might give their proposals for change a more sympathetic reception. Even before the election of a reformist Whig government in Britain in 1830, British authorities had shown some willingness to receive those who spoke for the disaffected in the province. John Rolph, for example, travelled to Britain in 1825 to speak with British officials on the alien issue. He was followed by Robert Randal in 1827 and thereafter by a number of other emissaries offering advice on religious and political questions in the province.

Lacking the entrenched power base within the provincial political structure enjoyed by their opponents, however, oppositionists hit upon an alternative source of legitimation to back their appeals to the British government: public opinion. To be sure, public opinion periodically expressed itself in general elections. But the limited powers of the Assembly, the restrictive franchise under which its members were elected,[43] and the infrequency of general elections detracted from their usefulness to oppositionists. Petitioning, on the other hand, offered a much wider constituency and the additional advantage of controlling the timing of demands for reform. Moreover, the upsurge of petitioning in favour of reform in Britain during the early 1830s, condoned and even encouraged as it was by leading officers of the government, encouraged Upper Canadian oppositionists to adopt similar tactics. Fearful that such evidence of public support for change would influence the British government, supporters of the Upper Canadian government followed suit. Under these circumstances, it is not hard to understand why petitioning the British government, the favoured route for those who sought political change, was also adopted by supporters of the status quo.

The petitioning movements, the strongest extraparliamentary force in Upper Canadian politics, played an important role in ensuring that the political culture of the province would remain essentially British rather than American. As Jane Errington has pointed out, Upper Canadians were not wholly hostile to the United States. They greatly admired its economic progress after the War of 1812. Moreover, as Gerald Craig showed long ago, oppositionists drew political inspiration from American practices in land-granting, education, banking, government spending, and many other areas.[44] The truth is, however, that as long as appeals to Britain dominated the oppositionist agenda, the petitioning movements would unmistakably speak the language not of American republicanism, democracy, and revolution but of British constitutional reform. The imperial context of the petitioning movements, then, ensured that oppositionists as well as government supporters would articulate their demands, as David Mills has shown, in the framework of "loyalty" to the British connection.[45]

While the necessity of appealing to the British government for support exerted a moderating influence on the substance of oppositionist demands, the reality of British power also acted to some degree as a check on the more extreme anti-opposition activities of government supporters. The British government, committed by the late 1820s to (moderate) political reform in England, objected to some of the means adopted by the Upper Canadian elite to control political opposition, notably the repeated expulsions of Mackenzie from the Assembly. Moreover, the fact that British officials were sympathetic to manifestations of public opinion gave government supporters a strong incentive to engage in peaceful efforts to attract expressions of public support in addition to their efforts to suppress their opponents by force.

At a more prosaic level, the political reality of British hegemony helped shape the nature of oppositionist demands. This is perhaps most striking in relation to the question of patronage distribution. Leading authorities on Upper Canadian history are agreed on the centrality of the patronage system to the operations of the provincial government and on the fact that patronage was distributed with a view to strengthening the existing regime. In other words, few oppositionists could hope to achieve positions of substantial power. It has also frequently been said that the ranks of the oppositionists were notably swollen by disappointed office-seekers. Under these circumstances, it might be expected that patronage distribution would be a key grievance in the petitions of reformers.[46]

Yet patronage distribution did not receive the attention in oppositionist petitions that its centrality to Upper Canadian government would suggest it deserved; the subject was never a major focus of complaint in oppositionist petitions. Part of the reason may be that oppositionists expected that changes in patronage distribution would follow from responsible government, so that their demand for the latter essentially included the former. Moreover, other oppositionist demands, like the request for elective local government, certainly had important patronage implications. Perhaps the most important reason, however, is that most Upper Canadian appointments were made internally, without the active participation of the Colonial Office – so that there would have been little point in the petitioners approaching the British authorities on this issue. The exception was appointments to the Legislative and Executive Councils, and thus some petitions, like Mackenzie's in 1831, asked that judges and clergymen be excluded from these bodies.

Both sides in Upper Canadian politics may have shared a common British political idiom, but this does not imply that the differences between their political programs were insignificant. It simply means that they both employed a shared language of political legitimation.[47] As in mid-nineteenth-century Ontario, as Jeffrey McNairn put it, "issues were constructed around competing interpretations of what was 'British.'"[48] The richness of the British political tradition ensured that both sides in Upper Canadian politics had ample material: for every tory hero like Wellington, there was a radical tribune like Wilkes. The inherent ambiguity of the province's constitution also lent itself to controversy over the character of its British content. Was its essence the governmental structure as set out in the Constitutional Act of 1791, as government supporters claimed? Or should Upper Canadians enjoy responsible government on the British model, as oppositionists maintained? The use of a common idiom of political discourse should not obscure the reality of the struggle in Upper Canada over the nature and functioning of the state.

Though petitioning was not an overtly party-building activity, it nevertheless helped in several ways to lay the foundation for political parties in the 1840s. Under the onslaught of oppositionist petitioning, politics burst forth from the constraints on public participation originally imposed by the authorities. One result was that even the ceremonial functions of lieutenant-governors, particularly the ritual of replying to addresses, became politicized. Another was that supporters of the government felt compelled to adopt the methods of their opponents and engage in competition for public backing. Moreover, the petitioning movements were, like the political parties of later decades, based to a considerable extent on the mobilization of various ethnic, religious, and economic groups behind competing political factions. Although neither side overtly espoused the cause of a fully democratic political system, the effect of the petitioning movement was to democratize Upper Canadian politics.

As they reached out to the public for support, by the 1830s, both sides in the petitioning movement harnessed the friction generated by the social changes of the previous generation, especially immigration and the growth of religious dissent. Because petitioning was more widespread than the reach of political parties in Upper Canada, it was largely through this movement that political alignments began to manifest themselves on a province-wide basis.

As historians have shown, the primary fault lines in Upper Canada were those of national origin and religion.[49] Oppositionists could count on the support of the North American-born when government policies restricted their rights or appeared to favour recent immigrants from Britain. Government supporters, on the other hand, were confident that the postwar British migrants, whom they regarded as generally sound politically, would outweigh the elements that appeared to be too prone to disaffection, too American. Religious divisions often parallelled these differences. Protestant immigrants from Ireland joined the Orange Order here, partly in the expectation that the Order's outspoken endorsement of the status quo would improve their own standing in Upper Canada. Similarly, the government often received notable assistance from the Anglican and Roman Catholic clergy. The Methodists, on the other hand, a growing sect whose adherents had by and large been born on this side of the Atlantic, were by the late 1820s a critically important source of oppositionist support.

Members of the elite viewed Methodism as a special threat. It was politically suspect because it had spread to Upper Canada from the United States. More than this, however, the Methodists, along with other dissenting Protestants, challenged the status quo in a number of other ways, notably by their attack on religious establishment (particularly the clergy reserves) in Upper Canada. The Methodist political agenda threatened the established authorities because the Anglican Church was considered to be a critical bulwark against revolution, an argument used to justify its special privileges as essential. The Methodist agenda also struck at the cherished religious vision of influential Anglicans like John Strachan, who almost until the time of the Rebellion of 1837 entertained the highly unrealistic but nevertheless sincere expectation that the entire population of the province might espouse the Anglican faith.[50] In addition, Methodist reliance on lay preachers challenged the place of learning in established religion, and their revivalism contradicted notions of religious decorum. Moreover, their enthusiasm for temperance threatened the customary ways of a society where alcohol played an important role in both economic life and recreation. Nancy Christie has pointed out, too, that the dissenting evangelical culture had political implications: "Methodist and Baptist evangelicals offered a persuasive critique of established ecclesiastical and political institutions by erecting a renewed spiritual and egalitarian social order."[51] It may also be true of Upper Canada, as Rhys Isaac has suggested of colonial Virginia, that the extemporaneous preaching of the Methodists was "a form of rebellion against the dominance of the literary culture of the gentry."[52] The rapid spread of Methodism in the 1820s and 1830s was thus a source of alarm to the authorities, though its political force was often blunted by internecine quarrels.

In a society that was overwhelmingly agricultural, political divisions along class lines were less clear than those drawn according to national origin and religion. Nevertheless, the supposedly humble circumstances of most oppositionists provided a frequent target of scorn. Reformers in turn condemned the "ruffled shirts" and aristocratic pretensions of their opponents and simultaneously derided efforts of government supporters to buy the allegiance of the indigent with whiskey and soup kitchens. The petitioning campaigns, however, did not pit the haves against the have-nots in Upper Canada: both sides received support from a wide cross-section of the social structure.

The broad scope of the petitioning movements contributed significantly to the emergence of a province-wide political culture. By bringing key issues almost literally to the doorstep of every inhabitant, they had a powerful impact on the creation of a broadly based sense of political consciousness. In other words, the petitioning movements ensured that Upper Canadians would share a common understanding of the character of the issues before them. This was a precondition for the emergence of more firmly rooted political parties in the 1840s.

The petitioning movements, of course, mobilized public support both for and against political change. At the same time, therefore, as they promoted a province-wide sense of political awareness, they also clarified and hardened political divisions. They encouraged ordinary Upper Canadians to make political choices. The range of alternatives, however, was limited. In fact, the petitioning movements essentially demanded that the people choose either to support the government or to oppose it. The result was the polarization of the province along lines that were clear and well-defined. Such divisions provided a basis for the organization of extraparliamentary political parties in the 1840s. They encouraged the popular dissemination of two competing ideologies, helped familiarize ordinary Upper Canadians with important policy issues, and promoted ongoing political activism well beyond the boundaries of the capital. They also prompted the emergence at the secondary level of individuals who would take an active part in the politics of the 1840s. In a very real sense, the petitioning movements laid the foundations for the developments that transformed Upper Canadian politics in the 1840s.

1 Early Upper Canadian Petitioners, 1800–1831

By the early nineteenth century, the right of petitioning was firmly entrenched in the British constitution. Since the early Middle Ages – the days of King Edward I – British subjects had been required to put their requests to the monarch in the form of a petition. Centuries later, this practice gained formal sanction in the 1689 Bill of Rights. Originally, petitioners sent their requests directly to the monarch or, in judicial cases, to the Chancellor. By the nineteenth century, however, English petitioners more often approached the British Parliament, deluging it with almost twenty-five thousand petitions from 1826 to 1831.[1] Upper Canadians were no strangers to this process, making use of it even before the founding of the province in 1791. The first petitioners were the Loyalists, who, in mid-1780s, petitioned the King for a Loyalist settlement – separate from Quebec – where they could enjoy British laws and land tenure. Like other Upper Canadian petitioners in the succeeding half-century, they requested the benefits of the British constitution, and were "profuse in their expressions of loyalty and gratitude to the British government."[2] In other petitions, they sought "improvement of the court system, the election or appointment of township officers and local officials, and more clergymen and school masters."[3] Significantly, unlike those who petitioned for changes to the system of government in the 1820s and 30s, Loyalist suppliants were not treated as enemies of the regime. In the fluid political situation between Britain and its former colonies in the 1780s, British authorities were determined to procure inland areas that would be safe from American depredations. They were therefore anxious to show the Loyalists "that the rewards of loyalty were greater than those of rebellion," and responded in generally positive fashion to demands for changes to the Quebec Act.[4]

Loyalists also petitioned the government for favours of a more personal nature. The Revolutionary War had left many of them in straitened circumstances, and they responded by petitioning government authorities for the basic necessities of life. As Potter-MacKinnon has shown, these petitions are an important source of information on the Loyalists' sense of identity and provide valuable clues to the image and role of women in early Upper Canada.[5] Later settlers were no less persistent in their use of this method to secure a variety of government favours. J.K. Johnson's study of this process concluded that "during the whole Upper-Canadian period the use of the personal petition continued to be extraordinarily prevalent, in some cases even routine."[6] Petitions to the lieutenant-governor most often involved matters relating to land, jobs, pardons, pensions, and payments said to be due from government, as well as requests for various forms of assistance.[7]

While petitioning usually focused on personal matters such as these, the process was also used by members of interest groups trying to modify government policy. By the 1820s, petitioning was used for this purpose in Great Britain also. In Britain, from 1760 to 1830, as the power of public opinion increased, fledgling extraparliamentary organizations persistently attempted to harness this popular force to oppose the government. It began with supporters of the radical parliamentarian and agitator John Wilkes: they used petitioning to protest alleged threats to electors' rights and to spread Wilkes's anti-government cause across Britain in 1769–70.[8] A decade later, the moderate Yorkshire clergyman and reformer Christopher Wyvill headed an oppositionist petitioning movement known as "The Association." This extraparliamentary organization, which advocated moderate parliamentary reform, also petitioned on a national scale.[9] In the late 1780s, religious freedom for Protestant dissenters was linked to parliamentary reform by the Society for Constitutional Information, another organization that relied heavily on petitioning.[10]

The French Revolution cast a shadow over oppositionist appeals, and public support for parliamentary reform all but vanished. Members of evangelical groups, however, actively opposed particular government policies in spite of the inhospitable political climate. The evangelical Anti-Slave Trade Association, for example, overcame government resistance to the abolition of the foreign slave trade in 1807.[11] Leaders of the principal dissenting Protestant religions continued their struggle against the laws that prevented them from holding municipal, civil, or military office under the Crown, and also against other discriminatory policies. For example, in 1813, members of a number of dissenting denominations united to launch a successful petitioning campaign that persuaded the government to allow them to send missionaries to India.[12] Even at the height of the Napoleonic Wars, then, British organizers attempted to mobilize public opinion in order to convince the government to change established policies. The government, meanwhile, embarked on its own form of extraparliamentary organization as early as the 1790s: through its support of the counter-revolutionary "Association for the Preservation of Liberty and Property," it implicitly recognized the political usefulness of harnessing public opinion.[13]

The post-Loyalist oppositional petitioning movement that flourished in Upper Canada prior to about 1830 focused on political and religious reform (echoing British oppositional petitioning, as described above). The development of the movement, however, has been obscured (to the extent that historians have considered it at all) because Upper Canadian oppositional petitioning of the British government has been almost exclusively identified with the efforts of one man – Robert Gourlay. Such are the rewards of martyrdom. Gourlay enjoyed the dubious distinction of being the only individual banished from Upper Canada for promoting extraparliamentary agitation. Gourlay's cause was kept before the public for more than a generation by his own tireless efforts at publicity, and by a network of vocal sympathizers.[14] Historians, too, attracted by the obvious injustices Gourlay suffered, have made his career the subject of scrutiny.

It is true that Gourlay's activities are central to an understanding of the developing political culture of Upper Canada. But it is also important to remember that Gourlay was neither the first of the oppositionist petitioners nor the most successful. Oppositional political petitioning began not with Gourlay in 1818 but a decade earlier with members of a group of genteel British expatriates.[15] And while Gourlay essentially failed in his bid to effect changes in Upper Canadian government, some of his successors in the period before 1830 achieved notable victories. In particular, a group of political and religious reformers based in the provincial capital, York, launched a remarkably successful series of petitioning campaigns on behalf of religious and political causes in 1827–31.

THE THORPE-WILLCOCKS GROUP

An examination of the first oppositionists illuminates how petitioning moved from the periphery to the forefront of Upper Canadian politics. Petitioning the British government was very much an afterthought on the part of the Thorpe-Willcocks group, the first group to oppose the government of Upper Canada on a systematic basis. This group, which flourished from 1805 until the War of 1812, focused primarily on the Assembly, using it as the launching-pad for its criticisms of Upper Canadian government policies and practices – though the group's members did try to rouse public in various other ways. When it came to petitioning, however, their efforts were defeated not only by the modesty of their efforts but also by the unresponsiveness of the British government.

The group's core consisted of five individuals, all relatively affluent and all recent immigrants from Ireland and England.[16] They included Robert Thorpe, a judge of the Court of King's Bench from 1805 to 1807, Joseph Willcocks, sheriff of the Home district from 1804 to 1807, Charles Burton Wyatt, surveyor general from 1805 to 1807, John Mills Jackson, and William Weekes. Thorpe, Willcocks, and Wyatt were ultimately fired for speaking out against the Upper Canadian government. Thorpe and Wyatt left the colony as a consequence. Their crony John Mills Jackson, an Englishman, was another malcontent whose stay in Upper Canada proved brief. He returned to England and wrote a pamphlet, published in 1809, condemning the government of Upper Canada.

The first member of the group to oppose the government in the Assembly was William Weekes, a lawyer who campaigned against the Sedition Act of 1804 in a by-election held the following year. In the session of 1806, Weekes and other MPPs assailed the government, accusing it of financial mismanagement and other deficiencies. They found an ally, strangely, in the newly arrived judge of the Court of King's Bench, Robert Thorpe. Thorpe frequently attended sittings of the Assembly to offer counsel to opponents of the government, meanwhile informing British officials that he was doing his utmost to quiet provincial discontent.[17] Weekes also sponsored an address on the occasion of Lieutenant-Governor Sir Francis Gore's arrival in York in August 1806. This address, signed by "301 inhabitants of the Home District," complained of the previous authorities' neglect of public interest and the arbitrary nature of the government.[18]

When Weekes was killed in a duel in late 1806, Thorpe took his place in the Assembly. There, Thorpe's "allegedly inflammatory behaviour"[19] attracted unfavourable attention from the lieutenant-governor. Gore also considered that Thorpe's activities on circuit showed him to be a "factious demagogue" and disapproved of his involvement with Willcocks in the establishment of an opposition press that one correspondent claimed would revolutionize the province.[20] All these factors contributed to Thorpe's dismissal from the bench in October 1807.

Willcocks, an electoral supporter of Thorpe's, was also disciplined: he lost the office of sheriff of the Home district in April 1807, partly as a result of his attacks on the Upper Canadian government in private conversations.[21]

Freed from the restraints of appointive office, Willcocks quickly established an opposition newspaper in Niagara. He entered the Assembly following a by-election in 1808, representing the riding of West York.[22] Gore then attempted to silence Willcocks with a charge of seditious libel. This effort was dropped when the trial site was moved from York to the Niagara district, where the authorities feared he would be acquitted. Instead, it fell to the Assembly to convict Willcocks of the offence; he was thereupon sentenced, as Barry Wright has said, "to imprisonment in the district's common gaol for the duration of the session."[23]

Victimization, however, proved to be a career-booster, and Willcocks went on to lead an increasingly powerful opposition in the Assembly between 1808 and 1813. He must have been an able parliamentary organizer: at the height of his power in 1812, he briefly secured reliable support against the government from about half the Assembly. The War of 1812, however, nipped this nascent opposition in the bud, and Willcocks's defection to the enemy in 1813 did nothing to enhance the prestige of his cause. He was formally expelled from the Assembly in February 1814, seven months before his death in battle.[24] The result was that a decade of oppositional activity by the Thorpe-Willcocks group ended with more than a whiff of treason attached to its memory.[25]

Supporters of this short-lived and rather eccentric series of anti-government activities were pioneers in their efforts to rouse public opinion in Upper Canada, employing a wide variety of methods to this end. Perhaps the most unusual of these methods was Robert Thorpe's effort to use the institution of the jury as a focus of opposition. As a judge, Thorpe exploited to the full the fact that various juries offered him a captive audience, lecturing them on such subjects as "the means of increasing our wealth"[26] and "the principles of social order."[27] Members of these juries sometimes responded by enumerating grievances of their own.[28] It annoyed Lieutenant-Governor Gore that these addresses and answers were circulated in the public newspapers.[29] On the other hand, Thorpe, perhaps disingenuously, disclaimed any intention of stirring up the population. Indeed, he informed the Colonial Office that the goal of his efforts was to prevent the population from "meet[ing] in all the counties to address the King."[30] Such disclaimers carried little weight with Gore, however, who considered Thorpe's behaviour towards the juries as attempts "to poison the minds of the lower order of the people."[31] By the end of the year Thorpe went from soliciting the approval of juries to running for election to the Assembly.

Willcocks and Thorpe also reached out to the populace by holding public meetings – Thorpe in York county and Willcocks in Niagara – where "the Thorpe-Willcocks agitation had its deepest roots."[32] Thorpe's supporters held public meetings prior to his election in 1807, and later – in the summer of 1807 – to protest the omission of his name from the commission of assize.[33] There is no evidence, however, that there was any effort to mobilize a larger portion of the population on the judge's behalf. Willcocks's meetings appear to have been advisory ones, at which he solicited his constituents' advice on issues and sought their mandate to pursue subjects of local importance in the Assembly.[34]

Not content with simply responding to public opinion, however, Willcocks attempted to shape it. From Niagara he edited the province's first opposition newspaper, the *Upper Canada Guardian; or, Freeman's Journal,* between 1807 and the outbreak of war in 1812. Willcocks's biographer notes that the few surviving issues of this journal "contained remarkably little editorial matter," in contrast to later newspapers.[35] It was nevertheless, according to historian Bruce Wilson, a valuable weapon in Willcocks's struggle to forge an effective local opposition to the mercantile-official elite of the Niagara district.[36]

It was only after the dismissal from office of Robert Thorpe that this group of early malcontents considered petitioning the British government. At that time, according to Jackson, petitioning was stifled by official repression: "On the people's declaring their intention to petition the King for redress of their many grievances, it was publicly declared, that any man should be sent to prison who signed any petition or address whatsoever."[37] In a pamphlet published in 1810, this assertion was categorically denied by judge and executive councillor William Dummer Powell.[38] In any case, petitioning the British government was delayed until 1811, after a persistent campaign for redress that relied heavily on the privileged access to British officials enjoyed by Wyatt, Jackson, and Thorpe.

Once returned to Britain, Wyatt and Jackson used their connections to continue their struggle against Gore. In 1807, Wyatt obtained a personal interview with the secretary of state for the Colonies, but his complaints were not sympathetically received.[39] Jackson meanwhile used his pamphlet to lobby for a motion to be brought in the British Parliament in 1809–10. In this connection, Jackson wrote Willcocks in July 1809, asking him to forward "a true & correct statement of the proceedings of the Executive, & such as you might vouch for even you [*sic*] on oath &

endeavour to get as many signatures to it as you can." Jackson also requested "letters from the principle [*sic*] inhabitants which may give a true & impartial view of the present situation." He noted that he had already obtained "many documents & Letters."[40] It was in this same context, apparently, that Thorpe contacted a Mr Cheniquy in February 1810, noting that he was composing a petition "for Mr Jackson."[41] The petition that resulted in 1811 was signed by almost two hundred of Thorpe's former constituents. It duly condemned the provincial administration for "Partiality and Corruption."[42] This modest effort, however, even in conjunction with the dissidents' other activity, proved insufficient to persuade the British government to redress the petitioners' grievances – a sorry result that offered little encouragement to continue with the practice of oppositional petitioning.[43]

Thorpe and his allies had faced almost insuperable obstacles in their efforts to effect change in Upper Canada. Recent immigrants themselves, they failed to develop strong ties with the centres of power within the province. Moreover, they lacked an organizational infrastructure, relying primarily on personal contacts for support. Most important, members of the British government offered them little encouragement. No doubt the persistent hostility of Lieutenant-Governor Gore to the group,[44] as well as the exigencies of wartime, accounted for the lukewarm reception accorded colonial grievances before the War of 1812. In spite of their lack of success, however, Thorpe and his associates did leave a mark on the politics of Upper Canada. Thorpe received full credit from Robert Gourlay for his role as a pioneer in the petitioning movement. In addition, their other efforts to achieve reform, and the high-handed treatment to which they were subjected, secured for Thorpe and his associates an honourable place in the "martyrology" of Upper Canadian reform.[45] Beyond this, their influence was perhaps transmitted somewhat more directly. Historian Fred Coyne Hamil has noted that "the chairman and secretary of a public meeting of Thorpe's supporters in York county ... reappeared as active adherents of William Lyon Mackenzie two decades later, thus bridging the gap between the pre-war agitation and the reform movement of the 1820's."[46] Moreover, Willcocks's home territory – the Niagara district – was also the region from which the next leader of the petitioning movement, Robert Gourlay, drew his greatest strength.

ROBERT GOURLAY AND PETITIONING

Like his oppositionist predecessors, Gourlay was well-born, the son of a landed Scottish gentleman. Gourlay had attended St Andrews University and studied scientific agriculture at Edinburgh University in the late

1790s. He and his family, however, had fallen on hard times by the end of the Napoleonic Wars, and in 1817, at the age of thirty-nine, Gourlay decided to emigrate to Upper Canada, where he and his wife owned land.[47]

Gourlay's cultural baggage included considerable exposure to British radicalism. He was an admirer of William Cobbett, champion of the rural poor and editor of the radical journal the *Political Register*.[48] Gourlay also followed the career of Henry "Orator" Hunt, a famous supporter of parliamentary reform; in late 1816, he had actually heard Hunt speak at the notorious Spa Fields meeting in London. This petitioning meeting turned violent, prompting the British government to suspend habeas corpus and introduce a series of repressive laws known as the Gagging Acts.[49] (Gourlay, however, failed to draw from this series of events the obvious conclusion about British government's attitude towards reformist extraparliamentary agitation).

Gourlay's own sympathy for the rural poor and his support of parliamentary reform were proclaimed in a series of pamphlets written after 1808. In connection with these progressive concerns, he was particularly interested in the device of petitioning. As he said at his trial at the Kingston Assize in 1818, "The right of free petitioning, has, for years, engaged my own special attention: – it is a subject which I have again and again agitated, at home by my writings."[50] Gourlay's strengths as an oppositionist leader lay largely in his exposure to the currents of reformist thought that were sweeping Great Britain in the postwar period and in his familiarity with British radical organization.

He travelled to Upper Canada in 1817, however, not as an agitator but as a prospective settler. Despite the personal nature of his voyage, he occupied his time aboard ship by drawing up a questionnaire. He hoped the answers would provide the basis for a statistical account of Upper Canada that would also serve as a guide for immigrants.

From the first, Gourlay made good use of highly placed relatives of his wife. In particular, he worked with her cousins William Dickson and Thomas Clark, both legislative councillors from the Niagara region with impressive mercantile and landholding interests. Letters of reference from these worthies were among the factors which secured Gourlay permission from Samuel Smith, the administrator of the province, to publish his questionnaire and an accompanying address in the *Upper Canada Gazette* in October 1817. He demonstrated his command of publicity techniques by distributing an additional seven hundred copies of the address to township officials throughout the province. The address urged the respectable farmers of Upper Canada to complete the questionnaire, preferably at specially called township meetings. Gourlay proposed to publish the results of this collective effort in Britain, where its account of the province's abundant resources and promising future would surely attract capital and settlers to Upper Canada.[51]

As Gourlay was well aware, for Upper Canada to prosper, the province urgently needed settlers. Immigration from the United States had essentially dried up during and after the War of 1812, a result of the British government's policy of restricting the landholding rights of "aliens." In 1817, this policy was the target of criticism from the Assembly, particularly by former government supporter Colonel Robert Nichol, whose attack on the government was so severe that it prompted Lieutenant-Governor Gore to prorogue the House.[52] Other opponents of the land policy included speculators, among them Gourlay's relatives by marriage, who bent his ear with bitter complaints. They were so vehement that Gourlay became convinced that the connection with England was in serious danger.[53]

Thus prompted, Gourlay issued his second address to Upper Canadian landholders February 1818. The address was polemical in tone, and political in content. It took particular aim at Lieutenant-Governor Gore, who was condemned as both idle and arbitrary and whose conduct, Gourlay claimed, merited impeachment. It also condemned the "system of paltry patronage and ruinous favouritism" in government administration. Gourlay's greatest fire, not surprisingly, was reserved for the land-granting policies that were discouraging immigration from the United States.[54]

Having condemned the inadequacies of the Upper Canadian government, Gourlay proposed a solution: a parliamentary inquiry into the state of the province, the results of which would be carried to Britain by special commissioners. This inquiry was to be supplemented by popular petitioning. Though at this stage petitioning was secondary for Gourlay, he believed it was a crucial element in the campaign to impress the British government with the necessity for change. "Petitions," Gourlay urged, should be sent "from every quarter ... it should appear, if possible to be the unanimous desire of the whole population."[55] The strategy of an inquiry supplemented by petitioning had to be abandoned, however, when the legislature was prorogued in early April without having taken effective action on the land question.

Petitioning then moved to the forefront of Gourlay's strategy, as revealed in his third address, on 2 April 1818. Outraged by the proroguing of the legislature, Gourlay heartily denounced the system of government. The constitution, he contended, was in danger. "*For three years the laws have been thwarted, and set aside by executive power* ... Till the system is overturned, it is vain to expect any thing of value from *change of,* [*sic*] Representatives or Governors."[56] The solution, he maintained, was to be found in petitioning.

More remarkable than the shift in strategy was the extraordinarily detailed and comprehensive character of Gourlay's plans. Petitioning was organized on a three-tiered basis. The first tier called for township meetings to choose representatives. These representatives were to meet at the second tier: district meetings where they would compose petitions to the prince regent. The petitions were then to be circulated for signature. The third tier was a provincial convention, where representatives selected by the district meetings would organize succeeding stages of the campaign: the dispatch of commissioners to Britain with the petitions, and correspondence with the imperial government. Funding was to occur at the grassroots level, with clerks elected at the township meetings acting as local treasurers for the movement. This organizational plan was much more detailed, elaborate, and systematic than anything Thorpe and Jackson had attempted.

The first of the meetings was held in Niagara township on 13 April 1818, less than a week after the publication of the third address in the *Niagara Spectator.*[57] Meeting participants unanimously approved Gourlay's third address. They elected a representative and a clerk. They also appointed a committee "to forward the views of the meeting." The participants then organized the rest of the district: the other townships of the Niagara district would meet on the following Monday, and the district gathering would take place on 27 April in St Catharines. The committee undertook to publicize these later meetings. They must have done their work effectively: fifteen representatives gathered in St Catharines on 4 May for the district meeting.[58]

Gourlay continued to attract the support of local notables, despite his increasingly inflammatory language. William Dickson and Thomas Clark, his foremost contacts in the Niagara district, had approved his third address prior to publication. They had also made a financial contribution to the project of sending a petition to Britain. Also, the fifteen representatives and clerks in attendance at the Niagara district meeting included four magistrates, two doctors, two individuals identified by military rank, and several "esquires." Among the group were members of the locally prominent Hamilton and Clark families, as well as William Hamilton Merritt.[59]

As planned, participants in the Niagara district meeting chose representatives to attend the provincial convention in York. They also approved in principle a draft petition and referred it to a committee for final changes in wording. The committee, they directed, was to have the final draft printed, with a view to soliciting public input. The petition was then to be given the widest possible publicity throughout the province. Another important organizational initiative of the Niagara district meeting was to clarify the timing of subsequent meetings elsewhere. Township meetings were to be held on 6 June, district meetings on 13 June, and the provincial convention was to take place in York on 6 July. In little more than a month, the Niagara district had been fully organized, and arrangements made for the spread of the petitioning campaign throughout the province.

Publicity was crucial to Gourlay's strategy. The first step was the publication of one thousand copies of the "Principles and Proceedings" of the Niagara district meeting. This pamphlet included some material on the district meeting itself, as well as the text of the petition. The petition highlighted abuses relating to war losses and to land-granting: the failure of the government to make payment for losses sustained in the War of 1812; broken promises of land grants to those who served in the militia during the war; and the "system of patronage and favouritism, in the disposal of Crown lands." Other evils of the provincial administration were not included in the petition, but were left to the commissioners to explain in person to members of the British government. Early responses from the Niagara district were encouraging: nine hundred individuals made financial contributions to Gourlay's crusade.[60]

Personal proselytization was also a key element of the petitioners' strategy. In order to publicize the township meetings, it was decided to distribute literature throughout the province, particularly to areas beyond the reach of newspapers.[61] Unlike some of his successors, Gourlay was primarily concerned with attracting the support of "respectable men," individuals who were presumably literate. Hence the major focus of this campaign was on the dissemination of print materials; attracting support through public meetings appears to have been an afterthought.[62] Accordingly, four riders were "dispatched ... to lodge [the pamphlet] for sale and distribution through different quarters of the province."[63] In this manner the Western, London, Gore, Newcastle and Home districts were covered. Gourlay himself undertook to distribute the material in the eastern part of the province, though he assigned part of the task to "an attorney, who very completely did the business of the Midland district."[64] Gourlay ensured that both his journey and the petitioning meetings would receive widespread publicity. His accounts of his journeys in the eastern part of the province were published in the *Kingston Gazette*, which also carried reports from the petitioning meetings.[65] No stranger to the benefits of advertising, Gourlay ensured that these accounts speedily appeared in pamphlet form as well.

By this time, Gourlay's activities were arousing suspicion and hostility at several levels in the province. John Strachan, the leader of the province's Anglicans and a member of the Executive Council, had been leery of Gourlay from the first.[66] Samuel Smith, the administrator of the province, who had initially supported Gourlay's proposed statistical account, now became similarly hostile. In April 1818 Smith instructed Attorney General John Beverley Robinson to be on the alert for an opportunity to prosecute Gourlay and thus stop him in his tracks. More ominously for Gourlay, his chief supporters in Niagara turned against him. Thomas Clark, alarmed by the thought that Gourlay's activities might be seditious, hastened to dissociate himself from his relative by marriage.[67] Before long, another of Gourlay's former supporters, the powerful Niagara figure William Dickson, followed suit.[68]

Gourlay's roster of enemies increased as a result of his tour of the eastern part of the province in the early summer of 1818.[69] His activities offended powerful figures there, particularly once he began holding public meetings. His opponents retaliated with a combination of obstruction, demonstrations of public disrespect, and physical attacks on Gourlay's person. The first of these occurred at Prescott at the end of May, where Gourlay called a meeting in response to a hostile letter that had appeared in the *Kingston Gazette* two weeks earlier. Here his chief opponent was Jonas Jones, MPP for Grenville, whose refusal to surrender the floor utterly disrupted the meeting. Philip Vankoughnet, MPP of Stormont and Russell, then began following Gourlay about, tearing down placards advertising the meetings. Two meetings in Glengarry county, held shortly after the Prescott meeting, were relatively uneventful in spite of the obstruction elsewhere. This, however, was the calm before the storm that occurred in Cornwall after a parade on 4 June, militia muster day. Having bought up all of Gourlay's available promotional material, the militia denounced the petitioning movement and burned the literature in a great bonfire.

Thus provoked, Gourlay armed himself with "a plentiful supply of Printer's amunition [*sic*]" and began attending township meetings in the Johnstown district. By this time, Jonas Jones had recouped his forces sufficiently to call another a public meeting opposing Gourlay's petition. Gourlay himself attended the meeting, held in Prescott on 25 June. He spoke for nearly three hours before rushing off to another engagement; in his absence Jones circulated a counter-petition of his own.

More ominously, Gourlay became the target of personal violence. Just after the Prescott meeting, he was assaulted by a crowd outside a Cornwall inn; he was shocked to be told that the first to strike had been a magistrate, Duncan Fraser.[70] Not long after, Christopher

Hagerman, a rising star in the legal firmament of the province, horse-whipped Gourlay in the streets of Kingston because he intended to publish information about the criminal activities of one of Hagerman's brothers.[71] This incident occurred in front of the house of a magistrate who initially watched the assault with indifference, then intervened with a demand that Gourlay – not the aggressor Hagerman – keep the peace.

Officials also resorted to legal tactics in their efforts to silence Gourlay. On the initiative of Attorney General John Beverley Robinson, Gourlay was charged with seditious libel on 11 June. Significantly, Christopher Hagerman acted as Robinson's agent in relation to the warrant for Gourlay's arrest. Freed on bail, Gourlay was arrested on the same charge two weeks later in Cornwall on the initiative of magistrate Duncan Fraser. Gourlay believed that the combination of legal action and violence against him was no coincidence, and that "lawyers and magistrates" from Kingston to Cornwall were "striving to hasten [my destruction] by the foulest means – not by slander only, but by arrests and violence."[72] Bailed out again, he was able to attend the convention in York from 6 to 10 July 1818.

The much-heralded convention was not a revolutionary assembly intent on substituting its rule for that of the constituted authorities. That much was clear from its name: "The Upper Canadian Convention of Friends to Enquiry." As Gourlay had suggested, it was an organizational meeting of the petitioning movement. Accordingly, the representatives adopted a slightly modified version of the Niagara petition, deciding to delay sending it to Britain until they could present it to Sir Peregrine Maitland, the incoming lieutenant-governor of the province. However, petitioning-related activity continued – even after the convention – under the auspices of a permanent management committee. Regional conventions with representation from several districts met in Ancaster in late July and in Kingston at the beginning of August. The petition, however, failed to reach Britain, though Gourlay continued to entertain hopes for this result into the 1820s.[73]

Official efforts to suppress Gourlay's movement now entered a critical stage. When juries in the Midland district acquitted him of seditious libel in his two trials of August 1818, the authorities resorted to other means. Maitland's speech from the throne in mid-October asked for a new law to ban seditious meetings. Gourlay responded with a call for township meetings, and eleven were actually held in the vicinity of Kingston. The people at these meetings declared that the population of the province lacked confidence in their present Assembly and asked Maitland to hold elections for a new Assembly. In the meantime, Maitland declined to receive the petition endorsed by the July convention on the grounds that the convention had been unconstitutional. A week later, the Assembly passed the law against township meetings, which were said "to encourage riot, tumult, [and] disorder."[74] Though some of Gourlay's supporters in the eastern part of the province responded with petitions asking for the dissolution of the Assembly, the backbone of the petitioning movement had essentially been broken.[75]

Having stilled popular protest, the authorities moved to silence the Gourlayite press. Bartemus Ferguson, the new editor of the *Niagara Spectator*, had published the first instalment of a letter from Gourlay which protested the law against allegedly seditious meetings. Ferguson was arrested for seditious libel on the initiative of William Dickson, who had decisively turned against Gourlay, and William Claus, a member of both the Legislative and Executive Councils, from the Niagara region.[76] Three days later, Gourlay himself was arrested under the Sedition Act of 1804. Under the terms of this act, according to G.M. Craig, "anyone who had not lived in the province for six months and who had not taken the oath of allegiance might be arrested and required to prove that his words, actions and conduct were not intended to promote or encourage disaffection."[77] It was possible to apply these provisions to Gourlay because he had recently been out of the province on a brief visit to the United States. In addition, he had not taken the oath of allegiance in Upper Canada (though he had in Britain). Predictably, Gourlay failed to convince a panel of magistrates, which included Dickson and Claus, that he was not a threat to the status quo. When he refused an order to leave the province, he was jailed under the Sedition Act without possibility of bail on 4 January 1819. There he remained, tormented by the close quarters and oppressive summer heat, until his trial on 20 August. Charged with failing to leave Upper Canada, he was found guilty. The next day he left the province for the United States and returned to Britain by the end of the year.

Though Gourlay was gone, he was not forgotten. One reason was the publication of a book, written by John Strachan – a rising figure in the established church and member of the Executive Council – under the name of his brother James.[78] The book, purporting to be the record of a visit to Upper Canada in 1819, devoted an entire chapter to assassinating Gourlay's character and justifying his treatment by Upper Canadian authorities. Gourlay, Strachan claimed, was "half insane," a debtor, and an associate of turbulent characters in Britain. Though a stranger to the country, he had the audacity to call public meetings. Worse still, he had organized a convention that conjured up "the horrors of a revolution." Such activities, Strachan maintained, "struck … completely at the root of all civil government … The mischief which this man would have accomplished," he continued, "under a less firm and intelligent government ... is incalculable." Not the least of Gourlay's offences was that "the grievances were chiefly imaginary." Happily, however, Gourlay had now been banished from the province, and as a consequence the population was "sensible that the interests of the government and the governed is [*sic*] the same." Significantly, many of the charges Strachan levelled against Gourlay were resurrected more than a decade later and used against William Lyon Mackenzie and his associates. Such charges were part of a generic vocabulary of abuse on which government sympathizers drew in response to criticism of the provincial administration.

Gourlay's memory was also kept alive by others with connections to the Upper Canadian government, which embarked on a campaign to punish his followers; many delegates to the convention of 1818 lost their jobs, or were denied the land that had been promised to them for war services.[79] Gourlay was remembered, as well, at the election of 1820, when eight Gourlayite candidates were elected in Niagara and elsewhere. The publication of his *Statistical Account*, "easily the best compendium of information about Upper Canada for his period" according to S.F. Wise, also kept Gourlay's name before the public.[80] So too did the efforts of his sympathizers to secure the repeal of the Seditious Meetings Act (repealed in 1820) and the campaign to repeal the Sedition Act of 1804 (repealed in 1829). For all these reasons, Gourlay's name and career remained fresh in the minds of Upper Canadians in the 1820s.

Gourlay was also significant because he was the first to identify a number of targets in government administration that later petitioners would also criticize. These included the system of land-granting and the disposition of patronage, though oppositionists of the 1820s and 1830s added substantially to the list. Gourlay's solution – a commission of inquiry – was not among the demands of his successors. In a sense, however, his objective was ultimately realized in 1838, when the British government appointed Lord Durham to make recommendations on potential government reform in the Canadas.

It has been suggested that Gourlay's chief importance was as a "martyr" to the cause of reform.[81] Other aspects of his career as a political activist, however, are also significant. He overcame the obstacle of being a stranger to the province by cultivating his ties with men of importance like Dickson and Clark. The history of Gourlay's relationship with these individuals, however, illustrated an emerging truism in Upper Canadian politics: such alliances were inherently unstable because officials were vulnerable to pressure from the highest levels of the provincial administration. Indeed, Gourlay was the last of the Upper Canadian oppositionist petitioners who attempted to work closely with officials of the provincial government.

Gourlay's experience offered additional lessons, ones in organization. Though his use of the press and other publicity techniques was an unprecedented success, his method of fine-tuning the wording of the petition by having it pass through multiple tiers of meetings was both cumbersome and unnecessarily alarming to officialdom. Later petitioners streamlined the process and dispensed with the idea of a provincial convention, that red flag to the authorities. This was true at least until the late 1830s, when William Lyon Mackenzie considered holding a similar gathering prior to the Rebellion of 1837. Another organizational lesson was the importance of speech-making to the task of publicizing the cause; Mackenzie, for one, ensured that this tool was included in his organizational strategy from the start, and not as an afterthought.

There was a third lesson to be learned for those who followed Gourlay's career. From the viewpoint of British politics, Gourlay's timing could hardly have been more unfortunate. Between 1815 and 1820, Britain experienced harrowing postwar economic dislocation. At the same time, working class antagonism to the established order, no longer restrained by wartime patriotism, burst forth in a series of demonstrations that filled the governing classes with alarm.[82] The result, as we have seen, was repressive action on the part of the British government. A ministry intent on suppressing reform in Britain was hardly likely to look with favour on similar movements in the colonies. Gourlay's initiative was doomed not so much by the hostility of the Upper Canadian authorities as by the anti-reform climate of the British government. Contrastingly, the oppositionist petitioners who succeeded him in the late 1820s were blessed with more receptive British ministries.

PETITIONING AGAINST THE 1827 ALIEN BILL

The oppositional petitioning of 1827–31 has all but escaped the notice of historians. The best-known aspect of these campaigns is the 1827 mission to London of MPP Robert Randal, who succeeded in persuading the British government to disavow provincial legislation on the rights of the American-born (the so-called "alien question"). The importance of oppositionist petitioning in these years, however, went well beyond that particular victory. Located in York, the organizers of Randal's mission soon joined with others to launch a series of challenges to government policies on religion and government. One important result was the fusion of a number of different strands of opposition into a common movement. Also, the ongoing petitioning helped develop an organizational infrastructure and exposed Upper Canadians more than ever before to this type of political activism.

One of the leading figures behind this series of petitions was Jesse Ketchum of York, a wealthy tanner and real estate investor. In addition to his business interests, Ketchum was a philanthropist with a particular interest in education. As a prominent dissenter, he had tangled over educational questions with John Strachan, whose support for the Anglican Church, particularly the clergy reserves, was anathema to Ketchum.[83] A so-called "late Loyalist," he had emigrated from New York state in 1799 at the age of seventeen. Hence, Ketchum had a personal interest in issues relating to the rights of the American-born in Upper Canada. Indeed, he was a prime mover in the agitation against the Alien Bill in 1827.

Another leader of the movement was William Warren Baldwin, whose family had emigrated from Ireland in 1798. Baldwin was a multi-talented and ambitious individual: after graduating as a doctor of medicine from the University of Edinburgh in 1797, he broadened his opportunities five years later by qualifying as a lawyer in Upper Canada. By the 1820s, having achieved considerable professional success with his legal practice in York, Baldwin also became active in politics. He was elected in the constituency of York and Simcoe in 1820, and in Norfolk in 1828. While a member of the Assembly, he spearheaded resistance, both there and out-of-doors, to the British government's proposed Union Bill of 1822, which would have united Upper and Lower Canada into one province.[84] Though he served only six years in the Assembly, Baldwin enjoyed great prominence among opponents of the Upper Canadian government, contributing to their efforts both his social standing and his unwavering support. His son Robert, a junior lawyer who had been called to the bar in 1825, was a loyal supporter of his father's many causes.[85] The Baldwins and Ketchum were typical of the growing middle class of merchants and professionals in York who were poised to assume leadership roles in provincial affairs.

Like Ketchum and the Baldwins, William Lyon Mackenzie was a prominent figure in York, but unlike them his reputation had more than a hint of notoriety. Born in relatively humble circumstances in Scotland in 1795, Mackenzie emigrated to Upper Canada in 1820. Four years later he founded a newspaper, the *Colonial Advocate*, in Queenston, but transferred it to York shortly thereafter. His vicious personal journalistic attacks on members of the governing elite and their families met with spectacular retaliation when a group of young lawyers and law students destroyed his press in 1826, throwing his types into the bay. In the aftermath of this "Types Riot," a civil jury awarded him £625 in damages – enough to give him a degree of financial stability he had not previously enjoyed. Like Ketchum and Baldwin, Mackenzie harboured political ambitions and was quick to associate himself with extraparliamentary activities that opposed the established authorities.[86]

By the 1820s, opponents of the Upper Canadian government could realistically entertain hopes of success in their dealings with the British government. The visible tensions that had agitated British society and panicked the governing classes in the immediate postwar years had dissipated in the more prosperous 1820s. The tory government began in the 1820s to institute a domestic policy of economic and judicial reform. These "liberal tories" were also sympathetic to religious reform. They responded in 1828, for example, to the formidable petitioning campaign organized by British dissenters by repealing the Test and Corporation Acts, those "badge[s] of social inferiority and a barrier to political office."[87] The following year marked an even more significant turning point with the achievement of Catholic emancipation.[88]

The issue that first revived extraparliamentary agitation in Upper Canada, however, was not a major question in British domestic politics. It was, nevertheless, a subject of extraordinary interest to Upper Canadians. The alien issue dominated Upper Canadian politics in the 1820s. It had a rather long and tangled history, well before it attracted the attention of Jesse Ketchum and his associates in 1827, having been contentious since at least the 1790s. Officials were always fearful of the potential democratic tendencies of these newcomers, though others, as Mills has shown, argued that "loyalty could develop naturally through settlement in the province."[89]

Although American immigration to Upper Canada had been an issue for some time, the specific question of the rights of these immigrants arose during the War of 1812. This conflict engendered antagonism towards the American-born residents of Upper Canada, whose loyalty seemed lukewarm at best, at least to supporters of the government. The authorities responded by trying to discourage American immigration after 1815, refusing to allow Americans to take the oath of allegiance, a necessary prerequisite for the holding of land.

Within a few years, the question of the rights of the American-born in Upper Canada had become both complicated and politically volatile.[90] The complexity was in part a result of differences in attitude between members of the British government and the colonial administration. The former took a narrow technical view of the question, and their conclusions were dismaying to the "late Loyalists" (those who had entered the province after the end of the American revolutionary war in 1783). London argued that anyone who had come to live in Upper Canada after 1783 and had not conformed to the Naturalization Act of 1740 was not entitled to hold land in the province, as British subjects were. This view found favour with the British courts in a decision rendered in 1824. The administration of Lieutenant-Governor Sir Peregrine Maitland, on the other hand, had no desire to interfere with anyone's property rights, but, because they considered American immigrants politically unreliable, he and his advisers were keen on preventing the American-born from voting.

Either position was extremely difficult to implement in Upper Canada. Here, the Naturalization Act of 1740 had never been enforced, and thousands had been lured to the province from south of the border on the understanding that they would afterwards enjoy the rights of British subjects. Late Loyalists who had endured the hardships of the early pioneer days, who had taken a full part in civic life, or who had fought in the militia during the War of 1812, were insulted that the British government considered them aliens. There was also considerable panic at the thought that their landholding rights – the basis of their livelihoods – appeared to be in jeopardy. The late Loyalists wanted a declaration from the government guaranteeing both their property and their political rights.

The issue began to attract public attention in 1821, after Barnabas Bidwell's by-election victory in the riding of Lennox and Addington. Political opponents challenged Bidwell's right to sit in the Assembly, partly on the basis that as a former office-holder in the United States he had taken oaths abjuring his allegiance to Great Britain. He was ultimately ejected from the Assembly, however, on the different issue of moral turpitude: he had stolen public money in Massachusetts. His American-born son, Marshall Spring Bidwell, who had never held public office in the United States, offered himself to the electors in his father's stead. The younger Bidwell was elected to the Assembly in 1824, after having his candidacy rejected by the returning officer in two by-elections on the grounds that he was an alien. In spite of the Assembly's acceptance of the junior Bidwell, the British government took the view that neither Bidwell was eligible for a seat in the Assembly because both were aliens. Efforts to settle the issue in the Upper Canadian legislature in 1825 proved unavailing; the Assembly and the Legislative Council were hopelessly deadlocked.

Extraparliamentary agitation around this question, somewhat surprisingly, began when Maitland ventured a rare sally into the realm of popular politics. Touring the eastern part of the province in early 1826, he was greeted with a deluge of loyal addresses, many of them applauding his actions and condemning champions of the late Loyalists in the Assembly. An address from the county of Durham, for example, condemned opponents of the government's alien policy in strong language: "Unprincipled and designing men, under the dark mantle of specious patriotism, have dared to malign the purity of Your Excellency's impartial administration, and excite the frenzy of popular commotion in the untutored and unreflecting mind, by appealing in strong language to the passions of the ignorant, and thereby deluding the many."[91] Such strictures on supporters of the late Loyalists were combined with high praise for Maitland's administration of the province. The addresses, in fact, were so laudatory as to raise suspicions that they had been manufactured by Maitland's own advisers.[92] Whether or not this was the case, it is significant that the administration had actively solicited public support. Maitland, moreover, used the addresses as a basis for arguing to the Colonial Office that he indeed enjoyed the backing of public opinion.[93] By the 1830s, government supporters would increasingly solicit evidence of public approval in their efforts to influence policy-making in Britain.

From the standpoint of popular politics, the most important consequence of the alien question arose on the other side of the issue. It was prompted by the passage in February 1827 of an Upper Canadian Alien Bill conforming to the instructions of the British government. This bill was profoundly unsatisfactory to the late Loyalists, largely because it required them to retake the oath of allegiance and to register. Opponents of the bill lost no time in organizing their resistance. With remarkable efficiency, they orchestrated a province-wide petitioning campaign against the Alien Bill, and laid the foundations for the next decade of anti-government activity.

The initiative came from the provincial capital, where Jesse Ketchum organized a meeting on 21 February 1827 to prevent the British government from approving the Alien Bill.[94] Ketchum was no stranger to political organization. The year before, he and some colleagues had taken an active part in organizing public support for two individuals – Charles Fothergill and Robert Randal – they considered victims of injustice at the hands of the provincial government.[95] Building on this experience, Ketchum and his associates in the meeting of February 1827 appointed a committee (later called the Central Committee), chaired by Ketchum himself and also including Thomas Styles, Alexander Burnside, and Joseph Shepherd. Among their allies was William Lyon Mackenzie, who read the petition in draft form and assisted in transmitting it across the province.[96]

This committee, charged with supervising the signing of a petition to the British Parliament against the Alien Bill, acted with extraordinary speed and decisiveness. In little more than a week, they had arranged for the printing of one thousand copies of the petition, and had sent them throughout the province for signature. Shortly thereafter, supporters organized township meetings in the Niagara, Gore, and Newcastle districts.[97] As befitted a group with strong representation from the business community, the organizing committee did not fail to make provision for the collection of money to defray the expenses of a mission to London. The committee ensured the distribution of great quantities of literature advertising their campaign and summarizing the issues involved in the alien question. As hostile commentator Samuel Peters Jarvis observed, "Circular letters/printed/and fictitious bills [*sic*] ... have been transmitted in thousands to the most remote parts of the Province."[98]

In many quarters, the petition may have circulated privately. In other cases, opponents of the Alien Bill held public meetings to discuss the issue, obtain signatures to the petition, and collect money. Such gatherings occurred in Port Hope, Hamilton, St David's, Whitby, Prince Edward, and Belleville, and likely elsewhere as well.[99] The most colourful of the meetings documented in the press was in Port Hope, where developments foreshadowed the more dramatic encounters between oppositionists and government supporters in the Newcastle district in the 1830s.

The Port Hope gathering to obtain signatures on the petition against the Alien Bill was called by the oppositionists for 10 March at the Wellington Hotel.[100] Government supporters, wanting to minimize attendance, considered holding a militia drill at the same time, which would have diverted the attention of all able-bodied men between the ages of sixteen and sixty. This idea, however, was rejected, and government supporters simply decided to attend the meeting themselves. So great was the attendance, in fact, that the floor of the hotel threatened to collapse. It proved difficult, however, to secure alternate accommodations for the meeting because an auction sale was in progress in the only room large enough to hold the entire crowd.

Once finally underway, the meeting was addressed by Charles Fothergill, MPP for the county of Durham and a prominent opponent of the government, who denounced the Alien Bill.[101] Local officials, in turn, spoke in its favour, undeterred by the fact that an effigy of one of their number hung all day at a fork in the main road. Opponents of the bill claimed a victory, noting that the York petition had been approved at the meeting and that a committee had been appointed to circulate it. Further gatherings were scheduled for the front townships of the Newcastle district. Supporters of the bill told a very different story (omitting all mention of their opponents' gathering): they simply noted that an address to Maitland approving the terms of the Alien Bill had been arranged at the Port Hope meeting.[102] Evidently, supporters of the bill had gone ahead with a meeting of their own.

The readiness with which signatures against the Alien Bill were obtained no doubt owed much to the urgency of the issue and the large numbers of individuals throughout the province who were affected by the bill. These factors also contributed to the high number of signatures (fourteen thousand) on the petition that Robert Randal took to London in mid-April 1827.[103] In a population totalling about 186,500 this was an impressive figure. It is particularly striking in light of the number of active voters at the time. According to the calculations of Elwood Jones, there were approximately sixteen thousand voters in the Upper Canadian general election of 1828.[104] Thus the number of signatures on the oppositionist petition was equal to about eighty-seven per cent of the number of voters in the provincial election of the following year. It is highly unlikely, however, that all the signatories were eligible to vote. Although it is not possible to determine reliably what percentage of them were also among the electorate, it seems fair to conclude that a very large number of them indeed were among the unenfranchised. In their effort to demonstrate the strongest possible public resistance to the 1827 Alien Bill, oppositionists spread their nets as widely as they could. The result, in all likelihood, was to attract the participation in the petitioning process of thousands who were barred from exercising the franchise.

The breadth of support for the oppositionist petition delighted its sponsors and outraged the provincial administration. The number of signatures on the petition prompted a warm reception for Randal at the Colonial Office. Moreover, the British government instructed York to pass a bill that essentially met all of Randal's objections. Before the end of 1827, Randal was back in Upper Canada with his mission nearly completed. The only remaining loose end was taken care of when, in 1828, the Upper Canadian legislature passed an alien bill more acceptable to the American-born. When the bill passed, its proponents shocked government supporters in the Assembly by giving, as one sourly noted, "Three hearty Cheers to the King."[105] Given the snail's pace at which the Colonial Office customarily operated, this amounted to virtually instant success.

The final passage of this bill in early 1828 did not go unremarked by members of the Central Committee. The *Colonial Advocate* reported that the event was celebrated with the music of "national airs" and the illumination of many houses in York. Jesse Ketchum spared no expense in his contribution to the festivities, displaying two large transparencies painted by Mr Craig, an artist. One showed Joseph Hume presenting the petition to the British House of Commons on 12 June 1827, and the other an interview between Randal and Colonial Secretary Lord Goderich. The *Advocate* office boasted a lantern displaying three transparencies, inscribed "The People's Rights," "Success in Randal," and "Long live Lord Goderich." There was a darker side as well to the celebrations. An effigy, said by some to be that of Attorney General John Beverley Robinson, was suspended from a poplar tree opposite a picture of the premier of Britain. After suffering numerous indignities, the effigy was "anatomized" by the crowd, apparently in exuberant good humour.[106] Not long after, similar celebrations in the village of Port Hope (without an effigy but with the addition of a spectacular fireworks display) marked the final passage of the revised alien bill.[107]

The official houses of York likely remained dark during these festivities. The provincial administration, which had courted unpopularity in 1827 by supporting a bill endorsed by the Colonial Office, felt that the ground had been taken out from under them.[108] The capitulation to Randal was particularly insulting, in the view of Lieutenant-Governor Maitland, because of the low social status of the organizers of the petitioning campaign. The lieutenant-governor stigmatized them as "men of low station, and questionable character as to loyalty" and described their deficiencies of character to the Colonial Office in considerable detail. Ketchum, for example, was accused of discreditable conduct during the war of 1812, and condemned as "wholly illiterate."[109] This would not be the last time that the cause of the provincial government's opponents would be attacked because of the allegedly low social status of its promoters.[110]

Maitland also demonstrated concern about the long-term effects of the actions of the Colonial Office. He hotly penned a series of dire predictions that their capitulation to an irregular ambassador like Randal would seriously destabilize provincial politics. "If a petition ... is considered and treated as an expression of public feeling," he maintained, "and if in deference to it any reasonable measure of the Government is abandoned, then indeed an importance will be conferred upon the few political agitators who are industrious to sow dissentions."[111] Before long, in fact, a flood of petitions deluged the province.

Maitland may have been correct in attributing this outpouring in large measure to the encouragement offered not only by the actions of the Colonial Office but also by the advice of British radical MP Joseph Hume. In a widely reprinted letter to Robert Randal, Hume advised the establishment of an ongoing grievance committee in York to maintain contact with an agent in Britain.[112] By late 1827, the committee that had organized the petitioning campaign against the 1827 Alien Bill had christened itself the "Central Committee," suggesting aspirations towards permanency.[113] It lost no opportunity to trumpet to the world the success of Randal's mission; this too suggests that its members were following Hume's advice and looking to the future.

PETITIONING ON RELIGIOUS AND CONSTITUTIONAL QUESTIONS, 1827–31

The Central Committee continued to function after the resolution of the alien question. One reason was that its members were involved in an ongoing effort to cover the expenses of Randal's mission. In December 1827 the Committee issued a circular noting that they were still £100 short on Randal's account. They also needed money to pay for two thousand copies of their first report, which they intended to disseminate throughout the province. This report contained a thorough coverage of Randal's correspondence with the Colonial Office and with Joseph Hume. Subscription lists were drawn up for supporters to carry throughout the province in search of generous donors.[114]

Members of the Central Committee, however, were not content simply to finish up the details of the campaign against the Alien Bill. Their success on that issue prompted them to use the same methods to tackle other grievances as well – and in the same manner – by appealing to the British government. The alien question had given them a natural constituency among the American-born. Many of this group, as dissenters, were also aggrieved by the exclusive privileges that had been given to the Anglican Church under the Constitution Act of 1791. The appeal of this issue, however, reached beyond the ranks of the American-born to include dissenters from Great Britain as well. In the aftermath of the alien question, religious issues were given a special potency because of the newly aggressive pretensions of the Church of England in Canada.

The prominence of religious issues during the late 1820s was in large measure the result of the efforts of John Strachan, Archdeacon of York, to entrench and solidify the role of the Anglican Church in Upper Canada. His actions enraged his opponents, the voluntarists, who believed that there should be no connection between church and state. The voluntarists – whose membership included, among others, the Methodists (the largest denomination in the province) – were an increasingly vocal and active segment of the population during the 1820s and 1830s. Their chief complaints concerned the clergy reserves and the provincial university. The clergy reserves were extensive lands set aside by the imperial government at the founding of the province for the support of the Protestant clergy. But in fact, the Anglican Church was essentially the sole beneficiary of this imperial largesse. The voluntarists argued that the reserves should be secularized, with the proceeds from the sale of the lands going to education and perhaps to strengthen the economic infrastructure (then called "internal improvements").

The grievance was an old one, but, in 1825, voluntarists were goaded into action by John Strachan's attacks on their loyalty and the quality of their preachers in his sermon on the death of Bishop Mountain.[115] In addition, after departing for Britain in 1826 to lobby on behalf of the Anglican Church, Strachan produced in 1827 an "Ecclesiastical Chart" which soon became notorious for its alleged exaggeration of the numerical strength of the Anglicans and the corresponding weakness of other denominations.[116] The Sales and Improvement Acts (1827), passed by the Imperial Parliament with Strachan's endorsement, appeared to protect the financial interests of the Anglican Church.[117] At the same time, Strachan further inflamed non-Anglicans when he obtained, in England, a charter for King's College – a provincial university that was to be Anglican-dominated.[118]

The voluntarists, perhaps inspired by the ongoing campaign for the repeal of the Test and Corporation Acts in Great Britain, quickly became expert organizers. Religious issues soon drew thousands of Upper Canadians into the political process. In late 1827, once Strachan's strictures on members of other churches became known in Upper Canada, petitions of protest poured into the Assembly, including one bearing six thousand signatures asking for an inquiry into Strachan's charges and into the university question.[119]

An alliance with the voluntarists had both advantages and drawbacks for political oppositionists. The large number of voluntarists was definitely one of the advantages. Between 1828 and 1832, the number of Methodists in Upper Canada rose from 9,678 to 14,999.[120] Among the drawbacks was the widespread view that Methodist loyalty was suspect. The early Methodist ministers in Upper Canada had been American. Though the denomination was progressively Canadianized, and its leadership tended to be profoundly conservative on political as opposed to religious questions, as late as the 1830s, government supporters continued to denounce its adherents as a danger to the state.[121]

One such detractor was John Willson, MPP for Wentworth and sometime speaker of the Assembly. In 1831, Egerton Ryerson, a young Methodist minister who, in the decades to come, played a leading role in Upper Canadian religion and education, complained that Willson "had been frequent and long, and loud, and boisterous in his unfeeling criminations of the Methodists and the Conference in his place in the house of Assembly, and spared no pains or labour to impress upon the house that the Methodist were under a foreign controul, [*sic*] and that the measures of their Conference were nothing but a system of 'TREACHERY.'"[122] John Strachan, too, believed that the Methodists intended "to pull down all establishments, undermine the loyalty of the people and constitute us a province of the United States."[123] Strachan was hardly a disinterested observer, but his views were nonetheless extremely influential.

The politicization of the voluntarists provided a basis for co-operation between political activists – whose primary concern was political reform – and preachers impressed with the urgency of educational and religious matters. In December 1827, the Central Committee swung into action again to orchestrate protests in York against both the existence of the clergy reserves and the sectarian character of the university. That same month, Jesse Ketchum, hero of the fight against the 1827 Alien Bill, chaired a public meeting to protest Strachan's ecclesiastical chart. Ketchum's name also stood at the head of a list of Home district residents who, in 1828, petitioned for a more liberal charter for King's College.[124] This group brought together religious and lay figures, including two ministers and oppositionist stalwarts Jesse Ketchum and T.D. Morrison.

A report of a district meeting in Newcastle indicates how signatures were obtained for these petitions. On 31 December 1827, a gathering took place in the Methodist chapel in Cramahe to petition the Imperial and Upper Canadian legislatures regarding Strachan's statements on the strength of the Anglican Church. The main speaker was Egerton Ryerson, under whose guidance participants passed a series of resolutions contradicting Strachan's assertions of the numerical superiority of the Anglicans and emphasizing the loyalty of the major dissenting denominations. They further asserted that Strachan's charter for an Anglican-dominated college had been obtained by misrepresentation and contrary to the wishes of a majority of the population. They asked for the establishment of a non-denominational college instead of the Anglican-dominated King's College and urged that the proceeds from the clergy reserves be devoted to secular purposes. Participants also adopted the petitions of the Central Committee in York. To promote the petitions, they established district and township committees. Members of these committees would receive copies of the resolutions and petitions, which were to be returned to the committee's secretary before the end of January 1828.[125]

A month later, on behalf of various non-Anglican denominations, the Central Committee deputed Reverend George Ryerson to travel to England and present a petition against the claims of the Anglican Church in Upper Canada.[126] By June 1828, the Committee was able to report that the petition had obtained some eight thousand signatures before being sent to England; it was presented to the British Parliament by the Scottish radical Joseph Hume in May. This event coincided almost exactly with the establishment of a select committee of the British House of Commons to inquire into Canadian affairs. Upper Canadian oppositionists were encouraged by the support that members of that committee offered to their proposals.[127] For a variety of reasons, however, no progress was then made towards secularizing the reserves or amending the college charter.

Members of the Central Committee acquired new allies when they joined with the Baldwins in a secular protest concerned with legal and political problems that surfaced in the summer of 1828.[128] The crisis began when John Walpole Willis, Judge of the Court of King's Bench, was dismissed by Lieutenant-Governor Maitland after he objected to the court sitting in the absence of the Chief Justice, who was on sick leave in Britain.[129] Reform-minded lawyers agreed with Willis that the efficiency of the courts was gravely imperiled by an incomplete bench. But more than purely legal issues were at stake here: there were concerns that the dismissal of a "learned, independent, and just judge" – allegedly without cause – was a serious abuse of executive power.[130] Moreover, the incident triggered more general anxieties about the Upper Canadian constitution at a time when it was under consideration by a committee of the British Parliament.

These factors help explain how the Willis case brought together three emerging strands of oppositionist thought in the persons of Jesse Ketchum, Dr W.W. Baldwin, and William Lyon Mackenzie. It was Ketchum who offered his premises for a private meeting to prepare for the public meeting of 5 July 1828. As for Dr Baldwin, he was the featured speaker at the 5 July meeting and the principal promoter of the petition thereafter. Mackenzie, who had already been closely associated with Ketchum in the protests against the 1827 Alien Bill, was not among the primary organizers of the meeting, but he did give the initiative considerable coverage in his newspaper, the *Colonial Advocate*; the promotion of oppositionist popular politics was evidently complementary to his ongoing journalistic crusade against provincial officialdom.

Supporters of Willis, dubbing his dismissal an "alarming crisis," advertised a public meeting to be held in York on 5 July 1828.[131] The event, said to have been the largest public gathering in the town's history, attracted farmers from as far away as forty miles. This show of interest heartened the organizers. Dr Baldwin began his address to the crowd by commenting that county meetings had not been held often enough. By assembling in this manner, the people of Upper Canada were exercising their rights as British subjects – and following the British example. Such meetings, he hoped, would become a regular occurrence in the province. This statement prefigured Baldwin's own role in promoting, for the next decade onwards, peaceful public participation in political affairs.[132]

The *Canadian Freeman*, a stalwart supporter of Judge Willis, was confident that an expression of public opinion in Willis' favour would carry great weight in England: "This voice," it said, "has only to be heard in England, to be respected."[133] Those at the meeting were not as confident of success as the editor of the *Freeman*. Their petition began by expressing frustration with the uncertainties of gaining the ear of British officials. In particular, the petitioners confessed that they were discouraged by the privileged access to British officialdom enjoyed by their opponents, as shown in the circumstances surrounding recent threats to civil and religious liberty (a reference to John Strachan's ecclesiastical chart).

The petition has been called "the most comprehensive public declaration yet made of Upper Canadians' grievances against the form and style of their government."[134] In fact, questions relating to the administration of justice were front and centre: more than half of the eleven grievances related directly to this question.[135] Among them were "the frequent want of a deciding voice on the Court of King's Bench" and inadequate judicial independence. Other complaints relating to the legal system involved the monopoly of prosecutions by the crown law officers, the "imperfect jury system," and terms of tenure of both major and minor judicial offices. Beyond this, the petition inveighed against the policies of the Legislative Council, the spending of revenue without the consent of the Assembly, extravagant official salaries, unsuitable officeholders, and the lack of accountability in government. The restoration of Judge Willis, and the redressing of these grievances, were among the demands of the petitioners.

This petitioning meeting inspired numerous hostile handbills, at least one of which suggested that the judge's supporters had invented a crisis in order to win support in the week before a general election.[136] The crisis was real enough, but the Baldwins and their supporters certainly tried to use it to electoral advantage. The petitioning meeting, in addition to passing a sympathetic address to Judge Willis, nominated Robert Baldwin to run for the county of York.[137] Not long after, government supporter Robert Stanton also charged that W.W. "Baldwin has become a regular *travelling Stump Orator* – going about the country from place to place."[138] This may have been a reference to the fact that the senior Baldwin had been recruited at the last minute to run, successfully as it turned out, for the county of Norfolk in the same election.[139]

The petitioning campaigns were turned to electoral benefit for others as well. Jesse Ketchum returned to the Assembly as one of two members from the county of York in the 1828 election. As Samuel Peters Jarvis sarcastically reported, "Jesse Ketchum is becoming quite an important political character amongst us – he ... calls public meetings, and harangues the [mob?] in a most magnificent style."[140] According to the *Canadian Freeman*, "The Alien Bill has been the chief cause of putting Mr Ketchum into [the Upper Canadian] Parliament – the Anglo Americans have elected him."[141] The *Freeman*, moreover, claimed that Ketchum and the Central Committee had been instrumental in soliciting support for William Lyon Mackenzie in the same constituency, and thus securing his election.[142] The evidence does not, however, sustain any suggestion that the primary purpose of this petitioning campaign was to further the political ambitions of its leaders.

That petitioning was not simply a means to achieve political office is illustrated by the aftermath of the 1828 elections. By mid-August, long after the elections were over, supporters of Judge Willis held a "constitutional meeting" to organize a committee for "the preservation of our constitution unimpaired." This "Constitutional Committee" included the two Baldwins, Jesse Ketchum, Dr Burnside, Mr Cawthra, and Dr Morrison, thus overlapping somewhat in membership with the committee on religion and education.[143] It was resolved at the meeting to send the petition to a host of British political figures, including Lord Goderich and Joseph Hume, for presentation to the British Parliament.[144]

Although the inhabitants of three townships of Gore met as early as 14 July to sign an address to Judge Willis,[145] the petition itself did not circulate around the province as quickly or effectively as its supporters might have wished. From Kingston, journalist Hugh C. Thomson reported to W.W. Baldwin in mid-August that the relevant documents had only reached him at the end of July. Thomson regretted that their arrival occurred after the elections, a prime time for collecting signatures.[146] From Niagara, lawyer Bartholomew C. Beardsley declined to participate in circulating the petition because of a falling-out with Mackenzie and some of his associates in the Assembly over Beardsley's "parliamentary conduct."[147] John Rolph, a lawyer as well as a doctor and MPP, was a willing supporter of the petition, but his energetic efforts in circulating it took place as late as December 1828.[148] Faulty timing and an apparently tenuous network of supporters may explain why the petition appears to have garnered only slightly more than three thousand signatures by the time it was finally presented in the Imperial Parliament in May 1829.[149]

The real problem, however, may have lain with the cause itself. The issue closest to the hearts of the Baldwins, and of other legal activists such as John Rolph and Marshall Spring Bidwell, was the constitutional one. The Baldwins' commitment to responsible government needs no elaboration here. Their analysis was evidently fully endorsed by their political associates. In 1828, for example, the younger Bidwell wrote to W.W. Baldwin about the "crisis in the affairs of this Province. Power," he continued, "unaccompanied with any real responsibility, any practical accountability, can never be confided safely to any men." Bidwell gloomily (and presciently) predicted, however, that "I do not … expect that the sound principles of our excellent constitution will obtain a triumph without encountering a violent struggle."[150] Several months later, John Rolph expressed the fervent wish "that the L.C. Patriots would join in asserting the principle and the practice that advisers who have neither the confidence of the governor nor of the people should be dismissed!"[151] The relatively small number of signatures gathered on the petitions suggests, however, that constitutional reform lacked the broad popular appeal of religious issues in Upper Canada. The constitutional issue did not attract widespread support until, as we shall see, it was combined with other demands and promoted systematically in the press and in public meetings throughout the province.

The following year, the committee, now calling itself "The Constitutional Committee of York," urged the province to greater efforts in the wake of the report of the Select Committee of the British House of Commons on Canadian affairs. This British Committee, they pointed out in a general circular, had been sympathetic to their rights and privileges, but its members had insufficient material on Upper as opposed to Lower Canada. Since the committee could be expected to engage in further investigations in the following session of the British Parliament, it was necessary to combat the misrepresentations of the supporters of the colonial government and to reiterate the grievances enumerated in the previous petition. Moreover, they reported that a sympathizer who had appeared before the Canada Committee had urged that "nothing will better ensure the complete redress of our grievances, than a general expression of opinion, by the people of this colony, a petition numerously signed."

Members of the Constitutional Committee had fully thought out the question of the organization of this petitioning campaign:

> We beg to suggest the calling of public meetings for the appointment of committees in each district, and sub-committees in each township, to ensure general success in obtaining signatures, and to direct that they be properly made to the several petitions, so as to enable this committee to attach them to the general Petition of the same tenor, to be transmitted to the several high authorities addressed. … you must be aware that numbers of signatures are the only means by which they have, in England, of judging of the extent of public feeling and opinion. Five copies of this petition are forwarded – one for each body addressed, and we take the liberty of recommending that the signatures

be taken on paper, attached to each petition successively, filled on one side only ... or on the printed paper to prevent confusion, and as much uniformity as possible in the petitions sent to England; it is also very essential that every individual should make his own signature, or mark, as the case may require.[152]

The Constitutional Committee ended these instructions with the injunction to avoid the public postal service because of the expense and to send the petitions by private conveyance to York. This form of organization, with significant variations from time to time, would become, for more than a decade, the standard method of mobilizing the Upper Canadian people on political matters.

A petition was indeed forwarded to the Constitutional Committee, though it is unclear if there were more signatures than the five thousand from the inhabitants of the county of York that Mackenzie mentioned in his 1833 petition to the British House of Commons.[153] The Constitutional Committee continued to be active in 1830, when W.W. Baldwin wrote Joseph Hume in London on behalf of its members. Baldwin reiterated the "evils" of which the petitioners complained and fretted about inaction on the part of the British government.[154] Despite the relatively low number of petitioners, however, the response of the British government to the petition's demands for greater judicial independence was in fact favourable.[155]

More public support was forthcoming for a renewed effort to combat the clergy reserves and sectarian education in the colony. The background to this was a growing (though still small) movement in favour of admitting the Church of Scotland to some of the privileges enjoyed by the Anglicans. On 16 December 1830, a meeting held at the Presbyterian church in York provided the first public evidence of the existence of the interdenominational committee of the "Friends of Religious Liberty." This group opposed state aid to religion, including benefits such as stipends for the clergy and land grants to religious organizations. At the meeting, a standing committee was appointed to circulate petitions. Among the three ministers on the twenty-three-member committee was Egerton Ryerson. Membership, however, was predominantly lay, and Presbyterians accounted for fully half of the lay membership. Among this group were Jesse Ketchum and W.L. Mackenzie, MPPs for the county of York. The committee chair was W.W. Baldwin, whose son Robert was also a member. They, along with wealthy merchant Joseph Cawthra, were the only Anglicans. Other future oppositionist stalwarts included James Lesslie, Dr T.D. Morrison, John McIntosh, and Edward Thomson. The petition that emerged from this meeting, then, had the backing of a substantial group of professionals and merchants of York.[156]

The petition, which was drafted by Jesse Ketchum and Egerton Ryerson,[157] began by noting that the evils of an established church continued to plague the province, despite the petition of 1827 and messages from the provincial legislature. The petitioners hoped, they said, that their efforts would mean that "the representations which are secretly made to His Majesty's Government, and which shun the light of public investigation in the colony, will no longer be listened to."

At the heart of the petition was an argument against ecclesiastical establishment. Anglicans, it said, made up only a minority of the population. In any case, establishment was "repugnant" to the majority of Upper Canadians, as a select committee of the Assembly had reported in 1828; continuing to support an established church would simply invite ongoing civil strife.[158] Moreover, since the increase in the value of the clergy reserves was the result of the labour of the whole population, it was not fair that the benefits from their sale should go to a select few. Appealing to history, the petitioners made the ingenious argument that the ministers of churches that were neither Anglican nor Presbyterian were not really dissenters. In the early years of the province's history there had been nothing to dissent from; the established churches of Britain were the johnny-come-latelies here.

On the basis of claims made by adherents of the Church of England, the petitioners viewed grants of money to that denomination as unfair. Indeed, they were "powerful weapons, unjustly put into the hands of one class of persons, to carry on a proselyting [*sic*] warfare against the conscientious opinions and civil liberties of other numerous and equally loyal and deserving" citizens. The charter and endowments of King's College were "partial and exclusive." In sum, the petitioners remonstrated against the "manifest injustice, impolicy, and evil of thus appropriating so large a portion of the Province, and of making such invidious distinctions on account of religious opinions." They concluded by asking for the separation of church and state: there should be no established church; in education, no denomination should benefit from any kind of favouritism – including financial; no ministers should sit in political institutions; ministers of all denominations should have the right to perform marriages; and the proceeds from the sale of the clergy reserves should go to education and internal improvements.

Significantly, instructions for the collection of signatures closely parallelled those given by the Constitutional Committee the year before. Members of the Standing Committee, for example, were to correspond with members of other committees and associations throughout the province.[159] Before long, the petitions were circulating extensively in the Home and Gore districts and in the Bay of Quinte area.[160] They did not do so without opposition. Mahlon Burwell, for example, the MPP for Middlesex, denounced the petitions in the Assembly, proclaiming that the people who signed it "did so to their degradation."[161]

By mid-January 1831, the committee was instructing supporters that they had until 15 February to return the petitions with signatures. They further directed: "the circulation of the petitions should be extended with all possible vigilance until the inhabitants generally shall have had an opportunity of signing them."[162] Indeed, so extensive was their circulation that one newspaper charged they had been "transmitted to all the Methodist meeting houses in the country."[163] Having received some ten thousand signatures, the petition was ready, by early March 1831, to be transmitted to England, where the faithful Joseph Hume presented it to the British House of Commons in October 1831.[164]

The Anglicans did not seriously attempt counter-petitioning. Since their numbers were greatly inferior to those of the dissenting denominations, there would have been little point. The Anglican clergy did draw up a petition, but failed to circulate it. The one recorded effort to do so, called by Reverend A.N. Bethune at the Newcastle Court House, was a dismal failure.[165] The public grounds adopted, however, were that "the peace of society, and the interests of religion" would best be served by avoiding public petitioning.[166] Instead, the issue was pursued by high-level negotiations. The Bishop of Quebec and the Reverend A.N. Bethune travelled personally to Britain to represent the episcopal cause. Notwithstanding the petitions in favour of change, these worthies persuaded British authorities that no compromise was possible on the university question. On the clergy reserves issue there was similarly no real progress, in spite of support for reform from both British and Upper Canadian sources.[167] Anglican intransigence, gubernatorial stonewalling, and revolving-door occupancy of the Colonial Office together ensured that these issues resisted settlement for years.

Though the religious reformers failed to achieve their objectives, as a whole the oppositionist petitioning movement had, by the early 1830s, achieved some remarkable results. Their greatest visible triumph had been the repeal of the 1827 Alien Bill. Behind the scenes, meanwhile, the movement had mobilized a disparate constituency for extraparliamentary agitation: the American-born who were offended by the Alien Bill; opponents of the pretensions of the Anglican Church; and judicial and constitutional reformers. The constant procession of petitions, meanwhile, had familiarized Upper Canadians with the practice of petitioning the British Parliament, and had no doubt furthered the political education of many inhabitants on the issues facing the province. It seems very likely, indeed, that such education extended in many cases well beyond the ranks of those who possessed the franchise.

The leaders of the movement in 1827–31 enjoyed a number of advantages that their predecessors had lacked. The movement had by the late 1820s developed a strong indigenous leadership. Its members, moreover, were able to deploy institutional networks like the Methodist connection, and individual professional contacts like members of the legal profession. They additionally benefited from a more active oppositionist press, including the *Colonial Advocate*, the *Canadian Freeman*, and Egerton Ryerson's religious journal, the *Christian Guardian*. Above all, perhaps, they received tremendous encouragement from the fact that the British government had become more sympathetic to the voices of reform. This was an advantage that William Lyon Mackenzie would soon exploit to the full.

2 The Petitioning Movement of 1831

The petitioning movement of 1831 was the most important outburst of popular political activity in the entire Upper Canadian period. Partly because it received the widest publicity possible in that society, it mobilized the greatest number of people yet in the cause of general political reform. Beyond this, the petitioning movement of 1831 acted as a catalyst that transformed Upper Canadian politics in fundamental ways. The explosive reaction it provoked among government supporters led to the repeated expulsion of its organizer, William Lyon Mackenzie, from the Assembly. This high-handed treatment in turn triggered a chain reaction throughout the province which, more than any other events in Upper Canadian history, promoted the development of a province-wide political consciousness and dramatically linked the politics of the capital with emerging political and religious concerns elsewhere in the province.

Mackenzie's leading role in the petitioning movement belies his image among historians. Although some analysts have treated his political and social thought seriously, most commentators have been critical of his practical leadership skills. Anthony Rasporich trenchantly summarized this approach in 1972: "At the very least, he has been shown as an ineffective bog-jumper, running from clod to clod in search of temporary political victory. At worst, he is seen as a 'scandal-monger,' and his role in the rebellion as 'a cold comfort to the men and their families whose lives he had ruined and to the reform cause which he had greatly injured.'"[1]

Time has not greatly altered such assessments of the peppery Scot, though recent research on the administration of justice in Upper Canada has substantiated most of his criticisms of the judicial system.[2] "Persistent hero" he may be, but few historians would credit him with a talent for political leadership.[3] It is true that Mackenzie was not an effective party leader in the mould of later reform leaders (such as Robert Baldwin and Francis Hincks)[4] – nor did he prove to be an able military leader during the Rebellion of 1837. His role in the petitioning campaign of 1831–32, however, indicates a remarkable ability to mobilize the mass of ordinary Upper Canadians in the cause of political reform.

As a result of his many years of anti-government activity, Mackenzie was well placed to assume the role of political agitator in 1831. His credentials as critic of the administration of the Upper Canadian government were impeccable, though they were not acquired through formal education. It was in the realm of action – through his journalism, his parliamentary career, and his extraparliamentary activities – that he had established his reputation. His newspaper, the *Colonial Advocate*, had been a scourge of the Upper Canadian government since 1824. This journal had played a major part in securing for Mackenzie a presence in provincial politics, partly because it was a prominent critic of official policies in the provincial capital. Its role was highlighted in 1826 when it became the target of the wrath of the Types Rioters. The Types Riot of 1826, indeed, allowed Mackenzie to claim for himself a prominent place in the long line of Upper Canadians who had struggled for reform.[5]

In time, Mackenzie would employ his talent for self-dramatization to even greater effect in connection with his parliamentary career. That career, however, may be said to have officially begun with little fanfare when, in January 1828, Mackenzie presented a series of resolutions to an election meeting in Markham. These resolutions represented both a summary of his critique of the current government and a foreshadowing of the grievances he would later present in person to the British government.

Mackenzie painted the weaknesses of the colonial government with a broad brush, detailing its political, judicial, social, and economic failings. In the realm of politics, he believed that the provincial government was unresponsive to public opinion: he pointed out that the Legislative Council persisted in rejecting useful legislation passed in the Assembly. He objected to the membership of the Executive and Legislative Councils: these councillors had a vested interest in ensuring that their own salaries and fees remained high. Members of these councils, moreover, enjoyed far too much power, suggested the resolutions; the balance should be redressed in favour of the Assembly. In particular, no money should be spent without the Assembly's consent. In addition, the colony required better representation in Britain: it should have an agent resident in London to counteract representations made to the British government by the ignorant and the prejudiced.

The judicial system, too, was riddled with flaws, according to the resolutions. The judges were too highly paid and too closely tied to the executive branch of government. Justice in the civil courts, moreover, could be obtained only at an excessive price. At the local level, Mackenzie declared, magistrates should be chosen not by the government but by the people. In the social sphere, he crusaded against the privileges of the established church, calling for the secularization of the clergy reserves and a nonsectarian university. He felt the educational system was urgently in need of revision, since money earmarked for this purpose had been "partially and unequally bestowed." Taxes were too high and were misapplied to pay extravagant salaries to government officials. Too little money, on the other hand, had been devoted to the erection of an economic infrastructure, including roads, bridges, and the improvement of the St Lawrence river.[6]

Significantly, this series of resolutions included a number of references to the agitation against the Alien Bill of 1827, likely in an effort to attract the support of the American-born. One resolution celebrated "the wisdom, justice, and integrity of his majesty's ministers" but expressed "our decided disapprobation of the line of policy which has lately been pursued by the executive government at York." In an another resolution, it was pointed out that the results of the petitioning campaign of 1827 "afford strong and convincing proofs that the British ministry would willingly redress our grievances if made known to them."[7] The idea of launching a more wide-ranging petitioning campaign than that of the previous years was prefigured in Mackenzie's resolutions of 1828.

After his election for the county of York in 1828, Mackenzie continued to crusade for change as a member of the anti-government majority in that Assembly. He demanded improvements in the post office and the banking system, changes in the conduct of returning officers at election time, and the opening of chaplaincy of the Assembly to ministers of all denominations. Moreover, he brought in a series of thirty-one resolutions on the state of the province, articulating a wide-ranging program of reforms.[8] This activity evidently found favour with his constituents, since in 1830 he retained his seat in a general election that was disastrous for most opponents of the administration.[9]

THE GENESIS OF THE 1831 PETITIONING CAMPAIGN

By mid-1831 Mackenzie had broadened his focus to some degree, as he came to see the Upper Canadian scene in a wider framework – that of the colonial relationship with Great Britain. A number of factors prompted him to embrace extraparliamentary agitation to pressure the British government to institute changes in Upper Canadian government. First, in 1831 there was little hope that any change could be achieved by bringing pressure on the government of the province itself. Government supporters dominated not only the Legislative Council but the Assembly as well. With an election unlikely for some years to come, the prospects for reform within the province appeared bleak – at least for the immediate future.

This view was reinforced when, after the election of 1830, the Assembly majority acted in a manner particularly galling to their opponents. Mackenzie had been able to secure the appointment of a committee to examine how well the Assembly represented the people of the province, an issue that had assumed transatlantic significance with the rise of the British movement for parliamentary reform. Nevertheless, neither the report of Mackenzie's committee nor many other reform measures went far in the session of 1831. The majority rejected bills providing for the abolition of primogeniture in cases of intestacy, and for modifying the law of libel to make truth a defence.[10] When they passed a bill granting a permanent civil list, moreover, they hit one of the raw nerves in oppositionist sensibilities; as one correspondent of Mackenzie's argued, provision for payment of the province's judicial and executive officers should be made annually, rather than on a permanent basis, until those officials were made responsible to the people.[11]

To add to Mackenzie's frustrations, in February 1831 his enemies in the Assembly, led by Hamilton's representative Allan MacNab, had attacked him and attempted to expel him from the Assembly for distributing at his own expense one hundred and sixty-eight copies of the Assembly's *Journals*.[12] The motion that his actions constituted a breach of privilege was defeated and Mackenzie managed to turn the occasion to his advantage by lambasting his opponents for trying to conduct their business in secrecy.[13] In this instance, at least, they were unable to use the Assembly to prevent a wider dissemination of political information.

Mackenzie was not the only oppositionist who was discouraged by the political outlook in 1831. John Rolph, for one, had relinquished his role as a leader of the oppositionist forces in the Assembly since

1824, and "retired" to medical practice in Dundas.[14] From there, he wrote W.W. Baldwin that involvement in the Assembly "could do no practical good ... The few veterans of the public service remaining in the House," he continued, "can remonstrate against the prevailing corruption of the executive, and treason against the people: and as such remonstrances can be of no other avail than to sound in the ears of the country, they are fully sufficient for all practicable purposes."[15]

Like Rolph, other leading oppositionists, notably the Baldwins, succumbed to defeatism and exhaustion in the face of obstacles and the slow pace of change. Mackenzie, however, now stood ready to assume leadership of the oppositionist petitioning movement. He may have lacked the aura of respectability with which the Baldwins illuminated any cause they supported, but his abilities as a publicist and as an organizer were considerable compensation. Moreover, as Methodist leader George Ryerson recognized, the task of mobilizing Upper Canadians in the early 1830s required certain character traits: "The people of Canada," he informed Lord Goderich, "have to encounter many difficulties in making the government of this country [England] acquainted with the true state of things and of public opinion in that colony. One, and not the least of these difficulties, is, that few have the hardihood, to undertake, and still fewer, the perseverance to go through with, the ungrateful task."[16] Hardihood and perseverance were qualities that William Lyon Mackenzie certainly possessed in abundance. In mid-1831, no-one could have predicted just how far – armed with these qualities, his particular skills, and a popular programme – he would go. Certainly, no-one could have foreseen the ensuing consequences for the colony of Upper Canada.

Instead of organizing a new phase of the oppositionist petitioning movement, Mackenzie might have chosen to build up an effective extraparliamentary organization with the objective of securing greater anti-government representation at the next general election. With hindsight, it seems obvious that such a move would have been premature, given the divisions among oppositionists in the Assembly and the lack of a province-wide political culture. But Mackenzie was probably not even thinking in such terms. He was not primarily a party politician; on the other hand, he did have considerable experience in the provincial petitioning movement. Moreover, petitioning was proving remarkably successful at this time, as exemplified by the achievements the movement for British parliamentary reform. The temptation to secure similar gains in Upper Canada must have been irresistible.[17]

Though Mackenzie had quickly familiarized himself with the procedures and conventions of the Assembly, he was not first and foremost a party politician. Like most other political figures of that period, he did not think in terms of parties that might legitimately differ on questions relating to the public good. On the contrary, he stigmatized his opponents as members of "factions" motivated by no grander objective than pure self-interest. He argued, for example, that "had the Council of Upper Canada been designed for the express purpose of faction, it could not have been more skilfully framed ... with every opportunity, his Majesty's Council have every inducement to faction."[18] (Mackenzie's opponents in turn castigated political reformers as factious themselves, disappointed patronage-seekers of dubious loyalty stirring up agitation in the cause of personal gain.[19]) The low respect in which the idea of party was held by virtually all who were active in Upper Canadian politics was a powerful force ranged against the organization of political parties – both inside and outside the Assembly – in the late 1820s and early 1830s.

This is not to say that the various groups in the Assembly were entirely without organization. John Rolph, who had marshalled the forces of reform in 1824–30, was succeeded in this role by M.S. Bidwell in 1830. During the 1820s, moreover, government supporters had enjoyed effective leadership in the Assembly under John Beverley Robinson, though as we have seen they did not always follow him. After Robinson's departure for the bench in 1828, moreover, government forces in the Assembly fell into serious disarray.[20] Extraparliamentary political organization, meanwhile, had remained highly localized up to and including the election of 1830.[21] Historian Donald Akenson's comment on the county of Leeds in the 1830s was also generally true of provincial politics in the period: "provincially called elections were the arena but the fight was local."[22]

The most widespread and effective form of extraparliamentary organization since the late 1820s had been not electoral organization but petitioning. Petitioning, indeed, had been very much on Mackenzie's mind since 1827. Though he had arrived in Upper Canada after the departure of Thorpe and Gourlay, he was well aware of oppositionist history in the province. Indeed, through the columns of the *Colonial Advocate* he constantly kept the names of these alleged martyrs to the reform cause before the Upper Canadian public.[23] Not content with rehearsing historic defeats for oppositionist petitioners, however, he had bent his efforts to making the strategy a success in the more favourable times of the late 1820s. In addition to his participation in the Alien Bill conflict of 1827, he had signed the petition for constitutional reform from the county of York in 1829. Beyond this, Mackenzie had also promoted the Methodists' petition of 1828 and served as a member of the central committee of "Friends of Civil and Religious Liberty" that petitioned the British government in 1831.[24]

Thus Mackenzie himself had played a significant role in laying the groundwork for a much more ambitious objective: the organization of a more comprehensive, province-wide petitioning campaign. Discontents that had acquired a new potency since the days of Gourlay provided a powerful impetus for the injured to seek redress. Land policies, religious discrimination, education, bureaucratic inertia, and the administration of justice continued to cause profound dissatisfaction. Indeed, Mackenzie claimed that his contemporaries had even greater grievances than those of Gourlay's day, since the executive had progressively continued to restrict the people's rights.[25]

The success of the protests against the Alien Bill in 1827 pointed to the best means of securing political change: appealing once again to the British government for redress of grievances. By 1831 political reformers enjoyed, in their recently forged alliance with religious dissenters, a new basis of support. A movement that combined the political grievances championed by the Central Committee and its successor with a program of religious reform appealing to dissenters offered new possibilities for success in the realm of popular politics.

The appeal of petitioning was enhanced by the apparent success of this process not only in Upper Canada but in Britain as well. It was at the end of 1830 and in early 1831, in fact, that petitioning in support of parliamentary reform in Britain really "took off." Between November 1830 and March 1831, some 645 petitions in favour of parliamentary reform reached the British House of Commons. The *Colonial Advocate* provided detailed coverage of this burgeoning movement through early 1831.[26] Partly in response to such developments, the Whig government of Lord Grey, which was in any case sympathetic to the cause, introduced a reform bill on 1 March 1831. When the bill's future began to look doubtful, the Whigs themselves encouraged the unleashing of an unprecedented outburst of extraparliamentary activity on behalf of parliamentary reform.[27]

By early summer 1831, the future of parliamentary reform in Britain was still uncertain, at least to Upper Canadians, though supporters of the cause certainly hoped for the best. When the British reform bill ran into trouble in the British House of Commons at the committee stage in April 1831, the King dissolved the British Parliament. As if signalling his optimism for reform in Great Britain, Mackenzie announced his own petitioning campaign in the very same issue of the *Colonial Advocate* that he published the news about the forthcoming election in Britain.

Though he did not yet know that the election would produce an overwhelming vote of public support for the Whigs, Mackenzie was elated by the progress of the reform cause in Britain. "Never did a more favourable opportunity present itself," he crowed on 2 June 1831, "for the province to express its sentiments. ... Your King ... is with you; his ministers will cheerfully enquire into the sources of existing evils and strive to redress them, they too are with you." Thus Mackenzie argued that the British government's support for reform in its own country boded well for change in Upper Canada as well. From another perspective, however, he was shrewdly taking advantage of a relatively liberal climate in Britain to challenge restrictions on political participation by a local administration far more committed to maintaining the status quo intact.

In legitimizing his course of action, Mackenzie presented petitioning as a thoroughly British procedure, entirely free from the taint of disloyalty. His perspective was not without historical merit. As we have seen, since the days of Wilkes in the mid-eighteenth century, British subjects had petitioned in the cause of parliamentary reform as well as in defence of British freedoms. In support of this process, Mackenzie quoted the great Whig Chancellor, Lord Brougham. In a speech in the House of Lords in March 1831, Brougham had rehearsed the history of petitioning for parliamentary reform in Britain: "You will find that the table of this House was crowded with petitions praying for reforms in 1791; in 1817, your table was also loaded with petitions calling for reform, and now again, almost without the slightest concert, and certainly without preconceived arrangement, petitions flock in upon you in thousands, and as my Noble Friend admits, irresistibly overpower all objections to the granting of a large measure of reform."[28] Petitioning for reform was not only a hallowed tradition in Britain but very much a current practice. It was endorsed, moreover, by one of the highest authorities in the British government.

Mackenzie also used Brougham's words to suggest the necessity of capitulation to public opinion as expressed in petitions. Like most of the more intelligent members of the British governing elite, Brougham believed that timely concessions were the correct response to popular dissatisfaction: "I own that I fear the discontent of an unanimous people, and I should tremble at the thought of going no further without endeavouring to appease it, feeling as I do that they ask for their right, and that right, if withheld, and that wrong unredressed, might rouse their slumbering strength today."[29] Here was encouragement indeed for discontented Upper Canadians!

Such appeals to British experience reveal the extent to which Mackenzie felt compelled to justify the course of oppositional petitioning on which he was now embarking. Realistically, he could not have expected that his activism would be welcomed by the authorities in the way that the British government welcomed petitions advocating political reform. The British government was committed to change in their domestic affairs in a way that Upper Canadian officialdom was most certainly not. Unlike pro-reform petitioning in Britain, Mackenzie's efforts were neither solicited nor received enthusiastically by the local authorities. This was only partly because the administration opposed the substance of his demands. Equally threatening from their perspective was the fact that this renewal of oppositional petitioning meant a new level of public political activism that appeared to jeopardize their control of the province. It was more menacing than the movements for changes to the 1827 Alien Bill and education because it was not confined to limited issues. Moreover, this new petitioning campaign put an unprecedented emphasis on public involvement by encouraging attendance at widely publicized public meetings. Accordingly, Mackenzie may well have anticipated resistance to his movement from provincial authorities. This may explain why he justified his actions with reference to developments in Britain, where, though he didn't admit it, a very different set of circumstances existed.

Unaware, however, of just how controversial his activities would become, Mackenzie launched the opening salvo of his petitioning campaign. It was contained in a manifesto that occupied more than a full page of the *Colonial Advocate* of 2 June 1831. The main argument of this document was that Upper Canada was on the verge of financial ruin. The province already suffered under extraordinarily high levels of public and personal debt, exorbitant official salaries, and oppressive levels of taxation. The future looked bleaker still. Wheat would probably remain cheap, and lumber prices would fall. And the British government was unlikely to boost the economy with capital expenditures.

Much of the blame for the economic woes of the province, Mackenzie believed, rested on the system of government. "The prevalence of individual interests over the general welfare," he thundered, "is the fatal defect of this government." Too much power, he maintained, rested with the executive government, "render[ing] the constitutional check derived from the power of electing a branch of the legislature altogether nugatory." The problem, then, was not with the British government, which "deserves your esteem and confidence," but in the governing system of Upper Canada: a corrupt Assembly and an unresponsive Legislative Council. "The only enemy you have to contend with," he continued, "is the faction in power here, and its fellow workers the faction of disappointed state priests, pensioners, charlatans, and tax consumers."

While this document revealed a keen awareness of the benefits of the British constitution, it did not depend for its force on an idealization of conditions of life in Britain. On the contrary, Mackenzie appealed to immigrants from Britain on the basis that the many evils of life in the country of their birth should not be duplicated in Upper Canada. These included "lords spiritual, national debt, poor's rates, game laws, rotten boroughs, state religions, high salaries, enormous pensions, [and] an educated *few* and an ignorant *many*."

Underlying this critique of Britain lay a kind of rough-hewn version of British country-party ideology. The intellectual historian Pocock has summarized this ideology in the following terms: "What may be termed the ideology of the Country was founded on a presumption of real property and an ethos of the civic life, in which the ego knew and loved itself in its relation to a *patria, res publica* or common good, organized as a polity, but was perpetually threatened by corruption operating through private appetites and false consciousness."[30]

Mackenzie's manifesto reflected this ideology, endorsing the complaints of Upper Canadians that "your interests, the great interests of the province, are sacrificed in order to promote the interests and augment the profit, pleasure, and immediate advantage of a few." Under the present system of government, he charged, the Assembly had become an arena "for promoting individual and partial interests at the sacrifice of the public good." According to Mackenzie, these few – comprising the great landowners, merchants, and officials – "have pawned the industry of the poor, the ignorant, the unborn, for immense sums to be expended upon schemes in which the good of the country was the last and least consideration."

The solution to Upper Canada's problems seemed clear to Mackenzie: "*Petition the King:* ... from every town, township, village and hamlet in the colony; humbly yet firmly recapitulate your grievances, and patiently but perseveringly seek redress."[31] He urged Upper Canadians to "UNITE AS ONE MAN," and insist on a number of reforms: Assembly control of the civil list; control of local assessments by electors at town meetings; equal representation of qualified electors in the Assembly; reduction of legal expenses; the establishment of a court for the trial of impeachments; and abolition of all reserves except those for education, roads, and bridges.

THE 1831 PETITIONING CAMPAIGN IN THE HOME DISTRICT

With this general call for reform, Mackenzie launched a new phase of petitioning in the summer of 1831. His constituents in York were not slow to respond; before the end of the month, the *Advocate* was publishing requisitions from "respectable inhabitants" of Markham, King, and Whitby townships requesting the town clerks to call the inhabitants together to ask the King to remedy abuses.[32] Mackenzie cheered them on and announced that he intended to attend each of the meetings "to consult with them for their interest upon subjects connected with the general welfare; to learn their opinions, desires and intentions." He noted that the gatherings were to be held in public: they were not "done in a corner, nor in secret."[33]

Mackenzie's arguments in favour of the meetings suggest that he had encountered resistance from the farmers of York County. It might be a hardship for the farmers to leave their fields for an afternoon at that time of year, Mackenzie observed, but it was no less inconvenient for him to leave home for nearly a month.

The time was now propitious: Mackenzie had consulted repeatedly with Mr Viger, the London agent of the Lower Canadian legislature in the spring of 1831, and secured Viger's promise of support. Mackenzie also noted that "the petition of many thousands of the people of this province, to Great Britain, against the upholders of spiritual tyranny, has been placed in the hands of Mr Hume."[34] Finally, Mackenzie spurred on the faint of heart by issuing a challenge to John Strachan and the Executive Council of Upper Canada: either find a majority in any township who approve of their policies, or "admit to the whole world ... that public opinion is universally against them – all because they have contemned and utterly disregarded its salutary admonitions."[35]

The first of these new meetings, and the one to set the tone for the rest, occurred not in the wheat fields of the countryside but in the Market Square in York on 16 July 1831. It had been called by the town clerk, Joshua Van Allen, at the request of 108 "respectable inhabitants." According to the *Advocate*, a large crowd of between 350 and 450 people attended. Mackenzie himself read the draft of a petition and address to the King; his motion was seconded by T.D. Morrison, and the motion was unanimously passed.

The address opened with flattery: "We are blessed with a patriot king who has already enthroned himself in the hearts of his people." It went on to ask for an enquiry into the administration of the province, "so that, forming an integral portion of the British empire, we may at length fully share in its equal and exalted justice." It harked back to Simcoe's assurances that the constitution of the province was "the very image and transcript of that of Great Britain." The promise, the address maintained, had not been fulfilled: "There is not now, neither has there ever been in this province, any real constitutional check upon the natural disposition of men in the possession of power, to promote their own partial views and interests at the expense of the interests of the great body of the people." This contention was substantiated by a catalogue of mismanagement and self-aggrandizing conduct on the part of members of the provincial government and administration. The address concluded: "Deign, Most Gracious Sovereign, favourably to listen to our supplications for a practical recognition of the principles and usages of the established constitution; and to adopt such measures for the future equitable government of this province as may be within the limits of Your Royal Prerogative, and best calculated to maintain the unity of the empire, promote the happiness of your subjects, and establish on a sure foundation all public and private felicity."[36]

On the surface, the address sent the authorities a reassuring message, redolent of the spirit of sincere loyalty and expressing attachment to British institutions; indeed, there was nothing misleading about presenting the petitioners in this light. What was deceptive – to a degree – were the frequent references to hallowed traditions of the British constitution and the polity of Upper Canada. These references were misleading because the petitioners in fact sought political change, a demand that was pleasingly decked out in the request for the restoration of ancient rights. In this sense, the address stood firmly in the tradition of popular constitutionalism which both British and American critics of government had been expounding for generations.[37] Using the rhetoric of constitutionalism, they nevertheless articulated a counter-definition of loyalty to the one put forward by government supporters.

The petition that followed was a catalogue of requests for changes on political and economic matters that followed no obvious organizational pattern.[38] First, it said that the petitioners felt "deeply aggrieved" by the passage in Britain (where they had no representatives) of laws affecting them, particularly those relating to the internal affairs of the province. Second, the petition objected to the East India Company's tea monopoly and asked that the company's charter not be renewed. Third, the petitioners requested fair and equal representation in the Assembly. Fourth, no religious groups should be allowed special privileges. Fifth, the crown and clergy reserves should be abolished. Sixth, the operations of the land-granting department should only be regulated by law. Seventh, the Assembly should have control of all monies coming into the hands of the government – from taxes, duties, or crown lands. Eighth, elected officials, not appointed magistrates, should control local government. The ninth item argued for economy in the operations of government. The tenth objected to the banking monopoly enjoyed by the Bank of Upper Canada. The eleventh argued for Assembly control of the civil list. The twelfth requested a more efficient and less costly system of justice. The thirteenth demanded the abolition of primogeniture in cases of intestacy. The fourteenth item asked that the right of impeachment and the mode of trial be fully and effectually recognized and established. The fifteenth item asked that judges and clergymen be kept out of the Executive and Legislative Councils, and out of government more generally. The final resolution called for responsible government, or, as the document put it, "that the Executive Council of this Colony may be composed of those persons only who possess the confidence of the people."[39]

The bare recital of the main points of this petition does not do justice to its value as a magnet for popular support. More than any previous document in support of reform, Mackenzie's petition of 1831 embraced all the grievances of Upper Canadians. In particular, for the first time it combined the interests of dissenters (those inveterate petitioners) with the concerns of oppositionists more concerned about the structure of government. Dissenters could rejoice in the petition's attacks on religious privilege. At the same time, the petition appealed, as Mackenzie's electoral platform of 1828 had not, to "constitutional" reformers because of its support of responsible government. The petition of 1831, then, was the most comprehensive popular critique yet produced against the system of government in Upper Canada.

At the York meeting the cause was advanced immediately by the appointment of a committee to carry out its work. Mackenzie was joined on the committee by pillars of previous petitioning efforts like Joseph Shepard, T.D. Morrison, William Cawthra, John Edward Tims, Alexander Milne, and Jesse Ketchum. These individuals assigned themselves the following set of responsibilities: they were to receive signatures to the petition and address; to correspond with the British government; to send the petitions to British radical Joseph Hume, as well as to Denis Benjamin Viger and George Ryerson (now in London to forward Methodist aims); to circulate the petition among the Upper Canadian government; to correspond with other areas of Upper Canada; and to raise money to defray expenses (accounts to be presented at the next town meeting in January). They were also to correspond with people of other townships, to place copies of the proceedings in their hands, and to invite them to do the same.

The most pressing of the immediate duties of committee members, however, was to ensure that residents of York could sign the petitions. Before the week was out, the "General Committee on the State of the Province" gave notice that the petition and address to the King had been left for signature in charge of Mr McLellan of the firm of Henderson & McLellan, Bible Society's Warehouse, Market Square.[40]

Next, the committee set out to widen the exposure of the petition and address. Accordingly, following the York meeting of 16 July, Mackenzie made another appeal to the people of the Home district, urging them to attend the township meetings. In following this course, he said, "you will prove to your enemies that you perfectly understand your true interests, and mean no longer to be farmed out for the advantage of attornies, pensioners, favourites, church and state parsons, and sycophants of all grades."[41]

Following the meeting of 16 July, eighteen further gatherings were held in the county of York during July and August. After this, there were an additional twenty township meetings throughout the province, lasting into November. The geographical scope of these meetings was unprecedented in the history of the province. Though Gourlay had aspired to mobilize the entire province, his personal efforts were largely confined to the Niagara district and the eastern part of the colony. Mackenzie's meetings covered not only these areas, but the Gore and Home districts as well. Unlike Gourlay, Mackenzie aspired to reach not only the respectable part of the population but all who might respond to his message. Accordingly, verbal communication in the form of speeches was from the start an integral element of his petitioning strategy.

The meetings in York County had something of the character of constituency meetings, with Mackenzie, one of the York representatives in the Assembly, attending as he had promised. In addition, the other member for York, Jesse Ketchum, was specifically recorded as attending the meetings in Markham, Whitby, and Pickering, and committee member Milne was present at Markham.[42] The *Advocate* did not provide full accounts of these meetings, but more than half of them were called by the town clerks on requisitions from a number of inhabitants.[43] Others were called on the basis of handbills and of notices placed in county newspapers or posted in public places. Eleven of them took place in or near inns or taverns; three at schoolhouses; one at a store and one at a mill; and one at a Baptist meeting house in Whitby. (Two locations went unrecorded.) They seem to have proceeded uneventfully, with no opposition evident in Mackenzie's home territory.

Attendance at the township meetings is, in some cases, documented. In Etobicoke, Whitchurch, and Scarborough, 50 to 60 people were reported to have turned out, 150 to 200 for the East Gwillimbury meeting in Hope, and a gratifying 200–300 in Markham. At the Brock meeting, it was reported that there were 52 signatures on the petition and, in East Gwillimbury, 81. Altogether, Mackenzie claimed that 2,000–3,000 people attended these meetings in the Home district, noting that "now the people will have their associations also."[44]

Typically, these gatherings were chaired by township clerks, and the resolutions were presented by local residents. The meeting that made the greatest contribution occurred in Whitby, where on 21 July two additional resolutions were added to the rather full list of grievances already contained in the petition. The first called for more polling places at election time, and the second asked for juries to be chosen by more impartial methods. Township meetings held thereafter endorsed the Whitby resolutions as well as the address, resolutions, and petition of the York meeting of July 16. Printed copies of the York and Whitby resolutions, likely produced and made available by activists in York, were circulated to the meetings for endorsement by the chairmen and secretaries of the meetings.[45] Beyond this, a committee to circulate the petitions and collect money to defray expenses was appointed at each meeting.

There is little indication that these township meetings, in York County or elsewhere, indulged in ceremonial processions or in the hoisting of flags and banners, both of which were characteristic of public meetings later in the decade. Although there were variations in form between meetings, the reading of the petition and addresses at each of the meetings, and the presence of Mackenzie, gave the meetings a common focus. Occasionally reports indicated that "one of the members of the York General Committee delivered certified copies" of the petitions and addresses, which suggests a ritualistic element in the proceedings. The liveliest development occurred in Hope, the locus of the East Gwillimbury meeting. Here, after the meeting, the volunteer militia band marched up and down the streets of Hope, playing "cheerful and enlivening airs." The band included clarinets, French horns, bassoons, German and octave flutes, flageolets, violins, and cellos.[46]

Though the gatherings of 1831 may generally have been lacking dramatic flair, they nonetheless offered a notable contrast to traditional, officially sponsored public occasions featuring the governor or members of the Assembly. Mark Francis has stressed that ceremonial functions involving the lieutenant-governor were intended for a limited and elite audience, unlike the petitioning meetings which were open to the public at large. A lieutenant-governor could demonstrate his dignity and authority to the few, but the petitioning campaign's strength lay in the participation of thousands. In contrast to the silence surrounding the lieutenant-governor's ceremonial functions, events at the petitioning meetings were recorded by journalists in obsessive detail. And whereas the vice-regal presence was symbolic of the unity of the community, the petitioning meetings represented dissent from the official political culture.[47]

If the petitioning meetings bore small resemblance to traditional public ceremonies involving the lieutenant-governor, they were remarkably similar in form to the meetings that community leaders increasingly held in support of causes like public health and the diffusion of religious knowledge. In a society where social reform depended on private initiative, such meetings were the essence of middle-class public activism. They exhibited a high degree of formality in their published proceedings, which mentioned the reading of reports and the passing of resolutions.[48] In their similarity to such middle-class ventures, the petitioning meetings attempted to attract an aura of middle-class respectability, rationality, and order.

Staging the meetings was, however, only half the battle; it was then necessary to collect signatures to the petitions and forward them to York, whence they could be speeded to their several destinations. A report from the chair of the Etobicoke meeting indicated how this was done. At that meeting, held on 18 July 1831, a committee of three was appointed. Their duties were threefold: obtain signatures to the petitions; correspond with the committee in York and render assistance to the York activists; and receive money to defray expenses, "accounting [for] the same at the next Town meeting."[49] Before long, the York General Committee was calling on the members of the Home district township committees to return the signed petitions to the Committee by 23 September.[50] Duplicates, the notice said, were to be found at Mr Ketchum's, Messrs Lesslie and Sons', Mr Edward Parry's, Dr Morrison's, and Mr Bergis's. The task of collecting signatures in the Home district was far advanced, then, before the second wave of meetings – outside the Home district, beginning at the end of August – had been completed.

The first wave of petitioning meetings did not go unnoticed in the highest quarters of the provincial administration. Before the end of August, the Executive Council and the magistrates of York had passed comments on the addresses and petitions to the King, and Colborne lost no time in forwarding their contents to the Colonial Office.[51] Not surprisingly, the Executive Council cast aspersions on both the means of collecting signatures and on the substance of the complaints.

The petitions were suspect, according to the Council, because they were all expressed in the same language, and obviously came from the same source. Nevertheless, the demands were inconsistent. First, the complaints about the administration of justice dealt with issues that fell not within the jurisdiction of the provincial executive but within that of the Colonial Office or the provincial legislature. Second, the petitioners contradicted themselves in asking on the one hand that the imperial government refrain from legislating on Upper Canadian commercial affairs, but on the other hand asking that the British ministers intervene in a whole host of questions that were, in fact, under the control of the provincial legislature. Third, the grievances were undocumented: "No particular injury is brought forward to shew the necessity for a change." The report concluded that the meetings were called on the pretext of preparing a congratulatory address to the King (a claim that readers of the *Colonial Advocate* must have found ludicrous), and that most of those present were tricked into signing petitions asking for remedies which "if adopted would afterwards be held up, by the parties themselves, as an infringement of what has been considered the Constitutional rights of the people." There followed a detailed and unsympathetic commentary on eleven points contained in the resolutions (items 2–8 and 12–16). Members of the Executive Council, then, did not think that any one of the points contained in the petition had any validity whatsoever. Mackenzie, however, did not know this (because the Executive Council document did not circulate publicly), and in any case was looking to England and the pro-reform ministry there as his audience.

THE 1831 PETITIONING CAMPAIGN OUTSIDE THE HOME DISTRICT

The extent to which the inspiration for the next phase of the petitioning movement – outside the Home district – was in fact British was made clear in the correspondence of the York General Committee, published in the *Colonial Advocate* several months later.[52] It was only on the urging of British advisors, Mackenzie revealed in a letter of 20 August 1831, that this new phase of the petitioning movement had been launched. Joseph Hume, advisor to Robert Randal during the Alien Bill conflict in 1827, was one of the principal proponents of an Upper Canadian petitioning campaign. His enthusiasm for this method of bringing pressure on the British government was endorsed by a Mr Wilks, secretary of the British Society for the Promotion of Civil and Religious Liberty. The confidence of these two veteran British reformers in a reformed parliament, Mackenzie wrote,"has induced the Committee to re-consider their proceedings." The result was a decision to co-operate "all through the colony to offer Township and County Petitions to the Commons ... and several hundred petitions to the King and parliament ready for the next session."

The nineteen meetings that resulted – all outside the Home district – were considerably more turbulent than their predecessors. By the summer's end, when they began, Mackenzie's opponents had had an opportunity to assess the impact of his actions, and many of them had decided to go head-to-head with him in their own districts. For the most part, this involved not violence but attendance at the meetings and an effort – rarely successful – to sway the crowd against Mackenzie. Their most successful tactic was to filibuster – to keep the meetings going from noon or before until after six at night – in the hopes that most farmers would become impatient or hungry and drift away before a vote was called.

These meetings appear to have enjoyed considerable support at the grass-roots level. In mid-August, Mackenzie, who often used the *Colonial Advocate* as a substitute for correspondence, stated that he had received a number of letters "from places at a distance, chiefly in regard to intended township and county meetings throughout the province, in order to take measures in concert with the spirited inhabitants of the Home District." While he had answered some of these letters, he was unable to answer most. He did however announce that, "convinced that UNION and ORGANIZATION will soon effect" constitutional reform, he would visit every county and district in the colony, delivering certified copies of the proceedings he had witnessed in the Home district, and attempting to ascertain the state of public feeling.[53]

Mackenzie played a key role in arranging these meetings. Developments in the Home district, in which he had been a prime mover, had paved the way for the organization of petitioning elsewhere. Surely, too, it was no coincidence that the meetings that occurred before the end of November were staggered, allowing Mackenzie to attend them all. His leadership of the opposition forces throughout the province had evidently made his presence at these meetings a *sine qua non* of their success, at least in the eyes of their local organizers. Moreover, his role in these events was a central one. While it was usually local individuals who chaired the meetings, acted as secretary, and moved the resolutions, it seems to have been Mackenzie who did most of the talking on behalf of the petition and address.

Mackenzie's speeches make the "sound bites" of today's television coverage seem feeble indeed; he apparently never spoke for less than an hour and a half, and sometimes went double that length. He himself said of his tour of the eastern part of the province that he had been "teaching sound political doctrines in two and three hour discourses."[54] In giving speeches like this, Mackenzie was moving beyond the framework of the middle-class organizational meeting. He was making his message accessible not just to those familiar with the techniques of middle-class activism but also to ordinary citizens, including those beyond the reach of printed communication. It is also significant that political speeches in Upper Canada, apart from general elections, were a rarity. Mackenzie's activities implied that political activism was necessary at all times, not just during elections. Moreover, in seeking the support of the community at large, Mackenzie was conveying the message that all citizens, not just those with the franchise, were entitled to participate in political affairs.

The meetings outside the Home district were organized either by requisition or by giving some other form of public notice. In the Johnstown district, meetings were set up throughout the district on the authority of a single requisition for the counties of Leeds and Grenville. Although Leeds was a large county, only two meetings were held for the entire county. (This was a contrast to the Home district proceedings, where each township had held an individual meeting.) The meetings outside the Home district were typically announced in advance in area newspapers, in notices issued by town clerks, or in handbills – sometimes all three.

The first of the second wave of meetings took place in Hamilton, where Mackenzie's old antagonist Allan MacNab, was anxious to assert mastery of his home territory.[55] At the 29 August meeting, MacNab and his fellow MPP John Willson not only appeared in person but also spoke at some length. Indeed, this was the first of the filibustering efforts; the meeting, which had begun at the Court House Green in Hamilton around noon, adjourned after four hours to the front of Mr Bliss's Inn on the main street in Hamilton. No doubt all that serious political discussion was making both participants and observers thirsty!

The Hamilton meeting was given a special character because the courts were in session, bringing to Hamilton on 29 July not only lawyers but their friends and clerks – all of whom, the *Hamilton Free Press* alleged, supported MacNab.[56] The *Free Press* account of the meeting stressed the opposition between lawyers and their supporters on the one hand and farmers on the other, a theme that resonates throughout Upper Canadian history.[57] MacNab and his supporters were referred to as "gentlemen of the gown," who held their "canopy deliberations" beside Mackenzie in order to annoy him while he took first place in addressing the meeting. It was also they who led the heckling and hissing in response to Mackenzie's address to the crowd.

MacNab's speech was presented as an address to the jury on behalf of his client – in this case himself.[58] His argument that no one could make better laws than the lawyers who had expertise in the field evidently failed to carry conviction. One wag in the audience commented: "Who should be capable of making more *intricate* laws than those who are *paid for understanding* them?" MacNab closed by "pouring a shower of unmerited abuse on 'Mackenzie and his sattelites [*sic*].'"

MacNab was followed by his fellow MPP John Willson, the former speaker of the Assembly and critic of the Methodists. Willson went over nearly every item on the petition, and "solemnly admonished the meeting against its adoption, probably on no other ground that the rancour of party feeling." The newspaper account seized on Willson's comments on the incomes of lawyers. In defence of high legal salaries, Willson asserted that a talented lawyer in the Gore District could make £1,000–2,000 per annum. In the view of Mackenzie, and perhaps also of the crowd, it was an outrage that "lawyers, in this infant colony where so little cause of litigation should exist, derive $4,000, $6,000, and $8,000 a year for filling the sphere of a mere pettifogger."

One of the striking things about the meeting, even making allowances for the biases of the *Free Press*, is the lack of the common touch of Hamilton's representatives in the Assembly. Flying in the face of the anti-lawyer sentiment expressed in the petition, and evidently present in the crowd, MacNab had the temerity to compare lawyers interpreting the law to theologians interpreting the divine will. In a society so permeated by spiritual concerns, this must have struck MacNab's listeners as pompous at best and almost blasphemous at worst. Similarly, Willson's remarks about the inadequacies of £500 a year as a judicial salary cannot have been very convincing to the farmers of Wentworth, who might not see that much cash in a lifetime. It is not hard to understand why Mackenzie's brand of populism played better to this crowd than the elitism of the lawyers and their supporters. Indeed, the meeting divided after a long speech by Willson, and the Chair concluded that a majority of freeholders supported Mackenzie. (Willson then ungraciously began a hiss, "in which he was followed by the whole choir of *ruffled shirts*"). The *Free Press* reported that Willson had been burnt in effigy that night, but claimed that the offence had been committed by his own supporters in order to discredit Mackenzie's adherents.

Mackenzie's commentary on the meeting offered him an opportunity to endorse the participation in politics of all members of the community, not just the select few. His critics had charged that the Hamilton meeting had been attended "only by the children of the town, persons of no property, [and] the poor who never paid any taxes." To Mackenzie, however, the social status of those who signed the petitions was irrelevant. The signature of a lawyer carried no more weight than that of a labourer. What mattered was that the signatures on the petitions offered a public record of support for change.[59]

Mackenzie, annoyed by an opposing newspaper's claim that not many had attended the Hamilton meeting, took the opportunity to attack "'the associate judges' who left their judicial stations on the bench" to attend that meeting; in his view, they were "the *natural* opposers of every government devising improvements by which the working classes might be secured in the full reward of their labour; and the idle, worthless and profligate prevented from preying on their industry and rioting on their means – *under colour of law.*"[60]

The same occasion provided Mackenzie with an opportunity to showcase his attitude towards government supporters. Turning around accusations that he was stirring up party discontent, he argued that his opponents constituted "disloyal and factious opposers of His Majesty's ministers in this colony, the venal crew who desire to live in idleness and affluence upon the spoils of the people."[61] It was not he, Mackenzie argued, but his opponents who were subverting the true ideals of political order.

After the Hamilton meeting, the gatherings held west of York appear to have been much less controversial and attracted less attention in the press. At the end of August the townships of Ancaster and Flamborough met, followed by a meeting at the Beverly schoolhouse. In early September, there were meetings in Nelson, Trafalgar,[62] Galt, the town of Waterloo, Guelph, and Flamborough East. All endorsed the resolutions of the York and Whitby meetings, adopted the address to the King and the petition, and appointed committees to oversee the collection of signatures and of money to defray expenses.

Much of the real drama in the fall lay to the east of York, however, in the Johnstown and Eastern districts. Here, the notices proclaimed that Mackenzie, "agent of the York General Committee, will attend these meetings, with certified copies of the proceedings of the people of the HOME and GORE DISTRICTS."[63] The first Leeds meeting, in Farmersville on 11 October, proceeded uneventfully enough, typically approving the resolutions, address, and petition from the Home district, and appointing the usual committee.[64] Objections that the meeting was held in secret and that there was an attempt to "keep the Irish in the dark" were scornfully denied by Mackenzie's defenders.[65]

The Brockville meeting two days later, however, brought trouble from the start. As the original notice of the meeting had indicated, the sheriff had refused the use of the Court House. Stymied in their original plan, the organizers prevailed upon the trustees of the Methodist Episcopal Chapel to open their doors.[66] In addition to being advertised in the *Brockville Recorder*, the meeting was publicized through the distribution of three hundred handbills.[67] The chief excitement at the Brockville meeting was the encounter between Mackenzie, representing the York General Committee, and Ogle Gowan, leader of the Orange Order and would-be ally of the old tory elite of the Johnstown district.[68] The Orange Order, founded in Ireland in the 1790s, was identified in Great Britain with Protestant loyalism, military support for the established order, and anti-Catholicism. It spread to Canada before 1800, but it was only after the arrival of Gowan in Upper Canada in 1829 that numbers began to rise steeply in the province. Gowan's remarkable organizational skills were in no small measure responsible for the fact that by the early 1830s the order claimed the adherence of 18,000 members, many of them recent immigrants.[69]

The Brockville gathering began with Mackenzie delivering certified copies of the proceedings of the Home district meetings, then addressing the crowd in support of the resolution in favour of adopting the petition and addresses. Gowan then took the floor, objecting both to the petition and to the resolution. According to Mackenzie, he argued for the status quo in respect of the clergy reserves, and the representation of judicial and religious figures in the Legislative and Executive Councils. Gowan further disagreed with the petition because he supported the tea monopoly.

Moving beyond the subject matter of the petitions, Gowan cast aspersions on the entire petitioning movement when he pompously proclaimed that he "disliked to see ignorant people *bellowing* about reform in Parliament." Appealing to ethnic antipathies, he claimed that the petition to the King had been devised by "the half Yankee half Dutch committee at York" with the assistance of a few hundred Dutchmen in Markham. In an effort to attract the support of his fellow Irish Protestants, Gowan reminded them of their Orange lodges,[70] concluding his tirade by reading an amendment "declaring the petition and address uncalled for in the present circumstances of the country."[71]

Gowan was followed by a young lawyer, a Mr Bogart, who identified himself as a "no party man." Bogart also spoke against the petition, echoing the rhetoric of paternalism by asking why the people of Upper Canada should trouble the King of England with their affairs. Gowan and Mackenzie later addressed the assembled company anew, with Gowan allegedly trying to stir up the Irish against the resolution. According to Mackenzie, he was not entirely successful: many Orangemen voted against Gowan. The vote was not taken until sunset (the meeting having begun at noon), and the count had to be taken three times: once inside the chapel and twice outside. The Chair, Truelove Butler, determined that the resolution had been adopted by a majority of the meeting, and committees were established to circulate the petition throughout the county.[72]

The committee lost no time, sending out circulars over the signature of Andrew N. Buell three days after the meeting. The circular enclosed petitions, asking for their return by 14 November. In addition, it requested a "SMALL SUBSCRIPTION" to defray the expenses of the committee.[73]

This meeting occasioned a newspaper war between the two Brockville newspapers, the *Recorder*, which sympathized with the petitioners, and the *Gazette*, which denounced them. The *Recorder* found itself defending Mackenzie against the suggestion that his supporters "had defeated the supporters of British Laws" and threatened vengeance against every person who opposed the petition.[74] On the contrary, said the *Recorder*, "one of the most prominent objects of the Petitioners is to obtain a more correct administration [of British laws]."[75] As Mackenzie had done earlier, the *Recorder* denounced the opponents of the petition as a "faction," and identified their own cause with "the most liberal, the most patriotic King who ever filled a British Throne."[76]

The Grenville meetings that followed those in Leeds took place in a rather heated atmosphere because of a by-election following the death of the incumbent MPP, Edward Jessup (or Jessop). The Augusta meeting of 15 October was a kind of triple-header, since it occurred after the Cattle Show and Grenville Agricultural Society meeting and before a nomination meeting to choose a candidate for election.[77] There must have been complaints that the petitioners had taken advantage of a captive audience; the *Recorder* countered by arguing that "whether the people assembled for a Cattle Show or any other purpose, they were the same who might be expected to assemble at any other time, for any other object."[78] The two non-bovine meetings were chaired by the same individual, Samuel Heck, and Daniel McLeod acted as Secretary for both.[79]

After Mackenzie had urged "the necessity of a union and active co-operation on the part of the people of the province" in order to forward the purposes of the committee, the newly nominated candidate for Grenville, Hiram Norton, seconded by Thomas Sherwood, moved for the adoption of the petition and addresses. Samuel Heck placed an announcement in the newspaper listing the names of those with whom copies of the petitions had been placed for signature; they were to be transmitted to the York General Committee of management within a month.[80]

In this case, there was considerable overlap between electoral politics and the petitioning movement. They could never be entirely divorced, of course, because one of the chief complaints of the petition was the nature of representation in the Assembly. 1831 was not, however, an election year, so there are limited opportunities to examine the intersection between Mackenzie's activities and the electoral process. In the case of Grenville, however, Norton and Mackenzie must have seen an association as being to their mutual advantage. Mackenzie, for example, attended Norton's nomination meeting, where he was "warmly and enthusiastically cheered." Further, the first resolution of the nomination meeting called for an independent house of Assembly, a cause of the petitioners. As we have seen, Norton proposed, at the public meeting, the adoption of Mackenzie's petition, address, and resolutions. The personnel of Norton's election committee additionally showed considerable overlap with the committee appointed to receive signatures to the petition. While the former was larger than the latter, every member of the petitioning committee also sat on Norton's election committee.[81]

Mackenzie could not have been expected to keep quiet on the issue of the Grenville by-election and in fact endorsed Norton as a candidate.[82] He also ran in the *Colonial Advocate* extracts from a pamphlet to the electors of Grenville attacking Judge Jonas Jones (an associate of members of the Family Compact) who finally decided to run against Norton.[83] Norton returned Mackenzie's compliment in his speech on the hustings in mid-December, reading the prayer of the petition and address to the King adopted in York in July.[84] It is perhaps not surprising that at the ensuing by-election, Norton was stigmatized as the nominee of "a self constituted committee at York, by whose emissaries he [Norton] is put in nomination and by whom you are told you must elect Mr Norton."[85] In spite of this, Norton received 344 votes to the 126 of Jonas Jones, his chief opponent.[86]

The other Grenville meetings were also eventful. The second occurred in front of Adam's Hotel in Kemptville on 18 October 1831. If the Hamilton meeting had occasioned much discussion of the evil effects of the legal profession, the Kemptville meeting provided an opportunity for an attack on "priests," another of Mackenzie's *bêtes noires.* Mackenzie's chief antagonist at this meeting was one Daniel O'Reilly, whom Mackenzie associated with Twelve-Mile Creek in the far-away Gore District, where O'Reilly was a property-owner. It appeared that he owned land in Grenville too, which accounted for his presence at the meeting. O'Reilly announced himself as speaking "on behalf of the government," and suggested that the people consider the petition for two weeks before voting on it. O'Reilly and his supporters were at times "very riotous and quite abusive," according to the *Brockville Recorder,* interrupting the speakers until "the good sense of the people" brought them to order.[87]

From Mackenzie's viewpoint, however, O'Reilly's chief fault was not his rudeness but the fact that he was in league with a Mr Patton, the English clergyman of the area, with whom he had "caucused" before the meeting. In his account of the Kemptville meeting, Mackenzie referred to his opposition as "the priest's party." Patton, described as "a very good-looking young man," "threw every possible difficulty in our way," according to Mackenzie, objecting to the sale of the clergy reserves and the application of the proceeds to education. Moreover, after the petitions had been adopted by a "glorious majority," Patton "tapped people on the shoulder, and advised them not to sign when he saw them about to do so."[88] In the end, though, Mackenzie concluded that the opposition had not been harmful to his campaign. On the contrary, he observed, "as a general rule, I have found that opposition to the petitions enlisted the people more anxiously in their own cause."[89]

The next day, at noon, there was another Grenville meeting in Merrickville in "Hoffmans large room." It attracted 150 to 200 of the principal settlers and "a *sprinkling* of canal labourers and overseers &c." This was another blockbuster event, lasting from noon until past sunset. O'Reilly made another appearance, interrupting Mackenzie during his two-hour speech. When O'Reilly had a chance to speak himself, he began with an hour-long digression on the subject of politics in the far-away county of Halton. This so annoyed the crowd that they wouldn't give him any further attention, notwithstanding Mackenzie's efforts to secure him a hearing. About sunset, the villagers finally divided, with a majority in favour of the petition. After dark, O'Reilly congregated with about fifteen or twenty others at a tavern door and made a long speech about "the Black List," presumably an attack on Mackenzie's views on the subject of the Family Compact.[90]

The final Grenville meeting occurred in the courthouse of Johnstown on 22 October 1831. Reports in the *Colonial Advocate* noted the presence of magistrates, militia and military officers, clergy, and "strangers of respectability from a distance." Also in attendance were Mackenzie, Hiram Norton, and Colonel Fraser, the county member. Mackenzie spoke for one and a half to two hours, stressing the need for unity and asking his opponents to point out which statements in his petition were incorrect. Government sympathizers were represented by Colonel Fraser, MPP, who denounced the York address as false libel. One or two others spoke on the same side – harshly – but "the good sense of the people" prevailed and there was no disorder. Ultimately, the usual resolutions were passed at the meeting – in this case unanimously.

If the meetings in Grenville were given a special character by the coincidence of an election, those in the Eastern district were notable for the ferocity of the encounters between Mackenzie and the county members for Stormont and Glengarry, Philip Vankoughnet (Gourlay's old nemesis) and Archibald McLean. First, however, there was a meeting for the county of Dundas in Mariatown, which was something of a reprise of the last Grenville meeting. It was attended by Colonel Fraser with Ogle Gowan in tow for support.

Gowan distinguished himself by speaking for two hours against the resolution supporting the York proceedings. Mackenzie, in a remarkable example of the pot calling the kettle black, complained that Gowan was "neither a freeholder nor an inhabitant of the county." By sunset, Gowan wanted to continue, but the exhausted crowd voted to put the question. It was a triumph for Mackenzie, as Fraser was virtually alone in his opposition to Mackenzie. Fraser proved to be a sore loser. He called the Presbyterian minister a liar, and told Gowan at the meeting's end, "they don't want to hear you – a pack of d – d [*sic*] fools – let them go to h-ll [*sic*] their own way." Members of the crowd were not amused.[91]

The next meeting, at Bockus' Hotel in Santa Cruz, attracted 300 of the "yeomanry" of the upper half of the county of Stormont, along with Archibald McLean, speaker of the Assembly, and Philip Vankoughnet, MPP.[92] In addition to giving his usual pitch on behalf of the people acting in unison, and "the evils that had resulted from the divisions which had been created among them for party purposes," Mackenzie launched a withering attack on the legislative behaviour of the local MPPs and said that the majority in the legislature were "utterly adverse to marching with public opinion." His opponents were also vulnerable because of questionable personal financial transactions. After supporting a bill in the Assembly to assess and sell wild lands, McLean and his brother had bought 40,000–45,000 acres of wild land at auction for 4d. to 6d. an acre. This sequence of events had enraged McLean's highland constituents, one of whom commented: "You first assisted in making laws to sell our lands, and then followed the Sheriff to buy our inheritance with our own money!"

While both local MPPs attacked the resolutions supporting the York proceedings, to some extent Mackenzie forced McLean and Vankoughnet to defend themselves on grounds of his choosing. McLean for example felt compelled to justify his role in the defeat of the libel bill. He also found it necessary to defend the high costs of government; his argument that they were essential to the maintenance of the dignity of the government is unlikely to have been persuasive to his cash-poor constituents. Throwing caution to the winds, McLean even had the temerity to defend the legal profession. A lawyer himself, McLean denied that he, for one, had ever overbilled his clients. (There is no record of how this self-serving statement was greeted by the crowd.)

The prospect of a speech from Vankoughnet must have aroused few expectations among his fellow citizens, two-thirds of whom reportedly left the room when he began to speak. He too defended his record in the Assembly, then attacked Ryerson and "the Methodist and General York Committee," and abused both Mackenzie and his petition. McLean then got up to speak a second time but lost the audience after calling on the assistance of pro-government newspapers. The meeting hit a low point when a farmer called over his old one-eyed dog and informed Vankoughnet that he'd make a better representative than the Colonel, because at least he'd do no harm.

At about 7 p.m., the pro-petition resolution was passed with only six or seven dissenting votes. A "deafening" shout of approval went up from the crowd of about two hundred when the results were announced. Like Colonel Fraser in Mariatown, McLean proved unable to hold his tongue: he called his constituents "a parcel of PUPPETS," an "ill-timed epithet" which apparently "gave much offence."

The meeting of Glengarry County in Williamstown on 29 October was, Mackenzie noted, "the first political Assembly" of the Scots in that part of the province. It was also the occasion for the appearance of many of the usual participants in leading roles. McLean and Vankoughnet once again headed the opposition to Mackenzie, assisted by Colonel Fraser and Major McMartin, members for the Eastern district who opposed the petition. After Mackenzie had spoken, both McLean and Fraser argued against the adoption of the petition. McLean essentially supported the status quo, urging the people to work through their Assembly, not through petitions to the King. He supported the Canada Trade Act which had so alarmed the farmers of Upper Canada and defended his vote against a bill to give £7,000 for the education of the children of Upper Canada. At this the chair, Colonel Chisholm of Alexandria, assisted Mackenzie with the pointed remark that "you could find another £50,000 to the Welland Canal, Mr McLean, but it seems there was no money in the treasury to assist in educating the children of your Highland countrymen in Glengarry."[93] Undeterred by this cut, McLean proceeded to attack the York committee, saying he distrusted them, partly because they seemed to have an understanding with the Canadian party in Lower Canada.

The final battle in eastern Upper Canada occurred at Marshall's Hotel in Cornwall, where Mackenzie again faced McLean and Vankoughnet. For an hour and a half Mackenzie assailed his opponents' voting records in the Assembly and revisited the matter of McLean and wild lands. The members for the Eastern district responded by attacking Mackenzie, quoting York newspapers, including the *Canadian Freeman* of Francis Collins. According to the account in the *Colonial Advocate*, they filibustered for about five hours – until 7 at night – in an effort to outlast the farmers of the area. Mackenzie then had half an hour of rebuttal, followed by an hour and a half of more discussion by the area MPPs. By the time the question was finally put at 9:30 p.m., a bare majority of the hardy one hundred souls who remained voted in favour of adopting the York petition.

The MPPs from eastern Upper Canada did not enhance their prestige in these encounters with Mackenzie. In December 1831 a "Stormont Farmer" wrote Mackenzie in response to the Attorney General's statements that the protest meetings were "the expressions of a few people." "If these meetings were of such little significance," he asked, "how came five coalition members to attend so regularly and make use of all the arguments they were in possession of to convince the people that they had no grievances – and that they (the said members) had been the faithful guardians of the people, their rights and privileges. The people were not willing to believe them then, and I think they will be less inclined to believe them for the future."[94]

The final petition meeting of 1831 took place in the Niagara district on 5 November at the church in St David's.[95] The announcement of the meeting for the counties of Lincoln and Haldimand noted that the copies of the address and petitions had been "widely circulated in the District of Niagara." Mackenzie was in attendance, presenting copies of the petition and address, while William Woodruff, a former Gourlay supporter, moved the resolution. The petition and address were adopted at the meeting and the usual committee was established to complete the work.

By this time, Mackenzie had returned to York to attend the opening of the legislature. In the meantime, he had been forwarding signed petitions to the Colonial Secretary and to Lieutenant-Governor Colborne.[96] In mid-September, petitions from Wentworth and Halton counties – ten in all – were forwarded to Britain, along with duplicates of original certificates, signed by the Chairman and Secretary of each meeting.[97] Mackenzie sent a separate note to Goderich pointing out that at these meetings "votes of thanks to His Majesty's ministers were unanimously passed, for their wise, upright and uncompromising conduct in bringing forward the measure of parliamentary reform … and also for recommending to His Majesty to assent to the Marriage Act."[98]

While he awaited the fate of the petitions in Britain, Mackenzie could only hope that they fared better there than in Upper Canada. The Assembly referred the petition of Vaughan township to a committee whose members Mackenzie believed were hostile to his cause. This Mackenzie considered contrary to parliamentary practice: "the Parliamentary law is to refer a petition in the first place to those who are friendly to its propositions." Instead, the petitions were referred to a committee chosen by ballot; its members, Mackenzie argued, "have done all in their power against the petitions." Mackenzie further argued that the majority in the Assembly predictably wanted to make the issue disappear.[99] This hostility to reform in the Assembly, he believed, amply demonstrated the necessity of approaching the relevant British authorities, as well as the urgency of doing so as soon as possible.[100] Even as he wrote, Mackenzie reported, William Henry Draper was on his way to London on behalf of supporters of the provincial government, "to oppose the general petitions, and advocate the interests of the executive faction here with His Majesty's government."[101] These exhortations must have had their effect on Mackenzie's correspondents; not long afterwards, the *Colonial Advocate* proudly proclaimed that petitions signed by more than 10,000 people had been sent to London. Mackenzie noted, however, that many duplicates remained with "committeemen" throughout the province, and asked that they be sent "*without delay.*"

As they awaited the reaction to the petitions in Great Britain, Mackenzie and his followers may well have reflected on what they had achieved since July. Most obviously, of course, they had been instrumental in collecting a huge number of signatures on anti-government petitions from all over the province. That accomplishment, in turn, was a result in part of Mackenzie's own efforts in the cause. In addition to appearing at every petitioning meeting from the Niagara district to the eastern extremity of the province, he had made important contributions to the organization of the campaign through the *Colonial Advocate*. The paper had served as a device to broadcast reform grievances, as a means of publicizing petitioning meetings, and as a spur to complete the collection of signatures. Not coincidentally, it had also acted as a kind of oppositionist news service, available to be widely copied by sympathetic editors elsewhere in the province, including the Buells of Brockville's *Recorder*.

During the course of this campaign, Mackenzie had reached out to particular segments of the community for support. He sought to attract ordinary Upper Canadians, the farmers rather than the lawyers, the dissenters rather than members of the established church, and all those who believed that the cost of government was too high. On their behalf, he had engaged in verbal battles across the province with members of the Assembly, supporters of the established church, and the leader of the Orange Order. In the process, he was building a political coalition similar to those that political parties would later rely on.

Though Mackenzie's petitioning campaign was not undertaken with party interests in mind, it could not help but indirectly lay the foundations for political parties. One of the preconditions for the development of political parties is the emergence of a province-wide political consciousness. In assuming leadership of a new phase of the oppositionist petitioning movement in 1831, in carrying a common set of grievances throughout the province, and in mobilizing large numbers of people to participate in the political process, Mackenzie was unwittingly erecting a scaffolding on which other, more party-minded contemporaries, would later build. Mackenzie himself, of course, was in effect attempting to expand the narrow existing boundaries of political society, seeking support far beyond the relatively few who enjoyed the vote, and encouraging the unenfranchised also to participate in the political process.

As a result of these efforts, Mackenzie had positioned himself to serve as the chief target of the anger of government supporters. From their viewpoint, he was disturbing the peace of the province, stirring up grievances where none truly existed, and offering suggestions for change that were at best futile and at worst a serious danger to political stability. If this were not enough, Mackenzie had personally invaded the territories of numerous local notables with seats in the Assembly. He had attacked their conduct in the Assembly and ridiculed their arguments for the status quo. Worst of all, he had bested them on their own ground and advertised his victories to the world through the medium of his newspaper. The majority in the Assembly evidently did not agree with the adage that revenge is a dish that tastes sweetest eaten cold: they rushed to demonstrate their displeasure with Mackenzie as quickly as possible.

3 The Expulsion Crisis and the Oppositionist Response

The petitioning movement of 1831 offered a widespread and comprehensive challenge to the political status quo in Upper Canada. To supporters of the government, it appeared all the more threatening, no doubt, because it mimicked the highly effective movements for political reform then underway in Great Britain. And, given the receptivity of British political leaders to change in Great Britain itself, there was good reason to suppose that they would view with favour similar proposals emanating from the colonies. Under these circumstances, Mackenzie's opponents did not sit idly by awaiting the decision of the British government on Mackenzie's grievances. Instead, they launched a two-pronged attack on the oppositionist petitioning movement and its leadership.

Government supporters moved first against Mackenzie. In a striking demonstration of public disrespect, and in an effort to undermine his credibility at home and abroad, the Assembly majority expelled him from their midst in December 1831. This strategy, however, enjoyed at best mixed success. For one thing, Mackenzie refused to stay expelled, winning re-election within a month. His opponents re-expelled him a week later, but the result was the same. In all, Mackenzie would be expelled from the Assembly five times in two years, only to be triumphantly re-elected on each occasion.

Thus Mackenzie defied supporters of the status quo by emphatically refusing to submit without a fight to the humiliation of expulsion from the Assembly. He and his followers were also able to capitalize on the hostile actions of the Assembly majority. The expulsions gave Mackenzie a new prominence, and added more grievances to the already long list that he had delivered to the British government. In addition, the expulsions provided the occasion for new forays into the realm of popular politics, most notably in the provincial capital. These activities, in turn, helped provoke a second method of attack by government supporters. Like Mackenzie's followers in early 1832, government supporters (as chapter 4 reveals) engaged in a massive effort to mobilize public opinion in their favour. Like Mackenzie, their main purpose was to influence the minds of British statesmen on the question of the necessity for reform in Upper Canada. With these developments, a common sense of political awareness was established in the colony, thereby laying the foundations for the emergence of political divisions that formed the basis for political parties. Upper Canadians, then, demonstrated a province-wide political awareness well before the previously accepted date of 1836.[1]

It was the expulsion of Mackenzie from the Assembly on 12 December 1831 that produced this series of explosions in Upper Canadian politics. Mackenzie was not expelled in response to any instructions from Government House, much less from the British government. Instead, members of the Assembly majority took the lead; the instigators, according to Colborne, were for the most part "altogether unconnected with the Executive Government."[2] Expelling Mackenzie served the purpose of publicly demonstrating their contempt for him. In their view, he was unworthy of the honour of sitting in the Assembly. His expulsion stripped away the legitimacy to his criticisms of the government that holding public office conferred. There was a practical side to this action as well, for expulsion deprived Mackenzie of a superb platform from which to criticize the government.

The Assembly could not expel a member without cause, and the *Colonial Advocate*'s generally abusive articles supplied a ready pretext. Mackenzie's opponents speedily located comments in the newspaper that criticized the Assembly, thereby supplying a basis for charges that they constituted attacks on parliamentary privilege. Upper Canadian precedents encouraged the use of this particular method of suppressing political opposition. It had been used effectively against opposition journalist and MPP Joseph Willcocks in 1808, when he was convicted of seditious libel and imprisoned for the better part of the parliamentary session.[3] Nine years later, James Durand was similarly sentenced to jail for "'bring[ing] the government and legislature into disesteem'".[4] Durand evaded the warrant for his arrest, but was successfully expelled from the Assembly. Though expelling a sitting member for libel was a legally dubious proceeding,[5] in 1831 it was the least problematic way for government supporters in the Assembly to express their disrespect publicly and to suppress opposition.

There were Upper Canadian precedents, as we have seen, for alternatives to expulsion, but these expedients were even less satisfactory. There could be no return to the days of the Sedition Act of 1804 and the Seditious Meetings Act of 1818 that had been used successfully against Robert Gourlay and his supporters. Not only had these laws been repealed in the 1820s but there had also been a change in the political culture of the province. The right of public assembly appeared to be firmly established in the province by the early 1830s,[6] and thus it was no longer possible for Mackenzie's opponents to pass legislation to prevent his agitation.

An alternative method of proceeding against Mackenzie would have been to prosecute him for libel through the courts. This method of silencing opponents had been relatively common as long as the Sedition Act had been in force. After its repeal, however, the law officers of the crown had been reluctant to use the criminal courts for political purposes because jurors, reflecting public disapproval of this method of proceeding, were reluctant to convict.[7] Colborne was fully aware of the political hazards of following this course in Mackenzie's case. He informed the Colonial Secretary that "a prosecution on the part of the Crown, even recommended by the House, would have prolonged the excitement, and have embarrassed the local Government in a greater degree than any other mode of proceeding."[8] Expulsion was the method of choice for disposing of Mackenzie because his legislative opponents were unable to proceed either by legislation or through the judicial system.

The offensive accordingly began on 6 December when Mackenzie's old antagonist John Willson of Wentworth moved a resolution asserting that the privileges of Parliament were the foundation "for the free institutions which have been transmitted to us by our ancestors." The MPP for Hastings, J.H. Samson, followed this up by offering an amendment condemning two articles published in the *Colonial Advocate* on 24 November and 1 December 1831 as "a gross, scandalous, and malicious libel – intended and calculated to bring this House and the Government of this Province into contempt and to excite groundless suspicion and distrust in the minds of the Inhabitants of this Province as to the proceedings and motives of their representatives – and is therefore a breach of the privileges of this House." The resolution quoted the articles, the more highly coloured of which argued that "our representative body has degenerated into a sycophantic office for registering the decrees of as mean and mercenary an executive as ever was given as a punishment for the sins of any part of North America in the nineteenth century."[9]

Mackenzie responded to these charges in the Assembly on 8 and 9 December. One basis of his defence was that the libel charge had no merit whatsoever. The comments on which the charge was based, Mackenzie asserted, were well within the bounds of contemporary political discussion. His opponents, he claimed, used even harsher language in their newspapers and certainly suffered no punishment as a result. The libel charge, he maintained, was nothing more than a pretext for a politically motivated attack.

Mackenzie was not alone in this belief. The *Christian Guardian*, for example, sarcastically attributed the attack on Mackenzie to "the patriotism of personal hate."[10] There was much to justify this view. Mackenzie had a considerable history of conflicts with such pro-government luminaries as the Types Rioters and Allan MacNab. More important, however, he was the chief organizer and spokesperson for a petitioning campaign designed to channel popular discontent against the existing system of government. In this connection, his telling attacks on pro-government MPPs in their own constituencies no doubt contributed powerfully to the animus against him in the Assembly. It was surely no accident, for example, that John Willson of Wentworth, bested by Mackenzie at the Hamilton meeting the summer before, now took the lead in the movement to expel Mackenzie from the Assembly. Mackenzie's aggressiveness in the Assembly in the fall of 1831 on issues like banking and the Welland Canal was merely the tip of a rather large iceberg of behaviour his opponents considered offensive and deserving of censure.[11]

Mackenzie's defence, not surprisingly, proved unsuccessful. The majority of the Assembly declared that the defence in itself was "a gross aggravation of the charge brought against him," and on 12 December 1831 he was expelled.[12] This is an obvious example of intolerance for opposition on the part of Mackenzie's opponents. Mackenzie's articles may have gone well beyond the bounds of common sense and good taste, but they were far short of treasonable. Moreover, the political movement that he led had been characterized by the utmost decorum, constituting no threat whatsoever to public order.[13] In addition, the remedies that he and his supporters proposed for the redress of grievances were well within the scope of British practice. The effort to muzzle Mackenzie indicates how far his opponents were from accepting the legitimacy of opposition to the government, and how remote political practice was from a party system, which cannot flourish without a large measure of tolerance for political opposition.

Government supporters at the highest levels vociferously encouraged Mackenzie's opponents in the Assembly and out-of-doors. On 6 January 1832 the Legislative Council denounced the *Colonial Advocate* of the previous day as "a scurrilous and unwarrantable Libel upon the Legislative Council." It further suggested that if Mackenzie, a member of the Assembly, were really the publisher, then the Assembly should "view with just indignation the efforts thus made by one of their members for impairing the independence of the Legislative Council and diminishing the respect which is due to them as a part of the Constitution of this Province."[14] The Assembly majority was also very active in condemning Mackenzie. In the second half of January 1832, an Assembly select committee on grievances produced two reports on Upper Canada's most famous petition.[15] Its members expressed some sympathy with the petition's complaints relating to trade and commerce (items 1 and 2), agreed that the clergy should stay out of government, and condemned the method of jury selection then in use. Most of the grievances, however, they dismissed either as impractical or as contrary to public policy. In addition to these reports, the Assembly passed an address to the King on 27 January 1832, declaring their attachment to the monarch and his government, and conveying the gratitude of Upper Canadians for peace, the constitution, prosperity, and the impartial administration of the laws.[16] Lest the colonial secretary misunderstand its context, the lieutenant-governor found it necessary to explain that the address had "probably been called forth in consequence of the conduct of Mr McKenzie, the Editor of the 'Colonial Advocate.' "[17]

In his communications to the Colonial Office, Colborne was a far from dispassionate observer on the subject of colonial politics. Behind the scenes, the lieutenant-governor was doing everything in his power to discredit Mackenzie and his allies. Though he did not agree with the tactic of expulsion, Colborne's dispatches to the Colonial Office offered powerful support to Mackenzie's opponents. Indeed, Colborne's letters to Colonial Secretary Lord Goderich during the first seven months of 1832 blackened Mackenzie's character and denigrated his supporters whenever possible. Scurrilous gossip about Mackenzie and his allies was speedily relayed to Britain, regardless of its authenticity. Mackenzie, Colborne reported, had attempted to commit fraud.[18] He was also a "formidable demagogue," full of "perseverance, cunning, and falsehood."[19] By May 1832, Colborne was denouncing Mackenzie as "a seditious knave, who has been using his best exertions for six years to weaken the attachment of the Colony to the Mother Country, and to prepare it for a revolution."[20] The lieutenant-governor further explained why he had used social exclusion as a weapon against Mackenzie, the only member of the Assembly who had not been invited to dine with him. "Any communication on my part," he explained, "with a person of his character ... would have seriously injured the interests of the Province."[21] There was something more than a little personal in Colborne's attitude to Mackenzie; the lieutenant-governor believed that the journalist's "attacks ... have long been directed with a view to embarrass me and to diminish my influence."[22]

Mackenzie's supporters fared little better at Colborne's hands. The lieutenant-governor asserted (falsely) that Egerton Ryerson, Mackenzie's ally, had been educated in the United States and harboured democratic principles. Mackenzie's principal supporters were said to be American immigrants, made restless by Mackenzie's newspapers, and English mechanics who had spent some time south of the border.[23] Needless to say, these criticisms of Mackenzie and his supporters were not balanced by any comparable strictures about their opponents.

In their efforts to discredit Mackenzie, his opponents in the Assembly and elsewhere attempted to influence public opinion within the province, but their intended audience was also a transatlantic one. Well aware that the ultimate power over Upper Canadian politics lay in Britain, government supporters ensured that a full record of their activities and their censorious comments on Mackenzie reached the Colonial Office. If they believed, however, that this campaign would stop Mackenzie, they were very much mistaken.

MACKENZIE'S RESPONSE TO EXPULSION

The expulsions, in fact, had the opposite effect, prompting Mackenzie and his supporters to engage in new expressions of their opposition to the authorities. By targeting Mackenzie, they transformed him from a chronicler of grievances into a symbol of violated rights. Those rights – freedom of the press and freedom of representation – were ones that resonated deeply in British history. By raising these contentious issues, Mackenzie's opponents allowed reform discourse to soar beyond the petition's catalogue of complaints to embody an expression of ideology. These changes were speedily reflected in reform demonstrations and publications. The expulsions triggered three important reform demonstrations in York in December 1831 and January 1832, followed by a series of province-wide meetings in favour of Mackenzie that only ended when he left for Britain in April 1832.

Mackenzie immediately recognized the potential appeal of the issues of freedom of the press and of freedom of representation, highlighting them during his own defence in the Assembly. His opponents, he said, were launching an attack on important British rights, for the press was the best safeguard of good government. It was the press, he maintained, that provided electors with the means to judge the behaviour of their representatives in the Assembly. The expulsion, therefore, was significant not only because it was politically motivated but more importantly because it violated a fundamental principle of the constitution. This cry was quickly taken up by Mackenzie's supporters, including the *Christian Guardian*, which declared that the attack on the freedom of the press was "as dangerous to civil liberty as it is fatal to free discussion – an attack which is calculated to humiliate the press, or make it the enslaved and corrupted tool of arbitrary power."[24]

Mackenzie developed his critique of the provincial authorities more fully in an address "To the People of Upper Canada," published in the *Colonial Advocate* on 12 January 1832. This document, which ran to about four hundred lines, adopted, with its focus on traditional British liberties, the rhetoric of popular constitutionalism. In doing so, it was relying on eighteenth-century ideas of liberty whose opposite was arbitrary government.[25] Thus Mackenzie's "Appeal" accused members of the Upper Canadian Assembly of "becoming more and more the appendages, the best appendages of arbitrary power," and charged that the executive was "applying the absolute maxims of despotism to the affairs of freemen."

The issues of freedom of the press and freedom of representation that had been raised by Mackenzie's "trial" and expulsion from the Assembly were aspects of the concept of liberty as it had been understood in eighteenth-century British political society.[26] They were particularly associated with the name of John Wilkes, a newspaper editor and MP who had been arrested for seditious libel in 1763 and expelled from the House of Commons early the following year. This was but the first of five expulsions which, along with his legal troubles, would make Wilkes a champion and a symbol of both freedom of the press and freedom of representation.[27] His tribulations had aroused unprecedented interest all over Britain, and his career had called forth dramatic new manifestations of popular participation in British politics.[28]

Mackenzie identified his own cause firmly with Wilkes's chosen issues of freedom of the press and freedom of representation. Both issues had become familiar in Upper Canada. The Sedition Act of 1804 had focused attention on freedom of the press and the prosecution of Gourlay's publisher, Bartemus Ferguson, for libel in the late 1810s was but one of many examples of efforts to suppress newspapers perceived as hostile to the provincial administration. Mackenzie himself, as the victim of the Types Riot of 1826, was personally associated with this cause.[29] Moreover, Mackenzie's recent career, from his "Report on the State of the Representation" of 1831 to his organization of the petitioning campaign, constituted an effort to obtain freedom of representation for his adopted province. In his address of 12 January 1832, Mackenzie highlighted his own recent victimization at the hands of the authorities, who, he maintained, lacked respect for freedom of the press and representation, those touchstones of British liberty. "I am attempted to be degraded," he declared, "because [I am] the proprietor of a free press which chanced to contain an opinion unpleasant to a few individuals in authority." Moreover, he continued, "you have a right to be represented; that right is trampled on, because [of] the caprice of a few individuals."

Mackenzie tied his own travails to those of others in Upper Canada. "You have seen a Gourlay unlawfully banished," he thundered; "a Thorpe persecuted and degraded; a Randal cruelly oppressed; a Matthews[30] hunted down ...; a Willis dragged from the bench of justice ...; you have seen a thousand other less noted victims offered up on the altar of political hatred and party revenge." In addition, Mackenzie put the Upper Canadian struggle in the context of events in contemporary Britain: he represented his opponents as "a part of the old tory aristocracy which is now warring against the king and his ministers; and are not the reformers here," he asked, "fighting the king's battles and seeking to establish his throne upon a broad and sure foundation?"[31]

Significantly, this was the only mention of the terms tory and reformer in the entire "Appeal". Elsewhere, Mackenzie referred to his opponents in a great variety of ways: "the executive faction," "the government and its officers," "a few individuals in authority," "the executive of this colony," "our rulers," "the administration here," and "the faction I oppose." As Mackenzie presented the situation, these individuals, placing their trust "in official bribery, corruption, [and] unlawful influence," were intent upon "keep[ing] the many in ignorance that the few may pillage them under colour of law," partly by means of "ministering to avarice, pride and vanity." The administration, he maintained, stood in direct opposition to the will of the people, "slight[ing] alike petitions and remonstrances." His supporters were, he said, "the natural aristocracy of Canada, the hardy yeomanry who own the soil." These men, the backbone of the country, were disgracefully condemned as "the rag tag and bobtail who assemble at town meetings." This analysis, juxtaposing a corrupt administration against the will of a virtuous people, was not one that derived from a framework of party competition. Instead, it harked back to the earlier concepts of British country-party ideology.[32]

This "Appeal" enabled Mackenzie to firmly identify the cause of the people of Upper Canada with his own, making himself the symbol of resistance to tyranny. He was well aware of the extent to which his expulsion had been intended as an expression of contempt and argued that it was directed not only at him but at the people for whom he spoke. "My expulsion is yours also," he thundered. "The insult offered me is offered to you." To the extent that the people of the province shared his opinions, he maintained, they too had been incapacitated from sitting in the legislature, "or claiming respect in society." A supporter soon after picked up on this theme, putting the sentiments of Mackenzie's aggrieved constituents in rhyme: "But Yonge Street lads will ne'er submit/ To be degraded, as unfit/ And destitute of sense and wit/ To choose their member."[33]

This "Appeal," a key document in the reform response to the expulsion crisis, does not bear out Cecilia Morgan's contention that participants in politics in the 1830s "relied heavily on the notion of 'true manhood' to validate and legitimate claims to political power, while using concepts of woman and the feminine to undermine their opponents."[34] The word "manly," which Morgan sees as a key word of "reform" discourse, appears only once in this document, approximately two-thirds of the way through its more than 2,400 words.[35] "Independence," another key concept allegedly linked to masculinity, is not explicitly addressed in this appeal. Though undeniably critical of the administration of the province, Mackenzie did not frame his criticisms primarily in sexual terms. He did, it is true, comment sarcastically that the supposed independence of the Legislative Council "was somewhat akin to the honor of the courtezan." This one reference in about four hundred lines of print does not, however, establish the centrality of sexual imagery to the oppositionist critique of government supporters. The rhetoric of the document was not primarily metaphorical, but instead criticized Upper Canadian government on the country-party grounds that it was corrupt and arbitrary.

With this "Appeal," then, Mackenzie breathed new life into old grievances, firmly staked out an ideological position, and established himself as a symbol of liberty in Upper Canada. His new stature was reflected in a series of three demonstrations that took place in York in December 1831 and January 1832. Unlike the petitioning meetings, these demonstrations were electorally oriented, and they antedated almost all of the meetings called purely for the purpose of petitioning between January and April 1832. In addition to their significance as manifestations of popular politics, they were important to Mackenzie's ongoing petitioning movement because they clarified the issues, helping to shape subsequent popular political activity outside the capital.

POPULAR POLITICS IN YORK AND THE EXPULSION CRISIS, 1832

Mackenzie's expulsion not only triggered a new level of political tension in the province but also prompted his supporters to embark on initiatives in political theatre that were new to Upper Canada, though familiar in Britain and elsewhere. The first of the three early York demonstrations was organized during the second week in December 1831, while Mackenzie was under attack in the Assembly. Like the meetings of the previous year, this event involved the preparation of a petition. In other respects, however, it also now embraced the techniques of political dramatization.

While he defended himself in the Assembly, Mackenzie's supporters were busy preparing and obtaining the signatures of six hundred freeholders on a petition criticizing the Assembly majority. The lieutenant-governor, the petition said, should dissolve the Assembly, whose members spent their time on "matters of little or no consequence" while serious problems awaited solution.[36] Unlike previous petitions, the presentation of this one became a public occasion. On 13 December, the day after Mackenzie's expulsion, this document and an address were presented to Colborne at Government House by nine hundred freeholders. The delegation and its messages were met with suspicion and hostility, partly as a consequence of Colborne's conviction that Mackenzie was trying to "encourage a belief that his expulsion had been effected through my interference."[37]

Colborne had been alerted to the impending arrival of the delegation by the petition's organizers the day before and had also received a copy of the petition beforehand.[38] He chose to interpret these manifestations of public opinion as threatening; as historian Charles Lindsey related, "Government House was protected with cannon, loaded, served, and ready to be fired on the people."[39] Colborne's reaction may have reflected the skittishness resulting from the arrival, in Upper Canada, of news about the British reform movement. In mid-December 1831, for example, the *Colonial Advocate* carried an extended report on a meeting of the Birmingham Political Union of 31 October, which allegedly attracted one hundred thousand participants. This meeting featured a procession replete with banners, including ones reading "William the Fourth, the Peoples' hope," and "the liberty of the Press is the palladium of all your Civil, Political, and Religious Rights."[40]

More frightening, for opponents of reform in Upper Canada, was the news of the public disorder associated with such meetings in Britain. In Bristol, for example, the arrival of a particularly outspoken opponent of the British reformers triggered a riot that began on 29 October and continued, out of control, for three days. These events left even supporters of reform in Britain fearful for their lives and property, and discussing the possibility of converting the political unions into some form of semi-military defensive organization.[41] Mackenzie went out of his way to refer to this incident in a speech to the Assembly, saying he hoped that the rulers of Upper Canada would learn from this example.[42] Apparently, what Colborne learned (and shortly put to use) was the insight that military preparedness was the appropriate response to manifestations of popular discontent. Moreover, his response to the petition was as chilly as his military precautions would lead us to expect. He merely commented: "Gentlemen: I have received the petition of the Inhabitants."[43] This contrasted sharply with the welcome he afforded "loyal" addresses and petitions on later occasions.

Undeterred by this rude reception, the demonstrators continued to act out their political views in public, first in a procession of which Mackenzie was the centrepiece, and later at a public meeting. The procession was described in the *Colonial Advocate* of 15 December 1831:

> The freeholders, being joined by about a thousand of the townspeople, immediately afterwards proceeded in a body to the residence of Mr Mackenzie ... and chaired him thro' the town, in token of their approbation of his political career. The procession stopt and gave 3 cheers in the Market Square of the Parliament House, and opposite the [Christian] Guardian Office. Mr Mackenzie addressed the people from one of the windows of the Sun Hotel; and three warm and enthusiastic cheers were given in honour of "The Sailor King," three cheers for "Earl Grey and the Reform Ministry"; also three cheers in approbation of "the patriotic Governor, Assembly and people of Lower Canada," whose noble example of union and harmony in support of the principles of the British Constitution, we consider worthy of imitation. Mr Mackenzie then left the meeting, which was re-organized for the purpose of taking into consideration His Excellency's answer and ensuring the re-election of their late county member.

Three things are noteworthy about this sequence of events. The first is that Mackenzie appears to have acquired a new status. Whereas, in the past, his had been the visible hand of reform organization, he now appeared as a symbol of reform itself. The organizers of the petition, procession, and subsequent meeting were careful to note that Mackenzie was not involved in the organization, and indeed the function he served on this occasion was largely ornamental. The second noteworthy feature of this procession is that there was no demonstration here of any American political leanings. On the contrary, it was the King and the British prime minister who received the cheers of the crowd, notwithstanding the fact that members of the procession were defying the lieutenant-governor and the Assembly majority. Mackenzie's supporters were promoting a definition of loyalty different from that of government supporters, but they did so very much in the framework of British constitutionalism. The third point is that this was not a victory parade. Instead, it was more like a demonstration of popular support for the reform cause. In this context it is significant that newspaper accounts discriminated between the 930 freeholders who presented the petition and the thousand others who also paraded in support of Mackenzie. The cause of reform was not relevant only to those who possessed the franchise but to all Upper Canadians, a point Mackenzie's supporters would reiterate in another procession a few weeks later.

If it was not a victory parade, the procession can be seen as a celebration of the struggle for reform. The marchers showed solidarity with the Methodists, their much-abused supporters who were struggling so hard for voluntarism and for respectability.[44] Like Mackenzie, the centrepiece of the procession, they were objects of "persecution," but the message of the parade was that struggle would result in victory in the end. The marchers also cheered the Lower Canadians who had battled for fifteen long years – and achieved recent success – for control of their civil list. Also elevated to the oppositionist pantheon were members of the British ministry, which was on the verge of achieving parliamentary reform after more than a generation. At a relatively dark hour, then, Mackenzie's supporters reminded themselves that persecution and struggle were part of the process of achieving reform.

At the meeting that followed, the assembled oppositionists voiced their approval of the policies and career of Mackenzie, their satisfaction with his defence in the Assembly, and their annoyance with the inflammatory character of the proceedings against him. Participants declared that Colborne's answer to the petition was "insulting to the feelings and opinions of a body of freemen"; they accordingly demanded that the imperial government remove him. They also took steps to publicize the manner in which Mackenzie had been treated, announcing their intention of printing a report of the trial and expulsion of Mackenzie. This, along with a general address, was to be sent throughout the province, advertising the assault on the freedom of the press and the arbitrary conduct of the majority in the Assembly. Moreover, in response to the Assembly's symbolic humiliation of Mackenzie, participants at the meeting announced that they would confer on this controversial man the unprecedented honour of a gold medal. After thanking the minority of the house who resisted Mackenzie's expulsion, the assembled oppositionists approved the appointment of a large committee to promote Mackenzie's re-election. Here indeed was a dramatic intersection of street and electoral politics in York!

Before the ensuing by-election and the second major demonstration of Mackenzie's supporters in early 1832, the cause of reform was strangely aided by a remarkable *faux pas* on the part of the lieutenant-governor. In September 1831, the President and Secretary of the Conference of the Methodist Episcopal Church in Canada (W. Carr and

James Richardson respectively) sent Colborne some documents to be forwarded to the British authorities, and an accompanying address to the lieutenant-governor himself. The address wished Colborne well, and announced the intention of its authors to do "all in our power to promote the interests of morality and pure religion, the essential precepts of which are, Fear God and Honor the King."[45]

To this anodyne communication Colborne returned a vitriolic response. His approval of the intention of Methodist leaders to further "pure religion" was qualified by his reference to "the very unfavourable impression ... made from one end of the Province to the other as regards an imputed secular interference on the part of your Preachers." Colborne also observed that "the soberminded of this Province are disgusted with the accounts of the disgraceful dissentions of the Episcopal Methodist Church and its separatists." He then indulged in a snide reference to the supposed American origins of many Methodist preachers, a canard that had been shot down by a select committee of the Assembly as recently as February 1831.[46] With regard to Methodist concerns about the clergy reserves, Colborne observed that it would be "imprudent to admit the right of societies to dictate on account of their present numerical strength, in what way the lands set apart as a provision for the Clergy shall be disposed of." Also, the Methodists could not hope for much change in the educational policies of the province: "The system of education ... will not be abandoned here, to suit the limited views of the leaders of Societies, who perhaps have neither experience nor judgment to appreciate the value or advantages of a liberal education."[47] Colborne ended this offensive communication with the suggestion that the Methodists should "close their churches and chapels against all meetings for the transaction of secular business – and never permit their consecrated places to be profaned by the party spirit of the hour."[48] This was clearly a reference to petitioners using the Methodist chapel in Brockville earlier that year.

Reaction to this gratuitous attack on the principal religious denomination of the province was not slow in coming. Egerton Ryerson, the young but nevertheless redoubtable editor of the Methodist newspaper, the *Christian Guardian*, was among the first to enter the lists with a letter to Colborne's secretary, expressing the view that the lieutenant-governor's remarks "must produce the impression ... that the Methodist Clergy, as a body, are a company of ignorant political demagogues, alike divested of religious principle and public character."[49] Ryerson went on to refute Colborne's charges on a point-by-point basis.

The issue spread immediately from the religious to the secular sphere. By the time of the York by-election of early January 1832, Mackenzie made Colborne's reply to the Methodists a focal point of his speech from the hustings.[50] The question did not fade away: it became a matter of discussion at petitioning meetings elsewhere in the province. The address passed at the Lennox and Addington county meeting in February 1832, for example, took Colborne's attack on the Methodists as a point of departure for criticizing the provincial administration.[51] The matter rippled further outward, affecting citizens who had previously been hesitant to reveal their political opinions. G.M. Boswell, was one such individual, telling the editor of the *Cobourg Star* that although he was himself an Anglican, he found the lieutenant-governor's answer to the Methodists "unwise and illiberal."[52] A correspondent of the *Grenville Gazette* went further in his assessment of the significance of Colborne's action. Among the reasons for the extraordinary political ferment in his district, he reported, was "his [Colborne's] reply to the Episcopal Methodist address [which] was most assuredly uncalled for."[53] Indeed, Colborne's statement was a serious political mistake; he might as well have handed Mackenzie the support of the Methodists and their sympathizers on a silver platter.

That Mackenzie would be re-elected on 2 January was taken as a foregone conclusion by his organizers, who had planned a spectacular demonstration of York's reaction to the expulsion. Their efforts to bring out the population, and the vote, were evidently successful. The *Colonial Advocate* gloated that "the assemblage [of 2,000–3,000] was the largest that has ever been witnessed in the Home District on any occasion."[54] Egerton Ryerson's sister-in-law, Mary Ryerson, concurred: "I thought there never were so many people in the town of York before," she wrote her brother.[55] Only a small proportion of these actually voted, since Mackenzie's opponent, Mr Street, abandoned the contest when the vote stood at 119–1 against him.[56] Instead, their major role was as an audience for Mackenzie's speech at the hustings and as participants in the demonstration that followed.

The day began with a procession of forty sleighs which "came through the Town and escorted Mr Mackenzie to the Hustings." Mackenzie had already been busy, racheting up the tension level with the authorities by distributing handbills critical of the lieutenant-governor, the Executive and Legislative Councils, and the majority in the Assembly. Mackenzie had now firmly cast aside any pretence at deference to such officials and determined openly to challenge the patriarchal tone of provincial politics by appealing for public support of his defiance. Reading from one of the handbills at the hustings, Mackenzie urged the electors to show their support for his critique of the provincial administration with their votes.[57] He was asking them, in effect, to join him in his assault on political paternalism. His re-election would symbolize the extention of defiance from one isolated individual to the entire voting population of the provincial capital.

The high point of the day was the presentation of the much-touted medal to Mackenzie by Charles Mackintosh, one of the organizers of the petitioning campaign that followed Mackenzie's initiative in 1831:

After the close of the poll, a Gold Medal and Chain were presented to Mr Mackenzie by a committee appointed for that purpose, with an address read by Mr Charles Mackintosh to which Mr Mackenzie made a short reply. This medal cost $250 and is a superb piece of workmanship. On one side is the Rose, Thistle and Shamrock, with the words – "His Majesty King William 4th, the People's Friend." On the other side is inscribed – "Presented to Wm. L. Mackenzie Esquire, by his constituents of the County of York, U.C. as a token of their approbation of his political career, January 2nd, 1832."[58]

The rose, thistle, and shamrock were of course the symbols of England, Scotland, and Ireland, emphasizing the British and loyal character of the proceedings – as did the reference to the King. The entire ceremony, moreover, was a rebuke to Mackenzie's opponents in the Assembly, constituting as it did a striking demonstration of respect to a man the Assembly had so notably attempted to humiliate on the public stage.

The parade that followed picked up on the themes of the meeting. The keynote, however, was freedom of the press. The *Colonial Advocate* contained a full account of the victory parade:

A procession was then formed to escort Mr Mackenzie to the town. Mr Mackenzie was placed on the second story of an impressive sleigh belonging to Mr Montgomery which was drawn by four horses and carried between 20 and 30 men, and two or three Scots Musicians. From fifty to one hundred sleighs followed, and between 1 and 2000 of the inhabitants. The procession passed by the Government House, from thence to the Parliament House, thence to Mr Cawthra's, and then to Mr Mackenzie's own house – giving cheers at each of these places. One of the most singular curiosities of the day was a little *printing press*, placed on one of the sleighs, warmed by a furnace on which a couple of boys continued, while moving through the streets to strike off their New Year's Address and throw it to the people.

Over the press was hoisted a crimson flag with the motto,"The Liberty of the Press." The mottos on the other flags were – "King William IV and Reform," "Bidwell and the Glorious Minority," "1832, A Good Beginning," "A Free Press is the Terror of Sycophants," "Mackenzie and the People." The proceedings were conducted with general order and sobriety – though with much spirit. No treats were given ... Thus has the County of York ten times more than undone in one hour, what 24 vain inconsiderate men employed six days to doing at an expense to the province of 2 or 3000 dollars.[59]

This procession represented a kind of triple threat to Mackenzie's opponents. First, for those who had tried to expel Mackenzie from the Assembly less than a year earlier for publishing that body's *Journals*, this parade must have appeared as a monstrous affront. Dissemination of the Assembly's proceedings was at least an appeal to an educated audience, but the procession was calculated to reach a much wider spectrum of public opinion and stir discontent to a deeper level of society (though one confined, for the moment, to the Home district). As such, it represented a new kind of threat to the hegemony of the rulers of Upper Canada.

Second, the demonstrations before Government House and the Parliament buildings were gestures of defiance that represented an escalation of tensions in popular politics. Mackenzie was no stranger to defiant gestures. He had not only reinserted a copy of his alleged libel in the *Colonial Advocate* and distributed it to members of the Assembly; he had also ordered, for distribution throughout the province, two thousand copies of the Assembly proceedings relating to his expulsion in December.[60] The procession of 13 December, it is true, had involved presenting a petition at Government House, but the cheering occurred primarily at locations, like the *Christian Guardian* office and Mackenzie's house, that were dominated by Mackenzie's supporters. In January 1832, on the other hand, at least some of the cheering occurred at locations that were symbols of Mackenzie's opponents. Mackenzie's supporters were, at least temporarily, occupying the public spaces which their opponents generally controlled.

The third threat was represented by the banners of the Mackenzie supporters, which carried a clear message about Upper Canadian politics. The majority in the Assembly obviously had the power to expel Mackenzie, but the banners indicated that, in the eyes of the protesters, Mackenzie occupied the moral high ground. This was because he represented that time-honoured principle of the British constitution, the freedom of the press. Freedom of representation would also soon assume considerable significance at reform meetings.

Taken together, the processions of 13 December 1831 and 2 January 1832 constituted a new stage in the campaign for reform. In contrast to the sober rationality of Mackenzie's effort to distribute the journals of the Assembly and of the formality of the township and district meetings of 1831, the processions in York were more popularly oriented, more overtly defiant, and more ideological in their popular constitutionalism. Their provoking symbolism may well have played a role in precipitating the next episode in the Mackenzie saga.

The Assembly majority reacted swiftly to this series of events, and to other inflammatory activities of Mackenzie. Once again, it was what he published that attracted attention. In the early days of January, he published his election address attacking Lieutenant-Governor Colborne, along with a blacklist of those who had voted against him. He also republished one of the articles for which he had previously been expelled. Thus provoked, Solicitor General Christopher Hagerman had him expelled once again – this time for a new libel on the Assembly constituting a supposed breach of privilege.[61] The re-expulsion took place on 9 January, a mere week after Mackenzie's election.

When this new crisis arose, Mackenzie's supporters were fully prepared. On the very day of the re-expulsion, John McIntosh and T.D. Morrison issued a call on behalf of "certain inhabitants of the County of York" for a public meeting to be held on 19 January. The purpose of the meeting was to "wait ... upon His Excellency the Lieutenant Governor, and [to] request ... him to dissolve this Parliament forthwith."[62] This notice was circulated to newspapers elsewhere in the province, and also appeared as a handbill.[63] Mackenzie's response to expulsion was to demand that his attackers answer to public opinion at a general election.

In addition to this notice, the York meeting of 19 January 1832 received a great deal of advance publicity. The *Colonial Advocate* published both an appeal and an address "To the People of Upper Canada" a week before the by-election; the latter was published in handbill form under the title "Meeting of the Home and Adjoining Districts."[64] Mackenzie's opponents claimed that he had distributed "*millions* of inflammatory hand-bills, calling together the people of this and the neighbouring districts" to encourage attendance at the meeting on 19 January.[65]

The purpose of that meeting, according to the "Appeal," was to continue the agitation for redress from the imperial government. To this end, participants were to draw up an address to the King and the Imperial Parliament on the current state of the province; to consider whether Colborne should be asked to dissolve the Assembly; and to organize the co-operation of the country in supporting the proceedings of the meeting. Significantly, the use of violence was convincingly repudiated. Mackenzie carefully instructed his supporters to "subdue every passionate and angry feeling, forgetting personal injuries and burying all resentments and animosities against the men who have worked all this mischief."[66]

Notwithstanding Mackenzie's rejection of violence, Colborne and his supporters considered Mackenzie's electoral publications inflammatory, especially "the seditious Address to the people, and the soldiers of this Garrison," as Colborne put it.[67] Indeed, Mackenzie's "Address" had scoffed at the idea that the soldiers would march against the petitioners: "Do they expect to make butchers of British soldiers, the soldiers of liberty, the friends of freedom, the conquerors of the tyrant of France?" Mackenzie ridiculed the idea that "the bravest of Scotland's sons [would] sabre their countrymen merely because they do not conform to the doctrines of prelacy and follow the example of Archdeacon Strachan to apostacy and worldly wealth." The *Canadian Freeman* accordingly accused Mackenzie of "tampering with the troops – men who are bound by a sacred oath to do their duty – men who have supported in trying times, and will, we hope, ever support, the honour and high standing of British soldiery." Mackenzie, it warned, was very much mistaken if he thought that the troops would shirk their duty in a crisis.[68]

Mackenzie's comments on the troops opened the door to his opponents, who made a show of fearing that the meeting might turn violent. The magistrates of York issued notices to the householders to go to the Police Office to be sworn in as special constables.[69] But while the *Canadian Freeman* – and no doubt other government supporters – applauded the foresight of the magistrates, the *Colonial Advocate* ridiculed these supposed fears: "In order to produce an effect upon the election next Monday, for we can suppose no other reason, Dr Dunlop, D'Arcy Boulton, S. Washburn, Grant Powell, Col. Fitzgibbon, Dr Widmer, Mr Stanton and the rest of the worshipfulls had issued a handbill from Mr Stanton's office declaring themselves alarmed and requesting the people to come forward to be sworn in for that week as special constables. But the town's people laughed them out of it. During the day we saw no one individual either from town or country intoxicated or disorderly."[70]

An editorial in the *Colonial Advocate* suggested that the precautions taken by Colborne were little short of insulting, the result of a fundamental misunderstanding of the character of Mackenzie's supporters: "Had the Governor known the manly, quiet, peaceable character of the people of the Home District he never would have ordered the cannons to be set in their carriages in the garrison ready for service, nor would he have ordered the soldiers so many rounds of ball cartridges. The order for a grenadier's guard round his house to protect him from the rudeness of the farmers was countermanded." Mackenzie found it hard, however, to obtain precise information about the precautions taken to protect the lieutenant-governor, for "his underlings ashamed of the magistrates and the whole transaction strictly deny that such an order was given."[71]

The lieutenant-governor, as it turned out, need not have feared being besieged by the crowd. The demonstrators had concluded that they did not want to be insulted again and decided to take their grievances directly to the King.

The meeting of 19 January was held closer to the centre of York than previous events involving Mackenzie's supporters, and the choice of location may be interpreted as a move further into their opponents' territory. It took place outside the Court House, near the junction of Church and King streets, an obvious hangout of members of the legal profession so detested by Mackenzie's supporters. Mackenzie's "persecutor," Solicitor General Christopher Hagerman, was reported to have watched from the windows. Hagerman was only one person in a large crowd attending the meeting – some estimates placed attendance as high as three thousand. Newspaper accounts mention the presence of many of Mackenzie's other opponents, including Sheriff William Botsford Jarvis, members of the Legislative Council, and Sir John Colborne's eldest son. The windows and balconies of adjoining buildings provided a good view for the many women who chose to be present.[72]

The meeting took on the character of an all-candidates' gathering due to the presence of Colonel Washburn and James Small, who were running for election against Mackenzie. Mackenzie spoke first, going over the events of the past six weeks and urging that the crowd take their proceedings to the lieutenant-governor. Washburn could not get a fair hearing, in spite of the intervention of a number of leading participants, including Mackenzie himself, and after listening to one hundred interruptions in forty-five minutes, the participants voted that they had heard enough from him. Evidently they were afraid that he was reviving the old trick of filibustering the meeting. The *Canadian Freeman* declared that in refusing to let Washburn speak those at the meeting had "[acted] the part of a mob, refused to hear argument, and finally laid hands upon him, and put him down by *violence*."[73] Small, though present, did not attempt to speak. Dr Morrison proposed the resolutions, petition, and address to his Majesty, which were adopted. Mackenzie then addressed the meeting again, saying that the administration had sent William Henry Draper, a lawyer and protege of Chief Justice John Beverley Robinson, to London "with a green bag full of stories."[74] This, Mackenzie thought, strongly suggested that he himself ought to go "home" to present the case for reform.[75] It was a prospect which, as we shall see, thoroughly alarmed his opponents.

The second York by-election of January 1832, held at the Red Lion Tavern on Yonge Street,[76] seems to have been anticlimactic. Washburn withdrew after the second day's polling, having garnered only 23 votes; Small did somewhat better, but still lost to Mackenzie by 96 votes to

628. There is no indication that this event was followed by processions or other public ceremonials. The stage had been set, however, for the next phase of the petitioning movement.

OPPOSITIONIST PETITIONING, 1832

The expulsions and counter-demonstrations in York in 1831–32 unleashed an unprecedented wave of popular political activity throughout Upper Canada that fundamentally altered the political culture of the province. Surviving records document the holding of more than fifty public meetings throughout the colony. Almost half of these, and all the great district meetings outside York, were called on the initiative of government supporters (see appendix A). All of them – without exception – addressed the questions raised by Mackenzie and the petitioning movement. This, however, was only the tip of the iceberg of popular participation in politics. The agitation bore fruit for both sides in a truly astonishing total of signatures on petitions and addresses. Moreover, publicity was not limited to public meetings and personal contacts but was also provided by the newspapers of the province, which offered extensive coverage of these new petitioning campaigns. For a period of several months in 1832, then, Upper Canadian politics was undeniably dominated by issues relating to Mackenzie. The oppositionist meetings and petitions, which were closely related to the events just described in York, will be considered in the remainder of this chapter, while their opponents' activities will be covered in the chapter that follows.

Popular politics in early 1832 centered around public meetings, either township meetings or district ones. The procedures governing public meetings were well understood in Upper Canada. Typically, a district meeting would be initiated by a requisition signed by prominent members of the community asking the sheriff to call a public meeting. It was also the duty of the sheriff, as a supposedly impartial public official, to begin the meeting by holding a vote on who should take the chair. This was an important responsibility, since the chair normally determined matters such as who could take the floor and which side had a majority of votes on the resolutions. In 1832, Mackenzie's followers frequently charged that the sheriffs acted in partisan fashion, awarding the chair to government supporters even when a majority of votes had gone to Mackenzie's forces. In situations such as this, the silenced majority often withdrew from the public meeting to hold their own gatherings elsewhere. This happened frequently at public meetings in 1832, indicating the extent to which political issues were polarizing Upper Canadian society.

Many of the pro-government meetings, and all but one held by Mackenzie's supporters (the one in York on 23 March), took a different form: that of township meetings.[77] Township meetings tended to be smaller than their district counterparts and brought together like-minded individuals, with the result that only one set of resolutions or one address generally issued from such gatherings. Organizers used both types of meetings as an opportunity to obtain signatures on the addresses and petitions. Afterwards, the documents might remain for signature at a local tavern or store (in the case of Mackenzie's supporters), or at the sheriff's office (for their opponents). In addition, committees – whose members were responsible for carrying the documents around the district for signature, and for forwarding the completed petitions to York – were sometimes appointed.

The largest and most celebrated of the pro-Mackenzie meetings occurred late in the spring of 1832. A notice published on 12 March over the signature of some seventy oppositionists called the inhabitants of York together at the courthouse at noon on 23 March to express their views on the administration of the government. Because this meeting has been covered in considerable detail elsewhere, the following account will be brief.[78] Both Mackenzie and his opponents marshalled their forces beforehand, but only the latter are on record as threatening violence.[79] When the crowd could not agree on a chair, Sheriff Jarvis, himself a notorious anti-Mackenzie partisan, took control and asked for a division. He awarded a well-known government supporter, Dr Dunlop, the chair, a decision that Mackenzie and his supporter James Lesslie, who recorded the day's events in his diary, considered manifestly unfair in light of a two-thirds majority in their favour. It seems likely that Mackenzie and Lesslie were right, in view of Mackenzie's previously demonstrated strength in York.

Mackenzie's opponents made short work of the meeting. Thomas Carfrae's resolution endorsing the addresses that had just been delivered to Colborne was adopted by an "immense majority," and the meeting was speedily adjourned. In a move that was becoming increasingly common at public meetings, Mackenzie's dissatisfied followers decided to reassemble nearby. Two of the three accounts of the events that followed indicate that the pro-government forces attacked the platform from which the oppositionists were speaking. It happened to be a wagon, which was hauled down the street; its passengers were physically beaten by their abductors at the end of this unexpected journey.

The sheriff and the General Committee of government supporters then sensibly lured the disruptive forces away from the scene by sending them on a triumphal progress to Government House towards the west edge of town. Mackenzie and his supporters, meanwhile, persisted with their meeting. The chair, Jesse Ketchum, "strongly recommended moderation, good order, and the practice of great forbearance towards political opponents."[80] Under Ketchum's leadership, the participants then carried a set of resolutions acceptable to themselves, collecting numerous signatures on petitions displayed nearby.

When the marchers returned, they encountered another group bearing an effigy of Mackenzie, dressed in the cast-off clothes of the grandson of Chief Justice Campbell and wearing a gingerbread suspended around its neck by a yellow ribbon.[81] This apparition was carried around the streets for an hour, making an appearance in front of Bishop McDonell's home, where the crowd cheered, presumably in support of the bishop's efforts to counter Mackenzie's political appeal. Then the effigy was carried to the *Advocate* office and burnt. In the meantime, the marchers had taken offence at a flag, said by Mackenzie to read "The Liberty of the Press," flying from an upper window of the newspaper office. When Mackenzie's supporters refused to remove it, skirmishing broke out and some windows were shattered. An apprentice at the *Colonial Advocate* office fired a gun to frighten the crowd. Whether it contained merely powder, or types (as its targets claimed), it injured no one. Armstrong records that "a full scale attack was only prevented by the printers giving up the gun which was promptly smashed to pieces."[82] The authorities finally decided to swing into action. Captain James Fitzgibbon provided Mackenzie with an escort home, and later deterred a third attack on the *Advocate* office. Moreover, some magistrates made themselves available for action, special constables were sworn in, and citizen volunteers mounted guard over the *Colonial Advocate* office and Mackenzie's house. Though "mobs prowled the streets all night," no further outbreaks of violence occurred.[83]

Historians including Frederick Armstrong have expressed some doubts as to whether Mackenzie's supporters were simply, as they claimed, the victims of violence on this occasion. Such scepticism should be qualified in light of the general context of the popular politics of York (and indeed the rest of the province) in the 1830s and 1840s. Mackenzie had a remarkable record of conducting proceedings free of violence in the petitioning meetings of 1831. In addition, the demonstrations in York in December 1831 and January 1832 had taken place without incident. On the other hand, encouraged no doubt by their victory of March 1832, government supporters in York went on to sponsor a series of election riots and effigy-burnings in the late thirties and into the forties, as the work of Gregory Kealey has shown.[84]

It is also significant that such use of violence was widely condoned at the highest levels of the Upper Canadian establishment in York. This is illustrated by the views of John Strachan, spiritual leader of the province's Anglicans and former tutor of many leading officials. Strachan was also a member of the Executive Council from 1815 to 1835, and of the Legislative Council from 1820 until 1841. This eminent worthy was as keen a proponent of the use of violence as any Orangeman. In a private letter to protégé John Macaulay in March 1832, Strachan wrote of Mackenzie: "A man who goes about to disturb the peace deserves a horse-whipping every time he leaves his own county." The following day, commenting on the York riots, Strachan professed to regret the violence against oppositionists, but commented "it is hardly to be wondered at when you think of the provocation which [Mackenzie] has given."[85] As we shall see, Strachan's attitude was fully shared by the government press of the province in the 1830s. A willingness to endorse political violence in the interests of preserving the status quo was a widely shared element of the political culture of Upper Canada's office-holders and their supporters.

This point is well illustrated by the tone of a form letter generated by the newly founded "General British Constitutional Committee of York."[86] This organization was a transitional group arising out of the anti-Mackenzie petitioning in York and a predecessor of the British Constitutional Society founded shortly afterwards, in April 1832. At the end of March 1832, the Committee produced a form letter designed to mobilize supporters throughout the province. In addition to organizing the collection of signatures on a "constitutional address," this document made a highly laudatory if mildly veiled reference to the violence of 23 March: "You have undoubtedly heard of the success of the general committee in York – and of the total defeat of Mr Mackenzie's party at the great meeting in this town on Friday last the 23rd March. And the general committee have no doubt that if the same exertions are made in other parts of the province, the friends of constitutional British principles will be equally successful in every other part of the province." Given the widespread publicity of the violent treatment of oppositionists on that occasion, no one could have doubted that this letter contained an incitement to violence. As we shall see in chapter 4, this was an all-too-common attitude among supporters of the government.

Outside of York, the meetings in support of Mackenzie in 1832 were generally peaceful, but, in leadership and organization, formed a dramatic contrast to the petitioning campaign of the year before. In 1831, William Lyon Mackenzie had been the motive force behind the movement. He had compiled the list of grievances, printed the petitions, and literally carried them into the hinterland of the province. In 1832, however, the movement was almost entirely decentralized. Mackenzie was not even present at most of the meetings outside York, with the exceptions of those in Amherst and Hamilton. As in 1831, the *Colonial Advocate*, Mackenzie's newspaper, continued to carry notices advertising many meetings and to publish accounts of developments outside the capital. But the initiative in political organization had clearly passed from Mackenzie's hands.

In every district, the ball was now carried by local opponents of the government, whose functions were to call and organize the meetings, and then to circulate the petitions. These figures were sometimes MPPs, like Marshall Spring Bidwell and Peter Perry, who together organized a meeting in Lennox and Addington on 16 February.[87] In the Niagara area, it was William Woodruff, a former MPP, who acted as the principal organizer, a role he would frequently undertake in the future.[88] Even when those with legislative experience were not among the apparent organizers of a meeting, they frequently acted as key participants. At the Smithville meeting in Niagara, for example, John Clark, one of the MPPs for Lincoln, made an important speech.[89]

On other occasions, local leaders emerged. An early anti-government meeting in the London District, held at a Baptist schoolhouse in Malahide, was chaired by William Teeple, a radical of loyalist antecedents whose brother Pelham would join the rebels in 1837. Acting as his secretary was the American-born Asahel B. Lewis, who would later edit the *St Thomas Liberal.*[90] In the Johnstown district, P. Pennock, clerk of the township, reported that, at the Augusta township meeting of 2 January, a vote of thanks to Mackenzie had passed resoundingly. Pennock's role was likely more than reportorial, for before long his bid for civic office was opposed on the grounds that he was "a *Mackenzie man.*"[91]

In accordance, perhaps, with this decentralized structure, the oppositionist movement manifested itself in a series of at least nineteen township meetings in seven districts: the Eastern, Johnstown, Midland, Newcastle, Home, Niagara, and London. In addition, Mackenzie's supporters attended the major district meetings in Amherst, Brockville, Hamilton, and Niagara, breaking away from the tories to pass their own resolutions. They took the same course of action at township meetings in Bath, Belleville, Frontenac, St David, and perhaps Beamsville.

If the leadership of these meetings in 1832 differed from those of the previous year, so too, did the content of the resolutions. In 1831, the grievance petition had formed the focal point of Mackenzie's meetings. In 1832, however, the expulsion crisis and related issues formed the basis of the agenda. Resolutions from these meetings referred to the expulsion crisis in three ways. First, they commented on Mackenzie's conduct, either in general terms by approving of his political activities, or more specifically by condemning the expulsions. Second, they frequently mentioned constitutional issues arising out of the expulsion, including freedom of the press, freedom of the franchise, and civil and religious liberty. (The last of these was a catchphrase used by opponents of Anglican religious dominance).[92] Third, they often commented on the conduct of the minority or the majority in the Assembly, on the extent to which particular MPPs represented their constituents, and on whether Mackenzie's expulsion for libel by the Assembly majority was justified.

The records of virtually every documented oppositionist meeting of that period mention at least one of these issues, and sometimes all three. This response to the expulsion crisis – well beyond the borders of the Home district – derives added significance from the prominent position of these matters near the top of most sets of resolutions; references to Mackenzie usually followed a resolution justifying the meeting as an expression of freedom of assembly.

The Whitby meeting of 2 January 1832, attended by more than two hundred freeholders and inhabitants according to the *Colonial Advocate*, set the tone for a number of future meetings in support of Mackenzie.[93] Many of the resolutions concerned Mackenzie's expulsion. The second, for example, summarized Mackenzie's interpretation of events: the conduct of the majority in the Assembly was a threat to freedom of election, freedom of the press, and the principles of civil and religious liberty. The fourth resolution, not surprisingly, concluded that the Assembly had forfeited claims to public confidence. Mackenzie's view that the expulsions were the product of personal animosity was endorsed at that meeting. "The true explanation," the resolution asserted, "is to be found in the influence of personal hate and the predominance of arbitrary and exclusive principles."[94]

The same theme animated a reform meeting in a Scarborough schoolhouse which attracted 50–100 people. This group approved Mackenzie's parliamentary conduct, denounced his expulsion as an "outrage," declared their support of liberty of the press, and stated that the majority of MPPs were not proper representatives of their constituents. Also, arrangements were made to take the resolutions to Montgomery's Tavern on Yonge Street and to the secretary of the York meeting of 9 January.

The most striking aspect of the resolutions of oppositionist meetings outside the provincial capital is the degree to which they demonstrate how closely oppositionists in the districts of the province were attuned to

Mackenzie's rhetoric in York. Indeed, with remarkable frequency and faithfulness they reproduced interpretations of events which stressed Mackenzie's key concepts like freedom of the press and freedom of the franchise. It was not just that the issues under discussion were the same but that oppositionists in the hinterland were interpreting them in exactly the same way as Mackenzie was in York. The "rights discourse" that Mackenzie articulated in York was shared to an extraordinary extent by his supporters throughout Upper Canada.

This was true not only in the wording of the resolutions but also of the newspapers that supported Mackenzie. Journals outside York like the *Brockville Recorder* reinforced Mackenzie's potent mixture of country-party ideology and popular constitutionalism, reprinting material from the *Colonial Advocate*. We have seen that Mackenzie portrayed the political struggle as one between honest yeomen on the one hand, and office-holders, lawyers, and half-pay officers on the other. A sympathizer from Niagara offered a similar analysis of signatories of his opponents' address in that district: they consisted, he scornfully remarked, of "all the JP's, and other official characters, office seekers and time-servers who were present on the occasion together with their tools and lackeys."[95]

To be sure, journalists outside York acknowledged that their opponents commanded support amongst the lower ranks of society. Like Mackenzie, however, they denied that this contingent included the independent yeomen on whose backs the country rested. Instead, they charged, the government had attracted the political allegiance of the downtrodden by the corrupt method of buying it, albeit for lesser prizes than the glittering offices that attracted their social superiors. Charity, they maintained, lured the poor from the soup kitchens of York, and government handouts secured the support of pauper immigrants from England.[96] They could win over the canallers and Irish labourers even more readily, with only a "treat" of whiskey.[97] It was not the social status of such individuals that Mackenzie and his followers denounced but the allegedly suspect methods by which government supporters sought their loyalty.

Beyond the expulsion crisis, oppositionist resolutions, reflecting the decentralized character of the movement, covered a wide range of subject matter. In fact, in their assorted sets of resolutions, oppositionists expressed their views on twenty-four different matters. The high profile of the Welland Canal in the Niagara area was reflected in resolutions from Thorold and, more surprisingly, from Mariatown in the Eastern district. War losses were mentioned in Otonabee (Newcastle) and Niagara. The Legislative Council should be made elective in the view of oppositionists in the Niagara district, Otonabee, and

Mariatown. Secularization of the clergy reserves rated a special mention in Grimsby (Niagara) and Otonabee. Scattered resolutions from a variety of meetings condemned the Bank of Upper Canada and high official salaries, while endorsing responsible government and Assembly control of public revenue. Significantly, in the eastern county of Lennox and Addington, as Akenson notes, two Mackenzie supporters "cannily used the emigrant society meeting of 16 February 1832 to ... discountenance migration of the poor to Upper Canada." Pauper migration from Britain, they contended, would only increase the amount of "'crime'" and "'misery'" in the province.[98] There was less agreement on specific policy issues from one meeting to another than on the issues relating to Mackenzie, where there was a notable concurrence of opinion.

In the eastern part of the colony, particularly the Midland and Johnstown districts, issues related to ethnicity and immigration loomed large. The emigrant issue was an old one in the Midland district, where shortly after the War of 1812 local supporters of the government had founded the "Kingston Compassionate Society." Its purpose was to dilute the strength of the American element of the population by attracting immigrants from Britain to the district. Not surprisingly, the society was "bitterly resented by many of the region's American settlers."[99] A generation later, their successors were also on the alert when Colborne, on proroguing the Assembly in 1832, issued a call for the formation of emigrant societies.

Oppositionists in the Midland district, led by MPPs Marshall Spring Bidwell and Peter Perry, responded by calling a meeting for 16 February in Lennox and Addington to consider this proposal.[100] Although this was actually a grievance meeting in disguise, the question of emigration was first on the agenda. The first resolution began with a statement that it was unnecessary to bring in emigrants from Britain to reinforce British values, because the existing inhabitants were strongly loyal. Pauper emigration was condemned as offering dubious benefits, in part no doubt because Mackenzie's supporters believed that poverty-stricken immigrants were particularly susceptible to the political blandishments of government supporters. At the meeting, however, a resolution was endorsed, welcoming emigrants of "fair character and good principles, and of sober and industrious habits," those who might be expected to exhibit more independent political behaviour. Participants then proceeded to pass a series of resolutions condemning the activities of government supporters.

The process of collecting signatures on these petitions did not go entirely smoothly. For example, the winning margin for government forces at a public meeting in Otonabee (Newcastle district) on 13 March 1832 was powerfully aided, according to eyewitness John Cameron, by a number of fraudulent tricks. These included rumours that naysayers would lose their lands; organizers taking special note of those who had signed the oppositionist petition; and liberal doses of whiskey. Also, Mackenzie's voting behaviour in the Assembly was allegedly misrepresented in an effort to discredit him.[101]

In spite of such interference, the oppositionist petitioning campaign of 1832 apparently produced results which more than equalled Mackenzie's efforts of the previous year. In 1831, Mackenzie had claimed ten thousand signatures in favour of reform.[102] A revised list, however, compiled at the Colonial Office the following year, brought the number to more than twenty-two thousand.[103] If this figure is correct, then the oppositionists' activity in early 1832 had produced an additional twelve thousand signatures. (There is no way of telling, however, how many of those who had signed the petitions in 1832 had also signed the "grievance petition" of 1831). This was no mean achievement, particularly in view of the apparently decentralized character of the movement in early 1832 and the extent of official disapproval of such activity.[104] Under the circumstances, this number of signatures was a strong endorsement of Mackenzie, not only in York but also from outside the provincial capital.

The record of these petitions compiled by the Colonial Office provides some insight into the geographic distribution of oppositionist support in the 1831–32 period (see appendix B). This document needs to be treated cautiously, partly because Colonial Office recordkeeping appears to have been somewhat haphazard at the best of times.[105] On the understanding that this account may be incomplete, what it shows is that the heart of oppositionist strength lay in the Home district, which provided almost half the signatures on these petitions. Indeed, the York oppositionist total of more than ten thousand signatures greatly dwarfed their opponents' figure of 3,273 (see appendix C). No doubt this was in part a reflection of the faithful following that Mackenzie was developing in his own home base. Outside of York, moreover, it is significant that Mackenzie's supporters gathered more than six thousand signatures. The year before, Mackenzie himself had spearheaded the petitioning movement outside York. In 1832, however, there was no such strong guiding hand to spur local leadership to action.

Beyond the provincial capital, the greatest concentrations of oppositionist strength, in descending order, lay in the Niagara, Gore, Johnstown, Midland, and Eastern districts. From the London and Newcastle districts, on the other hand, the support for reform was negligible. It is not surprising that the oppositionists did well in the Niagara district. This area had demonstrated support for political change since the days when it had served as the heartland of support for Robert Gourlay. Moreover, oppositionist forces there were anchored by William Woodruff, an organizer of formidable talents. Significantly, the government did not fare nearly so well in this district, garnering only 1,172 signatures by comparison with the 3,224 that their opponents were able to collect (see appendix B). This is consistent with H.V. Nelles's finding that in the election of 1830 "majority sentiment in the peninsula ... supported reform," though by the election of 1834 political moderates were in the ascendant.[106]

Similarly, oppositionists successfully attracted significant numbers of signatures in other areas where opponents of the government had demonstrated electoral strength. The Johnstown district, where the Buells had long been a mainstay of reform, provided more than two thousand signatures, though this was less than half of the total collected by their opponents. Even if the dubious petition of the Johnstown Orangemen signed "on behalf of" 2,047 supporters is omitted, however, the oppositionists still ran second to their opponents in this district. In the Midland district, where oppositionist electoral strength had returned Marshall Spring Bidwell and Peter Perry in 1830, opponents of the government also obtained more than two thousand signatures, though again this total was greatly outweighed by the 5562 of government supporters.

Two of the results of this tally are somewhat puzzling. One is the extent of oppositionist strength in the Gore district, where Mackenzie's virulent opponents Allan MacNab and John Willson had been elected in 1830. In 1831–32, in this district, the oppositionists actually collected more signatures on their petitions than did their opponents, if only by a small margin (2,490 to 2,340). The political popularity of MacNab and Willson, then, was likely stronger among those who could vote than among the unenfranchised.[107] If the Gore district proved surprisingly supportive of reform, the London district must have been a great disappointment, providing the derisory total of only 260 signatures in spite of strenuous organizational efforts.[108] Perhaps the oppositionist petitions from this district somehow went astray, or failed to arrive in England in time for tabulation. An additional consideration is that the violence deployed by government supporters in the London district and elsewhere may well have significantly reduced the number of signatures on oppositionist petitions.

The oppositionists appear to have been slightly behind their opponents in the number of signatures they collected in 1831–32. It must be remembered, however, that their efforts were hampered both by threats and by violence. Nevertheless, the totals on their petitions suggest that their interpretation of the expulsion crisis had made a significant impact on public life throughout Upper Canada. The events of early 1832, however, also demonstrated the existence of extremely powerful counter-currents in Upper Canadian politics.

4 Pro-Government Popular Politics, 1832

On 23 April 1832, inhabitants of the village of St Thomas in the London district witnessed an unprecedented public gathering. It was called at the initiative of Colonel Thomas Talbot, "father" of the Talbot settlement – a huge tract of land extending more than 130 miles along the shores of Lake Erie.[1] Exceedingly disturbed by the progress of oppositionist forces within his domain, Talbot decided to stage a pro-government demonstration that would conclusively overawe the malcontents. The tone of the meeting was set by its date: the name-day of the patron saint of England. Significantly, the meeting place was an inn with the patriotic name of the "King's Arms." At the appointed hour, Talbot rode up to the inn and was greeted by a procession of two hundred men on horseback escorted by a bugler. The military theme was reinforced as Talbot passed through the cheering crowd (estimated at two thousand) to the sounds of a band playing "The British Grenadiers." At the inn, Talbot ascended a platform decorated with British flags and a scarlet banner embellished with a crown and the slogan "Sir John Colborne and the British Constitution."[2]

Talbot's impressive gathering in St Thomas was but one of a series of great district meetings that government supporters staged outside York between February and April 1832. These manifestations of political theatre were held in Amherst (24 February), Kingston (2 March), Brockville (17 March), Hamilton (19 March), and St Thomas (23 April).[3] Some of them attracted large crowds, with one thousand attendees reported at both the Amherst and the Kingston meetings, for example. These gatherings were carefully planned and executed.

In fact, they may well have been the result of concerted planning on the part of government supporters. Unlike the oppositionist meetings in the fall of 1831, they often featured parades, banners, and music designed to reinforce the theme of loyalty to the British connection. The addresses and resolutions of the meetings, too, reiterated the pro-government interpretation of loyalty that was centrally concerned with the expulsion crisis. These documents also attacked oppositionist figures, particularly Mackenzie and Egerton Ryerson, in both personal and political terms. The resolutions of these district meetings, and the township meetings held in other centres, were widely circulated throughout the province. Government supporters spared no effort to obtain signatures on these documents, and achieved brilliant success in this undertaking.

The importance of this venture by government supporters into the unaccustomed territory of popular politics, however, extended well beyond the number of signatures affixed to their resolutions. Efforts to combat Mackenzie's popular following in York also gave birth to a new, unprecedented and province-wide organization of government supporters, the British Constitutional Society. Accounts of the gatherings themselves provide powerful evidence of the penetration of provincial issues into the several districts of the province. An examination of the manner in which these meetings were conducted, and the events that occurred in their aftermath, exposes the darkest side of Upper Canadian politics: the ongoing deployment of political violence by government supporters. Though political violence was far from unknown in the province's history, never before had it been employed so methodically or so effectively. Government supporters were setting a very dangerous precedent for the future.

This activity fundamentally transformed the political culture of Upper Canada: everywhere it prompted the mobilization of public opinion in response to issues that had arisen in York. Throughout the province, activity was directed towards the common end of demonstrating to the British government the character of public opinion in the province. In the process, what occurred was the creation of a common sense of political awareness – though not, as we shall see, a single interpretation of political events that commanded universal acceptance.

LEADERSHIP OF THE PRO-GOVERNMENT PETITIONING CAMPAIGN, 1832

The real initiative in these months, then, lay not with oppositionists but with their political opponents. To a remarkable extent, the government offensive was marshalled by members of the Assembly. East of

York, at the kickoff of the movement in Amherst (Newcastle) on 24 February, George Strange Boulton and John Brown, MPPs for Durham, took a prominent part in the proceedings. In Kingston, James Samson, MPP for Hastings, was among the signatories of the requisition calling for the meeting in the courthouse on 2 March. Samson was also the leader of the pro-government forces at the Belleville meeting on 10 March. When oppositionists unexpectedly took control of the meeting, Samson and his supporters retreated inside the inn, where they passed a typical "loyal address."[4] Two days later, the Brockville meeting took place at the request of a group of notables including Henry Jones and Richard D. Fraser, MPPs for the town of Brockville and the county of Grenville respectively.[5]

West of York, MPPs Allan MacNab and John Willson took the lead in calling the Hamilton (Gore) meeting of 19 March with the help of the sheriff. In Sandwich, the MPP for Essex, William Elliott, was among those who signed the address.[6] In Niagara, H.J. Boulton's immediate predecessor as MPP for the town, Robert Dickson, took the lead in marshalling government forces.[7] It was only in the London district, still dominated by the powerful and eccentric Colonel Thomas Talbot, that members or former members of the Assembly were not conspicuously active; Talbot evidently embodied in his own person the spirit of respectability that elsewhere required the presence of MPPs.[8]

The prominent roles of so many MPPs at the anti-grievance meetings outside York may mean that their activities were planned before the proroguing of the Upper Canadian Parliament at the end of January 1832. Whether Lieutenant-Governor Colborne provided any direct encouragement is unknown, though it was clear by mid-February that such activity enjoyed his firm approval.[9] The oppositionist press certainly entertained strong suspicions of collusion among their opponents. In early March, for example, the *Colonial Advocate* took careful note of a recent dinner[10] hosted by Chief Justice Robinson and his wife and attended chiefly by "delegates who have been sent in with addresses to His Majesty, and His Excellency." One of the most honoured guests was Mackenzie's *bête noire*, John Brown, MPP, of Port Hope. Brown was already in very bad odour with oppositionists. For one thing, he had reportedly disrupted an oppositionist meeting in Whitby by carrying off the requisitions and the notice for convening the meeting, causing it to be rescheduled.[11] Moreover, as we shall see, he had played a leading role in the uproar at the Newcastle district meeting in February. "During the evening [of the Chief Justice's dinner]," reported a letter to the *Colonial Advocate*, "Dr Strachan, Mr Brown and the Chief Justice were occupied chiefly in close and earnest confabulation."[12] Mackenzie's supporters could not help but draw sinister conclusions from such evidence of consultation among their leading opponents.

Before long, supporters of the government could boast of a much more formal organization. The British Constitutional Society, founded to support the government in the crisis of 1832, originated in the efforts of residents of York, notably members of the Roman Catholic population, to collect signatures in support of the government. The activism of members of this group was consistent with a long tradition of support for the government among leading members of the denomination, particularly Bishop Alexander McDonell. The Bishop, who was seventy years old in 1832, was a master of political paternalism. He had spent much of his life showcasing the loyalty of his flock and receiving favours from the government in return, most recently an appointment to the Legislative Council. "He was," as his biographer put it, "an associate member of the governing elite and by the end of the 1820s was perceived by radical critics of the government as a pillar of its support."[13]

McDonell took full credit for mobilizing his co-religionists in support of the provincial government in early 1832. His view of the situation was that "by their tool Mackenzie the Methodists attempted to upset the Government of this country and drive or at least overawe the lieutenant-governor. Upon that occasion I must acknowledge to have united the Catholics of this town [York]."[14] Thus the Roman Catholics of York, inspired by the alliance between Mackenzie and the Methodists, enlisted on the government side in popular politics. It was not long, however, before this initiative on behalf of the government lost its distinctively Roman Catholic flavour and was absorbed into a more general movement in support of the government.

It was amongst highly placed Roman Catholics that this development began.[15] The *Colonial Advocate* of 8 March reported that a private meeting had recently been held at the home of Reverend Vicar General O'Grady to call the Catholics together for an anti-grievance meeting. O'Grady had been joined by Bishop Alexander McDonell, legislative councillor James Baby, and one Peter McDougal. These individuals had reportedly canvassed the town for signatures on a requisition asking Sheriff William Jarvis to convene a meeting in the Legislative Council chamber at noon on 6 March. Publicity, which included the widespread posting of handbills around the town, doubtless helped swell attendance on this occasion.

Jarvis assumed the chair at the meeting, flanked by the Bishop, Francis Collins, and James Baby. Doctor Dunlop of the Canada Company,[16] Thomas Carfrae Jr,[17] and Captain [probably Edward] O'Brien were also present. Francis Collins, editor of the *Canadian Freeman*, began by reading resolutions that were to form the basis of the address, stating that "the catholics came forward with reluctance as a religious body to correct the insolence of a faction, which they viewed with abhorrence, and to support Sir John Colborne's administration the measures of which they much approved." Patrick Handy, an auctioneer, and Maurice Malone, a teamster,[18] joined in opposing the resolution, but were told to wait until Collins had finished.

When Handy finally had his chance to speak, his remarks created an uproar. According the *Colonial Advocate*, he said: "he did not want any party business in America to be mixed up with religion. Irishmen had seen enough of the defects of stirring up one denomination against another, before they crossed the Atlantic, and he believed the government would not be able to pit them against each other in Canada ... He was as loyal to the King as any man in Canada, but against meddling with religious party work. He wished the meeting, as it was to discuss politics, to be open to his Protestant brethren who here possessed equal political rights with himself." Handy blamed John Strachan, Archdeacon of York, for this foray of the Roman Catholics into politics, arguing that Strachan wanted to be able to show the British government that both Orange and Green elements of the Upper Canadian population supported the present administration. He then moved an amendment to the first resolution which proposed that the meeting be adjourned.

As the meeting divided, Malone cried out "that there was nobody on the other side but the placemen and those persons who were dependent for their daily bread on Doctor Strachan's soup kitchen."[19] This statement was greeted with "much laughter." When a head count revealed that two-thirds of those present supported adjournment, "the sheriff put on his hat and the people immediately left the council chamber." The address was left for signature at the Steam-Boat Hotel.

Leading Catholics were not so easily deterred, however, and the meeting resumed on 12 March at noon at the York Hotel.[20] Disorder prevailed from the start, with great crowds flocking up the stairs, prompting the Bishop to threaten to send for the troops.[21] Patrick Handy was evidently an admirer of Daniel O'Connell, the Irish popular leader whose campaign for Catholic Emancipation had culminated in victory in 1829. Handy contributed to the rowdy atmosphere of the meeting by provocatively elevating Daniel O'Connell's colours, "Green & Red & Orange & Blue, on a staff, and said he would be for brotherly love and union as far as his voice would go." The colours, symbolic of the extraparliamentary pressure directed against the British government, were soon torn down. A shoving match started after Mackenzie, present by invitation as a journalist, suggested that the meeting should be adjourned in favour of a general town meeting. As participants pushed each other, the Bishop took fright and headed home with some of his followers.

A crowd of well-known government supporters, Protestants and Catholics, re-assembled at the Bishop's palace. Their numbers included York *Courier* editor George Gurnett,[22] George Duggan,[23] John Lyons (registrar of Niagara),[24] and Dr John King, a prominent lay Catholic. The Bishop took the chair, and Dr King read the resolutions. The *Colonial Advocate* reported that about one hundred people signed the address, "each one as he signed walking out at the Bishop's kitchen door."

The intervention in politics of Bishop McDonell and senior lay officers of the Roman Catholic Church proved a mixed blessing for the Church. On the plus side, they collected over six hundred signatures on a "loyal" petition to the King.[25] There were, however, many drawbacks to this religiously based support. Oppositionists, rebuked for their association with the Methodists, lost no opportunity to trumpet to the world Bishop McDonell's flagrant meddling in politics. Mackenzie, for example, charged that McDonell had denounced him from the altar, and had beseeched his congregation to sign the anti-grievance petition "for God's sake."[26] McDonell, who was known to be seeking favours from the government on behalf of the Church, was vulnerable to accusations that he had been bought for the price of a substantial pension and a large land grant for his brother.[27] This charge was particularly telling in view of the heritage of religious discord in Ireland, which many emigrants sought desperately to leave behind.[28] Moreover, it had the effect of further dividing the Roman Catholics of York, who had already been racked by conflict between established members of society and the new Irish poor, as well as by an incipient feud between senior officials.[29]

The crisis also provided an opportunity for upwardly mobile members of York's middle class to demonstrate their support for the government. Typical of these activists was George Gurnett, an immigrant from England who had, in 1830, founded the *Courier of Upper Canada* newspaper in York. One of Gurnett's political associates was Thomas Carfrae Jr, a merchant himself and the son of successful merchant who had immigrated from Scotland in 1805. From the mid-1820s, Carfrae became increasingly involved in the civic affairs of his adopted home, helping to establish a burying ground, and serving as the first chief of York's Fire Department.[30]

Carfrae was evidently interested in fighting political fires as well, and, accordingly, he chaired a meeting of support for the government at the Ontario House on 6 March 1832, with George Gurnett acting as secretary.[31] Prudently avoiding a public meeting in the heart of Mackenzie territory, they agreed to circulate an anti-grievance address. Carfrae, Dr Dunlop, and James F. Smith drew up the address, and, along with Gurnett, formed a general committee to receive it. A meeting the following day provided for the preparation of fifty copies of the address to be circulated around the city by the fourteen canvassers who were to work selected wards of York. These canvassers ultimately collected eight hundred and seventy-six signatures.[32] By the third week in March, both groups of government supporters had their petitions ready, and together their representatives met at the British Coffee House on 22 March. From there, they made their way to Government House, where Carfrae and Dr John King read the addresses to Colborne on behalf of their respective organizations.

A week later, members of these two groups celebrated their success with a "grand public dinner" at the Steam-Boat Hotel in York. More than two hundred tickets were issued for this affair, presided over by Sheriff William Botsford Jarvis, with Dr John King acting as Vice-President. Those present, according to the *Canadian Freeman*, were agreed on two matters: that the spirit of disaffection should be crushed, and that religious differences should be forgotten. The dinner was followed by thirteen toasts, saluting members of the royal family, the British army and navy, "the rose, shamrock, and thistle," Roman Catholic Bishop McDonell, Anglican Bishop Mountain (of Lower Canada), and Sir Wilmot Horton, "the father of the system of emigration." A topical toast to the "Loyalist" triumph of "the 23rd March 1832" received three times the usual number of cheers. "The champions of constitutional British principles in the Newcastle District" were also recognized with a toast. The only sour note was struck by Sheriff Jarvis, whose disparaging reference to the Lower Canadians offended the sensibilities of Catholics who were deeply grateful to their French counterparts for their defence of their common religion in Lower Canada.[33]

As part of the petitioning effort, pro-government forces had organized the "General British Constitutional Committee of York,"[34] which proved to be the predecessor of the British Constitutional Society founded shortly thereafter. At the end of March 1832, the Committee produced a form letter designed to mobilize supporters throughout the province. It began by announcing that the Committee "has taken the liberty of naming you one of a Committee for the Township of ____ for the purpose of obtaining signatures within the said Township to a loyal and constitutional address." Lest this statement seem too dictatorial, it was followed by a proviso: "should it be compatible with your views and your convenience to do so."

Along with this notification of their new political role, recipients also received a copy of the York address as a possible template for use in their own districts. They were, moreover, urged to form a township committee with a chair as well as a secretary whose job it was to correspond with the general committee in York. This effort may have inspired some of the meetings, petitions and addresses from government supporters in April 1832 (see appendices A and C). By that time, however, whatever the pretensions of these activists in York, the organization of government supporters in the province as a whole was very well advanced indeed.

The formal founding of the British Constitutional Society of York followed shortly. Not surprisingly, the prime movers were those who had taken an active part in the petitioning movement on behalf of the government, including Dr Dunlop, the president of the new organization, John King and Thomas Carfrae, two of the vice-presidents, and George Gurnett, the secretary. As Frederick Armstrong has pointed out, these individuals were part of York's expanding middle class, essentially the same social class that provided leadership for the York Central Committee. Significantly, unlike their rivals, many leading members of the British Constitutional Committee were recent immigrants from Britain.[35] It was thus natural that the purpose of the British Constitutional Society was to support the empire and the local government of the colony, and "to counteract the efforts of any ... faction ... whose principles and conduct, may be incompatible with the British form of Government, or dangerous to the peace, and true interests of the people of this colony."

Although this counterpart of the York Central Committee was founded too late to have much effect on the events of early 1832 (at least beyond organizing township committees in the Home district), its appearance was nevertheless a very significant development. For the first time, supporters of the provincial government had attempted to establish some form of permanent extraparliamentary organization founded not on national or religious distinctions but on essentially political criteria. Like its oppositionist counterpart, the York Central Committee, the British Constitutional Society was not simply, or even primarily, an electoral organization. As chapter 5 indicates, it was directed more broadly at mobilizing public opinion in support of the status quo, whether the occasion was an election or not. The organization evidently proved its usefulness, remaining intermittently active into the 1840s.[36] Among the consequences of the expulsion crisis, then, was the appearance of permanent political organization among supporters of the government.

RELIGION AND ETHNICITY

Issues relating to religion and ethnicity, as we have seen, were not confined to the provincial capital. Immigration was emerging as a significant factor in the eastern part of the province. While oppositionists were at best lukewarm about British immigrants because of the support they were expected to offer to the established authorities, government supporters welcomed them for exactly the same reason. Thus, at a meeting in Kingston on 2 March, John S. Cartwright, a lawyer and business leader of the town, responded to the meeting of 16 February in Lennox and Addington by railing at those who disapproved of British immigration. He charged that these critics feared that the loyalty of the newcomers would make it "difficult to mould them to their way of thinking." Cartwright also reached out for the support of impecunious immigrants, suggesting that their detractors did not understand that "this [was] a poor man's country," and that all British subjects had equal rights. Indeed, it was paupers who had undertaken the burden of taming the land and settling the province. Thus Cartwright neatly tied the locally important issue of emigration to the province-wide question of the grievance petitions, appealing for support from those who had recently arrived in the colony.[37]

In Leeds as well the issue of immigration was highly relevant, because of a recent wave of Irish immigration. By 1830, the Irish formed a majority in at least some of the county's townships.[38] In the conflicts arising between them and the old inhabitants, Ogle Gowan, himself a recent immigrant, smelled the possibility of his own rise to power in local politics. As early as 1830, he had begun manoeuvering to use his influence with his fellow countrymen – Catholic (if possible) as well as Protestant – to make a place for himself in the local establishment. With this in mind, he attempted in 1831–32 to organize "Independent Clubs" and "Patriotic Clubs" to counteract the growth in oppositionist strength.[39] His opposition to Mackenzie at the petitioning meetings in 1831 and his role in the district meeting of March 1832 were also means to this end.

Gowan was stirred to action by the report of the anti-immigration meeting in Lennox and Addington in mid-February. In addition, a local oppositionist's public attack on pauper immigration required an answer. Also, the recent news that Lower Canada was implementing a head tax against immigrants was a spur to action on behalf of the immigrant population of the district.

The stated object of the March 1832 district meeting, called pointedly for St Patrick's Day in Brockville, was to consider Sir John Colborne's suggestion for organizing emigration societies.[40] Oppositionists, however, were instantly suspicious, fearing this was merely a pretext for an anti-grievance meeting. Accordingly, they produced a handbill urging friends of equal rights and constitutional freedom to attend the meeting.[41]

In the end, there were three meetings, the first of which established an emigration society in Brockville.[42] It was followed by a political meeting, which unsurprisingly split along political lines. Each meeting dealt with the immigration issue, with Gowan proclaiming that the oppositionist newspaper, the *Brockville Recorder*, was utterly hostile to the newcomers. To his voice was added that of Henry Sherwood, an entrepreneurial lawyer whose family loomed large in the Johnstown district establishment. Sherwood had publicly demonstrated his political affiliation by participation in the Types Riot six years before.[43] On this occasion, he argued in favour of British immigration, saying that it would lead to the erection of "a Bulwark of British feeling ... against which the waves of Democracy may beat in vain for ages." Oppositionist lawyer A.N. Buell refrained from throwing a red flag before the Irish population of the district and simply contented himself with urging moderation on the question of immigration. This spirit was reflected in the resolutions of the oppositionist meeting, which condemned efforts to stir up religious and national feelings – a clear hit at Gowan's technique for improving his own political fortunes. Nevertheless, it is clear that the oppositionists spoke essentially for the old inhabitants of the region, with government supporters old and new reaching out to those who had recently come from Great Britain.

THE CONTENTS OF PRO-GOVERNMENT PETITIONS

Even without hard evidence of early formal organization of government supporters, collusion among them is suggested by the fact that, though the wording of their resolutions differed from one meeting to another, their message was essentially identical. The province was in a flourishing condition, the resolutions maintained. No unjust taxes were imposed, there were no threats to civil and religious liberty, and the administration of justice was totally impartial. The serpents in this veritable garden of Eden were a few designing malcontents who were wickedly deluding the ignorant by stirring up imaginary grievances. According to the pro-government addresses, the activities of these malicious and self-interested individuals posed a serious danger to Upper Canada; they threatened to disturb the tranquillity and the prosperity of the colony, and perhaps even to rupture the link with Great Britain.

Government supporters did not even attempt to answer the oppositionist critique of Upper Canadian government. On the contrary, they denied that there were any substantive grievances whatsoever. No doubt the intention was partly to deter the British from intervening in Upper Canada to implement any part of the oppositionist program.

Indeed, a number of pro-government addresses explicitly stated that the British government should stay out of Upper Canadian affairs. As they said in Bath, "we are satisfied that any change which may be required by us, or the removal of any real grievance which may be found to exist, can be effected by the local Legislature, through our own representatives; in whom the privilege has been granted to assist in [?] making laws for our peace and good government."[44] There is a certain irony in this attitude: though government supporters postured as die-hard opponents of responsible government, on occasions like this when their interests required it, they actually argued forcefully for local autonomy.

In contrast to the rights-based discourse of the oppositionists, government supporters spoke of politics in the language of paternalism and deference. This was an approach calculated to appeal to members of the British government, whose ears were always receptive to arguments in support of the British Empire, particularly when couched in paternalistic terms. Nowhere in Upper Canada was paternalism more obvious than in the London district, where Colonel Thomas Talbot liked to think of himself as the "Father of the Talbot Settlement."[45] "I gave my *Children* some wholesome advice"; thus in 1832 did Talbot describe his political harangue to a public meeting.[46] Not all government supporters were so literal-minded in their paternalism, but rhetoric associated with this concept permeated pro-government discourse through the 1830s.

In the view of paternalists like Talbot, politics was an ordered and hierarchical process, in which authorities manifested paternalism towards their subordinates and were rewarded with deference. Thus even local notables such as members of the Assembly and Legislative Council were required to defer to their superiors like the monarch, the British government, and the lieutenant-governor, and to express their appreciation of the benefits conferred by these authorities. The Kingston address, for example, expressed "a faithful and devoted attachment" to the person and government of the king, and gratitude for "the many signal acts of kindness performed for our behoof [*sic*], by the government of the parent state."[47] The township of Toronto put forward a common and similar viewpoint towards the lieutenant-governor; they offered "the warmest gratitude for your Excellency's constant endeavours to promote the welfare and prosperity of this province, and [asserted] that the temperate and impartial discharge of the duties of your high office, has merited their esteem and respectful approbation."[48]

A major thrust of the pro-government argument against their opponents derived from their paternalistic frame of reference. In this view, the oppositionists' attacks on Colborne and other officials failed to demonstrate the proper deference; on the contrary, they violated the paternalistic code that government supporters believed rested at the heart of politics. Referring to Mackenzie's demand for Colborne's recall, and the marches of his supporters on Government House, the *Canadian Freeman* complained that the oppositionists had "insulted the proper authorities, and attempted to intimidate the government."[49] Moreover, Mackenzie and his supporters had demonstrated disrespect to their elected representatives. The address from government supporters in Hamilton showed that even controversial assertions could be phrased to fit the paternalist mold: "We feel most thankful to Your Majesty and Your Imperial Parliament, for granting us the privilege by our Representatives in the Assembly to assist in 'Making laws for the peace, welfare, and good government of the Colony.' Thus affording us ample means of redressing any grievances that may exist."[50] The oppositionists, on the other hand, came right out and blatantly "mocked their representatives."[51] In the view of their opponents, then, the disrespectful attitude of Mackenzie and his supporters violated the paternalistic code that lay at the centre of the political order.[52]

By acting outside the boundaries of this code, oppositionists laid themselves open to attack, their suitability for political leadership questioned. Thus government supporters untiringly trained their spotlights on the allegedly unsavoury attributes of oppositionist leaders, their supporters, and their allies. Among their chief targets was William Lyon Mackenzie, whose standing among oppositionists had risen so greatly since his first expulsion from the Assembly in December 1831.

Mackenzie, his critics maintained, did not have the dignity or accomplishments that a leader should possess. Indeed, it was all too easy to make a mockery of him, with his diminutive size, red wig,[53] and checkered career. The *Canadian Freeman*, which was widely copied in pro-government papers outside York, launched a campaign of character assassination against "the little Knight of the *Red Wig*"[54] in January 1832 that was quite the equal of Colborne's slurs in his correspondence with the Colonial Office. Mackenzie, it said, was a former shop boy turned "mountebank." His newspaper was so scurrilous that it "got his office levelled to the ground" – an inaccurate reference to the Types Riot. He secured election to the Assembly by begging for funds, by treating the voters, and by catering to the "saddle-bag faction." He was expelled from the Assembly because he had become an "intolerable nuisance."[55] In the view of this newspaper, and other commentators as well, Mackenzie in no way demonstrated the gentility that was a fundamental precondition for political leadership.[56] The implication was that petitioners who could attract no better leadership material than Mackenzie surely did not deserve to be taken seriously. In this view, Mackenzie's alleged lack of the obvious attributes of leadership reflected adversely on the entire oppositionist movement.[57]

Such journalistic ridicule was another dimension of the disrespect his political enemies manifested towards Mackenzie in public demonstrations. In the York riot of March 1832, for example, his famous medal was mocked as gingerbread in the effigy his opponents paraded about the town. Efforts to fit him with a tar cap and to hang and burn him in effigy were other public demonstrations of contempt. These manifestations of popular politics echoed the public humiliation that Mackenzie had suffered at the level of high politics, when government supporters had expelled him from the Assembly.

It might be argued that it was Mackenzie's questionable social status that made him vulnerable to attacks of this kind.[58] After all, other, more "gentlemanly" oppositionist leaders were not subjected to this kind of treatment. The fact that the Baldwins, for example, prosperous lawyers of York, were not similarly punished for their leading role in petitioning on behalf of Judge Willis suggests that their relative affluence and respectability protected them. A more likely explanation is that the Willis agitation predated government supporters' full-blown revival of the twin strategies of character assassination and political violence that had been deployed with such success against Robert Gourlay. Events later in the decade indicated that even W.W. Baldwin was not immune from attack when he attached himself to a widespread movement advocating political reform. As we shall see, the Durham meeting of which he was an organizer was forcibly disrupted in 1839, and, in one of the most scurrilous of surviving Upper Canadian political broadsides, he was subjected to ridicule by being linked to rustic Irish rebels of the 1790s.[59] Much later, in 1849, his son Robert, then co-premier of the Canadas, was burned in effigy in Toronto on the occasion of William Lyon Mackenzie's return from exile.[60] After 1832, social status was small protection against political violence, and unfavourable references to social status were not statements of sociological reality but part of the repertoire of abuse directed against the political left.

Mackenzie was a major target of scorn, but pro-government newspapers sometimes also attacked the social composition of the oppositionist forces more generally. For example, in early 1832, the Kingston *Patriot* carried a letter from Middlesex county that cast aspersions on the local leadership of the oppositionist movement as well as the signatories to its petitions. "*Pedlars* and *strollers*," alleged the writer, constituted the movement's local leadership; presumably such creatures were neither respectable nor propertied. Moreover, according to the same correspondent, the signatories were "chiefly ... runaway negroes, and ... people who have neither habitation nor property in the country." The social status of the oppositionists, the writer believed, meant that their cause need not be taken seriously: "The sensible part of the community," he approvingly observed, "only laugh at such silly attempts to do mischief."[61]

Not surprisingly, Mackenzie's Methodist allies were targets of similar charges.[62] As we have already seen, in addition to their political activism, the Methodists challenged the established church in ways similar to those by which oppositionists threatened the established order in politics. The most common term of abuse was to refer to the Methodists as members of the "saddle-bag faction."[63] A letter in the *Brockville Gazette*, for example, referred to oppositionists at the Amherst meeting as "the disgraced and defeated dregs of the meeting, consisting of a few saddlebag disciples."[64] Methodist ministers, the term implied, did not travel in carriages like gentlemen but on horseback. The term "saddlebag" suggested not only poverty but also a kind of rootlessness associated with the itineracy of the Methodists circuit riders. There was perhaps more than a touch of envy in this charge, since it was their mobility that helped to make the Methodist clergy so effective in building and maintaining their flock.[65]

The Methodists were also condemned as disloyal because of their American origin; those who followed Ryerson and Mackenzie were ungrateful to boot, considering that they had been "so liberally treated by our Government." Methodists were also occasionally tarred with the brush of immorality because of rumoured incidents at camp meetings. At the Kingston meeting of 3 March, for example, Thomas Dalton, editor of the *Patriot*, made a snide reference to "those of the rabid Ryersonian Sect, frantically ... exhibit[ing] temptations at Camp Meetings, to debauch and corrupt the youth of the other sex."[66] The main focus of attack on the Methodists, however, was directed at their supposed disloyalty rather than at alleged sexual transgressions.

The Methodist journalist and minister Egerton Ryerson was a particular target of hostility. The *Niagara Gleaner*, for example, took exception to his conduct in "stepping out of the duties of [his] Holy vocation, and attending to political manoeuvres ... McKenzie [*sic*]is only a tool made use of, to answer their purpose."[67] A letter printed in the *Canadian Freeman* also criticized Ryerson for leading the Methodists astray through political activism. He had, the writer said, "formed them into a political body, nearly alienated their allegiance – ruffled their peace of mind, divided the society by his pride, ambition, and persecution – rendered them odious in the eyes of other sects – while he upheld misrepresentations, and urged wicked and foolish men to acts, and endeavoured to render unworthy and degrade our superiors throughout the province."[68] This charge was not confined to Ryerson: Methodist circuit riders, in general, were portrayed as messengers carrying disaffection.[69] As "A.B." put it in a letter to the editor of the *Niagara Gleaner*, "the different travelling preachers perform all the functions of *political runners*, advocating a disorganizing faction, who have been a trouble and a disgrace to the Province."[70] There is no small degree of irony in these attacks in view of the activism of Anglican clergy and the Roman Catholic bishop on behalf of the government cause!

In the eyes of their opponents, the oppositionists would have been simply laughable had their activities not been so threatening to the body politic. In a context in which no true grievances existed, attempts to stir up popular discontent could only be regarded as seditious, or so government supporters argued. The address of the Brockville meeting on 17 March reflected this view. "We cannot but view with feelings of abhorrence and detestation," it proclaimed, "the wily machinations of a factious party in Religion and Politics, endeavouring by the most unhallowed means to sow disaffection in this happy land; and to bring into contempt and disrepute the Local Government." It hastened to assure the British government, however, that "we will, ALL of us, with equal alacrity, fly to arms (if need be) to repel foreign aggression or suppress domestic insurrection."[71] The address of Toronto township suggested that the promoters of the grievance petitions entertained "a wish to separate those fine provinces [the Canadas] from the British Crown."[72] Government supporters in Kingston similarly maintained that the agitators were attempting "to alienate their affections from their gracious Monarch, and to weaken, if not destroy their attachment to [British] institutions."[73] The issue as government supporters defined it, then, was not misgovernment of the province but the treasonable behaviour of opponents of duly constituted authority. The utter denial of the legitimacy of the oppositionists' demands was a key ingredient of the popular politics of their opponents.

POLITICAL VIOLENCE

Following Mackenzie's expulsion, in the midst of what they viewed as an alarming crisis, government supporters turned to extra-legal means with unprecedented zeal in order to preserve the status quo. The deployment of political violence, to be sure, was not entirely unknown to Upper Canada before early 1832. As we have seen, Robert Gourlay had been the victim of more than one assault; in fact, he was once horsewhipped in the streets of Kingston by William Lyon Mackenzie's future antagonist, Christopher Hagerman. Mackenzie too had gained fame as well as fortune as a result of the destruction of his press at the hands of the Types Rioters in 1826. These, however, were essentially isolated incidents. Their rarity is highlighted by the fact that the subsequent petitioning movements of 1827–31 transpired without any hint of repressive violence. By the early 1830s, changing circumstances promoted a different view among government supporters.

By this time, as we have seen, most of the legal bulwarks of government hegemony had crumbled.[74] Legislation that had been used so effectively to banish Gourlay and to suppress meetings in his support was no longer in effect. The Seditious Meetings Act was repealed in 1820, and the Sedition Act finally followed in 1829. In addition, by the late 1820s, the use of seditious libel charges against oppositionist newspaper editors and others was foundering under the weight of popular resistance in the jury box. By 1830, supporters of the government had essentially been forced to abandon this method of silencing their opponents.[75] Moreover, the fact that petitioning was universally acknowledged to be the right of every British subject precluded suppression of petitioning meetings by the legislature.

If dissent could not be controlled by law, many government supporters believed that it should be put down by force. This view no doubt owed a good deal to the example offered by the conduct of government supporters in Britain itself in times of perceived crisis. In the late eighteenth century, for example, when support for political reform spread rapidly, "church and king mobs," often incited by the authorities themselves, attacked the property of those suspected of republican and democratic sympathies. Again, in the five years or so following the Napoleonic Wars, the British government resorted to massive domestic repression, notably in the massacre at Peterloo in 1819.[76] On a smaller scale, a few supporters of the Upper Canadian government had used forcible means in their efforts to suppress Robert Gourlay's form of activism. The use of political violence in support of the established authorities, then, was firmly within the British tradition. The tendency was reinforced, as we shall see, by the activities of the Orange Order, a Protestant paramilitary organization that originated in Ireland and spread quickly in Upper Canada during the early 1830s.

The connection between Orangeism and political violence in Upper Canada is illustrated by the first of the great district meetings, which occurred in Amherst, near Cobourg, on 24 February 1832. It was widely covered by the provincial press, as befitted the first of the pro-government district meetings outside York and the first meeting in support of the status quo that included violence against the oppositionists. The repressive tactics of government supporters in Amherst owed much to the fact that their local leaders were recent recruits to the Orange Order. George Strange Boulton was one of these local notables. An alumnus of John Strachan's Cornwall school, he went on to become a lawyer and officeholder, and he represented the county of Durham in 1824–5 and from 1830 to 1841. In 1831, Boulton lent his support in the Assembly to his brother, Attorney General Henry John Boulton, by voting for the expulsions of Mackenzie.[77] The other member for Durham elected in 1830 was John Brown, a mercurial merchant and magistrate of Port Hope who was constantly embroiled with the legal system during the early 1830s.[78]

By 1831, leading government supporters in the Newcastle district, including Boulton, Brown, and an associate, Colonel John Covert, had determined to embrace Orangeism. This decision was doubtless facilitated by the political strategy of Orange leader Ogle Gowan. In the 1830s, Gowan's major focus was to establish the respectability of Orangeism. The method he chose was to throw the weight of the Order behind the government in its struggles with oppositionists. The inertia of the government in the face of Mackenzie's many public meetings of 1831 may have alerted Gowan to an opportunity to be of service. He and his colleagues were more than willing to draw on the paramilitary traditions of the order in Ireland and to employ violence against opponents of the status quo. The provincial government's willingness to accept such support is a telling commentary on the political culture of Upper Canada in the 1830s.

Though John Covert piously claimed that he had joined the order in the hopes of persuading its leaders to abandon their divisive anti-Catholicism,[79] more self-serving motives may have animated him and his colleagues. Like Gowan, they may have hoped to curry favour with officialdom and thus advance their careers by using the order to support the "loyalist" cause. The Amherst meeting was a testing ground, where Irish energy was deployed against oppositionists in "the first instance of a clash involving violence between Orangemen and reformers" in Upper Canada.[80]

A contingent of Orangemen was crucial in the efforts to deny oppositionists the use of public space in Amherst. Early on 24 February, Brown and Boulton sent sleighs to fetch Orangemen from the townships of Cavan and Peterborough.[81] They arrived on the scene about an hour before the meeting "with banners and a band."[82] The flags were of plain orange, and of orange striped with blue, bearing inscriptions favourable to Lieutenant-Governor Colborne. According to Mackenzie, who attended, this show of party and religious affiliation was unprecedented at a political meeting. The display was countered only by a flag bearing Mackenzie's name and a slogan endorsing freedom of the press.[83]

This panoply of Orange regalia was no doubt intended to overawe the crowd of about one thousand who had gathered despite the unseasonable cold and the short notice given for the meeting: Mackenzie reported that the occasion began with "the outrageous clamour and tumult of a mob excited and aided by several magistrates."[84] It was but one aspect of a series of efforts to deny a hearing to supporters of the grievance petitions.

The featured speaker was Charles Fothergill, MPP for Durham from 1825–30, who commented that this was the largest assembly he had ever seen in the district.[85] Fothergill had been one of the leading oppositionists in the Assembly in the late 1820s, but in reality his view of politics more closely approximated those of the paternalists.[86] This was reflected in his observations to the Amherst meeting, where he contended that it was absurd to promote agitation in view of the British government's obvious solicitude for the welfare of Upper Canadians. Moreover, it was wrong "to impose on our gracious sovereign and his Ministers in England." This was the time, he said, for "every honest man now coming forward to declare his creed." Fothergill concluded by moving a resolution that was carried by acclamation, declaring the attachment of the "vast majority of the inhabitants of Upper Canada" to the King and the British constitution.[87]

Suspected oppositionists who attempted to follow Fothergill as speakers were essentially shouted down. Such unfortunates included Captain Archibald Macdonald, MPP for Northumberland, and G.M. Boswell, a local lawyer,[88] who were "compelled to retire amidst hisses and groans."[89] One eyewitness reported that the magistrates present encouraged the mob "grossly to insult one of the county members [Macdonald] in barking like dogs, screeching like owls, and hissing like serpents."[90] Further disruption ensued when G.S. Boulton leaped to the platform as Macdonald addressed the crowd, saying "By G-d he shall not speak." At this, "the banners of the party were again unfurled which the Sheriff ordered away." Ruttan begged for order, unheeded, and repeatedly threatened to dissolve the meeting.[91]

Having denied Mackenzie's sympathizers a hearing, the sheriff took advantage of the tumult to ram through a series of resolutions favourable to the administration. According to Mackenzie, Ruttan "began to read a paper which I understand ... to be an address, but so great was the disorder and confusion that I can only say I heard none of it although close to the platform. After reading what no one then heard or could hear he appeared to put the question for its adoption, &

declared it carried by acclamation."[92] Ruttan added insult to injury by refusing to allow the meeting to divide on the dubious grounds that the address had already been carried by acclamation.

Barred from meaningful participation in the public meeting, oppositionists withdrew to discuss their own set of resolutions. These deplored Mackenzie's expulsion from the Assembly and supported the British constitution, freedom of the franchise, and the right of peaceful assembly. They also endorsed responsible government and criticized the composition of the Legislative Council. Even this activity, however, was not allowed to continue undisturbed. John Brown materialized with his supporters to denounce the proceedings before calling on his musicians to play the "Rogue's March." This well-known tune was customarily played on two military occasions, neither of them pleasant: when a soldier received a dishonourable discharge, and when military camps were cleared of prostitutes (a custom giving rise to the song's other name, "The Whore's March").[93] This unpleasant musical interlude was followed by what must have been a remarkable vocal rendition of "God Save the King" accompanied by a bugle. According to a report in the York *Courier*, "the assembled multitude ... then dispersed, leaving the disgraced and defeated dregs of the meeting."[94]

Not content with denying the oppositionists a public hearing and interrupting their counter-meeting, government supporters completed their activities by publicly denying any legitimacy to the oppositionist resolutions. Four district magistrates, including John Brown and John Covert, publicly stated that the resolutions of the second meeting had not been offered to the public meeting. Reports that they had, the magistrates solemnly intoned, were "utterly destitute of truth."[95]

In view of this campaign of intimidation, it is not surprising that both sides frequently cited the Amherst meeting as a pivotal one. One correspondent of the *Colonial Advocate* denounced "the violent and successful efforts to prevent discussion" there.[96] A few weeks later, another letter suggested that the meeting represented an effort to "suppress public and fair discussion and carry and enforce despotic measures by virtue of the *Shelaleigh*." The author asserted that "great exertions were made to collect disorderly characters." Some respectable inhabitants, he said, were "knocked down with clubs and otherwise injured." The event, he complained, "has every appearance of having been a connected plan of the high Tories of this District to trample on the rights and privileges, civil and religious, of the U.E. Loyalists, their children and grandchildren, and other old inhabitants."[97]

The Orangemen and other government supporters, on the other hand, were much encouraged by their "victory" in Amherst. In their view, the events of that day had greatly enhanced the prestige of the Orange Order. As Colonel John Covert later explained, "the Orange Lodges were at the time the only embodied associations in the province; and they had risen much in public estimation since the celebrated meeting at Amherst, where their prowress [*sic*] and exertions were well appreciated."[98] The alliance with the Orange Order brought government supporters willing allies in the campaign to suppress political dissent, and made it possible for them to employ political violence on a grander scale than ever before.

At the time of the Amherst gathering, Mackenzie in particular became a target of would-be attackers. A Hamilton newspaper reported that as soon as Mackenzie's presence in the neighbourhood was discovered, "the people surrounded the house he was in, and had not the Magistrates interfered, they would have pulled it down."[99] Mackenzie did not always enjoy the benefit of such protection, as an incident shortly after the Amherst meeting demonstrated. As Mackenzie returned to York, a group of "Irish wags" accosted his sleigh. Anticipating an unfriendly encounter, Mackenzie quickly sought refuge under the buffalo robes, and thus narrowly avoided being fitted with a tar cap. His would-be assailants departed only after insisting on "the John (driver) taking off his hat and assisting them in singing God Save the King and in giving 3 hearty cheers for Sir John Colborne."[100] At the same time, there were reports that Mackenzie had been burnt in effigy in Marysburgh.[101]

Not long after, Mackenzie was burned in effigy in Port Hope, along with Egerton Ryerson. The moving spirit behind this event was none other than John Brown, accompanied by three other magistrates and a sizeable crowd. This well-lubricated throng responded with alacrity when Brown offered "five pounds for a '*Mackenzie man's head.*'" They began their search at "Mr William's grocery," where they forced open the door and assaulted those within. Having thus breached the local stronghold of reform, the crowd initiated the effigy burnings. "Their dying confession," it was reported of the effigies, "was read by the constable ... during which time there were many hurras." According to the same account, "the hangman made his black appearance." This grim demonstration of public disrespect for Mackenzie and Ryerson was all the more menacing because it was conducted at the instigation of an MPP, and under the eyes of several magistrates. This was neither the first time, nor the last, that officialdom would implicitly sanction violence against the forces of reform.

Not all political violence in early 1832 was clearly connected to the activities of members of the Orange Order and their close associates. Two days after Gowan's meeting in Brockville on 17 March, government supporters struck again, this time to the west of York in the town of Hamilton. The capital of the Gore district, Hamilton, was a rival to York with distinctive commercial ambitions of its own. In spite of Hamilton's proximity to the provincial capital, as late as the election of 1830, local issues far outweighed "provincial" ones at elections.[102] It was Mackenzie's foray into the district with his petitioning meeting in 1831 that had forcefully alerted inhabitants of the district to developments in York.[103]

Hamilton had been a scene of triumph for Mackenzie in the fall of 1831, but in the following year the story was different. It was government supporters who called a meeting under the leadership of Allan MacNab, John Willson, and the sheriff. MacNab had a number of objectives in mind: to discredit the results of the 1831 petition meeting in Hamilton; to demonstrate public support for his own role in the expulsions of Mackenzie; and to improve his electoral prospects.[104] The crowd gathered in the Hamilton Court House, where Mackenzie's appearance, accompanied by a standard-bearer with a "provocative" blue and white striped flag, triggered pandemonium.

The mood of the oppositionists cannot have been improved by a resolution stating that Mackenzie had, "by his inflammatory and revolutionary principles and libellious [*sic*] publications rendered himself unworthy of a seat in the councils of the country," and requesting his removal from the meeting.[105] Pro-government accounts would have it that Mackenzie and his supporters responded by drowning out the voice of the sheriff, creating an uproar as he tried to read the notice of meeting. Oppositionist accounts, on the other hand, emphasized the unfairness in the process of choosing the chair, with two-thirds to three-quarters of the crowd being in favour of the oppositionist choice, William Sheldon rather than the sheriff, the pro-government candidate, who was actually awarded the chair.[106]

As long as Mackenzie and his followers remained at the meeting, chaos reigned. Mackenzie, attempting to address the crowd from a tabletop, was hauled down by William Johnson Kerr, a local magistrate. Another member of the crowd delivered a blow below Mackenzie's ear that would have knocked him down but for the density of the crowd. A rotten egg aimed for Mackenzie caught his supporter Caleb Hopkins with his mouth open.[107] Reaching the logical conclusion about the better part of valour, Hopkins soon after moved that the meeting adjourn to the Court House Green. The oppositionists accordingly seceded from the original meeting to pass their own address and petition. Their opponents, meanwhile, went on to endorse an address which contended that "certain unprincipled individuals are endeavouring to excite and mislead the people, and by a foul and organised system of misrepresentation, to persuade them that they are oppressed by many weighty grievances, in order to weaken if not destroy their attachment to [our] institutions."[108]

Not satisfied with having denounced Mackenzie and with having driven his supporters from the courthouse, some local detractors determined to silence him permanently. Once again, Magistrate W.J. Kerr, who had laid hands on Mackenzie earlier, took the lead. He lured the editor out of his lodgings in Hamilton and, along with some of his colleagues, gave the intruder from York the beating of his life. This episode attracted wide attention in the provincial press, not least in the *Colonial Advocate*, which mounted a running campaign on the subject.

The reaction to this violence depended greatly on the political persuasion of the commentator. From distant London, Upper Canada, the editor of the *Sun* argued that the involvement of Colonel Kerr, a pillar of the local establishment, was nothing short of disgraceful.[109] The pro-government *Canadian Freeman*, however, employed metaphor to suggest that violent means were necessary in order to suppress the threat offered by reform: "Are we to remain careless observers, until the serpent that we have nourished in our bosoms shed his poison? When we see the tyger crouching, are we to wait carelessly for his spring? No, crush the serpent in its coils – strike the tyger in his lair – and put down sedition in its infancy."[110] The conclusion of the affair doubtless gave more comfort to the editor of the *Freeman* than to his political opponents. When a friend of Mackenzie ultimately brought Kerr to trial at the Grand Assizes in August 1832, the offender was fined such a small amount that Mackenzie was outraged. His co-conspirators remained unindicted.[111]

Though Mackenzie providentially escaped death at the hands of his visitors, he took this episode very seriously indeed. Avoiding the threat to his personal safety from Orangemen and other political opponents, he put in only one more public appearance before his departure for Britain, at the ill-fated meeting in York on 23 March. Personal assault, increasingly the weapon of choice in the attempt of government supporters to seize control of popular politics in Upper Canada, was already having a discouraging effect on oppositionist activism. No doubt its proponents took careful note.

SIGNATURES ON PRO-GOVERNMENT PETITIONS

The pro-government analysis struck a responsive chord across much of Upper Canada, as appendices A and C demonstrate. Not only did government supporters dominate the roster of public meetings; they also collected more signatures on their petitions than did Mackenzie's supporters. While the Colonial Office could find no more than about twenty-two thousand signatures on petitions in support of reform, British officials credited the pro-administration forces with more than twenty-six thousand signatures. In the battle of numbers, pro-government forces had won an important though not a decisive victory. The achievement was all the more impressive because they had mounted their campaign from a standing start. (The fact that their triumph was achieved with the help of strong-arm tactics and the use of violence does not appear to have made their victory any less satisfactory.) The lieutenant-governor, for one, anticipated highly desirable results from such initiatives in the years to come: "I can assure you with great confidence," he informed the undersecretary at the Colonial Office, "that you will have little trouble with this Colony for some years on account of grievances if the factious party be discountenanced."[112]

Bearing in mind the usual caveats about the reliability of Colonial Office records, these documents suggest a relatively wide distribution of support for the government throughout the colony. While oppositionist strength was concentrated emphatically in the Home district, government supporters received approximately twenty per cent of their signatures over three districts: Midland, Newcastle, and Johnstown. This strongly suggests that the heart of government strength lay to the east of the provincial capital – though there was notable support from the Niagara and London districts as well. It is also noteworthy that government supporters carried the politics of York as far afield as the Bathurst district in the northeastern part of the colony, an area that had been beyond Mackenzie's reach in 1831. They had not only foresworn their customary reluctance to engage in popular politics but had also acted as the agents for taking the petitioning movement into areas apparently untouched by their opponents. They had successfully collected signatures in nine districts of the province, one more than their opponents.[113] If the public meeting in Sandwich (Western district) is taken into account, government supporters had made their presence felt in all regions of the colony except the remote and underpopulated Ottawa district.[114] Thus in 1832 government supporters proved themselves the most effective agents yet in taking issues of provincial significance to the furthest reaches of Upper Canada.

The validity of the process of collecting signatures on pro-government petitions was frequently challenged by oppositionists, who charged both that the documents had been signed by those ineligible to do so and that signatures had been obtained by trickery. Though women routinely signed petitions on other matters, both sides in the petitioning movement of 1831–32 evidently considered that it was not legitimate for women to sign petitions on political affairs. Mackenzie, for example, complained that in York "women were induced by false representations to affix their husbands' names in their absence."[115] In Otonabee, oppositionist John Cameron charged that his opponents "got signatures from the cradle upwards, it made no matter if they were of the male kind."[116] A report from Whitchurch indicated that the pro-government canvasser had "asked the wife ... whether the child at the breast about five months old was a boy or a girl, as if it was a boy he would take down its name." The canvasser was thwarted: "it was a girl."[117]

The charge that government supporters sought the signatures of women balanced similar charges made against oppositionists. Charles Fothergill insisted in Amherst that oppositionist forces circulated "a petition full of *generals* and *no particulars* ... for the signatures of women and children, (for surely no man of sense would sign such a farago)."[118] Also in the Newcastle district, Dr Connin, a magistrate and chair of the meeting, made a more specific accusation against participants at the oppositionist meeting in Otonabee on 6 March. Connin was evidently scandalized that among those who had voted in favour of the reform resolutions were three women![119] The comparative rarity of such accusations suggests, however, that the participation of women in the petitioning movement was very limited.

Oppositionist complaints about their opponents' methods of collecting signatures in the Home district were particularly bitter, with charges of unfair tactics, undue influence, and outright fraud. The *Colonial Advocate* alleged that Colonel Thomson of Toronto had taken "a few blank leaves of paper," telling the people that their signatures were "to be tacked to a petition for road tax money in order to build a certain bridge." In fact, however, the pages were attached to a pro-government petition.[120] Signatures gathered among the Roman Catholics of the Home district were highlighted as especially questionable. Handbills circulated "extensively" in York maintained that McDonell had taken the petition on a tour of the townships and obtained signatures by misrepresentation.[121] Such charges were substantiated in 1833 when a petition to the King signed by more than two hundred and forty Roman Catholics of Upper Canada pleaded that they were "unknowingly led to oppose the Petition of our fellow subjects, by the inexcusable misrepresentations of Bishop McDonell, who induced us to believe that we were only signing an Address to your Majesty for the good of our Church and Holy Religion."[122]

Although some signatures on petitions in support of the government may have been of questionable provenance, there is no reason to doubt that the great majority of them were legitimate. This certainly casts doubt on Mackenzie's contention that he spoke for the people of Upper Canada against a small and unrepresentative clique of office-holders. The reasons for that support doubtless varied. Some signatories no doubt were genuinely pleased with the status quo: they did not consider themselves oppressed by partisan magistrates and did they not see any need for changes in the privileged position of the Church of England. Others perhaps feared that Mackenzie represented a threat to the British connection. Still others may have signed for reasons of friendship or for personal advantage. Whatever the reason, the number of signatures indicates that the government did not exist in a state of political isolation.

Let us assume that the signatures on petitions – both for and against the government – represent at least an approximate reflection of the numbers of male Upper Canadians who had been exposed to publicity surrounding the expulsion crisis and its aftermath. If this is true, the most significant fact is that between them the two sides had collected almost fifty thousand signatures on their petitions. Obviously, an awareness of the crisis had spread well beyond the ranks of those who customarily voted in elections. Elwood Jones has indicated that approximately 17,600 Upper Canadians went to the polls in the election of 1834.[123] The total number of signatures on petitions two years earlier, however, was almost three times that number! The expulsion crisis, then, had been the means of mobilizing a larger public than the relatively narrow electorate. Moreover, the fact that only about four thousand signatures separated the two sides suggests a sharp political polarization of the population.

SIGNIFICANCE OF THE EXPULSION CRISIS

The expulsion crisis of 1831–32 was truly a turning point in Upper Canadian history. Like the banishment of Robert Gourlay in 1819, the expulsions of Mackenzie from the Assembly 1831 and 1832 provided opponents of the administration with a prominent victim of government oppression. Unlike Gourlay's opponents, however, Mackenzie's were unable to shut down the engines of protest though legislation banning public meetings of protest. Moreover, in the transatlantic context, the impending triumph of parliamentary reform in Britain suggested that Mackenzie's complaints would receive a far more sympathetic hearing than had Gourlay's. In response to this threat to their hegemony, government supporters for the first time launched their own popular campaign to demonstrate support for the status quo. The results transformed the political landscape of the province.

It is true that the expulsion crisis did not result in tangible legislation, like the Reform Bill in Britain, or even in electoral change like the triumph of Jacksonian democracy in the United States in 1828. Perhaps that is why previous historians have missed its significance. The change was nonetheless real. It took place, as John Adams commented of the spread of revolutionary sentiment in the Thirteen Colonies, "in the minds and hearts of the people."[124] The expulsion crisis, indeed, resulted in the crystallization of a common awareness of provincial politics in Upper Canada. It helped fix political loyalties that would endure through the end of the Upper Canadian period in 1841 and beyond.

The crisis unleashed a barrage of publicity the likes of which Upper Canadians had never seen. It dominated the newspapers. It appeared in handbills that circulated widely throughout the province. It was the subject of countless speeches, resolutions, and public meetings. Such publicity achieved spectacular success in awakening inhabitants everywhere to the issues it raised. At the Niagara meeting of 31 March, for example, Robert Dickson, a government supporter, testified to the name recognition Mackenzie had already achieved. "Small children throughout the country," he explained, "know the name of William Lyon Mackenzie as well as they did that of Papa or Mama."[125] A letter to the *Colonial Advocate* from Yarmouth in the London district confirmed the degree of political excitement in that region: "I am an old inhabitant, but never saw the Talbot Settlement in such a ferment as at present. The Lion is roused."[126] From the other end of the province, meanwhile, a correspondent of Mackenzie's who was collecting signatures on a petition in Grenville commented: "I have never known the yeomanry of these townships, in so high a state of political fermentation."[127]

The events of 1831–32 brought ordinary Upper Canadians to public meetings in unprecedented numbers, and prompted thousands of them to sign petitions for or against the administration of government. Indeed, the numbers who signed the petitions exceeded by some measure the entire voting population of the province. There could be no clearer evidence of the widespread penetration of these issues in the popular consciousness of Upper Canadians.

This outburst of public opinion, of course, was not entirely spontaneous. Members of the Assembly played a key role in mobilizing public support both for and against the administration. Moreover, the crisis prompted government supporters to found an extraparliamentary organization of their own, the British Constitutional Society. At the same time, the spread of oppositionist support manifested itself in a strong but more decentralized organization operating under the loose supervision of the York Committee. Both of these organizations, in one form or another, would enjoy a more than transitory existence.

The importance to Upper Canadian politics of the petitioning movements and Mackenzie's expulsions extended beyond the fact that the public became alerted to a particular set of issues on one occasion. In many districts, the politics of the expulsion crisis acted as a catalyst, fundamentally and permanently transforming political life. We have already seen that the grievance meetings of 1831 were instrumental in bringing, for the first time, the oppositionist message of the post-Gourlay years to some areas, including the Eastern and Gore districts. The great district meetings of 1832, along with their township counterparts, often performed the same function for pro-government forces, as it did in the Gore, Newcastle, and Johnstown districts. The similarity of the resolutions endorsed by government supporters throughout the province, moreover, points to the beginnings of a widespread integration of district and provincial politics.

It is also clear, however, that the spread of a common sense of political awareness did not mean that a single viewpoint on politics had triumphed throughout the province. Instead, two distinct ideologies and two interpretations of events found expression virtually everywhere. In ideological terms, the oppositionists relied on a discourse of rights, while government supporters articulated a discourse of paternalism. Whereas oppositionists interpreted the expulsions as a manifestation of oppressive political behaviour, government supporters viewed it as a measure necessary to suppress unacceptable dissent. Behind the expulsion crisis lay two distinct views of Upper Canadian politics. While the oppositionists challenged the power of appointed elements of the Upper Canadian government, the system of representation, and the special privileges of the Anglican Church, government supporters emphatically defended the status quo. Though voices of political moderation would soon appear on the scene,[128] in 1832 the polarization of Upper Canadian politics was almost complete. Moreover, the two perspectives that emerged in 1832 would dominate Upper Canadian politics for years to come.

As these divergent viewpoints were taking shape, they were reflected by changes in political terminology, particularly in the case of the oppositionists. As we have seen in chapter 3, as late as January 1832, Mackenzie's "Appeal to the People of Upper Canada" basically described political conflict in the province in terms of a struggle between "the people" on the one hand and "the government and its officers" on the other. Within a matter of months, this began to change. In accounts of the York riot of 23 March 1832, for example, the *Colonial Advocate* consistently referred to the oppositionists as "reformers."[129] This term suggested, of course, a similarity between the goals of parliamentary reformers in Great Britain, who referred to themselves as "Reformers," and the oppositionists in Upper Canada.[130] At a time when oppositionists were under attack as pro-American revolutionaries, this identification with British reformers served to underline the message that despite their quarrels with the administration of the province, they were indeed truly loyal. Moreover, use of the term "reformer" allowed the oppositionists to portray their opponents in a negative light, as "anti-reformers."[131] By the fall of 1832, however, the term "anti-reformers" was being dropped in favour of the epithet "tory."[132] Thus the oppositionists tarred their opponents with the same brush as hidebound reactionaries in Britain who had resisted in vain the achievement of parliamentary reform.

Government supporters, not surprisingly, did not adopt the same terminology. The *Niagara Gleaner* provides a good example. In the spring of 1832, its editor referred to the oppositionists as "Mackenzieites alias, the Ryersonites," "the Republican Faction," "the radical faction," the "grievance mongers," and "the *grievancers.*"[133] The *Cobourg Star* called the oppositionists "radicals," "revolutionists," "the malcontent faction," a "miserable crew of malcontents," and "brawling grievance-mongers," while the Brockville *Gazette* condemned them as "Provincial Republicans," and the "Yankee Party."[134]

As government supporters struggled towards consistent terminology for their opponents, by the end of 1832 oppositionist newspapers like the *Colonial Advocate* were commonly referring to a struggle between "reformers" on the one hand and "tories" on the other. The use of these terms, moreover, suggests a development that extended beyond the identification of provincial struggles and those taking place in Great Britain. The new terminology, in fact, strongly reflected a sense of province-wide political awareness. It furthered the impression that reformers across the province were engaged in a common struggle against opponents who also shared a distinctive world-view. Developments of the next decade confirmed this insight, entrenching the polarization that had first emerged clearly during the expulsion crisis and its aftermath.

This is not to say that these changes meant the establishment of political parties in Upper Canada, much less a party system. Whereas political parties are oriented towards capturing executive power, the two sides in 1832 were primarily concerned with bringing public pressure to bear on the British government. Party systems, moreover, are characterized by a basic acceptance of the legitimacy of the other side. Such acceptance was clearly lacking in 1832, as the rhetoric on both sides and the violence of government supporters clearly demonstrates.

The pro-government organizational triumph of 1832 was a remarkable one, but it was achieved, it must be remembered, partly through the use of intimidation and violence. The less savoury of these methods cast new light on George Ryerson's remark that oppositionist organizers needed to demonstrate the qualities of "hardihood" and "perseverance." This was particularly true in the case of Mackenzie, the primary target of hostility. In the first four months of 1832 alone, Mackenzie was publicly shamed by expulsion from the Assembly; he was mocked in effigy in the streets of York; he was burned in effigy elsewhere in the province; he was assaulted in York and nearly beaten to death in Hamilton. Yet historians have been slow to recognize the extent of Mackenzie's personal courage in the face of such hostility. Mackenzie, however, was only the most obvious victim of the wrath of government supporters; others who promoted the cause of reform were offered all too many opportunities to exhibit similar qualities. Through the remainder of the 1830s, events would continue to demonstrate that political organization in the cause of reform was truly not a task for the faint of heart.

5 Political Unions and Electoral Organization, 1832–36

In the aftermath of the tory[1] onslaught of 1832, the reformers faced a series of challenges that fully taxed their capacity for "self-denial and unwearied perseverance."[2] Circumstances forced opponents of the government to demonstrate a new flexibility, though always in the framework established by the petitioning movements, and always with an eye to influencing the British government. Their first new efforts, after a period of quiescence in mid-1832, were directed at institutionalizing the oppositionist petitioning movement by founding political unions based on the British model. These efforts, however, were squelched by the strong-arm tactics that had been so effective in early 1832. Violence also made it impossible for reformers to hold public meetings in Upper Canada, and they were forced to resort to circulating their petitions privately. Frustrated in their attempts to revive the petitioning movement and to organize political unions, the reformers resourcefully tried yet another means of attracting attention to their cause: electoral organization. In spite of a series of blows that hammered the movement in 1833–34, their efforts paid off handsomely with the return of a reform majority to the Assembly in the fall of 1834. Notwithstanding this triumph, however, the achievement of the changes they sought appeared once again to be as far distant as ever.

Mackenzie's opponents did not underrate the tenacity of reformers. They were not lulled into a false sense of security because of Mackenzie's absence (he was then in Great Britain), or by the quiescence of his supporters in Upper Canada. Instead, they filled the hiatus with ongoing abuse of the reformers and all their works. The *Cobourg Star* provides a good example. During August and September 1832, this journal carried a series of articles written by the district sheriff, Henry Ruttan, and addressed to the people of Newcastle. Ruttan took this opportunity to launch an attack on the oppositionist petitioning movement, arguing that the circulation of grievance petitions was the thin edge of the wedge of revolution. Nor did Ruttan believe that reformers' campaign for change had truly ceased, though they were presently inactive. Opponents of the government, he maintained, would lead the people on, "bit by bit" and "step by step, until they have become entangled in the cause of rebellion."[3] Tories like Ruttan were ever vigilant for the signs of a reform revival.

As it turned out, they didn't have long to wait. Reform inactivity ended late in 1832 with the initiation of a political union movement. Like the petitioning of 1831, this movement began in York, though its real inspiration was British. During the struggle for parliamentary reform in Britain, political unions were the means of channelling and expressing public opinion. They were not political parties geared to electoral victory but organizations intended instead to harness the power of public opinion in favour of political change. In modern parlance, they were intended to act primarily as pressure groups – ones with a bulging agenda – bringing their influence to bear on the Assembly and the British government.

Government supporters might try to stigmatize political unions as revolutionary associations, but reform journals were quick to defend the legitimacy of such organizations. The *St Thomas Liberal*, for example, proclaimed that the constitutionality of political unions was "admitted by all parties in the Mother country ... clearly recognized there, and countenanced by the British monarch and his enlightened statesmen."[4] "Had it not been for these Unions," it maintained, "the broad banner of Reform would not now wave triumphant in Britain."[5] The *Brockville Recorder* echoed this view, observing that political unions "in Britain have had a most powerful effect in giving success to the cause of the people and securing to them a constitutional representation in their own House."[6] The movement in Britain had not only been constitutional but successful to boot!

As early as January 1832, Mackenzie's supporters had called for the establishment of such institutions in Upper Canada.[7] Mackenzie himself, however, had put a damper on this activity until, as he informed Lord Goderich, "it had been ... ascertained whether His Majesty's Ministers would or would not favourably listen to our prayers against colonial oppression."[8] By the end of that year, though, even Mackenzie was urging the launch of another petitioning movement.[9] The pressure in favour of unions became too great to resist and, in late November

1832, the "Upper Canada Central Political Union" was finally established in York.[10] At a further meeting at the end of January 1833, the objects of the Union were refined and its officers selected.[11]

This organization was important not simply because it was the first reform effort to launch a political union but also because its founding showed that the reformers were not entirely dependent on Mackenzie to initiate political organization. (Mackenzie would not return from Britain until August 1833.) The composition of its executive also reveals the success of York reformers in reaching out for support throughout the Home district. Its executive brought together not only professionals from York like Dr John Tims and lawyer John Elliot but also business figures with interests north of the city, including John Montgomery and Jesse Lloyd.[12] This was no narrow group based exclusively in York; its reach extended well into the town's northern hinterland, the home of a number of distinctive religious communities. Members of such groups, including the Children of Peace based in Sharon, had already shown themselves receptive to the reform program because of their vehement opposition to the clergy reserves.[13]

A more radical political agenda accompanied the geographic expansion of the Central Canadian Political Union. Its statement of objectives, issued after a meeting on 26 November 1832, reveals the emergence in Upper Canada of a strand of radicalism quite different from the dominant British constitutionalism of most reform publications of the mid-1830s. To be sure, it began with loyal references to the British constitution, and included many of the grievances highlighted in Mackenzie's petition of 1831. But the document differed from previous reform publications in its appeal for public support in language reminiscent of the French and American revolutions. Specifically, it declared that the objects of the Union were to further the rights of man – the right to "liberty, equality, security of person and property and the full enjoyment of the produce of his labour." In keeping with this, the statement of objectives endorsed a theory of government quite at variance with the monarchical system of Upper Canada. "All law," it said, "should be based upon the free and decided expression of the PUBLIC WILL." This democratic thrust was confirmed by a further provision, later rescinded, that called for manhood suffrage. Finally, the document specified that "when any government violates the just rights of the people, constitutional resistance becomes the imperative and indispensable duty" of the population.[14] This radical credo strikes a discordant note in a political dialogue hitherto dominated by variations of British constitutionalism and offers a preview of the reform movement's increasing radicalism of the following years.

The reformers of Middlesex, who began their own political union movement early in 1833, were more moderate than their counterparts in the provincial capital. The Middlesex Political Union's statement of objectives of January 1833 was more firmly anchored in the mainstream of reform constitutionalism than was the corresponding declaration of York unionists. In keeping with the tenor of most previous reform literature, it declared that the primary object of the organization was to preserve the connection with Great Britain,[15] though it contended that there were abuses in the system of government that required correction. Among the desirable changes were the exclusion of officeholders from the Assembly; the election of "men of talent, integrity, and liberal political feelings" to the Assembly; vote by ballot; economy in government; a parliamentary investigation into the administration of government; abolition of the laws of entail and primogeniture; changes to the jury law; and the appropriation of the clergy reserves to educational purposes. The major focus of the Union's activities was to act as a channel for the expression of public opinion on an ongoing basis, through the preparation of petitions, addresses, and remonstrances.

Organizers were careful to stress the Union's peaceful character. Indeed, nothing received greater emphasis in its declaration of objects. An important goal of the organization, the declaration stated, was "to promote peace, union and concord among all classes of His Majesty's subjects." Accordingly, their efforts on economic questions were to be achieved through "legal and Constitutional means." Similarly, their attempts to bring about change relating to the clergy reserves and the legal system were to be pursued only by "proper means." More generally, they were "to collect and organize the peaceful expression of the Public Opinion so as to bring it to act upon the Legislative functions, in a just, legal and effectual way."[16] Violent behaviour of any kind, the declaration made clear, was totally inconsistent with the objects of the Union. Members were "to be good, faithful and loyal subjects of the King"; "to obey the laws of the land"; to conduct themselves peaceably at meetings of the Union; "and to depart to their respective homes as soon as the chairman shall leave the chair." They were also "to bear in mind that the strength of our Society consists in the Peace, *order, Unity* and Legality, of our proceedings"; anyone who promoted violence was to be considered as an enemy.

In spite of the Union's obviously peaceful and constitutional orientation, its opponents quickly announced their intention to disrupt one of its early meetings. A handbill circulated before a meeting of the Union scheduled for 17 January ominously urged "THE Ripstavers, Gallbursters, &c, with their friends" to attend the meeting. "The Doctors are requested to be in readiness," it continued, "to heal the sick and cure the broken headed."[17] It is not recorded whether the doctors were present, but the other parties mentioned in the handbill were certainly there in force.

The meeting itself took place without incident; it was afterwards that the trouble began. The tories, according to the *St Thomas Liberal*, assembled in front of a tavern where they were addressed by Reverend Donald Frazer, a Wesleyan Methodist minister who was also the editor of the local tory newspaper, the *Journal*.[18] Then, inflamed by drink as well as Frazer's address, a gang of fifty men composed primarily of "Irish Orangemen from Port Talbot," armed themselves with clubs and went in search of political opponents. "Whenever they discovered a person that did not belong to their party," the *Liberal* account continued, "the whole crew of desperadoes would immediately start in pursuit – if they overtook their victim, he was left for dead ... The row was kept up until late at night." What particularly disturbed reformers was the connivance of the authorities in these proceedings: the gang was accompanied by a magistrate. Moreover, though forewarned by the circulation of inflammatory handbills, the magistracy had failed to take any steps to control the violence.[19]

Colonel Thomas Talbot took a very different view of the incident. On 26 January he zestfully reported that "my rebels ... were frustrated by my royal guards, who routed the rascals at all points and drove them out of the village like sheep, members with broken heads leaving their hats behind them – the glorious work of old Colonel Hickory [wooden clubs]. In short, it was a most splendid victory." Talbot's satisfaction with the conduct of his "royal guards" owed much to his expectation that the political union movement in the area had been effectively suppressed. "I scarcely think," he gloated, "[that] they will venture to call another meeting, at least, not at St Thomas."[20]

In spite of Talbot's hopes, another meeting did take place in the area, in South Yarmouth on 5 February 1833. This time, supporters of the political union were better prepared for their opponents. Anticipating another attack, about two hundred unionists armed themselves with white oak sticks and awaited the onslaught. Nearly an hour passed without incident before the unionists realized that their opponents, expecting an ambush, had taken refuge behind a hill half a mile away; there they remained until the reformers left the scene.

The *St Thomas Liberal* indulged in some spirited editorializing as a result of this incident. "What surprised us the most," said the journal, "was to see the LAWYER of the village, and several Merchants, and others who appear to the character of *gentlemen*, accompany the mob." This new example of lawless law prompted a demoralizing conclusion:

"Justice and *British Law* have FLED – not a vestige of these strong bulwarks of society remain. The property, nay even the LIVES of peaceable men are no longer safe." The *Liberal* did not miss this opportunity to turn the tables on the tories by casting doubt on their self-proclaimed loyalty: "Can that party be loyal who pay no respect whatever to British Laws? ... Who would rule the land by mobs instead of law?"[21] Not surprisingly, the political union movement was stopped in its tracks.

Mob rule in Middlesex and elsewhere owed much to the activities of members of the Orange Order. The presence of Orangemen at the rout of 17 January offered but a hint of the future importance of this organization in suppressing reformers' popular politics. The Amherst meeting of early 1832 had shown how effectively Orange forces could put down the public meetings of their opponents. By June 1832, the Grand Orange Lodge was broadly hinting that this should be no isolated occurrence. In the proceedings of a meeting held in Brockville on 5 June 1832, the Lodge urged that "every good orangeman, sworn 'to defend his King and country ... ' ought to be on his special guard against the traitorous and wily machinations and schemes of a pack of united Democrats." At the same time, the Orangemen approved an address to the people of Upper Canada, urging that they rally round the constitution, and pledge "to support our good King against all his enemies, whether they be rebels to their God or to their country."[22] By the fall, a meeting of the Grand Orange Lodge in Port Hope was recommending the formation in each county of a club that could include Roman Catholics as well as Protestants, "to unite the loyal and concentrate their energies and resources, to maintain the integrity, and uphold the Constitution of the Empire."[23]

Ogle Gowan's newspaper, the *Antidote*, used condemnation of the popular politics of reformers as a springboard to argue for these new clubs. In Gowan's view, a few "insignificant and inconsiderable" individuals including Bidwell, Ryerson, and Mackenzie, had acquired "BY THE FORCE OF CONCENTRATION AND UNION ALONE a power and influence truly alarming," to the peril of the political and religious institutions of the province. The efforts of Orangemen and other so-called "patriots," had, however, effectively neutralized the influence of reformers. The *Antidote* accordingly supported the call of the Port Hope meeting for clubs in each county "to frustrate the machinations of our cunning and artful adversaries," and to strengthen the hand of the majority in the Assembly against any popular outcry in favour of reform.[24] The means of achieving this goal, however, was not to be through the foundation of separate organizations in the counties. Instead, the militants worked through the Orange Order itself (and to a lesser extent through the British Constitutional Society in York). Members of the

Order and their relatives were closely involved in efforts to suppress public meetings called under reform auspices in the eastern part of the province in early 1833.

The inspiration for these meetings was a long-awaited sign of support for reform grievances in Britain. In January 1833, Lord Goderich's dispatch of 8 November 1832 arrived in Upper Canada. Though this document was not uniformly flattering to Mackenzie,[25] the colonial secretary exhibited considerable sympathy for some reform grievances, in particular those relating to electoral representation, the composition of the Legislative Council, the independence of judges, and education. Mackenzie's supporters, anxious for evidence of success, therefore hailed the dispatch as a great victory. As the *Colonial Advocate* said, it "concedes the main principles contended for by the Canadian Reformers."[26] Mackenzie's opponents were predictably enraged, with both the Assembly and the Legislative Council censuring Lord Goderich's communication.[27]

In the aftermath of this heartening communication from Britain, the Newcastle district was one locus of reform activity. Reformers had held public meetings in Port Hope on 9 February, and in Cobourg on the 20th, without incident.[28] It was otherwise when they tried to hold a similar gathering near Cobourg at the end of February to thank the King for Lord Goderich's dispatch.[29] The day of the meeting, J.G. Bethune,[30] a prominent Cobourg merchant and Colonel John Covert's son-in-law, sent wagons to bring supporters of the tory cause from surrounding townships. About an hour before the meeting, these worthies processed into Amherst in twenty or thirty sleighs and wagons, accompanied by tin horns, drums, and flags. When they arrived at the meeting place, a schoolhouse in nearby Cobourg, however, they discovered that the reformers had prudently adjourned the meeting. Nonchalantly knocking down the schoolhouse door, the tories held a meeting of their own instead.

Prominent among the speakers there was leading Orangeman John Brown, that notorious scourge of reformers. Brown announced to the crowd that he held in his hand a resolution "that will – G-d d-m them all, d-m Mackenzie, d-m the Methodists, and d-m the whole saddle-bag party."[31] Thus incited, the gathering went on to condemn the holding of "clandestine political meetings." One resolution declared that "any man, or number of men less than Twelve substantial freeholders, who shall at any future time presume to call a public meeting, for the purpose of agitating any political question, within this district, shall be considered enemies to the peace thereof, and shall be treated as such." According to the threats uttered soon after by the "mob," this meant bloodshed.[32]

Tory violence indeed extended beyond the verbal. Later that night, there were two assaults on J.T. Williams, a magistrate and well-known reformer. The first was perpetrated by Samuel Wainright, identified by a correspondent of the *Reformer* as "*a bully and nephew of John Brown.*"[33] Before the night was out, Williams was attacked a second time. This offence was all the more egregious because it was committed at William's own home, this time by "a number of ruffians in Brown's employment." Only the timely intervention of public-spirited neighbours saved Williams from what promised to be a severe bludgeon attack.

Mackenzie's supporters did not allow these incidents to pass without complaint. Erasmus Fowke, a veteran of petitioning in the Port Hope area, explained the situation in some detail to Lord Goderich in a letter accompanying a copy of the Port Hope address.[34] While the Port Hope meeting had been peaceful, he explained, this had not been the case elsewhere. "The Abettors of corruption," he explained, "had been roused – *Club Law* established, daring characters were assembled; and Magistrates, Legislative Councillors, and Members of the House of Assembly, were seen leading them into action." Incited by an inflammatory press, and by the circulation of placards calculated to provoke violence, these desperadoes had "abused, beat, and most shamefully maltreated" loyal British subjects. This behaviour had achieved the desired result: the suppression of public opinion in favour of Lord Goderich's dispatch. "Thousands of His Majesty's dutiful and loyal subjects," Fowke asserted, "[have been] deterred, by the constituted authorities, from attaching their signatures to [similar] addresses."

Orange violence was even more clearly in evidence when the reformers of Leeds convened a public meeting in Farmersville on 9 March 1833. According to the *Antidote*, about two thousand people attended.[35] They must have been a brave group, given the inflammatory character of the handbills that had been "industriously circulated" beforehand. Under the title "NOW OR NEVER!" "friends of the King, the Laws and the Constitution" were urged to join a "*Grand Procession*" in which "the friends of the Constitution [will] march to Farmersville, with *Music* and good *Shillalaghs.*"[36]

Ogle Gowan was one of the first speakers at the Farmersville meeting. The tone of the Grand Master's speech, and no doubt the presence of a number of his less respectable followers, prompted the reform contingent to adjourn to a nearby store.[37] A formidable gang of two or three hundred followed them, demanding that the meeting disperse. When this request was ignored, the tories dragged the chairman, a painter by the name of David Fairbarn, from his chair and, with grim humour, "*varnished* [him] with *paint* 'red as blood.'" Several others were also badly beaten on this occasion.

This time Orange violence did not go unpunished: six of the Farmersville rioters were subsequently tried in the courts, and all received jail terms and fines.[38] The tone of the Orange press, however, must have given reformers cold comfort. The *Antidote*, Gowan's newspaper, concluded its account of the Farmersville events with the defiant conclusion that "it was only such conduct as unprincipled demagogues had reason to expect."[39] Any satisfaction that reformers might have taken from the punishment of the malefactors was punctured when the two ringleaders were released from jail on the orders of the lieutenant-governor after serving only ten weeks of a four-month sentence, with the added bonus of having their fines remitted.[40]

The MPPs from Leeds, William Buell and Matthew Howard, persisted in spite of this violence in their own backyard, calling a meeting in Brockville a week after the Farmersville incident.[41] When the meeting was cancelled at the request of a number of magistrates and the Board of Police of Brockville, Ogle Gowan seized this opportunity to stage, with 350–400 of his followers, a demonstration in the town of Brockville. The Orangemen marched through the town, then assembled at the Court House. After passing a number of resolutions, they were addressed by Judge David Jones, Charles Jones, Henry Sherwood, and Gowan himself. Gowan and Judge Jones were then elevated on the shoulders of the crowd, and "carried through the principal streets of the town." This brazen display of force, and the complicity of legal authorities in Gowan's activities, outraged reformers. As one of them exclaimed, "What will be thought of such proceeding[s] throughout the country? A judge and expounder of the laws riding on the shoulders of an armed multitude, in company with the prime disturber of the quiet of the District!"[42]

While the political meetings of reformers were the most celebrated target of their opponents, the reform press also suffered. The best-known precedent for such activity, of course, was the destruction of William Lyon Mackenzie's press in the Types Riot of 1826. The militants who took over the Cobourg meeting acted in this tradition when they threatened "to demolish the Editor, Press and Types of the *Reformer*."[43] In 1833, the press of the *St Thomas Liberal* was wrecked by tory activists.[44] The following year, the editor and proprietor of the *Kingston Whig* was assaulted by Henry Smith Jr, an aspiring lawyer who would go on to represent the county of Frontenac as a conservative from 1841 to 1861.[45] The tory onslaught against the reformers, then, was frequently directed against their presses as well as against their public meetings.

This series of attacks on reform meetings, political unions, and newspapers achieved their obvious purpose – the suppression of demonstrations on behalf of reform. Such incidents gradually petered out in the late spring of 1833. Nothing much came from the founding of a political union in the township of Bertie in the county of Lincoln in early 1833. A public meeting in Mosa township, Middlesex county, to thank the King for Lord Goderich's dispatch, evidently also failed to prompt imitators. A reform meeting in Bath (Lennox and Addington) in March was suppressed, though apparently without bloodshed.[46] It was too risky for opponents of the government to seek public support for their cause.

If violence made it almost impossible for reformers to meet in public, it did not prevent the private circulation of petitions. Charles Thompson, president of the Central Canadian Political Union, informed Lord Goderich of his organization's progress in May 1833.[47] More than twenty thousand signatures,[48] he told the colonial secretary, had been collected on a petition containing "the almost unanimous thanks of the inhabitants for the paternal attention of His Majesty to the recent petitions [of 1831–32]." The petition thanked the King for "inquir[ing] into our grievances and giv[ing] us assurance of redress." It also censured the conduct of the majority in the Assembly for their reception of Lord Goderich's dispatch, and for their repeated expulsions of Mackenzie. It similarly deplored the Legislative Council's reaction to the dispatch. At the same time, the petitioners urged the King "not to relax the impartial measures which we understand your Majesty has been graciously pleased to take for our final and complete deliverance from a system of injustice and misrule."

The Central Political Union's activities in early 1833 were not confined to the circulation of this petition. As this document was making its rounds of the province, members of the Union were assisting the Methodists in obtaining signatures on another widely disseminated petition against the clergy reserves.[49] Egerton Ryerson was entrusted with the task of taking this document, which, like that of the Central Canadian Political Union, received the remarkable total of twenty thousand signatures, to England for presentation before the British House of Commons.[50] Thus, though reformers were unable to meet in public, they nevertheless pursued a vigorous program of petitioning through the first half of 1833. This ongoing activity allowed them to maintain the momentum that they had previously achieved, and to keep their political grievances firmly to the forefront in the public mind.

Other supporters of political change occasionally found ways to express their views without public meetings, as the reformers of Kingston did in May. The tories of Kingston had just held a large public meeting in support of Christopher Hagerman, the former solicitor general.

Hagerman, along with Attorney General H.J. Boulton, had just been dismissed from office for his role in expelling Mackenzie from the Assembly. The reformers of the town were not anxious to court violence, "having before their eyes," as they said, "the late breaches of the public peace at Brockville." Rather than risk a public meeting, therefore, they drew up an address in support of "the liberal tone of policy avowed in the late despatches," and circulated it privately. Even this unconfrontational mode of proceeding, however, was not allowed to pass without a demonstration of public disrespect. A copy of the address was "posted upon the butcher's shambles, with some vile personal allusions to a highly respectable individual."[51]

Reformers also developed other private forms of organization. In June 1833, they formed vigilance committees in the Home and Niagara districts "to watch over the interests of the province in general and their own neighbourhoods respectively in particular."[52] These look very much like a revival of the political union movement. Hopes of change ran so high in these months, however, that reform newspapers carried a letter from Mackenzie in England advising his followers to cease petitioning and to wind up the activities of the political unions.[53]

BLOWS TO THE REFORM CAUSE

Such optimism was short-lived. In late 1833 and early 1834, the reformers suffered a series of three setbacks that would surely have killed any less resilient cause: the loss of support from the Colonial Office, the defection of Egerton Ryerson, and the publication of Joseph Hume's "baneful domination" letter. Apparently undaunted, however, the reformers shifted their efforts to electoral organization. This change in focus was not a repudiation of the political union movement, however, nor a renunciation of the struggle to secure attention from the Colonial Office. Reformers were, for the moment, simply pursuing the same objective – mobilizing public support for political change – by other means.

The new drift of British policy became evident not long after Edward Stanley, Lord Derby, replaced Lord Goderich at the Colonial Office in March 1833.[54] Before the year was out, the Colonial Office reinstated Mackenzie's most formidable legislative enemies. H.J. Boulton was kicked upstairs as chief justice of Newfoundland. Even worse, perhaps, was the reinstatement of Hagerman as solicitor general by the new colonial secretary. Symbolically, at least, Upper Canadian reformers had been firmly rebuffed.

Most important, there had been no real change of British government policy on any of the issues raised in Mackenzie's petition of

1831. As Mackenzie's old ally, British radical Joseph Hume, indicated in August 1833, the sitting British parliament was not one from which reform could be expected.[55] In spite of their good intentions in relation to Upper Canada, the Whig government in Britain was essentially ill-informed on Upper Canadian subjects and preoccupied with other matters.[56] Accordingly, the clergy reserves remained intact, education issues stagnated, and abuses in government continued unchecked.

Evidence of disenchantment among reformers was not far to seek. In October 1833 the *British Colonial Argus* of St Catharines argued "that the people of this Province have nothing to expect from the present Ministry ... but insult and injury – insult, in promoting the repudiated crown lawyers – and injury, by imposing upon the people of Canada a dominant church."[57] Mackenzie, meanwhile, signified his frustration with British policy by renaming his newspaper the "*Advocate*," removing the term "*Colonial*" from its title.[58] Evidently, his sentiments were widely shared. By mid-January 1834, a number electors of the Home district agreed "to cancel the address of thanks to his Majesty of 15th May last, signed by many thousands of the freeholders." The explanation for this unprecedented action was that the "the subsequent conduct of the colonial office [has] greatly weakened our confidence in the disposition of his Majesty's present advisers to redress our grievances."[59]

Another demoralizing development for the forces of reform fell late in 1833 and struck at the heart of their most important political alliance – their co-operation with the Methodists. To the amazement and horror of reformers, Egerton Ryerson experienced a change of political allegiance during his 1833 sojourn in Britain. Returning to Upper Canada in the fall of 1833, he published his "Impressions" in the *Christian Guardian*. In these articles, Ryerson recorded his critical views of British radicals, particularly Joseph Hume, who had so long supported the cause of reform in Upper Canada. At the same time, he lauded the moderate tories of Great Britain.[60] The result was an uproar. Mackenzie, who, for many years, had assisted the Methodists in their popular campaigns for religious reform, was predictably outraged, expressing his sense of betrayal in his usual inflammatory manner. Many ordinary Methodists appear to have shared Mackenzie's anger, and to a degree that was quite remarkable. As Ryerson's brother Edwy reported in November 1833, "The Guardian has turned 'tory' is the hue & cry, and many appear to be under greater concern about it, than they ever did about the salvation of their souls."[61] Ryerson clearly had not swayed all of his co-religionists when he changed his politics, but his defection nevertheless meant serious damage to the cause of reform.

The third major setback for reformers during this period, unlike the others, was largely self-inflicted. It was an indirect result of yet another expulsion of Mackenzie from the Assembly, this one in December 1833. When Mackenzie was re-elected later that month, the Assembly majority prevented him from taking his seat. This sequence of events prompted Joseph Hume to write Mackenzie a letter of sympathy. These further trials, Hume wrote, "must hasten that crisis which is approaching in the affairs of the Canadas, and which will terminate in independence and freedom from the baneful domination of the Mother Country and the tyrannical conduct of a small and despicable faction in the colonies."[62] Mackenzie unwisely rushed this "baneful domination" letter into print, thereby leaving reformers open to charges of actively seeking separation from Great Britain. They spent the summer backtracking, arguing that while they endorsed Hume's condemnation of colonial misrule, they utterly rejected republicanism and rebellion.[63]

These events eventually prompted considerable public response from Mackenzie's opponents. The tories, however, having vanquished their foes on the battlefield, largely stayed out of popular politics until early 1834. The public meetings in Kingston and Niagara in the summer of 1833 to support local Assembly representatives – Christopher Hagerman and H.J. Boulton respectively[64] – were highly localized and were not part of any general tory agitation. Early in 1834, Mackenzie's publication of the "baneful domination" letter prompted further anti-reform activity. The tories responded by roundly denouncing Hume and Mackenzie in the Assembly, the press, and in addresses from Toronto, Gore, and Leeds.[65] Even this provocation, however, did not prompt an effort on the scale of the petitioning movement of 1832. The *Cobourg Star* explained the reason: Mackenzie and Hume weren't important enough to justify the bother of calling a meeting.[66] More likely, quiescence reflected the ongoing tory distrust of popular agitation. Whatever the reason, the *Star*'s belief in the unwisdom of public meetings was apparently widely shared.

ELECTORAL ACTIVITY, 1834

Popular politics may have seemed less turbulent than usual during the spring and summer of 1834, but there was a great deal of activity beneath the surface, as both sides organized their forces for the forthcoming general election. Prompted no doubt by the reform vigilance meetings and by the publication of Hume's celebrated letter, the tories reactivated and reorganized the British Constitutional Society in Toronto in early July 1834.[67] Among the moving spirits in this enterprise were W.H. Draper, an influential lawyer and protégé of such tory stalwarts as John Covert and John Beverley Robinson,[68] and George Gurnett, an associate of Ogle Gowan.[69] The stated object of the Society was "to sustain and cement, by all the means in its power, a perpetual connexion between Upper Canada and the United Kingdom." The Society, then, was not narrowly conceived as an electoral organization, though certainly electoral victory was among its objectives. Membership was to be open to every adult male of the city "who will pledge himself to support this connexion, and who will also pledge himself to oppose by all lawful means, every attempt to weaken that connexion." Members of the Society were also to oppose the separation of the province from Great Britain (a reference to the "baneful domination" letter). Those who shared these views were urged to establish similar societies in every township, county, and district elsewhere in the province and to enter into correspondence and co-operation with the Toronto organization. Two weeks later, the secretary, George Gurnett, had already collected names of suitable members from township committees and was set to initiate contact with them. In spite of this bustling beginning, however, there is little indication that the Society was very active outside of the Home district prior to the election of 1834. Nevertheless, it is significant that Toronto tories had shifted the orientation of the British Constitutional Society towards electoral organization.

The reformers, meanwhile, had also turned their energies to electoral agitation. This is not to suggest that they had given up on political unions. In late 1833, notwithstanding previous reservations, Mackenzie had taken to promoting such institutions on the basis of their achievements in Britain. "Political Unions of bad men for war, bloodshed, and plunder," he argued, "brought England to the verge of Ruin. Political Unions of honest farmers and tradesmen achieved the reform bill and averted civil war and a violent revolution."[70] Electoral agitation was simply one of many ways to manifest public opinion. Not all of Mackenzie's supporters believed that electoral organization would be very productive. The *British Colonial Argus*, for example, maintained that a reform majority in the Assembly "would be as powerless as their constituents ... The people," it continued, "*may* elect a house of assembly, but what is the use of it?" Given the powerlessness of the Assembly under the provincial constitution, the ongoing importance of political unions was more than apparent to the editor of that journal, and doubtless to many other reform sympathizers as well.[71] Electoral organization was a supplement, and not necessarily a very promising one, to other forms of extraparliamentary agitation.

Despite the drawbacks of electoral organization, Mackenzie was quick to promote it. As early as July 1833, he was urging reformers to be vigilant in anticipation of a forthcoming general election. "We advise every Reformer," he said, "to be wide awake and standing at his post; for depend upon it the tories will leave no stone unturned in their attempts to secure an election of the tools of the York official faction."[72] Accordingly, in the spring and summer of 1834, reformers embarked on a series of electorally oriented township meetings all over the province.[73]

The reformers' electoral activities of 1834 demonstrated several clear links to their petitioning campaign of 1832, and particularly to the issues raised by Mackenzie's expulsions from the Assembly. In fact, it was Mackenzie's re-expulsion from the Assembly in December 1833 that prompted the revival of the Central Committee that had secured his re-election after his first expulsion in December 1831. This committee in turn evolved into a form of central political organization for the reformers in the 1834 election.

Connections between electoral organization and the petitioning movement did not end there. The Central Committee began its campaign with a reference to Colborne's interference with constitutional rights, "particularly with regard to freedom of the press, and of private opinion and the right of the people to a free representation."[74] In a number of reform nomination meetings outside Toronto, other issues raised by Mackenzie's expulsions were prominent on the agenda. At one township nomination meeting in Leeds, for example, the "tyrannical, arbitrary, and illegal expulsions of Mr Mackenzie" was condemned. In addition, the participants went on to offer thanks to Mackenzie "for his strenuous exertions in promoting equal rights and privileges, his unwearied diligence in exposing the abuses of our Provincial Government, and his unremitting attention to the general interests of the province."[75]

If the issues of previous petitioning movements remained fresh in reformers' minds through 1834, it is also clear that they did not expect petitioning to be eclipsed by electoral activity. Thus at the December 1833 meeting in York, a petition to the British House of Commons asking for an inquiry into Colborne's actions was called for, as was an address to the King asking for further consideration of the petitions of 1831 and 1832.[76] Similarly, at the Halton county meeting of February 1834, it was proposed that a petition in favour of responsible government be sent to Britain.[77] Reformers, then, saw petitioning and electoral organization as complementary, rather than as competing activities.

The revived Central Committee, under the leadership of John McIntosh and Dr T.D. Morrison, reappeared as the "Central County Committee" on the occasion of Mackenzie's electoral comeback in

December 1833. Participants at a meeting held on 16 December 1833 urged members of the Committee "to continue their useful services on behalf of the people of Upper Canada." But larger plans were afoot. Members of the Committee were also urged "to call ... the attention of the other townships throughout this province" to the deplorable conduct of government officials in promoting Mackenzie's many expulsions and "to recommend the people to send delegates to the provincial and county conventions, with reference to the ensuing general election."[78] Accordingly, participants drew up a circular that was to be sent "to every township in the Province together with the county resolutions and address, for their concurrence."[79] By March, York reformers had taken the further step of establishing a constitutional tract society, with Mackenzie acting as secretary,[80] and Reform organizations elsewhere sometimes founded local tract societies as auxiliaries to this body.[81]

The tories believed that there were other dimensions to Mackenzie's organizational influence. A correspondent of the *Canadian Emigrant* reported from Kent, in the western part of the province, that one of the organizers of township meetings in that county had attended political meetings in Toronto and obtained resolutions from Mackenzie; he also surmised that Mackenzie had provided written instructions on how to hold the meetings. Another contributor reported that an envoy from Kent had attended the York convention, where he obtained the authority to call township meetings in his home county.[82] Mackenzie's own newspapers also indicated that he sometimes attended nomination meetings outside his own riding, and even conducted campaign activities beyond the boundaries of Toronto.[83]

Under some form of central direction, then, reform electoral organization for the election of 1834 evolved into a four-stage process. First, delegates to a county convention were selected at township meetings. Second, acceptable candidates for election were chosen at the county conventions. The most highly publicized of the county conventions was the one held in York in February 1834, the grandiosely named "General Convention of Delegates of the Metropolitan District of Upper Canada." Four candidates – one for each of the four ridings of York – were selected at this meeting. In some constituencies there was a third stage, which involved the establishing of the county convention as a permanent body. The fourth stage involved various types of ongoing activity at the township level. Sometimes, for example, participants held township meetings to endorse the candidates; in other instances nomination committees took charge of electioneering.[84] Evidence of reform electoral organization was very widespread. As historian S.D. Clark indicated, "by the spring of 1834 township meetings called to elect delegates to county conventions had been held in almost every part of the province."[85]

As every political campaigner knows, however, there is often little resemblance between the organization chart and the reality of mobilizing supporters. In fact, this pioneering effort at electoral organization was considerably less impressive than the reformers' petitioning campaigns. The fact that both reformers and Methodists were each readily able to obtain twenty thousand signatures or more on their petitions to Britain in the summer of 1833 suggests that the organization of this activity was very smooth indeed. The same could not be said of the reformers' electoral organization the following year, notwithstanding the fact that it represented a great advance over their previous electoral efforts.

Not all of the nomination meetings, for example, contained a clear partisan agenda. The experience of the first riding of Lincoln illustrates this point. The township nomination meeting held in Beamsville in that constituency lacked much of the usual reform rhetoric. For example, the incumbent (John Clarke) was rejected on the grounds that he had disappointed hopes that he was "an independent middle man"; Dennis Wolverton of Grimsby received their votes instead. Though "independence" was frequently required of reform candidates, so was "support for liberal principles," not something specified at the Beamsville meeting. The only policy issue on which participants expressed themselves was that of road appropriations, which had allegedly benefitted favourites at the expense of the public welfare. Touchstones of reform including responsible government, jury reform, and reductions in government spending were similarly absent from the published resolutions. Reports of this meeting, then, suggest that the institution of the nomination meeting had spread in some instances beyond the reach of York activists.[86]

If not all nomination meetings were clearly of reformist orientation, it is also true that the nomination process did not always function as smoothly as Clark's account suggests. In the third riding of Lincoln, for example, reformers evidently nominated not one but two different candidates at their township meetings. The *British American Journal* was aghast that "the Reform electors of this riding have tho't it necessary, or expedient, to nominate two candidates in opposition to each other," particularly as the two evidently entertained similar political views.[87] Such divisions of opinion are not inconsistent with reform organization, but they do suggest that the nomination process did not always proceed smoothly.

One solution to differences on candidate selection was intervention by well-known leaders. This method of conflict resolution, however, did not necessarily meet with universal approval. One of the disaffected in Markham, for example, wrote a long letter of complaint to the *Toronto Patriot* about Mackenzie's alleged interference in the nomination process in the third riding of York. Under the unwieldy pseudonym "Whiggissimus," this same correspondent reported dismay at Mackenzie's behaviour in Markham after the township nomination meeting in December 1833. "Our resolutions were suppressed," he complained, "our injudicious choice of a candidate was set aside, and our little pecuniary item was patriotically merged in the funds of the Central Committee." Mackenzie's interference at this meeting was but the opening salvo in his allegedly numerous instances of interference in the nominating process. The culmination of Mackenzie's efforts was the imposition at the county convention of Dr Thomas D. Morrison as candidate for the third riding of York. Morrison was so little known in Markham, Whiggissimus complained, that Mackenzie himself felt compelled to introduce the new candidate to the electors at a public meeting held specifically for that purpose.[88]

Variations in the nomination process, and the difficulties in establishing clear guidelines for conflict resolution, confirm the experimental nature of reform electoral organization at this time. Though the pioneering efforts of 1833–34 could not have been undertaken without a very substantial measure of commonality in the political culture of various regions of the province, they fell somewhat short of a province-wide party organization. Reform forces were without recognized leadership, organizational focus, or a clear province-wide political platform. Candidates were appointed by the approved nominating procedure in only half the ridings, and even then did not identify themselves with party labels. The financial question was dispatched with the pious hope that it would go away. (A hope shared by more soundly established parties since!)[89]

The incomplete penetration of partisan organization prior to the general election of 1834 is demonstrated by the holding of bipartisan nomination meetings in several constituencies, including Lennox and Addington,[90] Frontenac, Wentworth, and the first and second ridings of York.[91] The purpose of the gathering in Lennox and Addington was to nominate two candidates for the county for the next general election. According to the *Kingston Whig*, strenuous efforts were made beforehand to pack the event with supporters of John S. Cartwright, who had taken a prominent part in the Midland district anti-grievance meeting of March 1832. In his speech at the nomination meeting in April 1834, Cartwright identified himself as a supporter of the clergy reserves and a man with "a great interest in these counties" (thereby "bragging of his property," according to the disapproving *Whig*). Peter

Perry then spoke in defence of his own voting record in the Assembly and that of the county's other representative, Marshall Spring Bidwell.

Bidwell's nomination was evidently beyond challenge, but a tory resolution proposed that Perry retire in favour of Cartwright. Cartwright's nomination, however, was vulnerable to defeat on several counts. In addition to being a wealthy "outsider" from Kingston, he was perceived as both anti-Methodist[92] and in favour of British immigration to Upper Canada. At a meeting dominated by reform sympathizers, these factors were enough to secure Cartwright's defeat. Unbowed, Cartwright insisted that he would continue in his efforts to represent the riding and, in fact, ran a strong third in the 1834 election.

Perhaps these bipartisan meetings are the most surprising of all the political developments of 1834. After the violence and bitterness of the preceding two years, this degree of peaceful co-operation between reformers and tories is striking. Moreover, the tory press seems to have ignored the nomination meetings rather than attacking them. Evidently the ideological storm of the province had calmed somewhat.

Several factors may explain this development. The apparent absence of violence during the spring and summer of 1834 may have been partly a reflection of the change in reformers' strategies. The township meetings did not offer the same dramatic challenge to constituted authority as the much larger-scale meetings of the oppositionist petitioning campaigns. Nor did they offer as easy a target. Much of the organizing for these meetings must have occurred privately and therefore beyond the reach of tory shock troops.

Moreover, by the time of the election in the fall of 1834, the tories may have decided that the reformers were unable to compete effectively for public support. Mackenzie had certainly suffered some serious reverses. His mission to the Colonial Office had produced no lasting results of any consequence. Moreover, his strategy of appealing to British radicals for assistance had been denounced by the powerful Methodist leader, Egerton Ryerson, in the most public fashion. The reform-Methodist alliance, though far from dead, appeared to be seriously damaged. Mackenzie's additional expulsions from the Assembly in 1832–33 had produced only a limited public outcry.[93] The expulsions also had the effect – one desired by his opponents – of depriving him of a superb platform for agitation until February 1834, when he was finally able to reclaim his seat in the Assembly. His attention to the provincial scene, however, was somewhat diverted by his election as the first Mayor of Toronto in the spring of 1834. Perhaps his opponents believed that under these circumstances the reformers were incapable of mounting a serious challenge for control of the Assembly.

A third possibility is that the tories did not view their opponents' electoral organization as a very serious threat to their own hegemony. Of all the major institutions of government, the Assembly had the least power. Its decisions could be overruled by the Legislative Council, the lieutenant-governor, and the British government. Even if the reformers won a majority there, they would not be seizing the reins of political power. Electoral organization, then, offered a much less serious challenge than petitions to the British government.

If this is true, then it is necessary to explain why the reformers went to so much trouble to secure an electoral victory in 1834. Like the tories, they knew that it would not bring them true political power. On the other hand, it would allow them to show the British government that their criticisms of the existing system of government were endorsed by the provincial electorate. Control of the Assembly would also provide reformers with an excellent platform from which to launch attacks on the political *status quo*, and one that would have considerable credibility in Britain. This was perhaps particularly important in view of the fact that tory violence had essentially deprived them of any other public platform. There was a further strategic consideration for reformers. If the measures passed by a reform Assembly were scotched by the Legislative Council, this would offer further evidence of the serious limitations of the existing Upper Canadian constitution. For all these reasons, then, the reformers had far more to gain from control of the Assembly than did their opponents.

Whatever the reasons for reformers' focus on electoral organization in 1833–34, their efforts paid off handsomely. After the election of 1834, for the first time in the decade, they dominated the Assembly.[94] This victory, however, had not been achieved without bloodshed. In Leeds, Ogle Gowan's forces took control on the second day of polling, assaulting reform voters with impunity in the presence of magistrates. After three days of this, the reform candidates, William Buell and Joseph K. Hartwell, retired, leaving the field to Gowan. The grand master's victory, however, was brief; the election was declared void, as was the by-election held the following March, for similar reasons. Not until March 1836, after the passage of a special act by the Assembly to control elections in the county, did Leeds secure representation without conflict at the polls, with victory finally going to the reform candidates.[95] Reformers could take considerable pride in this rare and hard-won – if short-lived – victory over the forces of lawless law.[96]

In at least one other constituency, violence was threatened against opponents of the tories. In the aftermath of the election, W.B. Robinson, who had won the Simcoe county seat, publicly praised the efforts of "Mr Duggan's '*True Blues*' on one of the days of his Election." This force of tory supporters, Robinson said, "struck terror into the enemies ranks," thereby earning a large share of the credit for his victory.[97] Robinson's public celebration of electoral violence offered a striking contrast to reformers' attitudes to armed confrontation, as revealed for example in the declaration of objects of the Middlesex Political Union.

The electoral victory of 1834 did not turn reform attention entirely towards the Assembly. Mackenzie, for one, continued to focus more broadly on popular politics, as did some of the more radical reformers in Toronto.[98] The result was the founding of the Canadian Alliance Society in December 1834, with Mackenzie as corresponding secretary and James Lesslie as president. Its "Appeal to the People" of 23 December 1834 referred to the organization as a "union."[99] Thus it was not narrowly focused on electoral victory, nor was it primarily an electoral organization. Its purpose, according to the "Appeal," was to "strengthen the hands of a liberal [Upper Canadian] parliament." In addition, it was intended to "keep in check ... evil influences," among them such "unions" as the government, the Legislative Council, the Welland Canal Company, the Law Society, and the British Constitutional Society.

The "Objects and Rules" of the Alliance set forth a program that bore a strong resemblance to Mackenzie's petitions of 1831. Both documents argued in favour of responsible government, the non-intervention of the British government in local affairs, fair representation in the legislature, Assembly control of revenue, economy in government, judicial reform, and a thorough overhauling of the Crown and clergy reserves. Clearly, more than three years of effort had brought few of the changes reformers sought.

In the meantime, new and more radical measures had been added to the list. These included a written constitution, abolition of the appointed Legislative Council, vote by ballot, property tax equality, and less tax on labour. The first three items, leaning as they did in the direction of greater democracy, appeared to reflect American influences. The items regarding taxes suggest that the reformers were deliberately cultivating members of the non-elite, though the "Appeal" argued that the Society spoke to no "prejudices of individuals or classes."

Though the Alliance Society was not narrowly electorally oriented, it was certainly partisan. One might wonder at the logic behind its being founded almost immediately *after* a general election. Clearly, its major object was not electoral organization. Instead, it was designed partly to promote reform by maintaining continuous public pressure on the government. In accordance with this objective, the question of the election of a new Speaker in the House of Assembly was considered at one of the Alliance's earliest meetings. At the meeting, Marshall Spring Bidwell was chosen for this position. In order to express popular support for this choice, it was ordered that circular letters be sent to township officers "throughout the Province," asking them to obtain "an expression of public opinion on this important subject at the ensuing January Town meetings." Township officers were also "to urge the yeomanry to be alive to their public duty and to watch with conscientious anxiety whenever their representatives will by their absence, or otherwise, disappoint the ardent expectations of the country."[100]

Beyond this, however, the "Appeal to the People" revealed that reformers had been concerned that the founding of such a political union during the previous Upper Canadian parliament, dominated as it was by government supporters, would have invited "a gagging bill to put down meetings and petitioning, as in 1818." The "Appeal" also carefully pointed out that it was not necessary to call a public meeting in order to form a branch society; everything could be organized by mail. The Society's organization, in other words, was designed to avoid politically motivated violence.

The Alliance's "Objects and Rules" foresaw the widespread foundation of branch societies, and indeed it is credited with having enrolled 104 branches by May 1835. In Upper Canadian history, the organization was unique in soliciting the attendance of women – but the number of female members is not recorded. Membership in individual branches appears to have ranged from under fifty to over one hundred, and to have been concentrated mainly in the Toronto area.[101] Though this fell short of the stated hopes of the society's founders, it nevertheless represented a great advance in public participation over the abortive attempt to found a political union in 1833. Still, the reformers' hearts may not have been entirely behind the initiative. As Mackenzie later commented, "so long ... as Reformers here rested their hopes on the justice of the English Government, a Society of this sort could not be very extensively useful."[102]

Now that the reformers had control of the Assembly, they had a new focus of attention. The Assembly majority promptly elected Marshall Spring Bidwell as speaker, and passed an address emphasizing their loyalty to the British connection. The past was rewritten: the record of Mackenzie's expulsions from the Assembly was ceremonially expunged. Mackenzie himself was quickly occupied in the self-appointed task of documenting injustice and evil-doing in the government as chair of an Assembly committee on grievances, before turning to a similar task in relation to the Welland Canal.[103] His colleagues in the Assembly, meanwhile, laboured to further the objectives outlined in the manifesto of the Alliance Society. Discouragingly, but hardly surprisingly, most of their legislative initiatives were blocked by the Legislative Council.

These efforts, however, were not entirely in vain. In fact, they indirectly achieved one of the objectives reformers had long sought – the replacement of Lieutenant-Governor Colborne. The election of a reform-dominated Assembly, and the report of Mackenzie's committee on grievances, were critical in persuading Lord Glenelg to shift Colborne from his position at the end of 1835.[104] The election victory and subsequent actions of the Assembly majority had served, then, not as ends in themselves but as acts of political theatre which successfully influenced their intended audience in Britain. Like the petitioning movement of 1831–32, the electoral activity of 1834 was acted out on a transatlantic stage.

As the reformers set about using their electoral victory of 1834 to best advantage, the tories began to use the Constitutional Society for much the same purpose as the reformers had tried to use the political unions in earlier years. Thus the Society became in 1835 a vehicle for bringing pressure from out-of-doors on the Assembly. In February 1835, for example, its members met in Toronto to protest the actions of an Assembly committee in the controverted elections in Toronto and Leeds.[105] In April, they met again to express displeasure at the conduct of the Assembly majority. One resolution of the meeting condemned the "evasive manner" in which the Assembly majority had declined to express an opinion on Hume's "baneful domination" letter. Another resolution professed outrage at the decision of the committees on controverted elections, especially those in Lincoln, Toronto, and Leeds. More generally, the Assembly majority's "spirit of hostility to the institutions of our parent land, a decided leaning towards the anti-British party of the Lower Province, and a fixed determination to oppose the progress of British emigration" was denounced at the meeting. Not surprisingly, participants further applauded members of the Legislative Council for their stand "against the vicious and revolutionary inroads sought to be effected upon the Constitution."[106]

The organizational initiatives taken by the British Constitutional Society at this time also paralleled the activities of the Canadian Alliance. At the April meeting of the Society, it was agreed that delegates should be sent to the counties of the province "to explain the views of this meeting, and to form where practicable and necessary Branch Associations." By the end of the summer, a number of branch societies had been formed in the counties of York and Leeds, and no doubt elsewhere as well.[107] These gatherings showcased local displeasure with the conduct of the Assembly majority in much the same way as the parent society had done. Thus, for example, the conduct of the Legislative

Council and the minority in the Assembly was approved by a meeting of the Esquesing branch.[108] The meeting at the front of Yonge township was inclined to stronger action, moving to petition the lieutenant-governor for a dissolution of the Assembly.[109] Just as the tories had followed the reformers in organizing popular political activities connected with the petitioning movement in 1831–32, they now mimicked reform efforts to found political unions. Significantly, these activities were not narrowly directed towards electoral victory. Instead, they were aimed at eliciting public opinion more generally and bringing pressure to bear on the Assembly and the lieutenant-governor.

In the aftermath of the petitioning movements of 1831–32, the reformers had been more active than their opponents in trying to arouse public support for their political objectives. Their efforts to found political unions, to circulate petitions, and to promote electoral organization kept the issues they considered most important constantly before the public, and offered ordinary Upper Canadians the opportunity for continuous involvement in the colony's political life.

Through all the vicissitudes of these years, reformers never forgot their primary objective: to secure British approval for changes to the constitution and to the religious establishment. This task was proving to be more difficult than reformers had likely imagined. Events during 1832–33 had shown that it was virtually impossible to mount another campaign of public meetings to demonstrate popular support for their program, and that was it impractical to found political unions to maintain ongoing pressure for reform. Under these circumstances, it was control of the Assembly that offered reformers the last, best hope for change.

6 Popular Politics and the Rebellion of 1837 in Upper Canada

In the two years before the Rebellion of 1837, the story of popular politics was one of a persistent downward spiral in reform fortunes, and of a corresponding series of triumphs for reform's opponents. One explanation is the appearance on the Upper Canadian stage of Sir Francis Bond Head, who arrived in the province in early 1836. Head, Upper Canada's first civilian lieutenant-governor, was an unconventional choice for this position. He was dubbed "a strange person" by John Beverley Robinson, and "a damned odd fellow" by Lord Melborne.[1] Head's most recent position prior to his appointment in Upper Canada was the minor post of poor law commissioner in the English county of Kent. Before that, he had been an officer in the army, a mining supervisor, and a writer of light travel books. He won his knighthood 1831 by demonstrating the military uses of the lasso, an interest he had doubtless acquired during his extensive travels across the pampas of Argentina. Though well-traveled in Europe and South America, Head was so far out of the political loop that he had never voted in an election. Nevertheless, he proved to be one of the greatest masters of popular politics in the history of Upper Canada.

Neither this unsuspected talent nor the extent to which it would be enlisted in the tory cause were immediately apparent. Head's instructions from the Colonial Office reassured tories that the British government stood firm in resisting fundamental political changes, such as the introduction of responsible government. On the other hand, they raised the hopes of reformers by pledging non-interference in matters of local concern, urging Head to reform the patronage system, and mandating that he make every effort to accommodate the Assembly.

Moreover, in February 1836 Head appointed two well-known reformers, Robert Baldwin and John Rolph, to the executive council, along with J.H. Dunn, a moderate official. These appointments were not unnaturally seen as a precursor of a form of responsible government. Such hopes were quickly dashed, however. Three weeks after the new councillors had joined, the entire Executive Council resigned over the issue of responsible government.[2]

The Assembly responded by launching an inquiry into the affair. In April, the appointed committee returned a stinging attack on Head. Its tone owed much to the reformers' infuriation at the recent disclosure of Colborne's parting gesture – the establishment of forty-four rectories – an incident that further cemented ties between the Anglican Church and the state. The Assembly promptly approved the committee's report on 15 April and voted to stop the supplies. Five days later, Head prorogued the legislature. His answer to the stoppage of supplies was to refuse his assent to the money bills that had already passed; this measure, as G.M. Craig noted, "was far more crippling to provincial prosperity than was the Assembly's rather empty gesture."[3] In May, Head inflamed the situation further by dissolving the Assembly and embarking on a spirited election campaign in which he personally headed the government forces.

POPULAR POLITICS AND THE RESIGNATION CRISIS, 1836

The institutions of popular politics were active at virtually every stage of this political uproar. Popular involvement began as soon as the additions to the Executive Council were announced in February 1836. "A universal joy and satisfaction," Head himself recorded "was expressed by the radical party, and I received addresses from various places" expressing enthusiasm for his initiative.[4] Such an address, for example, emanated from the township of Thurlow in the Midland district.[5] The press also carried reports of similar addresses from the Home and London districts. Though none emanated formally from branches of the Alliance Society, and the meetings held were announced as public meetings, these addresses came from areas where oppositionist organization had historically been strong.[6] Head later recorded that he received them ("from places of no importance") with some scepticism; not only were they similarly worded but many were also presented by the same two members of the Assembly. Moreover, the support offered by the addresses to the idea of responsible government convinced Head that many Upper Canadians did not understand the true nature of the constitution (at least as he interpreted it).[7]

Not all of the addresses to Head from reform sources expressed "universal joy and satisfaction," as Head put it. For example, the appointment of the new executive councillors was approved at a public meeting held on 5 March in Albion in the Home district, but the retention of the old council members was denounced.[8] Not long after, a meeting held at the Alliance Room in Toronto on 10 March 1836 was considerably more critical of Head. Its participants attacked his patronage policy and his interference in matters of local concern and demanded that he dismiss the old executive councillors, who "have deservedly lost the confidence of the great body of the people of this province."[9]

This public response to the new appointments to the Executive Council was a mild foretaste of the popular reaction to the resignation of the entire Executive Council in March 1836. Toronto reformers took the lead less than a week after this event. In addition to the city council passing an essentially reform address to Head,[10] a great public meeting was held at city hall on 19 March, attracting a crowd of fifteen hundred according to the *Correspondent & Advocate.* Significantly, it was the name of Jesse Ketchum, that venerable petitioner, that headed the list of names on the requisition calling the meeting. The proceedings were peaceable, except for the opposition of Sheriff Jarvis and McLean from Cornwall, who interrupted "in a low and vulgar manner."[11] The chair was taken by veteran reformer, T.D. Morrison, who was now the mayor of the city. James Lesslie, another pillar of the Alliance Society, acted as secretary.

The resolutions of the meeting presented the core of the reform case. They maintained that Simcoe, the province's first lieutenant-governor, had said that Upper Canada possessed the image and transcript of the British constitution. According to a resolution proposed by James Small, the new MPP for Toronto, an "essential and inalienable feature" of the British constitution was responsible government. Further resolutions expressed sorrow at the resignation of the reform members of the council, and declared "our firm and unalterable determination to resist every attempt to *mutilate* and deform our constitution" by the denial of the principles of the British constitution. The new Executive Council was denounced, and the Assembly was encouraged to stop the supplies. At the meeting, a committee of correspondence was nominated to communicate with the districts of the province. It was also decided that, a few days later, a deputation should take an address to Head based on these resolutions.[12]

Accordingly, on 22 March a deputation of Toronto citizens met with Head and presented their address. The group included such well-known reformers as George Ridout, Jesse Ketchum, J.H. Price,

W.J. O'Grady, Dr John Tims, John Doel, James and William Lesslie, and Timothy Parsons. Head's reply to this delegation was both condescending and politically astute.[13] "Having reason to believe," he began, "that the meeting from which you are a deputation, was composed principally of the industrious classes and being persuaded that the liberal principles of the British Government in whatever climate it may exist, is the welfare and happiness of the people, I shall make it my duty to reply to your address with as much attention as if it had proceeded from either of the branches of the Legislature. Altho' I shall express myself in plainer and more homely language."

The remainder of the reply was an extraordinarily well-crafted public document. In it, Head turned reform rhetoric about liberty on its head, maintaining that the Constitutional Act of 1791, was "the great charter of [your] liberties"; any modification of it would result in Upper Canadians being deprived of their "property, ... freedom, and independence." The reformers' claims that responsible government had long since been promised to the province were hollow ones: the Constitutional Act did not provide for a responsible Executive Council. Demands for one, according to the lieutenant-governor, were nothing more than an attempt to obtain the power and patronage of the crown.

The old system, Head acknowledged, contained abuses, and the reformers, he claimed, had "feathered their nests" under that system.[14] Discontent had therefore arisen, but Head would act to allay it: "The Grievances of this Province," he maintained, "must be corrected – impartial justice must be administered." He himself, Head asserted, had "come here for the avowed purpose of Reform," and to "encourage, to the utmost of my power, internal wealth, agriculture, commerce, peace and tranquility."

This powerful appeal to the public wish for economic prosperity was coupled with a caution against political agitation hostile to Head himself. Such agitation, according to him, was bound to fail; familiarity with "the yeomanry and industrious classes" of Britain had convinced him that individuals from these backgrounds would in fact rally to his side if he were attacked. Moreover, he continued, "if intimidation be continued, it will soon be made to recoil upon those who shall presume to have recourse to it."[15]

With this one swift stroke, Head had assumed leadership of what he touted as the forces of true reform. He had also provided a refutation of reform constitutionalism, and wrapped his own interpretation of the constitution in the British flag. In partisan fashion, he had condemned the reformers as seekers after patronage, and issued a preemptive strike against hostile political organization. Small wonder that this speech, with its colourful metaphors about the feathering of nests, would serve as a basic political text in the electoral campaign that followed.

More than this, however, Head had stepped outside the traditional role of the lieutenant-governor as a figure beyond politics. In intervening in political debate in such a high-profile fashion, he was qualitatively changing the role of his office. He was in effect removing the cloak of secrecy from the functioning of the highest political office in the land and leaving his conduct open to public scrutiny and criticism in an unprecedented manner. In this way, his conduct contributed to the enlargement of the public sphere.

Head's reply was not calculated to reassure the experienced reform politicians of Toronto. Within the week, they responded with a waspish rejoinder which began: "We are deeply sensible, in receiving your Excellency's reply, of your Excellency's great condescension, in endeavouring to express yourself in plainer and more homely language, presumed by Your Excellency to be thereby brought down to the lower level of our plainer and more homely understandings. ... Any supposed necessity for this great condescension of your Excellency, could not have existed, in any degree, had not past administrations sadly neglected our claims to the blessings of general education."

The rejoinder went on to reiterate the grievances of reformers, including the failure to secularize the clergy reserves, the lack of responsible government, interference from Britain in local affairs, and the monopoly of office by ultra-tories. It also referred to past injustices, touching on the misfortunes of Gourlay, Matthews, Willis, Collins, Randall, and Mackenzie. It ended on a sober, even threatening note. In asking that the Upper Canadian constitution operate on British principles, the reply thundered: "If Your Excellency will not govern us upon these principles, you will exercise arbitrary sway – you will violate our charter, virtually abrogate our law, and justly forfeit our submission to your authority."[16] Like Head's reply, this document was widely circulated and commented on in the provincial press.[17]

Toronto tories responded with gusto to this popular challenge to Head's position. Indeed, they answered it with a "Great Constitutional Meeting" on 30 April. The meeting was chaired by Captain Macaulay, with John Strachan acting as secretary.[18] A string of resolutions was passed, and an address to Head was approved. This address was featured in an issue of the *Kingston Chronicle* under the impressive title "Address of 1622 of the Clergy, Gentry, Mechanics, and other inhabitants of the City of Toronto." Predictably, the address condemned efforts to create "an excitement and disturbance in the Colony which is calculated to produce the most injurious and fatal effects." Like Head, the address inverted reform constitutional rhetoric, maintaining that "the prerogatives of the Crown are only a sacred trust for the protection of the rights and liberties of the people." It similarly paid homage to Head's "declared desire to carry into effect the liberal intentions" of the British government.

The momentum of this occasion was carried forward a few days later when a public meeting was held at the Toronto Court House. Here, a committee was chosen to obtain signatures to the address. Soon after, "large placards were posted about the city," according to the *Correspondent & Advocate*, "inviting all who had signed the petition to meet at the Ontario House on Thursday last, at 12, to accompany the deputation to the Government House, with the address." The *Correspondent*, which minimized the importance of these events, claimed that only about one hundred people accompanied the address; they were "requested to walk as *far apart* as possible, in order to make them appear numerous." In spite of the newspaper's derision, this demonstration must have reminded Torontonians of the celebrated march on Government House by Mackenzie supporters in 1832. The subliminal message of the procession was that the tories had reclaimed the streets of the city from reformers, who had not even attempted a like demonstration in 1836.

Toronto tories resorted to a more unaccustomed method of speaking for the general population when the city's grand jury in mid-April processed to Government House with their own address to Head. This body included such tory stalwarts as George Gurnett and J.S. Macaulay, the foreman. Their address rejoiced at the "paternal solicitude" of the British government and deplored the extent of the "system of political excitement" evident in the province for some time. It further expressed the pious hope that the people would realize that they should avoid "consideration of abstract questions of government, and of theoretical changes to the Constitution." The grand jurors concluded by explaining that, though as grand jurors their function was purely judicial, they offered their views in the belief that these were widely shared by the freeholders of the Home district. Head, happy to receive support from whatever quarter, returned a warm and complimentary reply to this unusual document.[19]

Though Toronto activists spearheaded the movement in 1836, both reformers and tories launched a province-wide petitioning campaign over the issue of the resignation of the Executive Council. As in 1831–32, these movements combined the formal holding of public meetings with the informal circulation of petitions for signature. In 1836, however, neither side attempted to hold the mammoth district meetings that had attracted such violence in 1832; county and especially township meetings were the rule.

On the reform side, the initiative came from the Alliance Society in Toronto. Writing as secretary of "The Reform Society of Toronto," W.L. Mackenzie drew up and arranged for the distribution of a petition asking the Assembly to stop the supplies and praying for the appointment of a responsible Executive Council.[20] Hostile commentators claimed that some five thousand of these were in circulation "sent by mail – *franked* – by various members of [the Upper Canadian] Parliament of the same kidney [as Mackenzie], to all parts of the province."[21] Among the intended recipients were the clerks of the various townships and, no doubt, tried supporters.[22] By the end of March, two weeks after the start of the crisis, these petitions were in the hands of reform sympathizers.[23] These local agents could either hold public meetings to publicize the cause or simply circulate the petitions in the locality; sometimes they did both. The petitions were to be returned by mail to reform MPPs or to Mackenzie himself.[24]

Newspapers provide accounts of at least twelve reform meetings in the Home, London, Gore, Johnstown, Bathurst, and Niagara districts in late March and early April 1836.[25] Most of these were called to approve the "Reform Society" petition, but assumed the character of public meetings rather than gatherings under the auspices of the Alliance Society. As in the election of 1834, it was charged against the reformers – in this case specifically the Alliance Society – that "unfair and sinister efforts have been made ... to raise public excitement at a distance." Accordingly, the chair of the Alliance on one occasion wrote a public letter to organizers of a meeting at Dundas, asking them to contradict such charges.[26]

The most closely watched of the reform meetings was called by the four Assembly representatives of York for 2 April. This was the only recorded county reform meeting; the rest occurred at the township level. The meeting at Davis's Temperance Inn, Yonge Street, was extensively advertised under the heading "The Constitution in Danger!!!" There, a series of resolutions passed and the Alliance petition to the Assembly was endorsed.[27] This process was not uneventful. The *Correspondent and Advocate* reported the disruption of the meeting "in the presence of several magistrates" by about thirty well-lubricated tory enforcers under the leadership of Dr McCague of Yonge Street.[28] Sir Francis himself relayed the tory version of events to the Colonial Office. Mackenzie, he said, "totally failed in gaining attention." His colleague Dr Morrison, Head gloated, was "collared and severely shaken, and the whole affair was ... completely stifled by the indignation of the people."[29] In fact, the meeting was so seriously disrupted that the reformers continued it at another location. On the basis that Mackenzie's supporters had successfully been routed, the tories argued that Mackenzie's gathering had been a great failure.

Contests for control of public meetings occurred on two other occasions during this petitioning process. In early April, the inhabitants of the townships of Montague, Wolford, and Oxford (Grenville and Lanark counties) met in Merrickville to consider the petition forwarded by Mackenzie. To the disappointment of reformers, bad roads and inclement weather kept attendance low. The tories, however, "were untiring in their efforts," and two leading Orangemen of the area, with a few supporters, "had the complete monopoly of the business of the day."[30] Another struggle for control of a meeting occurred in Whitby at the end of the month. Here, reformers attended a meeting held by their opponents, who insisted that the gathering was a private one. Turned out of the house at the request of the tories, the reformers held a public meeting next door, with the tories surprisingly in attendance during the passage of anti-Head resolutions. After the meeting, the *Correspondent & Advocate* reported, "the poor tories returned to their old hole and locked themselves in."[31]

The Esquesing Alliance Society apparently defied the common pattern in early April when it held a private meeting to prepare its own document. Their bitter address to the "liberal members in the House of Assembly" occupied two columns of closely spaced print. "We have looked on for years," the address stated, "and seen our persons abused, our characters traduced, our wishes misrepresented and our property squandered away." The address, like Head's reply to the Toronto address, resorted to the world of nature for abusive analogies. "Ministerial favourites and dependents," it declared, were "hungry Ravens, crowds of whom flock around a minister in office like so many crows around a dead carcass." The signatories had given up hope that either the Colonial Office or the new governor would freely meet the demand for reform: "We have no confidence that any good is to rise from either till you carry every thing to the last extremity." Radical talk indeed! The address further urged that the Assembly stop the supplies immediately. Moreover, MPPs were to press the case for reform with the British government: an elective Legislative Council; a responsible Executive Council; an accountable officialdom; and the separation of church and state. The address ended with a note of encouragement: "Persevere and you will be successful."[32]

The results of these initiatives were disappointing. Instead of more than 20,000 signatures, as on the petitions of 1831–32, the reformers' petitioning campaign of 1836 netted only some 4,700 signatures, according to reports in the *Journals* of the Assembly. Significantly, more than half the signatures attributed to a particular locality in the *Journals* came from the Home and London districts; in these districts, which would be the scene of rebellion the following year, reform organization and sentiment was particularly strong.[33]

Why did the reformers obtain so comparatively few signatures on the 1836 petitions? Part of the explanation may have been that the personal touch was lacking; in 1836 Mackenzie himself did not tour the province in support of the cause as he had in 1831. It may also be that the breach with Egerton Ryerson deprived the reformers of an accustomed means of circulating petitions. Moreover, the issue of the resignation of the executive councillors lacked the dramatic public appeal of the expulsions of Mackenzie. It may also have been that public support for the reformers was simply lacking on this issue. Perhaps Upper Canadians were willing to give the new lieutenant-governor more time to show that he could indeed "remedy all practical grievances" before they sought the intervention of the British government yet again. Whatever the reason, the reform campaign fizzled badly.

For the tories, on the other hand, a corresponding sally into the realm of popular politics was a resounding success, garnering approximately 27,000 signatures by the end of May[34] (see appendix D). Though their meetings were organized a few weeks later than those of the reformers, they appear to have been very widely held, most of them from mid-April to early May. The correspondence of the civil secretary records public meetings that produced loyal addresses in the following townships and towns: Augusta and North Crosby (Johnstown); Peterborough and River Trent (Newcastle); St Thomas, Woodstock, Bayham, and Goderich (London); Niagara Falls (Niagara); Bytown, Beckwith, Nepean, and Richmond (Bathurst); Trafalgar (Gore); Napanee (Midland); and Kent (Western). The press also reported meetings in St Catharines (Niagara), Middlesex (London) and in Kingston and Hallowell in the Midland district.[35] These were more limited affairs than the great district meetings of 1832. While some were billed as county meetings,[36] the majority appear to have taken place at the township level.

The lieutenant-governor himself was likely the motive force behind this massive public campaign. This is suggested by the fact that its chief organizer was Head's private secretary, John Joseph. Joseph's correspondence contains numerous letters from individuals across the colony reporting on the progress of gathering signatures on the petitions.[37] But Head was too shrewd to proceed without considerable assistance from Toronto tories. Henry Ruttan, sheriff of Newcastle, for example, informed Joseph late in May that "having understood from a Friend in Toronto that our address was expected immediately we determined upon leaving Cobourg on Sunday evening next."[38] R.B. Sullivan, a new executive councillor who may have been the "Friend," evidently monitored incoming petitions; Daniel O'Connor reported to Joseph that he had received a letter from Sullivan noting that only one address had been received from Bytown."[39] Another well-wisher was

A.B. Hawke, the emigrant agent in Toronto, to whom at least two tory addresses were forwarded.[40] Moreover, many extant copies of the petitions were printed ones, suggesting that the forms had been sent ready-made, probably from Toronto.[41]

The number of signatures on the pro-government petitions of 1836 exceeded even the remarkable totals of 1832. This was a striking achievement, as organizers struggling with rainy weather and muddy roads would have testified.[42] The civil secretary's correspondence provides information on the perils and successes of local organization in the remote Bathurst district. Here, there had been a county meeting on 26 April, "when some gentlemen from Bytown volunteered to obtain signatures and forward the address." For reasons unknown, the volunteers had neglected to do their duty, and "in the mean time, a great many Freeholders who are in the Lumber trade have gone off with their Timber for Quebec."[43] In the township of Nepean, the omission was remedied by the holding of a local meeting to pass a new address.[44] In Bytown itself, Daniel O'Connor was watching the press to confirm that all petitions from the city had been received in Toronto.[45] In the end, addresses from Bytown, Nepean, Richmond, Lanark, and Beckwith met the cutoff date of 25 May.[46]

The organizational efforts paid off: every single district in the province contributed signatures to the tory addresses. The largest number – almost 6,000 – came from Newcastle, which outdid even the more heavily populated Home district. The Midland and Johnstown districts contributed more than 3,000 signatures each. These documents gave Head firm proof for the British government that his actions met with the warm approval of the people of the province.

The exact language of the various addresses differed, but taken together they provide some insight into the temper of public opinion on political issues in the spring of 1836. Typically they expressed attachment to Great Britain, and sometimes fear of disruption of the colonial tie that could result from the agitation of democratic and republican forces. Similarly, they stressed an awareness of the benefits of a paternal government and appreciation of Head's role as their protector. The maintenance of the tie with Great Britain, the addresses asserted, could best be maintained through a rigorous defence of the existing constitution. As the address of the session and congregation of St Andrew's Church put it, "Liberty enjoyed must be *the power* and *the Liberty* defined by the Law."[47] A number of the other addresses picked up on Head's identification of the existing constitution with true liberty.

The addresses, like those of 1832, condemned reformers – often in colourful language – as factious and self-interested. The address from Plympton, for example, elaborated on Head's ornithological reference to reformers, comparing them to "the ominous Birds of the Storm, [who] delight in the Breakers of the sunken Ledges and the treacherous Reef, but mourn at the laughing Bosom of a quiescent World."[48] The stopping of the supplies was generally deplored, and the dissolution of the Assembly sometimes recommended. Agitation, it was frequently asserted, was seriously retarding the prosperity of the province.

The contents of the addresses indicate that the signatories were firmly behind the lieutenant-governor in his stand on the constitution. This does not mean, however, that they thought the Upper Canadian government was beyond reproach. A number of them spoke with approval of Head's determination to remedy practical grievances, according to his Instructions. The Inhabitants of the town of Woodstock and county of Oxford were among them. Their address identified them as anxious "to claim a Participation in the Desire to witness the Removal of every acknowledged Abuse, and the administration of pure and impartial Justice."[49] The inhabitants of Camden East wistfully stated: "Constitutional Reform we earnestly desire."[50] Those who signed the address in Nichol and Woolwich in the Gore district were eager for changes to the land law in order to facilitate immigration.[51] From Pickering came encouragement for Head's insight "into the Nature and effects of that *Metropolitan* and *baneful Family Influence* to which so large a Portion of our Provincial Complaints are justly attributable."[52] An address from the Midland district approved Head's stated "Determination to remedy any real Grievances ... On this Promise implicit is our Reliance."[53] It looks very much as if Head's presentation of himself as a practical reformer did in fact have the desired result of attracting the maximum amount of public support.

If the addresses and public meetings of the spring of 1836 suggested that support for Head was contingent on his implementing practical reforms in the long term, they were nonetheless extremely useful in the short term. In the transatlantic context, they allowed Head to indicate that he had the documented support of the vast majority of Upper Canadians who chose to express themselves on political issues.

Within Upper Canada itself, the meetings held to promote the signing of petitions served almost as pre-election rallies. The many who signed petitions, even if they could not attend the meetings, were taking the opportunity to express their political views. Surely, given the overwhelming victory of the tories in the petitioning campaign, it was a foregone conclusion that their supporters would win a majority in the Assembly if an election were called. Indeed, the degree of support evinced in the addresses supplied a pretext for Head to call a general election in May 1836.[54]

THE GENERAL ELECTION OF 1836

The lieutenant-governor himself was the undisputed leader of Tory forces during the election. In a series of public statements, Head defined the contest as a "moral war ... between those who were for British institutions, against those who were for soiling the empire by the introduction of democracy."[55] He was ably assisted by a newly reorganized British Constitutional Society, which had been revived yet again in Toronto in April 1836. Although its organizers claimed that they were not organizing "for any party purpose," their Declaration of Views and Objects made clear the urgent necessity of electing "men having better ... claims to the title of Patriots" than those presently in the Assembly. The Assembly majority, according to the Declaration, had contributed in two major ways to the political crisis. First, they had stopped the supplies, which was resulting in the paralysis of economic activity. (As we have already seen, however, Head's refusal to assent to money bills was a far more serious matter for the provincial economy). Second, the Assembly majority had allegedly "adopted the anti-British and Revolutionary doctrines of the Ninety-Two Resolutions, and of Mr Papineau." The evidence for this was that the Assembly majority had failed to denounce a letter from Papineau which had been laid on the table of the Speaker of the Assembly the night before the Assembly was prorogued. On these feeble pretexts, then, the British Constitutional Society prepared to do battle with reformers at the hustings.[56] A rash of township constitutional societies was founded shortly thereafter in the Newcastle district and elsewhere.[57]

The Toronto headquarters of the British Constitutional Society, meanwhile, distributed campaign literature very effectively during the 1836 election. Robert Stanton of Toronto, an officer of the society, circulated a number of publications and transmitted encouraging rumours from one part of the province to another.[58] It is unlikely that he acted alone. In later years, the society would claim to have distributed 107,600 copies of "Loyal and Constitutional Documents," including some in German and one in Gaelic, at the very considerable cost of £404 14s. 2d.[59]

The reformers' Alliance Society was somewhat slower off the mark. At a meeting on 5 May its members voted that the correspondence committee get in touch with branch societies across the province to obtain a fuller expression of public opinion.[60] The news they received may have been discouraging, for when they addressed the reformers of Upper Canada on 16 May, their tone was decidedly defensive. The address explained the motivation behind the Seventh Report on Grievances, defended the conduct of the reform executive councillors, and justified the stopping of the supplies. Part of the document did however take the offensive against Head, accusing him of a number of instances of bad faith. Moreover, it attacked the lieutenant-governor for appealing to the British-born and Loyalists at the expense of Canadians. The document hopefully evoked Admiral Nelson's instructions at Trafalgar: "At the coming Election, North America expects every man to do his duty."[61]

By the end of May, the magnitude of the tory onslaught had flushed Toronto's moderate reformers like W.W. Baldwin and Francis Hincks[62] out of their voluntary political obscurity. The support of Baldwin, in particular, was an important advantage for the reform cause; as we have seen, he was a man of no little social prominence who lent an aura of respectability to any cause with which he was associated. At a meeting on 30 May, Baldwin assumed the chair of a public meeting of reformers, with Hincks acting as secretary. The group promptly founded the "Constitutional Reform Society of Upper Canada" and urged James Small to agree to accept the reform nomination for Toronto at the forthcoming election. Further communications from the "Constitutional Reformers" under Baldwin urged the voters to support reform candidates, complained about the choice of polling places in a number of constituencies, and expressed concern about the possibility of violence at the election.[63]

It is not clear, however, that the "Constitutional Reformers" mounted any very effective campaign organization in the 1836 election. In part this may have reflected a continuing reliance on the British government for redress of grievances. As a reform address of 1 June 1836 put it, "we confidently await the views and pleasure of his Majesty's Government on the subject, satisfied that the Constitutional Sovereign of the British Empire will ever uphold the constitutional rights of his loyal Canadian subjects, and will require that his representative so exercise the prerogatives of the Crown, as to ensure the peace, welfare and prosperity of the People."[64] The upheaval in their organization, the absence of the long-range electoral planning that had characterized their efforts of 1834, and the effectiveness of Head's appeals were likely also factors in the weakness of reform organization at this time. Moreover, as their campaign literature indicated, they had slim hopes that the election would be fairly conducted.

A formidable alliance of groups, both secular and religious, was arrayed against the reformers at this election. Among the most important were recent British immigrants, whose influx into the province, as we have seen, had been championed by the established authorities in the expectation that they would support the political status quo. This hope appears to have been amply realized in the 1836 election, when the lieutenant-governor made a point of appealing to this group. In the exceptionally immigrant-rich constituency of Toronto, for example, Paul Romney found that "only 31 of the 276 voters whose nationality is known had been born in North America." Here, "a large majority of the British-born" supported the government candidate, W.H. Draper; and those who had arrived since 1827 voted more than two to one in Draper's favour. Among the English and Irish Protestant immigrants, the pro-government vote was even more pronounced, coming in at more than five to one. There was a slight majority among the North-American born, on the other hand, for the reform candidate, J.E. Small.[65] Religious support for the government was also forthcoming, with the Methodist leadership firmly espousing Head's cause, though there is evidence that the voluntarists who would become Canadian Wesleyans voted decisively for the reformers, along with other voluntarists.[66] More striking was the very public alliance of Orangemen and Roman Catholics to defeat the reformers. The Grand Orange Lodge issued a manifesto approving evidence of Roman Catholic loyalty, and Bishop McDonell in return issued an address of thanks. Moreover, members of the two groups co-operated at the hustings; it has been estimated that the alliance accounted for between one third and one half of the change in seats in this election.[67] The Anglican vote was also important. In Toronto, where more than half of the voters whose religious affiliation is known belonged to this denomination, the vote for Draper was 115 to 15.[68] Clearly, the ethnic and religious divisions that had manifested themselves during the recent petitioning campaigns were also significant at the polls.

In some cases, however, the election figures of 1836 were less the outcome of the unfettered expression of public opinion than the result of questionable campaign tactics on the part of the tories. In individual constituencies, to be sure, tory electioneering was energetic without being corrupt. Anthony Manahan in the Bay of Quinte area and Alexander Ross in the London district were among those who oversaw the progress of conservative interests in their regions over a period of weeks.[69] When election day finally came, tories engaged in almost heroic exertions in some constituencies where the vote was expected to be closely divided. Particularly strenuous efforts were made to defeat Mackenzie in the 2nd riding of York. From the hustings in Streetsville, tory organizer T.W. McGrath kept the government informed of a veritable relay team of wagons sent to collect voters from Hamilton, Grimsby, Stoney Creek, Caledon, and Albion. "The other party leave *no means* untried to keep [illeg] ground," he stated.[70] But McGrath and his associates, according to one of Mackenzie's supporters, were not themselves beyond reproach in their electioneering techniques: "All kinds of intimidation," he reported, "all sorts of seduction – all the patronage and power of the banks & the Government – all the menaces of hired bullies – and all the prayers of the wolves in sheep's clothing, were arrayed against [Mackenzie]."[71]

Indeed, these and other illegitimate tory strategies were all too common. As reformers had feared, elections in many constituencies were corruptly conducted. For one thing, electoral violence could have been confidently predicted in light of the lieutenant-governor's refusal to take action against the Orange lodges.[72] In professing ignorance of Orange violence against reformers, Head was in effect declaring open season on his opponents. At the election, Orange activists took full advantage of this. They attacked reform election agents and assaulted other reformers in the London district (where the tories lost). Moreover, they severely disrupted the polling in three locations in the Johnstown district (where the tories won four out of five seats).[73] In the county of Simcoe, too, tory violence was such that the reform candidate, Lount, withdrew from the contest after the first evening, saying "that blood should never spilt on his account."[74]

Tory electoral manipulation, however, extended beyond this and included the manufacture of votes through the issuing of patents for land to those not entitled to receive them. These were targeted at areas where the reformers were expected to put up a strong showing: Simcoe, the 2nd riding of York, and the county of Middlesex. Moreover, returning officers sometimes denied the vote to former Americans who were unable to produce a certificate that they had taken the oath of allegiance.[75] This was but one example, according to Charles Duncombe,[76] of an electoral process that had been firmly rigged against the reformers, as further evidenced by the selection of supporters of Head as returning officers and the location of the polls in areas that would favour the tories.[77] Corrupt practices were also said to have included open-handed spending for electoral purposes. In the 4th riding of York, for example, it was alleged that Captain Macaulay spent £600 on the election: "his voters were all brought to the hustings free of *any* expense, and allowed 3s. 9d. per day for the time they were absent from home."[78]

Duncombe produced further allegations of the corrupt conduct of the election in a letter to Lord Gosford of 30 September 1836. Duncombe maintained that the Constitutional Society had received the considerable sum of £500 of public money to aid the tory cause. "Another sum," he said, had been given to the clerk of the Assembly, who was instructed to spend it "to best advantage" in the Eastern district. Moreover, Head had "openly allowed and encouraged all persons under him to interfere with and influence the elections by every means in their power." The result was that more than one third of the new MPPs were sheriffs and other paid officers of the government. Head had also influenced the election results by "denouncing a large proportion of the truly loyal people of the province as 'our enemies,' and allowing, if not actually encouraging Orange Associations ... to interfere with the elections ... by violence and outrage." Head and his secular officials were not the only ones guilty of improper interference in the election, however. According to Duncombe, "the newly created Rectors of the Church of England were indecently actively [*sic*] electioneering for the tory candidates, often among the crowd with their hats in their hands urging on the enemies of reform."[79] To say the least, the election of 1836, in the view of reformers, had not been a fair test of the strength of their cause.

Duncombe, supported by the reformers, took his petition to Britain, where the colonial secretary, Lord Gosford, refused to receive him. When the petition was referred back to the tory-dominated Assembly, a select committee, as Craig put it, "found no truth in it."[80] Head's brand of popular politics had triumphed, leaving reformers bitter and disillusioned. It was a poor portent for the future peace of the province.

PRELUDE TO REBELLION

What a difference a year makes! At the beginning of 1836 reformers had entertained high hopes that the arrival of Sir Francis Bond Head would lead to the achievement of many of the changes they had championed for so long. Before the year was out, their hopes had been crushed beyond anything they might have imagined. The appointment of reformers to the Executive Council had been a disaster. Their opponents had not only triumphed in the following campaign for public support, but had also hammered the reformers in the general election. And the Colonial Office, it appeared, offered no hope of redress. Reformers' best efforts to achieve reform through a decade of peaceful agitation had ended in failure.

It is not surprising that some reformers, frustrated by the disappointment of their legitimate hopes, should ultimately have turned to rebellion. More striking is that, in 1837, they made one final effort to revive the political union movement. It was only when tory violence confirmed the futility of such initiatives that the most extreme of the reformers finally resorted to violence themselves.

It was not Mackenzie, but moderates like W.W. Baldwin who began reorganizing reform forces after the rout of 1836. When the City of Toronto Political Union was founded on 10 October 1836, Baldwin himself became its new president.[81] Like the Middlesex Political

Union of 1833, this organization was designed to forward the cause of reform "by all constitutional and peaceable means." Detailed provisions were made at the meeting for the founding of a "Political Union of Upper Canada," with at least one branch to be organized in every township, city, and town of the province. Unlike previous unions in Upper Canada, this one was concerned primarily with electoral organization, no doubt a result of reformers' frustrations with the proceedings at the 1836 election.

Mackenzie soon took this organization in a considerably more radical direction. In December 1836, he organized the voters of his own constituency to challenge the results of the 1836 election in the second riding of York.[82] Progress was slow, however, until the summer of the following year,[83] with Mackenzie complaining in May that the "first cause" of the "present distress" was "want of Union and Intelligence among the People."[84] Resolved to do something about this, in July 1837 the more radical reformers issued a "Declaration of the Reformers of the City of Toronto to their Fellow-Reformers in Upper Canada."[85]

Although this document demonstrated considerable continuity with the reformers' previous rhetoric of popular constitutionalism, it also contained unmistakable and provocative references to the American Revolution. The language of popular constitutionalism explained the key problem: "The affairs of this country have been ever against the spirit of the Constitutional Act ... the due influence and purity of all our institutions have been utterly destroyed." The situation had deteriorated with the passage of Lord John Russell's Ten Resolutions of 1837, which denied all the major demands of Lower Canadian dissidents.

The "Declaration" also contained unmistakable echoes of the 1776 American Declaration of Independence.[86] The very use of the word "Declaration" in the title was one indication of this. Moreover, the Toronto reformers, like the signatories to the Declaration of Independence, launched a direct and personal attack on the King, holding him personally responsible for many of the evils afflicting the province, including unrepresentative government and the partial administration of justice. This was a radical departure from the convention of Upper Canadian oppositionist discourse that generally placed responsibility for such evils primarily on the heads of the local administration, and secondarily on members of the British government. There could be no more direct affront to paternalism than this personal attack on the monarch, couched moreover in terms reminiscent of one of the great documents of the American Revolution.

Significantly, the Toronto reformers also expressed exasperation with the failure of the British government to act on the demands of petitioners for political change. "In every stage of these proceedings,"they said, "we have petitioned for redress in the most humble terms; our repeated petitions have been answered only by repeated injuries." This was a direct quote from the Declaration of Independence, though it was not acknowledged as such.

The Toronto reformers, however, stopped short of declaring independence from Britain. They did conclude that control of Upper Canadian affairs from Downing Street "ought to be abolished," and that "the domestic institutions of the province [should be] so improved and administered by the local authorities as to render the people happy and contented." The moves they made in this direction were to express solidarity with the reformers of Lower Canada, and to urge Upper Canadians to organize political unions to promote co-operation with Papineau and his compatriots. They also recommended the holding of meetings throughout the province to elect delegates to a convention that would "seek an effectual remedy for the grievances of the colonists." These meetings were not designed to foment rebellion, according to Read and Stagg but "to demonstrate [the participants'] resolution to have reform."[87]

The holding of a convention was not, strictly speaking, illegal. It was, however, extra-constitutional: there was no provision for such a gathering in the Upper Canadian constitution. Moreover, conventions were tainted, in the minds of tories at least, by associations with democracy, republicanism, and other threats to the established order, as Robert Gourlay had learned to his sorrow. Lacking any legal means of suppressing Mackenzie's public meetings, the tories and Orangemen once again responded with the use of force.

The episodes of violence associated with the political union movement of 1837 differed from those of previous occasions in two ways. First, the reformers were considerably more persistent than they had been in the past. In 1832 and 1833, a few violent incidents had convinced them to abstain from public meetings. In 1837, however, the meetings persisted in spite of Orange violence. In part, this was because of the second difference: a new strategy adopted by the reformers, who now took steps to protect themselves – including resorting to arms.

In the summer and fall of 1837 Mackenzie called a series of fifteen meetings in the Home and Gore districts. The purpose of these gatherings was "to appoint Delegates to the approaching Convention of the People of the two Canadas" and "to form associations to aid in obtaining the redress of our grievances."[88] As in the petitioning movement of 1831, Mackenzie himself was in attendance at these meetings to speak on behalf of reform. Similar gatherings took place in the London district and in Prescott county.[89]

Initial meetings in Newmarket on 3 August and Lloydtown on 5 August proceeded without incident. Alerted to rumours of Orange violence to come, however, fifty farmers from King township appointed themselves as escorts to Mackenzie on his way to the meeting of 7 August in Boltontown.[90] As soon as the meeting opened, "the Orangemen declared their intention of putting down the meeting, and of resorting to force if necessary." According to the tory *Toronto Patriot,* "no sooner had little Mackenzie mounted the *fatal* cart, with his chairman and secretary, than ... with a shout of '*Faugh a Ballagh,*' (anglice '*clear the way*'!) the whole concern was shoved into the Humber [River], and the rebel army was made to feel the power of an Irish Shillelagh."[91] Reform accounts, on the other hand, maintained that Mackenzie's escort had been attacked after the meeting on a bridge over the Humber and had vanquished their foes "with rails, sticks, and their heavy fists."[92] Wherever the victory lay, the significant development was that the reformers were in the process of abandoning their previous policy of avoiding violence and were retaliating with force themselves.

A week later, a meeting in Churchville on 15 August was disrupted by another outbreak of violence. A correspondent of Mackenzie's recalled a few days afterwards how an "Orange brute who first climbed the hustings with his shillelagh, crying 'No Popery! – No Surrender!' tried to throw you [Mackenzie] down, below the knives, whips and clubs, of his enraged and infuriated banditti."[93] According to another correspondent, this was a very deliberate attempt to murder Mackenzie.[94] Tory newspapers now openly threatened that Mackenzie would in fact be assassinated if he held any further meetings.[95]

Accordingly, four days after the Churchville affray, reformers came to the Vaughan meeting "each man with a solid oak or hickory stick." These precautionary measures had the desired effect, and the Orangemen "sneaked off without beat of drum."[96] Mackenzie's biographer recorded that Mackenzie and David Gibson were escorted from the meeting "by a cavalcade of about a hundred horsemen and some thirty carriages; and it appears to have been understood that, in future, the Orangemen, if they disturbed any more meetings, should be met by their own weapons."[97] Indeed, those invited to the Pickering meeting on 14 September, according to the *Toronto Patriot,* were "*recommended to come armed.*" To the delight of the tories, however, Mackenzie failed to appear, and they used the occasion to adjourn to a tavern and pass their own set of resolutions.[98]

Further incidents followed in the London district, where a riot occurred at a public meeting of the township of Bayham on 23 September to which both sides had come armed. The reformers were attacked on their way home, and another brawl ensued.[99] Two weeks later, a group of four hundred tories, apparently unarmed, marched to the site of a reform meeting in the town of London and dispersed the reformers.[100]

Predictably, the publications of both sides reviled the conduct of the other. The *Patriot*'s account of the Boltontown meeting sympathized with the Orangemen, who were "disgusted and enraged beyond all endurance at the impudence of those who had '*dared to invade the borders of their realm*' to preach sedition against our gracious Queen and glorious Constitution."[101] It was hinted at a tory meeting in Whitby that the government should take action against the reformers: "it is a matter of surprise to all our well-disposed inhabitants, that such men and Mackenzie, and his associates and adherents ... are *permitted* so long and so often to annoy by their pernicious fooleries and rank sedition, an enlightened and loyal people."[102]

The reformers were equally vehement in their denunciations of the extra-legal measures taken by tories and Orangemen to suppress their meetings. The *Hamilton Gazette* correctly observed that "the laws afford you no protection."[103] A correspondent of the *Constitution* argued that the people could now see "that what gives the government the power of countrouling and enslaving them, is the preservation of the existence of an organized armed banditti amongst them."[104] The resolutions of the reform meeting of 6 October in Middlesex condemned the aggression of the tories in no uncertain terms: "We find no language in which we can adequately express our indignation at the conduct of those Magistrates of the Home District, who having collected a mob of ignorant and misguided men, so disgracefully disturbed by the most brutal outrages the Reformers of that district, when convened for the purpose of peaceably and Constitutionally deliberating upon measures for the public good ... we look upon [such incidents] as almost tantamount on the part of the Government to a declaration of civil war."[105]

By the fall of 1837, then, it had become virtually impossible for reformers to hold lawful political meetings in the province. Their range of options had narrowed almost to the vanishing point. The peaceable reform meetings tapered off in October, to be replaced by instances of men drilling for battle, as the most exasperated and discouraged of the reformers turned to rebellion.

In the short term, then, conservative political violence played a critical role in the outbreak of rebellion in 1837. Its most obvious significance was as one of many grievances entertained by opponents of the Upper Canadian government. In general, as Paul Romney has argued, "the maladministration of justice [of which political violence was a part] was only a particularly glaring feature of a more general maladministration of the province by an elite that was politically unaccountable to the people."[106] The powerlessness of the Assembly, the strength of the Legislative Council, the bias of successive lieutenant-governors against reform, and the unresponsiveness of the Colonial Office were also a part of the lack of accountability. In the often-reiterated view of reformers, it was for this reason that the province suffered under an established church, exorbitant taxes, an inadequate educational system, a lack of prosperity, and many additional burdens. Political and economic developments of the late 1830s, including the recession of 1836 and the British government's treatment of Papineau and his supporters in Lower Canada, were additional factors that caused reformers grave concern.[107]

Beyond its importance as a grievance, the repeated and savage resort to arms by supporters of the government, as well as the failure of the administration to secure the right of free assembly, played a key role in undermining the legitimacy of the Upper Canadian state. As Mackenzie had put it as early as 1836, "The government is above all law."[108] This view received popular endorsement when the Lloydtown meeting of 5 August 1837 emphatically upheld the right of peaceful assembly. Its resolutions argued forcefully that any government which failed to protect this right "is founded upon usurpation, and not upon the sanction of a free people; therefore, not fitted to freemen, but to slaves."[109] Reformers meeting in Brock on 2 September 1837 shared a similar perspective; one of their resolutions declared that reformers were "without representation and virtually without *law.*"[110] Opponents of the government were increasingly of the view that a state that could not ensure the right of free assembly had forfeited its claim to the allegiance of its citizens.

Behind this rather theoretical critique lay a stark political reality: conservative violence blocked the only available route to reform. Reformers knew that their political opponents were firmly in control of the higher echelons of the provincial government. Accordingly, the only real hope of change lay with the British government. For a decade, reformers had tenaciously pursued the strategy of influencing British policy by organizing the expression of public opinion in Upper Canada. Time and again, however, violence had silenced their supporters. By the summer of 1837, it was virtually impossible to hold a public meeting in favour of reform in Upper Canada. There remained, therefore, no effective peaceful means of seeking the redress of grievances. Accordingly, a small minority of the disaffected[111] – as a last resort – chose the desperate expedient of rebellion.

THE REBELLION OF 1837 AND ITS AFTERMATH

The rebellion in Upper Canada (that is, the risings in Toronto and in the London district) were not a continuation of the reform petitioning movement by other means. It is true that William Lyon Mackenzie, who had been a moving spirit of among reform petitioners, was the leader of the rebellion in Toronto. It is also true that he was joined by many from that region who had supported his more peaceful initiatives. Similarly, Colin Read has found that in the London district, 80 of 197 identifiable insurgents had attended political meetings in the fall of 1837, and 24 of these are recorded as politically active before that date.[112] In two critically important respects, however, the rebellion represented a clear break from the reform petitioning campaigns. First, the insurgents' declared support for independence was an utter repudiation of the previous reform tradition of loyalty to Britain. In addition, the resort to violence was a dramatic departure from the peaceful means reformers had invariably adopted to forward their cause. The rebellion had important repercussions on the political culture of Upper Canada, consequences that would have a significant impact on subsequent efforts to effect political change.

The rebellion in Upper Canada was much less serious than its counterparts in Lower Canada, owing partly to the remarkable lack of preparedness on both sides.[113] The government's ability to defend itself was limited by Sir Francis Bond Head's decision, in October 1837, to send all the British troops quartered in the colony to Lower Canada to assist government forces there. This gesture did nothing to dampen Mackenzie's enthusiasm for radicalism. By mid-November he had not only published a draft constitution for the State of Upper Canada but had also persuaded some of his rasher followers to undertake plans for an armed rebellion. The outbreak of rebellion in Lower Canada fixed his resolve, though some of his less sanguine followers, including T.D. Morrison and John Rolph, "in every way ... tried to cover their tracks in the event of failure."[114]

Mackenzie's chances of success were much reduced by a last-minute change in the date of the rising, a result of the news that the Patriotes had met with defeat. Still, his attempted coup might well have succeeded, given the unprepared state of the government. The death by shooting of Anthony Anderson, the only experienced military man initially present among the rebel forces, and the dilatory behaviour of Mackenzie, who failed to press his advantage as his forces marched down Yonge Street on 5 December, sealed the fate of the rebels. By 7 December, the government had collected enough members of the militia to risk a confrontation with Mackenzie's forces. "The actual battle," as Read and Stagg report, "took only a few minutes."[115] Within a week, the smaller group of dissidents that Charles Duncombe had mobilized for revolt in the London district melted away under threat of a confrontation with the militia under the command of Mackenzie's old foe, Alan MacNab.

Though the risings were quickly suppressed, apprehensions of military disturbances in Upper Canada continued for some time.[116] Many of the movement's leaders, including Mackenzie himself, fled to the United States. Here, in alliance with sympathetic Americans, they busied themselves for the next year in plotting invasions of the colony. Mackenzie, occupying Navy Island on the Niagara River, proclaimed a provisional government for Upper Canada. This occupation soon led to serious tensions with the United States. In January 1838, MacNab ordered the destruction of an American steamer, the *Caroline*, which had been supplying the insurgents. The following month, a force of American invaders attacked Pelee Island in Lake Erie, only to be defeated in early March by a combination of British soldiers and militia. During the spring and summer of 1838, there were incidents in the Thousand Islands, where a Canadian-owned steamboat was burned, and on the Niagara frontier, where an invading force came to blows with a small detachment of cavalry. The province was once again thrown into an uproar after Prescott was invaded in mid-November 1838 and an invasion force arrived near Windsor a few weeks later. Many of these incidents triggered new rounds of civilian arrests, and, throughout this period, the province remained in a turmoil as a result of constant rumours of other projected invasions. Upper Canadians remained apprehensive of further unrest well into 1839.

In this scene of alarums and confusion, the activities of the authorities did much to diminish any remaining confidence in their even-handedness. Indeed, the aftermath of the rebellion was sometimes referred to as a "Reign of Terror." An early casualty was Marshall Spring Bidwell, a leading oppositionist since the early 1820s. Though there was no evidence that Bidwell was implicated in the rebellion, the lieutenant-governor persuaded him to leave Upper Canada on the grounds that his safety could not be guaranteed. His departure was a great loss, both for reformers and for the province's legal community. Other reform sympathizers with no direct connection to the rebellion also suffered, including James S. Howard and James Lesslie, who lost their positions as postmaster in Toronto and Dundas respectively. James and his brother William were also incarcerated for two weeks, though the evidence against them was too flimsy to support any charge.[117]

Plights like those of the Lesslies were all too common. Indeed, the roundup of hundreds of suspected insurgents in the aftermath of the rebellion featured a number of notable violations of due process. As Read and Stagg explain in regard to the Home district and surrounding areas: "people were brought in only because of their known reform sympathies, blank warrants were issued for the arrest of suspects, and individuals were taken up because of personal dislike on the part of a loyalist or loyalists. In some cases these professed loyalists appear to have been little more than bandits, looting and smashing as they searched for evidence of rebel activity or sympathy."[118] Malicious individuals cloaked in the garb of loyalty prosecuted private feuds with impunity; legislation passed in March 1838 granted immunity from prosecution to any who had assisted in suppressing rebellion, regardless of the legality of their actions.[119]

The ongoing process of the law kept the issues of the rebellion to the forefront of the public mind through 1838. The government's policy towards most of the offenders proved relatively lenient in the long run, though it was not immediately apparent that this would be the case. By March 1838 Upper Canadian officials had received instructions from Lord Glenelg at the Colonial Office urging that executions should be avoided if at all possible. Nevertheless, the Executive Council decided that two of the leading rebels from the Home district, Peter Matthews and Samuel Lount, should be punished by death. Public opinion, as expressed in petitions, was against their execution; the government received between 12,000 and 20,000 signatures on petitions for clemency on behalf of these men, who between them had fifteen children.[120] Nevertheless, Matthews and Lount were executed on 12 April 1838 in the courtyard of Toronto's jail, sacrificed to satisfy loyalist anger and to serve as a deterrent to others. These, however, were the only instances of execution in Upper Canada. Of the remaining prisoners, seventeen received a sentence of banishment. A further twenty were sentenced to transportation; those in this group who did not escape were released after arriving in Britain. By late 1838, the policy of issuing amnesties had begun, though it would be another eleven years before William Lyon Mackenzie would be free to return to Upper Canada.[121]

The fates of many lesser fry hung in the balance through much of 1838. While many of those imprisoned were quickly freed on bail, a good number of the remainder found that the wheels of justice turned very slowly indeed. Most of the trials were over by April 1838, but many who had decided to admit their guilt and petition for pardon remained in jail for months. For some, the wait proved fatal: they succumbed to the cold or to fevers like typhoid in the dank and overcrowded conditions of the jails in Toronto, Hamilton, and London. Other, more fortunate individuals, survived: fifty men endured the harsh conditions in Toronto until their release in May 1838. In June, eleven survivors were released in Hamilton, and twenty-four in London.[122] Yet more survivors were released in October.

The continuing relevance of issues relating to public security is illustrated by the misadventures of John O'Carroll and his family in Belleville. In 1838 O'Carroll began a fund-raising campaign on behalf of the local church. Members of the militia mistakenly concluded from the volume of his correspondence that he must be in league with the American Patriots. Accordingly, they commenced a campaign of harassment, repeatedly attacking O'Carroll's shop and threatening his family. O'Carroll not only suffered the indignity of imprisonment for eight weeks; he was also driven out of business.[123] As a result of incidents like this, it is not surprising that, as late as 1840, Mrs Moodie observed that "the ferment occasioned by the impotent rebellion of W.L. Mackenzie has hardly subsided."[124]

The outbreak of rebellion in Upper Canada, and the events that occurred afterwards, indicated just how far the province was from enjoying a party system featuring peaceful competition for office among contending forces.[125] Mackenzie's resort to armed conflict represented an utter denial of the legitimacy of the constituted authorities. Similarly, government forces were only too pleased to suppress by force of arms what they considered as sedition. More than a decade would pass before tories and reformers in Upper Canada reached a point of genuine mutual acceptance. The road to reconciliation had by that time been paved by the passage of time, major constitutional change, and a sustained public relations campaign by reformers on behalf of political parties.[126]

The immediate effect of the rebellion was that, as Read and Stagg put it, "the lines of division between tories and reformers hardened."[127] The gap between them, established during the petitioning campaigns of the late 1820s and the 1830s, was deepened and confirmed by the events of 1837 and 1838. This is not to say that time and circumstance could not alter political views.[128] But in some areas of the province, for some time, one's conduct during the rebellion served as a touchstone of political affiliation. In the western part of the province, for example, Colin Read found that "the revolt [provided] the Tories with a benchmark ... in that for years to come a man would be asked what he had done during the rebellion. If he had not turned out against the rebels, he must have been disloyal then and, in all probability, was disloyal still."[129] The rebellion, then, had the effect, at least in some quarters, of cementing political allegiances, helping pave the way for the emergence, in the Union period, of two political parties competing for power.

Another short-run effect of the rebellion was to put an end to efforts at reform, whether through popular politics or through other channels. The leaders who were not in exile or in prison were effectively silenced. Uncounted numbers of others, discouraged by economic as well as political prospects, joined the leadership in American exile. This exodus, along with the general hostility to reform activities, effectively shattered the organizations of popular politics.[130]

Before long, however, prospects appeared to be brighter, at least at the level of high politics. Sir Francis Bond Head was gone, replaced in early 1838 by Sir George Arthur. The most promising development, however, was the appointment in 1838 of the radical British peer Lord Durham as governor-in-chief of British North America, with a mandate to inquire into the causes of the rebellions in the Canadas. Indeed, the appearance of Lord Durham's Report early in 1839 provided the occasion for the revival of the popular politics of reform.

7 The Durham Meetings and Popular Politics in Upper Canada

"Lord Durham," commented Upper Canadian Lieutenant-Governor Sir George Arthur, "has thrown a firebrand amongst the People."[1] Aghast at Lord Durham's success in swinging Upper Canadian public opinion against the existing system of government, Arthur railed against the Durham meetings, powerful expressions of a new spirit of political reform. These Durham meetings[2] – sixteen in all – were held throughout the province in the summer and fall of 1839.[3] They attracted huge crowds in support of the principal recommendations of Lord Durham's recently published report: responsible government and the union of the Canadas.[4]

When the report became public in early 1839, prominent Upper Canadian tories lost no time in expressing to the British government their opposition to it. John Beverley Robinson, on sick leave in Britain, roundly denounced it in an extensive communication with the Colonial Office. In addition, select committees of both the Legislative Council and the Assembly produced scathing indictments of the report's principal recommendations, especially responsible government.[5] In response, the British government decided to postpone consideration of the "Canada question" for some months.[6] In the interim, Upper Canadian supporters of Durham's recommendations urgently seized the opportunity to impress the British government with the extent of popular enthusiasm for fundamental political change.

Though Durham had spent little time in Upper Canada, his recommendations did more than anything else to revive the movement there for reform. In the aftermath of the Rebellion of 1837, as we have seen, that movement was very much under a cloud. Its leaders had been exiled, its demands decisively rejected. Durham's Report changed all that. By endorsing responsible government, one of the key demands of the pre-Rebellion reform movement, Durham instantly legitimized it, and restored the credibility of moderate constitutional reform in Upper Canadian political culture. Correspondingly, the report created awkward difficulties for the tories, who had historically opposed this change. Divided amongst themselves, they were poorly situated to re-enter the arena of popular politics and launch the kind of counter-offensive that had buttressed their political positions in the past.

LEADERSHIP OF THE DURHAM MOVEMENT

Durham's Report allowed reformers to position themselves more advantageously than ever before in relation to imperial policy. Since the days of Gourlay, oppositionists had been in the position of mobilizing public opinion in opposition to the declared policies of the British government. This was true whether the issue was the payment of war losses, the Alien Bill, the clergy reserves, judicial issues, or constitutional reform. The fact that responsible government had now been endorsed by a high official of the British government, however, allowed reformers in 1839 to portray themselves as supporting a leading British proponent of political change. It is true that Lord John Russell, the leading member of the Whig ministry, wavered in his enthusiasm for the doctrine during the summer of 1839. This, however, only made it more urgent for reformers to demonstrate the support of Upper Canadians for this key recommendation.[7]

Robert Gourlay, temporarily returned to Upper Canada, was the first to call for petitioning on behalf of Durham's Report, illustrating the continuity of the Durham meetings with the oppositional petitioning of previous decades. His effort, however, to hold a meeting in Grantham in the Niagara district in early February 1839 failed to spark immediate imitators.[8] Four months later he took up the cause again, and, as he later said, "advised holding meetings in every township, to support it [Durham's Report] against the wretched opposition got up in the Assembly."[9] His subsequent role in the movement, however, appears to have been largely confined to publicizing the cause in the Niagara district and to appearing at the Thorold meeting in September 1839.[10] The torch of leadership in oppositional popular politics had evidently passed to a new generation of leaders.

The individuals who mobilized public opinion in favour of the report were not the most radical of those who had succeeded Gourlay in the decade before the Rebellion. Key members of the former Central

Committee – William Lyon Mackenzie, T.D. Morrison, and Jesse Ketchum, for example – were all in American exile. In their absence, reform political organizations had essentially fallen apart.[11] Into the vacuum thus created now stepped another core of organizers – moderates who were untainted by participation in the Rebellion of 1837. They were not, however, individuals without political experience. For example, W.W. Baldwin, the leading spirit behind the Durham meeting in the Home district, had been active in the province's politics for a generation. Moreover, Baldwin's experience in popular politics included petitioning on behalf of Willis and judicial reform in 1828, as well as mobilizing opposition to Head before and after the 1836 election. Baldwin was assisted by Francis Hincks, who had taken an active part in the Constitutional Reform Society in 1836, and who was now editor of the *Toronto Examiner.* In keeping with his new political prominence, Hincks was busy intriguing with Niagara reformers to promote a forthcoming Durham meeting. He was also forwarding reform fortunes by electioneering in the village of Markham, and doubtless in other centres as well.[12] The wily Hincks was thinking ahead as usual, hoping to use the Durham meetings as a springboard for future electoral organization.

The presence among Durhamites of a number of "Old Reformers" – long active in the cause – offered further evidence of continuity with the pre-Rebellion reform movement. Caleb Hopkins, who had twice represented the county of Halton in the Assembly (1828–30, 1834–6) was one of those "Old Reformers" outside of Toronto. Richard Woodruff, an MPP whose brother William had also been a strong supporter of the oppositionist cause during the 1830s, was one of the Niagara activists. The Durham movement also attracted a number of new recruits to the cause of reform, among them W.H. Merritt,[13] George Tiffany, W.H. Notman, and I.W. Powell. In the 1840s, all of these men would play a significant role in the reform party.[14] Indeed, a significant result of the Durham meetings was to mobilize new support for the cause of reform.

Like the meetings in support of Mackenzie in 1832, in most respects the Durham meetings remained a product of local initiative and organization. In every instance, local men took the chair and moved most of the resolutions.[15] Although the resolutions produced by the meetings conveyed similar concerns, their wording and content generally differed considerably.[16] Further evidence of the decentralized character of the movement is provided by the variety of forms the meetings assumed. In seven cases there was in effect a district meeting, usually called by the sheriff in response to a "requisition" from members of the public. District meetings occurred in the Newcastle, Niagara, Gore,

Talbot, and Home districts. The meeting in Galt, Wellington district, took place after the militia drill in early June and may also have had the character of a district meeting.[17] In nine cases, activists varied the format by holding township meetings. Such variations, much like those of the meetings in support of Mackenzie in early 1832, conveyed the sense that there was widespread grassroots support for the cause.

Organizers of some Durham meetings perceived the meetings as a springboard for the creation of organizations similar to political unions. The Niagara meeting in June 1839, for example, urged the establishment of a "Durham Constitutional Club."[18] At the Murray, Thora, and Mara Township meetings, on the other hand, the friends of responsible government were urged to hold future meetings to demonstrate their approval of Durham's Report.[19] The gatherings in Guelph and in the Talbot district adopted another strategy and established corresponding committees.[20] The Toronto activists formed a committee in the fall of 1839 to bring pressure on the authorities to allow a Durham meeting in the Home district. After the meeting was aborted, another committee was established to promote the objects of the organizers. The meetings, then, were seen as a prelude to further activity, although this was not always immediately forthcoming.

The meetings may have been orchestrated by reformers partly for electoral purposes, but their objective, like that of previous oppositionist petitioning campaigns, was to reach beyond committed and potential oppositionists to demonstrate that the wider public supported their cause. Accordingly, the Durhamites refined and improved upon accustomed methods of attracting widespread attendance. The meetings were open not just to freeholders but to all inhabitants. This was true in Galt, Halton, Beaverton, Gore, Guelph, Eldon (Newcastle district), Niagara, Cooksville, and the Home district.[21] The Niagara district meeting reportedly included "resident aliens and other non-voters."[22] The meetings in the Town of Niagara and for the Talbot district were probably also attended by non-electors, while the remainder were meetings of freeholders only. Therefore, at the largest and most important of the Durham meetings, the participation of non-electors was deliberately encouraged.

In addition, organizers of the Durham meetings made extensive use of publicity. Many of the meetings were preceded by the circulation of public requisitions signed by a sizeable number of inhabitants; there were 196 signatures on the Thorold requisition, for example.[23] Although only the most "respectable" of the inhabitants seem to have signed the requisitions, their circulation spread the message for the Durham meetings to excellent effect – as did the newspaper notices of forthcoming meetings. The widest possible publicity was given to the

Home district meeting; newspapers as far away as the *Brockville Recorder* published numerous records of the unsuccessful efforts of the Durhamites to encourage the sheriff of the Home district to call a public meeting.[24] Other forms of publicity included large posters, such as those printed for the Niagara District meeting,[25] and handbills like those announcing the meetings for Halton and for the Townships of Haldimand and Murray (Newcastle district). The Haldimand Township handbill proclaimed that "An adjourned meeting, for the purpose of taking into consideration 'LORD DURHAM'S REPORT', will be held at the Widow Brown's INN, Haldimand four corners, on the first day of July next."[26] Durhamites exploited the media of their day to the full in their efforts to attract widespread participation in the Durham meetings.

But perhaps the most effective means of attracting popular support involved the use of flags, banners, and processions to a much greater extent than at previous oppositionist gatherings. The reformers had evidently learned a good deal from such expert practitioners of popular politics as Colonel Talbot! Thus, in Cobourg a procession of wagons was accompanied by two flags inscribed "Lord Durham and Reform."[27] More modestly, the Haldimand township meeting took place, "under a Durham flag."[28] Two banners were raised after the Murray meeting, including one with the motto "Lord Durham and Reform."[29] After the Dundas meeting, participants marched into the town "preceded by a party with flags prepared for the occasion, bearing appropriate inscriptions, such as 'Victoria and the Constitution,' and 'Durham and Reform.' "[30] The Hamilton meeting began with a procession of forty wagons bearing three banners with the devices "Victoria and the Constitution," "Durham and Responsibility," and "Durham and Reform."[31] After the meeting, a group from Dundas departed under a flying banner. The flags at the Thorold meeting made a vivid impression on one observer: "Of flags we only saw a brace; one of pink calico ... upon which 'St Davids', 'Unity is Strength', and 'Durham and Responsibility' figured in amiable juxta-position; the other flag was a silk one, furnished as a substitute for speech by the Queenstonians."[32]

The most spectacular display was at the Talbot district meeting in Simcoe, with a procession both before and after the meeting: "There were at least 2000 persons present ... They consisted chiefly of the wealthy farmers of the district, having come to the place, in about 300 waggons, besides a number on horseback. One cavalcade from the Vittoria side, consisted of 137 wagons in one train: and 90 from the Waterford side. The remainder came from different parts ... There were no flags displayed, until the meeting broke up, when the *Union Jack* was hoisted in a waggon drawn by four horses, in which was a small band of key bugles, which preceded the returning party to Vittoria." In using flags, banners, and processions, the meeting organizers were not only imitating the example of the tories earlier in the decade; they were also quite deliberately incorporating well-known aspects of popular political theatre and consciously exploiting the traditions of British street politics, both of which dated back at least to the mid-eighteenth century and which had been adopted in the United States as well.[33]

THE DURHAM MEETINGS

The message of diversity enhanced the effectiveness of the Durham meetings by emphasizing the broad nature of support in different regions and at different levels of society. In other respects, a show of unanimity seemed more effective. Organizers achieved this effect by highlighting the nonpartisanship of the meetings, the respectability of the organizers, the orderliness of crowd behaviour, and the loyalism of the movement.

Although these gatherings were organized largely by known reformers and supported reform policies, especially responsible government, strenuous efforts were made to showcase their alleged nonpartisanship. On some occasions the presence of well-known tories ensured that a diversity of views would find expression. For example, several speakers at the Halton meeting – including the chair of the meeting, the Honourable James Crooks – denounced responsible government. Sir Allan MacNab, arch-tory and anti-democrat, took a leading part at the Hamilton meeting the following day. MacNab moved resolutions in opposition to Lord Durham's Report, thereby lending credibility to Durhamite claims that the meeting was of a genuinely non-party character. The appearance of nonpartisanship was also highlighted by the actual content of a number of the resolutions and speeches.[34] The resolutions of the Niagara township meeting, for example, "deeply deplore[d] the lamentable state to which this Province has been reduced by the wicked machination of factious and designing men of all parties."[35] In Hamilton, moreover, Adam Fergusson began his lengthy speech by lamenting the extent of "vituperation and rancour" in the province since the Rebellion and commented favourably on the nonpartisan makeup of the crowd. At the Niagara district meeting in Thorold, W.H. Merritt similarly denounced party spirit as the product of the selfish designs of those in power. By way of contrast, Merritt himself touted the merits of "unanimity, organization, and the holding of similar meetings all over the province."[36] One newspaper editor was well aware that tactical considerations mandated public rather than party meetings. The editor of the *St Catharines Journal* wrote that to hold meetings of an overtly reform character "would give [them] the character of a *party*, instead of a publick, meeting, to the former of which, we are decidedly opposed. Constitutional Reformers are *not* a party, in Upper Canada: they comprise the PEOPLE."[37]

The emphasis on nonpartisanship, while somewhat misleading, was useful in the prevailing ideological climate. A second theme was the respectability of those behind the campaign. The leaders at the Durham meetings – those who moved the resolutions – were local notables, MPPs, doctors, lawyers, and other "natural leaders" of that society. The Halton meeting, for example, was chaired by the Honourable James Crooks, a former MPP for the county, and addressed by, among others, Dr James Hamilton, Dr Thomas of Hamilton, and Caleb Hopkins. The Hamilton meeting the following day was chaired by the sheriff, Allan Macdonnell. Among those who addressed the meeting were Mr Aikman, the MPP for Wentworth, and the Honourable Adam Fergusson, who had recently been appointed to the Legislative Council.[38] The Thorold meeting on 14 September was chaired by a military hero, John A. Ball, "who managed the only field-piece engaged on Queenston heights, on the memorable 13th October, 1812, with so much credit to himself, and usefulness to his country."[39] The meeting was addressed at length by Captain Eccles, who was followed by former MPP William Woodruff, MPP David Thorburn, and W.H. Merritt, MPP, local business leader, and erstwhile Welland Canal promoter. A week later, Merritt and William Notman, a future reform leader in Hamilton, addressed the Talbot meeting. The leadership of the Durham meetings, then, consisted for the most part of highly respectable individuals prominent in their own localities.

Sympathetic newspapers lost no opportunity to emphasize the respectability of those who took a leading role in running the meetings. The *St Catharines Journal* of 1 August 1839 highlighted the accomplishments of legislative councillor Adam Fergusson: "Mr Fergusson is a gentleman of high respectability, and great influence on the country, and his accession to the liberal cause, cannot fail to be of the greatest importance." The *British Colonist* was similarly alert to the social and political standing of Durhamites in Hamilton, impressing on readers that 3 MPPs signed the requisition that called the meeting, "as well as ... the leading professional and mercantile gentlemen of Hamilton."[40] As we shall see, however, this did not guarantee them immunity from the kinds of attacks to which Mackenzie and Ryerson had been subjected earlier in the decade.

In addition to nonpartisanship and respectability, the Durhamites put extraordinary emphasis on orderly behaviour. This stress on nonviolence was typical of oppositionist meetings, but it took on a new importance in the aftermath of the Rebellion. After more than a year of turmoil in Upper Canada, provincial authorities were preternaturally nervous about the possibility of armed insurrection and the threat posed by any kind of disorder. Durhamite organizers accordingly understood that any violent disruptions would greatly harm their cause. An episode of "riotous occurrences" in the historically volatile Newcastle district early in the summer heightened their sensitivity on this point. The occasion was the muster of part of the 3rd regiment of Northumberland militia in the village of Brighton on 4 June, and of the remainder of the regiment in Percy on the following day. On 4 June in Brighton, the colonel of the Regiment, Sheriff Henry Ruttan, ignited political passions by endorsing Lord Durham's Report in a speech to his troops.[41] An immediate flashpoint was a flag bearing the slogan "Lord Durham and Reform," which was flying in front of the local tavern at the time. Many wanted to tear it down, but Ruttan persuaded the man who had erected it to remove it in the interests of keeping the peace. After the militia had been dismissed, the flag was paraded through the street. Later in the day, several flags were "carried in wagons through the village."[42] The excitement continued into the following day, when a soldier was badly beaten in an incident involving an American flag. A riot later ensued involving about twelve loyalists and sixty "radicals."[43] The incidents gained a measure of more than local notoriety and served as a cautionary tale for organizers of meetings elsewhere.[44]

Accordingly, organizers of Durham meetings astutely determined to preserve their meetings from any taint of violence. This was a challenging assignment in view of the large numbers present and the contentiousness of the issues before them, but the Durhamites rose to the occasion. They were especially anxious to ensure that the symbols displayed at the meetings reinforced the theme of loyalty to Britain, giving opponents no pretext to attack them as disloyal or treasonable. In Simcoe, in the Talbot district, participants obeyed advance warnings "that no flag, standard, or insignia of any kind, *other than the UNION JACK* be permitted to be brought to, or displayed at the meeting."[45] As we have seen, many flags and banners at other meetings bore the names of Queen Victoria and Lord Durham, firmly associating the movement with the British monarchy and constitution rather than the republicanism and democracy of the United States. Above all, flags conveying even the slightest hint of Americanism were unacceptable to meeting organizers. Before the Thorold gathering, for example, a magistrate by the name of Adams discouraged would-be participants from parading with a provocative flag, said to have been "a tri-color, with three horizontal stripes running through it in the American mode, and a star figuring at the end of 'Durham and Responsibility', while a villainous caricature of Britain's cross was stuck in the corner as a kind of saving clause."[46]

Provocative symbolism by no means represented the only threat to organizers' efforts to impose order and enforce harmony. In Hamilton, a Mr Applegarth, who spoke to the crowd in an insulting way calculated to provoke violence, was repeatedly called to order by the chair. Then, when a Mr Holt proposed a resolution calling for the dissolution of the House of Assembly, he was frequently and loudly interrupted by opponents. At this point the organizers moved in and decided in the interests of preserving order to put the rest of the resolutions to the meeting in a body, together with Sir Allan MacNab's amendments.[47]

The procedures adopted at the Durham meetings were well calculated to reinforce the impression of orderliness. The meetings were generally called and advertised well in advance; they were run by a prominent individual who took the chair; and speakers made lengthy speeches before introducing resolutions to be endorsed by the participants. In adopting the ordered procedures of other formal public meetings, the organizers emphasized and enforced the orderly, nonviolent character of their proceedings.

The Durhamites' rejection of violence rested on more than one foundation. In a pragmatic sense, violence would have invited repression under circumstances in which their opponents enjoyed a monopoly of the legitimate use of force. The use of violence would also have been politically damaging to reformers insofar as it reminded waverers of the debacle of the Rebellion. The Durhamites rejected violence, however, for more than purely expedient reasons. Some, like W.W. Baldwin, a leading lawyer and politician, believed on principle that the use of violence against political opponents was "in the strictest sense uncivilized." Moreover, it violated the rule of law, a fundamental principle of the British constitution as understood by Baldwin and other reformers; for this reason also it was unacceptable.[48] The use of the unenfranchised as shock-troops and enforcers remained distinctly tory weapons. In offering a clear alternative to tory ruffianism, the reformers continued to discredit one of the most significant aspects of early tory governance.

If the form of the Durham meetings was dictated by the need to demonstrate nonpartisanship, respectability, and a sense of order, the content of the speeches and resolutions was powerfully affected by the necessity of stressing loyalty. The idea of "loyalty," as we have seen, was the essence of tory ideology in Upper Canada.[49] "Loyalty" meant focusing on the British heritage of the province; on the bond with Great Britain rather than on ties of geography with the United States; on the monarchy and the British constitution rather than on the democracy and republicanism which flourished south of the border.[50] The task of the Durhamites was to demonstrate their support for change without in any way leaving themselves open to charges of disloyalty. Their every effort was predicated on their understanding that it was possible to criticize the provincial administration only in a context of firmly delineated loyalty to British institutions.[51]

Caleb Hopkins, a former MPP, offered his personal interpretation of the relationship between loyalty and reform at the Hamilton meeting. Hopkins identified reform with the United Empire Loyalists, founders of the province, whose sacrifices for King and empire were the stuff of legend.[52] Among their numbers was Hopkins's father who had left the United States "from his attachment to the British Constitution." Bitter disappointment awaited his descendants in Upper Canada, for they were "deprived of those rights for which their fathers had abandoned their property and the land of their birth." The loyalism of Upper Canada's founders, however, had now found expression in the reform tradition in Upper Canada. According to Hopkins' vision of the colonial past, the "Mackenzie parliament" (1834–36) sought "the exercise of the British Constitution in its purity … a responsible Government." The obstacle to attainment of the true British constitution was not the British government but the provincial administration: the people "were loyal to their Sovereign, but they were disgusted with the oligarchy that ruled the country." Hopkins' analysis was a complete inversion of conservative interpretations of the loyalist myth; it offered a pertinent illustration of how a tory vocabulary could be adapted for the purpose of furthering reform goals.[53]

More colourful than Hopkins's effort was a speech to similar effect in Thorold by one Captain Eccles, who spoke in blank verse; the *Niagara Chronicle* transposed it into rhyming couplets that took up an entire column of tiny print. The speech included an attack on the tory House of Assembly, followed by an endorsement of responsible government as allegedly practised in Britain. Eccles argued that the cure for the evils of the province was responsible government, and lamented that the draft Bill of Union contained no mention of it. It was responsibility that distinguished England from continental and other despotisms. Eccles concluded:

> Responsibility … pulpits and presses …
> Should echo it, and Kings and Queens
> Obey it – maidens in their teens
> Should dream of nothing else, and every wife
> Of every sort, and size, and rank of life,

Ought to demand it – let the first faint cry
Of childhood be 'responsibility'.
In one full swelling chorus let it sweep
Across the billows of the mighty deep,
And rouse the British nation from its snooze,
Till Whigs and Tories tremble in their shoes.[54]

This speech was a hard act to follow, but other participants in the proceedings were equal to the task. For example, David Thorburn, MPP, insisted that responsible government was the British system of government and in no way inconsistent with the British connection. Further, Thorburn stoutly maintained that the loyalty of Upper Canadians was beyond reproach: "Every report that is sent home," he said, "applauds their courage and loyalty, and they have on every occasion, as they are now ready to do, shown themselves the enemies of republicanism and of that lawless democratic spirit to which it gives birth." No tory could have excelled Thorburn's denunciation of the United States and its twin evils of republicanism and democracy!

The resolutions of the Durham meetings echoed the themes of the speeches.[55] At all but one of the meetings (Toronto township), responsible government was explicitly endorsed, clearly identified as "the British principle of government."[56] The Hamilton and Eldon resolutions insisted that responsible government was the key to a closer relationship with Great Britain. It was maintained at a number of meetings that Upper Canadians without responsible government did not enjoy the same rights as other British subjects. As the Thorold resolutions plaintively put it, "The inhabitants of this province do not conceive that, by being transplanted from Great Britain to Canada, they become so debased, so degraded, so degenerated, as to be disqualified from enjoying here, the rights and privileges which their fellow subjects enjoy, in the parent land." The Murray resolutions put a more positive spin on the same point: "It is the inherent right of the people of this province as British freemen, to have their affairs directed by a government possessing the confidence of the House of Assembly."

Although the resolutions were passed by loyal subjects, the actions of some members of the British government did occasionally receive muted criticism. The Murray resolutions stated that remonstrances against the system had been in vain and expressed disappointment that the British government refused to assent to Lord Durham's Report. They also indicated dissatisfaction with Lord John Russell's declaration of 3 June against responsible government. Russell's proposed Bill of Union was condemned at the Lennox and Addington meeting. The Beaverton Durhamites disapproved of the evident reluctance of the British government to address Upper Canadian problems. Their counterparts in Thorold were unhappy that Lord Durham's recommendations were apparently not being given serious consideration. This gathering also expressed dismay that the British government would delay settlement of the Canada question as a result of the Assembly's report and disapproved of the draft Bill of Union because it did not contain provision for responsible government. The Toronto resolutions expressed concern that Lord Normanby, the colonial secretary, doubted the practical applicability of responsible government to the working of the provincial constitution.

Not the British government, however, but the government and administration of Upper Canada received the harshest criticism.[57] This is significant in view of claims that the Rebellion itself was first and foremost the result of the agitation of William Lyon Mackenzie and a few of his followers, as some recent historians of that event have claimed.[58] While the actual resort to violence may have been largely Mackenzie's work, the grievances he documented continued to be widely felt, as the resolutions of many of the Durham meetings confirm.[59] The Niagara resolutions were explicit "that great discontent and dissatisfaction still remain amongst the honest reformers of this Province," and they enumerated various problems: the monopolization of patronage by members of the Family Compact, the partisanship of judges, sheriffs, and magistrates, and the inadequacies of the educational system. They identified deficiencies in the educational system as a prime culprit in creating disorder in the province: "An erroneous system of education among the wealthy ... has left them in utter ignorance of the common principles of good government, and ... the total absence of all means of obtaining education among the great body of the working classes ... [means that] many have been made the dupes of the designing, and the wicked." The shortcomings of the provincial government did not end there, however. The banking system and the land department were condemned at the Niagara meeting, where participants urged that the clergy reserves question should be settled by the provincial legislature in accordance with the wishes of the people.

Although the resolutions of other meetings were less specific about particular grievances, most commented strenuously and adversely upon the administration of the province. The Murray resolutions melodramatically described Upper Canada as "a land of pestilence and famine" and attributed the problems of the province to the "absence of all constitutional government, and the substitution in its place of the despotism of an oligarchy at Toronto." They continued: "A few metropolitan families in Toronto, popularly known as the Family Compact, have for years directed the affairs of this Province, distributing the Executive patronage by their influence over successive Governors, and nullifying the labours of the peoples' representatives by their votes as Legislative Councillors." Participants at the Hamilton meeting expressed a lack of confidence "in those who are known to exercise an undue influence over the government of the country, and who are termed ... the Family Compact," while the Beaverton crowd opposed "the few who wish to enrich themselves at the public expense," identified as the only ones who continued to support the present government. In Talbot, the assembled participants expressed a lack of confidence in those "who are known to exercise an undue influence over the government of the country." Among specific grievances, emigration and the lack of public improvements were singled out at the Beaverton meeting, while regulations concerning land, trade, and education were condemned at the Toronto township meeting. Participants at the Talbot and Toronto meetings expressed concern about emigration from the province. The state of "this fast sinking and degraded country" was lamented at the Lennox and Addington meeting.

These Durhamite assaults on the government of a British colony endeavoured to avoid the taint of republicanism or democracy by adapting arguments perfected by adversaries of the British government in the mid-eighteenth century. British oppositionists of the 1760s had not held the King responsible for governmental abuses; instead, they attacked his ministers "behind the curtain," especially Lord Bute. Bute was condemned as an "overmighty subject," who was "unaccountable to others, and thereby threatening to the balance of the constitution."[60] Like those British opponents of the Ministry, Upper Canadian reformers reserved their heaviest artillery not for the British government, whose intentions were considered relatively benign, but for the local oligarchy, a kind of surrogate set of advisors "behind the curtain" who perverted the proper course of government for their own selfish ends. It was an argument that reformers would adapt and refine for some years to come.[61]

Closely allied to that local oligarchy was the provincial Assembly, another target of widespread complaint. In Niagara, Thorold, Lennox and Addington, and Toronto, resolutions denied that it possessed the confidence of the people. According to participants at the Niagara meeting, this was no doubt due in part to the corrupt means employed by tories to win the election of 1836. The Lennox and Addington and Toronto resolutions suggested that this gross abuse should be corrected by a dissolution of the provincial Parliament and a new election. This would have occurred in any case had the Assembly not prolonged its life in spite of the death of the King, an action roundly condemned in Niagara, Hamilton, Thorold, and Talbot. Because the Assembly lacked legitimacy, the imperial government would surely be safe to disregard the recommendations of the Committee of the Assembly which condemned Durham's report, as was urged at the Toronto township meeting. In contrast, the Murray resolutions looked to the future, promoting the election of "men of firmness and temper who will insist on the recognition of their inherent rights." Those in Hamilton and Eldon more specifically pledged themselves to support candidates favourable to Lord Durham's Report. The Durhamite critique of the provincial administration was in many respects harsh and unforgiving, but it received protective colouration from convincing protestations of loyalty on the part of organizers and participants.

The organization of the more crowd-oriented aspects of the meetings also built on the theme of loyalty. In deploying elements of popular political theatre the Durhamites were challenging the political views of the authorities; these elements, however, were employed in a way that stressed the message of loyalism. The symbols, as we have seen, were carefully screened to ensure that they reinforced the message of loyalty to Britain. The use of flags, banners, processions, and bugles bore considerable similarity to a military procession. Militia parades were a familiar sight to Upper Canadians, and British troops had staged their own parades in the province over the years. Reform loyalty to the British connection was thus emphasized by the appropriation of military symbolism.[62]

The Durhamites' use of public space carried a similar message. The meetings generally took place at the typical gathering places of the day: in the public squares where sheriff's meetings would normally be held and, in smaller centres, in front of the taverns which were also the meeting place for the militia. This use of public space helped to identify the Durhamite cause with the virtues of respectability, loyalism, and continuity.[63]

THE RESPONSE TO THE DURHAM MEETINGS

In organizing the meetings, the Durhamites were constrained by the need to balance demands for fundamental political change against the requirement that they demonstrate their nonpartisan, respectable, orderly, and loyal character. Strong leadership and clear messages were vital to protect the meetings from official suppression. The Durhamites were keenly aware that the authorities, opposed as they were to Durham's recommendations, would seize on any pretext to suppress meetings held to express support for political change. Provincial authorities, as we have seen, had never accepted the legitimacy of opposition.[64] In the aftermath of the Rebellion, their concern was accentuated by fears of the consequences of Durham's report. Supporters of the status quo were haunted by the ongoing possibility of internal subversion, American invasion by members of the Hunters' lodge, or both at once.[65] The right of public assembly, as in the summer of 1837, was again thrown into jeopardy.[66] In July 1839 Lieutenant-Governor Arthur discountenanced the public airing of political questions by issuing a militia general order condemning discussions about politics on militia training days. He further underlined his disapproval of any challenge to the administration, however remote, with the threat of military repression; on at least two occasions he sent troops in anticipation of disorder at Durham meetings.[67]

The tactics of the Durhamites, however, forced even the lieutenant-governor to grant the meetings a measure of legitimacy. Thus he did not actually call the military into action against any of the Durham meetings. In part that was because the highly ritualized conduct of the meetings had offered no pretext for official suppression. Beyond this, Arthur dignified the meetings by offering a public commentary. In answer to the Gore district meeting, Arthur made a statement on 24 August, stating that because the resolutions originated with "so respectable a meeting," they demanded a response.[68] In spite of this courteous beginning, Arthur rejected responsible government as inconsistent with the colony's relationship with Great Britain; moreover, he declined to dissolve the Assembly and submit the question of responsible government to the people. The lieutenant-governor did however indicate that the British government was anxious to accede to all reasonable demands, and expressed sympathy with a number of grievances, like those relating to education and trade. These apparent concessions were clear forerunners of the later Sydenhamite effort to co-opt the opposition.[69]

Though Arthur's answer to the Durhamites was less than encouraging, it is significant that it was offered at all. His predecessor, Sir John Colborne, as we have seen, reacted to oppositionist petitions and addresses in 1831 at best with exasperated non-committalism and at worst with vitriolic hostility.[70] The symbolic importance of the civility of Arthur's response to the Durhamites could not have been lost on anyone following Upper Canadian politics in 1839. Despite the oppositional nature of the resolutions, and notwithstanding the elements of popular participation at that meeting, the respectability of the Durhamites had forced the authorities to concede a measure of legitimacy to their meetings.

Nonetheless, at lower levels of the provincial administration, lesser officials vented their disapproval of the Durhamites through harassment of various kinds. This, of course, reflected their belief that the

Durhamites included among their numbers many"warm partizans," as Arthur put it, who were "engaged in the late Rebellion."[71] The *Kingston Chronicle* offered as the unvarnished truth the statement that "the first of the Durham meetings in the Newcastle District were [*sic*] principally composed of rebels and traitors, met for the purpose of encouraging the plunder and invasion of the country."[72] Similarly, the *Cobourg Star* asserted that the Haldimand Durham meeting was an "infamous attempt to rekindle the embers of rebellion."[73] The *Toronto Patriot*, meanwhile, revived the charge of disloyalty against those who had attended the Yonge Street Durham meeting. These imputations, in turn, were hotly denied by a group who had attended the meeting, including Elmes Steele, future reform candidate for the county of Simcoe.[74]

A broadside published by forces hostile to the Yonge Street Durhamites gave full vent to tory antagonism.[75] This classic example of Upper Canadian political invective showcased a remarkably varied array of anti-reform images, highlighting republicanism, disloyalty, military incompetence, social inferiority, religious irregularity, and sexual immorality. Entitled "GREAT DURHAM MEETING on Yonge Street," it purported to be an advertisement for the gathering, and addressed itself to "Friends of Responsible Government, Lord Durham's Report, Republican Simplicity, Free Institutions, and True Liberty." A procession, it announced, would be held prior to the meeting, and the event it described was a detailed parody of a military funeral procession.[76] In fact, it suggested a reversal of Mackenzie's march down Yonge Street in the 1837 Rebellion. Participants were to meet at the Toronto jail, where so many reform sympathizers had been incarcerated in the aftermath of the Rebellion. They would then march up Yonge Street, headed by an advanced guard with swords reversed, as in a military funeral. A band would play the pro-American tune, "Hail Columbia." The standard-bearer was to be "Mr EXAMINER HINCKS, in full uniform of the Hunter's Lodges, bearing on a pole ... the Declaration of Independence!!!" Egerton Ryerson would be the "trumpeter on horseback," carrying a bowie knife, a symbol of rough American frontierism and crude violence. He was to be followed by a Durhamite decked out in a cap of liberty, symbol of French revolutionary jacobinism.[77] Also included in the procession would be "MARTYRS OF LIBERTY," "consisting of those distinguished Patriots imprisoned for Political Opinions by Sir F.B. Head, during the Reign of Terror." A note at the end of the document observed that "Those Durhamites who have ever distinguished themselves as the slayers of Moodie, Burners of Dr Horne's House, Cobourg Conspirators, &c. are entitled to precedence." Moreover, the procession would halt at Gallows Hill, near the present St Clair Avenue in Toronto. Significantly, the encounter between Mackenzie's forces and the defenders of Toronto was often called "the battle of Gallows Hill."[78] At this location, Dr Baldwin would pronounce "a funeral oration on the first martyrs, LOUNT & MATTHEWS," the two Upper Canadians executed for their part in the Rebellion. The document ended with the supposedly republican slogan "GOD SAVE THE PEOPLE!!!" in place of the monarchist watchwords, "God Save the Queen."

In keeping with the strong implication of Durhamite support for the Rebellion were suggestions of military incompetence, allied with rustic ignorance,[79] on the part of the Durhamites. Flanking Dr Baldwin were two Durhamites mounted on jackasses, their coats turned, and "blowing a penny whistle." Baldwin's uniform was that of a general officer of the Vinegar Hill Croppies, a reference to the rustic Irish rebels of the 1790s. Later on, two other Durhamites would be preceded by a fife and drum playing the "Rogue's March," suggestive of both military disgrace and of the morals of camp followers.[80]

In addition to employing new symbolism associated with the Rebellion, the broadsheet exhibited continuity with the insults hurled earlier in the decade at Mackenzie's supporters among the non-Anglican religious denominations of the province. In the procession, the Methodists were to be represented not only by Egerton Ryerson but also by "TRAVELLING PREACHERS on Horseback with saddlebags," and a prominent place was to go to W.J. O'Grady, a one-time close associate of William Lyon Mackenzie. O'Grady was a defrocked priest who had been excommunicated from the Catholic Church in 1833 amidst allegations of sexual immorality. Significantly, O'Grady, who was unmarried and officially childless, was to be "attended by his numerous offspring."[81] The broadside claimed that another disreputable Irishman, Ogle Gowan, who had recently endorsed responsible government, would appear in the procession as "Clown of the Ring," and would "give a full explanation of the charge of having run away with the money from the Orange Lodge in Ireland."

Ironically, in view of the Durhamite stress on order and the behaviour of their opponents, this broadside suggested that the Durhamites intended to administer a sound beating to their political opponents. "No Bloody Orangeman," it declared, "Damned Tory, Compact Man or Irresponsible Loyalist dare shew his face, on pain of a sound cudgelling." Thus it crowned the many other insults against Durhamites with the accusation of being prone to violent behaviour. In reality, it was their opponents, often local officers of the government, who most clearly exhibited this characteristic at Durham meetings, in keeping with their practices earlier in the decade.

Sheriffs, who were typically requested to call public meetings in the first instance, were particularly well-placed to obstruct the Durhamites.

In Toronto and in the Talbot district, local officials refused to hold public meetings in spite of requisitions from many respectable members of the public, and the activists were forced to call the meetings on their own authority. There was also at least one incident in which the militia was apparently used to intimidate the crowd. In Hamilton, the 1st Gore regiment, with music playing and bayonets fixed, marched past the square where the meeting was being held. Few believed Sir Allan MacNab, the colonel of the regiment, when he said he had told the militia to stay away from the meeting. Not accidentally, perhaps, the pace of the meeting was speeded up immediately thereafter in the interests of avoiding violence.

There were a number of more serious incidents involving tory violence against Durhamites. One occurred in Cobourg, where a riot took place in the market square as a Durham meeting got underway. The *Kingston Chronicle* of July 13 described it this way:

> Here [in front of the Town Hall] they hoisted their flags, and appeared as if making preparations to commence the business of the day … . A few spirited old countrymen, principally Irish (Protestant and Catholic) without any preconcerted arrangement, some with shillalah and some without, advanced to the platform and demanded the surrender of the flags. An angry parley followed; one of the standard bearers, standing on the hustings, pointed a loaded pistol to the crowd beneath, and when charged with having done so, openly avowed it. He however put it up again, but with such a demonstration of course did any thing but allay the excitement. The demand for the flags became louder, and was accompanied with menacing gestures; upon which the Jack Cades on the platform, though armed with bludgeons, and, as it afterwards appeared, in more than once case, with firearms, gave up the flags to the justly incensed loyalists. The bunting, that bore Lord Durham's name was instantly torn into a thousand shreds and trampled upon with contempt.

The Durhamites were assaulted with a hail of stones and fled for their lives. A chase ensued, during which one hapless Durhamite was captured and carried around on a rail, a ritual that was also sometimes part of charivaris.[82] Another, the son of the Honourable W. Boswell, a legislative councillor, was severely wounded in the head.[83] Shreds of the torn-up Durhamite flags were sent to Toronto, likely to the lieutenant-governor, in a gesture of symbolic disrespect.[84] Not surprisingly, in keeping with pre-Rebellion practice, this attack, as well as the disruption of the Yonge Street meeting north of Toronto, were linked to the Orange Order.[85] Moreover, the presence of magistrates during this attack indicates that this incident, as well as other anti-

Durhamite violence, fitted into the well-established pattern of officially sanctioned popular violence in the province.[86]

The Durham flags were also a target of violence at the Gore district meeting. As some of the participants from Dundas were leaving, "they again unfurled their flag, and while passing through the Main street of Hamilton, the waggon which carried the flag, was attacked, and the flag torn to pieces. – the party succeeded in preventing their flag from being taken from them; but they were obliged in self defence to attack in turn, some of their assailants."[87]

The most celebrated episode of tory violence, however, and one that became permanently enshrined in reform lore, occurred in Richmond Hill, in the Home district. For years, Francis Hincks, the future Reform party cabinet minister and party leader, would tell the story of how he had barely escaped with his life.[88] More than any other events connected to the Durham meetings, the so-called "Yonge Street Meeting" demonstrated that many of the failings of the old regime continued unabated.

It all began with a requisition, dated 8 August 1839, from W.W. Baldwin and 222 other inhabitants of the Home district asking the sheriff, W.B. Jarvis, to call a public meeting on Durham's Report.[89] Toronto tories were swift to counter this with a requisition of their own, asking the sheriff not to call such a meeting on the grounds that it would promote "disunion." In any case, they argued, the inhabitants of the province were about to be consulted about the report very shortly. Not surprisingly, Jarvis succumbed to this logic. His arguments against calling the meeting included the observation that the reform requisition included "very few names of those who may be termed the influential part of the inhabitants." By way of comparison, he noted that the counter-requisition included signatures of the mayor and several other elected members of the city government. The comparatively low social status of reform supporters was not the only argument against holding a public meeting, however. Jarvis also noted that he feared that breaches of the peace would occur if such a gathering took place. In the end, the "friends of Responsible Government" called a meeting themselves and, on 15 October, met in Toronto at Finch's Tavern on Yonge Street.[90]

Accounts of the meeting predicably differed, depending on the political allegiance of the narrators.[91] A subsequent parliamentary inquiry, however, accepted the substance of the reform interpretation.[92] It recounted that among those present at the meeting were the sheriff, "followed by a large body of inhabitants of Toronto and its neighbourhood, including the Mayor of the City, several Aldermen, Magistrates, and other public functionaries, wearing badges, and assumed the lead in the business of the day, with a view to defeat the purpose of those at whose instance the meeting had been convoked." The inquiry further accepted that it was the sheriff's followers who were responsible for the ensuing riot.

The trouble arose, as it had so often at previous meetings in the province, as a result of dissatisfaction with the sheriff's procedures for determining who was to chair the meeting. The disgruntled reformers retreated a short distance from the scene and proceeded to hold a meeting of their own. Their opponents evidently feared that the resolutions from this gathering would be broadcast throughout the land as the opinion of the meeting as a whole. In order to prevent this, they launched a spirited attack on the Durhamites. As the report of the inquiry put it, "a rush was made upon them [the reformers] from the other party, who, in passing a board fence on their way ... broke part of it into weapons with the help of which they made a furious onset upon the unarmed and defenceless multitude, whom they dispersed, cruelly beating & wounding several of them." The day ended in tragedy with the death of one of the reform supporters, David Leppard from East Gwillimbury.

The committee of inquiry took pains to note that there was nothing unlawful about the original assembly. The resolutions, draft address, and other papers relating to the meeting, it said, "appear to be of a constitutional and loyal character." It further condemned the conduct of the sheriff and other government officials. These worthies, they noted, had arrived from Toronto with those responsible for the riot, led them to the grounds of the meeting, "were identified with their party – and wore badges." The committee regretted that such violence had occurred in the presence of officers of the government, "upon whom it is especially incumbent to preserve the public peace and maintain order, and to avoid taking an active part as political partisans." In a comment that echoed the complaints of oppositionists throughout the 1830s, the report also condemned the law officers of the crown and of the executive government, "who were well informed of those lawless occurrences, yet took no notice of them." No arrests were made on the scene, no one was tried at the ensuing Assizes, and no inquiry was held until 1841.[93]

The inaction of the authorities did not go unnoticed at the time. On the contrary, organizers of the meeting presented an address to Lieutenant-Governor Arthur, complaining of the conduct of the sheriff and the magistrates on the occasion of the Yonge Street riot and asking that an inquiry be held.[94] Arthur's unhelpful response was to direct them to appeal to "the legal tribunals of the country."[95] As reform newspapers tartly observed, the presence of many members of the grand jury among tory supporters on the occasion of the riot rendered this suggestion "useless and impracticable."[96] As had happened to reformers so often in the past, Durhamites had no recourse against the stubborn intransigence of proponents of government-supported violence.

Tory intimidation and violence may have temporarily frightened and discouraged the Durhamites, but on the whole these tactics backfired, as resolutions from the meetings and newspaper commentaries indicate.[97] The right of public assembly, which some obviously felt was in serious jeopardy, was reiterated at five of the meetings. The Galt resolutions argued that "it is a duty which free and enlightened people owe to themselves, their posterity, and their Sovereign, to express their sentiments publicly, freely, and in terms not to be misunderstood, upon all transactions of government which they may deem of sufficient importance to demand their attention." The Talbot and Toronto resolutions criticized the sheriffs of the respective districts for failing to call public meetings when requested to do so, and participants at the Talbot meeting reiterated the belief that it was the right of British subjects to meet and discuss matters relating to their civil and political rights and privileges.

Tory violence, moreover, attracted unfavourable comment from newspapers sympathetic to the Durhamites. Some observers attributed the violence at the Cobourg meeting to associates of the "family compact" and commented: "It is, therefore, plain, that the 'family compact' men are both enemies of the British constitution, and libellers of the intelligence and character of the inhabitants of the province. It is not surprising, then, that they are seeking the aid of mobs to conceal their weakness, and prolong their domination."[98] Two months later, the *St Catharines Journal* condemned "the tools of a Compact ... [who in Cobourg] committed the most brutal outrages upon the people who had assembled to consider the affairs of the province."[99] The *Toronto Examiner* implicitly condemned the "Yonge Street riot" of October 1839 with detailed accounts of the misdeeds of its perpetrators.[100] The violence of the tories contrasted unfavourably with the peaceful conduct of the Durhamites and undermined the legitimacy of their own cause by providing a basis for charges that the supposed defenders of the constitution were themselves behaving unconstitutionally. The head-bashing and obstructionism on the part of lower-level officials ultimately had the effect of discrediting the perpetrators themselves.

In the longer run, the continuation of tory political violence fuelled reform demands for meaningful change in local government. For months after the Yonge Street riot, the reform press complained of government inaction against its perpetrators. Moreover, as the *Toronto Examiner* noted in early 1840, "partizan magistrates are still oppressing the people in the most cruel manner, and no redress is afforded. "The solution was clear: "The Magistracy must be reformed." This perspective was echoed in the resolutions of township meetings early in 1840 that condemned the institutions of local government.[101] The perception of a need for change was reinforced by later incidents, like the attack on the offices of the *Examiner* in April 1840, in which a number of officials and their relatives were alleged to have taken part.[102] Reformers ultimately received a measure of satisfaction when, in 1841, the magistracy was stripped of its powers in local government, in favour of elected township councils.[103]

THE AFTERMATH OF THE DURHAM MEETINGS

The abortive Durham meeting in the Home district took place on the eve of momentous changes in the high politics of Upper Canada. Even as it occurred, a new Governor-in-Chief was already on his way to British North America. Charles Poulett Thomson, soon to be created Baron Sydenham, received his appointment in September 1839. It was well known that he had held high office in British politics as President of the Board of Trade. Moreover, he still enjoyed a close relationship with Colonial Secretary Lord John Russell, who was prepared to grant him a large measure of autonomy in settling Canadian affairs.[104] After a month in Quebec, Thomson took charge in Upper Canada at the end of November 1839. He quickly set about laying the groundwork in the upper province for the union of the Canadas, a multi-faceted undertaking that involved virtually every aspect of government.

In anticipation of Thomson's assumption of power, many of the Durhamites had evidently deferred sending their addresses to Britain, preferring in many cases to contact Thomson directly or even to await developments and withhold the petitions altogether.[105] In the Niagara district, for example, the committee of management appointed at the meeting of 14 September 1839 announced its decision not to send their petition, "under the impression that Your Excellency has in view the promotion of the objects to which the prayer of said Petition is mainly directed."[106] The Durhamites of the Talbot, Gore, and Home districts, on the other hand, submitted addresses directly to the new governor general. W.W. Baldwin and his associates in the Home district also forwarded a copy of the resolutions of a meeting called to express satisfaction on Thomson's appointment. They took advantage of this opportunity, as well, to declare that the existing Assembly did not represent the will of the people, and to heartily endorse responsible government.[107]

During the brief remainder of 1839, in the spirit of the Durham meetings, addresses in support of responsible government and the union of the Canadas continued to rain down on the new governor general, some of them clearly prompted by Thomson's appearance in their midst as he progressed through the province.[108] In addition to those that are clearly traceable to Durham meetings of the summer and fall of 1839, Thomson received nine other addresses approving responsible government, as well as six specifically in favour of the union of the Canadas. Geographically, the addresses approving responsible government came from the north and east of Toronto, including Simcoe county, the Victoria district, Peterborough, and the townships of Dummer (Newcastle district) and Richmond (Lennox and Addington). Support for the union was scattered from Sarnia in the west to Prescott and Ottawa in the east.[109]

Supporters of the government, meanwhile, were considerably less active in mobilizing public opinion than they had been in 1832 and 1836. Suggestions that public meetings be held to counter the activities of the Durhamites evidently fell, for the most part, on deaf ears.[110] As the editor of the *Cobourg Star* commented, "opposition to such schemes often clothes them with a kind of respectability which they really do not merit." Moreover, he confidently asserted, the British government was bound to disregard both Durham's Report and the meetings in its favour. Accordingly, "we have not deemed them of sufficient consequence to justify us in recommending a district meeting."[111]

The editor of the *Star* was whistling in the dark. In spite of the brave front he put on the inaction of government supporters, to a large degree it was a product not of indifference but of divisions within their ranks, notwithstanding the apparent unanimity of Toronto officialdom. Arthur unequivocally blamed Lord Durham: "With matchless imprudence the high Commissioner has proposed a Measure which has divided the loyal Party, & thereby given a vast preponderance to the Republicans."[112] Under such dispiriting conditions, schisms affected both the British Constitutional Society and the Orange Order, the twin pillars of pro-government agitation earlier in the decade. The *St Catharines Journal*, for example, gleefully reported in October that a number of officials of the "Constitutional Society" in Toronto had "come out openly against the 'Compact,' and in favour of 'responsibility.'"[113] The Orange Order was similarly divided. While their leader, Ogle Gowan, was sympathetic to responsible government,[114] most of his followers heartily opposed it. The Grand Orange Lodge of the County of York, meeting in September in Etobicoke, was particularly emphatic on this point. "We entirely eschew, condemn and repudiate every Doctrine, opinion and sentiment expressed or written by the Right Honourable the Earl of DURHAM, in his Lordship's REPORT," their resolutions proclaimed.[115] Thus the common front that government supporters had enjoyed in 1832 and again in 1836 was signally lacking during the 1839 debate over responsible government.

Local officials, too, were less ready than before to lend the high tories in Toronto their unqualified support on matters of province-wide significance.[116] This became apparent when the sheriffs and chairmen of the quarter sessions (leading magistrates) of the province were questioned by Lieutenant-Governor Arthur in October 1839.[117] The consensus among the respondents was that support for responsible government in the province had been powerfully aided by maladministration in the highest quarters. Indeed, it was largely a result, in their view, of faulty land granting policies, an inadequate educational system, and an undeveloped transportation network. Above all, they believed, it was a consequence of a patronage policy that was both corrupt and much too narrowly focused. Local officials, it seemed, were now finally ready to endorse many long-standing oppositionist grievances.

These local officials further believed that support for responsible government was widespread throughout Upper Canada. Under these circumstances, a campaign to mobilize public opinion against Durham's report might well backfire. What was needed was a show of support for change, but something less drastic than Durham's recommendations. Accordingly, the sheriffs and chairmen of the quarter sessions recommended a thorough programme of administrative reform. This, they believed, would blunt the force of the arguments for responsible government. Arthur agreed. Expressions of support for the status quo would have carried little weight against this united phalanx of imperial and local officials. Thus the Durhamites did not face an aggressive counter-campaign in their efforts to mobilize public support.

Under these circumstances, even the arrival of Thomson sparked only a modest spate of addresses from supporters of the old status quo. Of the six addresses opposing responsible government and/or the union, two came from longstanding centres of tory strength, Toronto and Brockville. The "mayor, corporation, and commonality" of the city of Toronto frankly stated their objections to any form of union with Lower Canada not "predicated upon the ascendancy of the loyal portion of the inhabitants." Though they dared not speak out openly against responsible government, they did urge the new governor general to "uphold the cherished constitution under which we live."[118] Signatories of the Brockville address were not so discreet.

On the contrary, they stated that they could not "but look with alarm and suspicion upon those new theories of Colonial Government which have lately agitated the public mind, as we are convinced that changes in Government should not be made by way of experiment, nor until the advantages to be hoped from them become morally certain."[119] This was one of the most numerously signed of all the petitions Thomson received at this time, with six pages of signatures in double columns. Also impressive was a printed address to the Queen from the "Irish Inhabitants of Upper Canada." This document rehearsed at some length the terrors of the Rebellion and its aftermath, along with the sacrifices made by the Irish community, before launching a plea for "a prospect of permanency to our institutions" – a veiled plea against the introduction of responsible government.[120]

Such entreaties reached official ears too late to affect the process of decision-making at the Colonial Office. By the end of 1839, indeed, the union of the Canadas was a foregone conclusion – one that was officially celebrated in February 1841. The responsible government question was more complicated. As early as October 1839 Colonial Secretary Lord John Russell had already instructed Thomson to avoid surrendering to the demand for responsible government on the grounds that it was inconsistent with the province's colonial status. What Russell took away with one hand, however, he partly gave with the other. Thomson, he indicated, was to ensure that the executive acted as much as possible in harmony with the Assembly. This task, moreover, would be facilitated by alterations in the terms of tenure of executive positions; the governor general would be able to change his advisers much more readily than in the past.[121] The British government, however, continued through most of the 1840s to insist on the primacy in Canadian affairs of the governor general, as the representative of the imperial government. This state of affairs still fell considerably short of responsible government, as the Metcalfe Crisis of 1843–44 illustrated.[122]

It was not, in fact, until 1849 – a full decade after the Durham movement – that surviving Durhamites could be reasonably certain that self-government in local matters was essentially assured. This realization occurred in the aftermath of the Rebellion Losses Bill, passed that same year in the Canadian legislature. This legislation was anathema to Upper Canadian tories. They strongly believed that rebels should not receive compensation of any sort and saw the Bill as a thinly disguised attempt to indemnify the Lower Canadian rebels of 1837–38, many of whom were claimants for compensation under the Bill.[123] In spite of their earnest entreaties, however, the British government declined to intervene. The British government, by not disallowing the

Rebellion Losses Bill, tacitly acknowledged that they were willing to permit the government of the United Canadas to exercise responsible government.

By this time, the trend in popular politics had already clearly moved away from its pre-Union focus on petitioning the British authorities, as it became increasingly apparent that policy was being made in North America rather than in Britain. As early as the end of 1839, the spate of addresses that greeted Thomson on his arrival in Upper Canada reflected the perception that his advent represented a new order in provincial politics and the belief that Thomson himself had the power to effect significant changes in the political status quo.[124] Similarly, the addresses presented to Governor General Sir Charles Metcalfe in the aftermath of the resignation of the reform ministry in late 1843 signified in part a recognition that Upper Canadian affairs were increasingly being determined in North America rather than in Britain.[125]

Only fleetingly during the Union period, when it appeared that British authorities might intervene in the politics of British North America, did popular politics revert to the transatlantic form of the Upper Canadian period. Significantly, this was on the occasion of the passage of the Rebellion Losses Bill. Hoping that the British authorities could be persuaded to disallow the bill, in 1849, Upper Canadian tories embarked on a petitioning campaign that gathered almost 13,000 signatures from Toronto, Kingston, and the Newcastle district. Ironically, it was Sir Allan MacNab, in company with William Cayley, who followed in the footsteps of Randal and Mackenzie, taking the petitions to Britain for presentation to the Queen.[126] Their failure had a far-reaching impact on Upper Canadian petitioning. The strategy of petitioning the British government on matters of local politics, so long the focus of popular political activity, had clearly outlived its usefulness. Accordingly, future petitioning would be directed primarily towards the provincial executive, and popular politics would focus more narrowly on electoral organization.

The Durham meetings played a crucial role in this transition, serving as a bridge between the petitioning movements of the 1830s and the party politics of the succeeding decades. On the one hand, the Durhamites harked back to the past in their adoption of the methods popularized by oppositional petitioners like Gourlay and Mackenzie. Moreover, their chief cause – responsible government – was also one that resonated throughout Upper Canadian history. The Durhamites' rhetoric of popular constitutionalism also recalled the manner in which earlier Upper Canadian oppositionists and their British counterparts of the early nineteenth century had argued for political change. The magic of popular constitutionalism lay in the way it masked demands for change in the rhetoric of loyalty.[127] The Durhamites crusaded for fundamental political change in the form of responsible government while declaring that their aim was no more than the implementation of the British constitution. The meetings sent clear messages to the effect that the Durhamites were nonpartisan, respectable, orderly, and loyal. In adopting the watchwords of the authorities but interpreting them in their own distinctive fashion, the Durhamites, like Mackenzie earlier in the decade, provided a counter-definition of loyalty.

Yet the Durhamites were also building for the future – a future that unequivocally included the existence of political parties. In 1839, noone understood this better than Francis Hincks, chief architect of the parliamentary alliance between Robert Baldwin, leader of the Upper Canadian reformers, and Louis-Hippolyte LaFontaine, Baldwin's counterpart in Lower Canada. Hincks, more than any of his contemporaries, served as tireless promoter of the institution of political parties (in spite of the antipartyism that continued to flourish through most of the 1840s). As an organizer for the Durham meetings, Hincks doubtless realized that they offered an opportunity for leading reform sympathizers to establish or re-establish networks of communication, extending the kinds of personal contacts that would be vital to reform organization through the 1840s.[128] More broadly, they helped reformers to extend the basis of their political support among the enfranchised, and to educate the public about the need for reform and the means of achieving it. They also provided a rallying-cry that could unite reformers as no previous cause had done. In all these ways, the meetings anticipated critical reform strategies of the following decade.[129]

The Durham meetings had another significance in relation to political parties. They illustrated that the political divisions that had emerged in Upper Canada in the early 1830s remained very much alive. In spite of the Durhamites' insistence on their loyalty, the tories persisted in labelling them rebels and revolutionaries. They also continued to demonstrate public disrespect by employing violence and verbal abuse against reformers. The Durhamites, in turn, revived the old charges of lawlessness, corruption, and oppression against their opponents. Though the Durham meetings revealed that the supporters of toryism were now on the defensive, Upper Canadians were entering the Union as divided as ever. This would have important implications for the emergence of political parties in the 1840s.

Conclusion

This study of popular politics casts a unique light on the history of Upper Canada. It shows well-known individuals from a new viewpoint and demonstrates that the public was far more involved in political affairs than has previously been suspected. Through the prism of popular politics, the colonial connection with Great Britain takes on additional significance. The pivotal event of Upper Canadian history, the Rebellion of 1837, also appears in fresh perspective in the context of a generation of oppositional petitioning in the face of violent suppression. More than this, however, this study shows that the impact of popular politics was very significant indeed. Upper Canadian popular politics assisted in expanding the public sphere in ways that promoted the emergence of a party system and, more generally, the bourgeois and capitalist state that took form by the middle of the nineteenth century.

This examination of the petitioning movements adds a new dimension to our understanding of a number of Upper Canada's oppositionist leaders. Robert Gourlay was not merely, as he is commonly portrayed, the most famous "martyr" to the cause of reform. In addition, he was the leading early proponent of the strategy of petitioning that would be the mainstay of oppositionist agitation for the better part of a generation. William Lyon Mackenzie was not simply the bumbling organizer of the failed Rebellion of 1837. His leadership of the oppositionist petitioning movement in the earlier 1830s, on the contrary, shows that he was a surprisingly able political leader, gifted with extraordinary personal courage, as well as a master of political theatre.

W.W. Baldwin, too, appears in an unaccustomed role, beyond his traditional guises as father of Robert Baldwin and of responsible government. This prosperous barrister, notoriously stuffy though he was, nevertheless placed himself at the forefront of popular political agitation on numerous critical occasions. Equally remarkable was Egerton Ryerson's role in the late 1820s and early 1830s as a stalwart supporter of political and religious reform.

Government supporters also recruited some surprising allies. Who would have expected John Strachan to emerge as a proponent, even privately, of political violence? He was a strange bedfellow indeed for the likes of John Brown, pillar of government support in the Newcastle district and promoter of effigy-burnings, beatings, and general mayhem. Another unlikely participant in this process was the venerable Bishop Alexander McDonell, who played a small but distinguished role in mobilizing the Roman Catholic population of the Home district against Mackenzie in early 1832. The role of Strachan and McDonell in popular politics reveals how thoroughly the petitioning movements had penetrated Upper Canadian society.

This cast of characters, along with uncounted associates, ensured that popular politics in Upper Canada would bc both robust and varied. Popular politics was conducted in two discourses, both of British origin. On the one hand, government supporters spoke the language of loyalty and paternalism. "Loyalty" was a political virtue that encompassed devotion to the monarch, the British empire, the British constitution, the established church, and the existing way of life in Upper Canada. It opposite was "sedition," represented by an attraction to the republican and democratic political values of the United States. Paternalism, the pillar of social thought among government supporters, reflected an idealized world in which power flowed down a great chain, originating with the monarch and descending through the British government, the lieutenant-governor, and Upper Canadian officials – ultimately affecting the general population. The discourse of paternalism assumed that the units in this chain were bound by ties of benevolence on the part of those above and deference on the part of those beneath them. Those who violated the paternalistic code automatically placed themselves, in the view of its proponents, among the ignorant riff-raff of the province.

Oppositionists, on the other hand, employed the discourse of popular constitutionalism, legitimizing demands for political change by claiming that what they sought was no more and no less than the British constitution. They professed no attachment to republicanism and democracy, except for a brief period during 1837. Instead, they provided a definition of loyalty that, though different from that of government supporters, allowed them to appear to be in fundamental agreement with the basic political values of their society. Complementary to this political discourse was a social ideology that pitted the honest yeomen of the province against the "ruffled shirts" of a corrupt, profligate, and self-interested set of appointed officials.

The political culture of Upper Canada was rich in the vocabulary of political abuse as well as in the practice of political theatre. It compelled extensive newspaper coverage, and the dissemination of news about popular politics in handbill form. It featured public meetings, illuminations, the circulation of petitions, processions, electoral organization, and riots. It called forth new institutions, like the Central Committee, political unions, and the British Constitutional Society. Moreover, it provided a new outlet for the energies of the rapidly expanding Orange Order. Through all of these routes, popular politics engaged the attention of a far greater portion of the public than had ever before concerned itself with political questions.

Indeed, popular politics was the vehicle through which not only the narrow electorate but a far more numerous segment of the population was drawn into the political process. Both oppositionists and government supporters contributed to this result, because both went after signatures on their petitions in a relatively undiscriminating way, at least among the male population. The result was that petitioning reached thousands of individuals who did not exercise the franchise. This was most evident in 1831–32, when the Colonial Office counted as valid a total of signatures about three times higher than the number of voters in the 1834 general election. The unenfranchised could also, of course, participate in popular politics through attendance at parades, demonstrations, and other public spectacles associated with the petitioning movements during the 1820s and 1830s.

Of the two groups engaged in the struggle for popular support, of course, it was the oppositionists who more actively and credibly sought the widest possible participation in politics. It was they who began the process and they who sustained it for more than a generation. They never exhibited, as government supporters did on numerous occasions, any reluctance to stir up the forces of public opinion. Moreover, particularly in the case of the Durham meetings, reformers deliberately offered the unenfranchised an important part in a process that was designed to associate them with the virtues of respectability, nonpartisanship, non-violence, and loyalty. Non-electors were no longer considered a unruly mob of the ignorant and illiterate street ruffians. Instead they had become welcome participants in a more general and orderly political movement. This attitude reflected both the increasing respect accorded "public opinion" in Britain and the growing emphasis on "respectability" that would soon pervade the very schoolhouses of Upper Canada.[1]

While the oppositionist attitude to the unenfranchised may have involved an element of bourgeois co-optation, its attractions soon became evident as members of this group joined the proliferating nonelectoral extraparliamentary organizations, including, among others, temperance associations, antislavery societies, groups supporting changes in the law affecting married women's property, and, later, women's suffrage activists.[2] Like the popular politics of Upper Canadian reformers, these organizations legitimized the participation in civic life of many ordinary people, harnessing the energies of a wider and more diverse constituency than the mid-nineteenth-century political parties themselves.

Far more than has ever been realized before, the popular politics of Upper Canada were shaped by the colonial tie with Great Britain. Indeed, in spite of oppositional debts to the Americans for some of their organizational policies and techniques, and to the long dominance of a distinctive form of Upper Canadian toryism in helping to establish a framework for discussion,[3] the British influence essentially dominated Upper Canadian popular politics – even among the oppositionists. This was largely a result of Britain's ultimate authority over key points of conflict (including the province's constitution, religious establishment, judicial system, and economy). If oppositionists wanted their pleas for change to succeed, political realities dictated that their demands be phrased in terms acceptable to the British authorities.

The British influence was important in other ways as well. Oppositionist leaders adapted British political discourse to the colonial situation, employing the strategies of British street politics and the popular political strategies of the elite. They drew direct inspiration from the demonstrations organized in support of the Great Reform Bill of 1832 and formed political unions on the model of similar British institutions. They also acted under the guidance of British leaders like Joseph Hume. It was the apparent receptivity of British officials to the influence of public opinion after the mid-1820s that spurred oppositionists to engage in repeated petitioning. It was only when oppositionists had given up hope that the British authorities would respond to their decades-long struggle for reform that they resorted briefly to appeals based on the American discourses of republicanism, democracy, and revolution.

That relatively brief departure from the traditions of the oppositionist petitioning movement, the Rebellion of 1837, appears in a new light when examined in the context of popular politics. It was certainly more than the inexplicable eruption of an eccentric agitator. Instead, it was a symptom of the exasperation of Mackenzie and some of his rasher followers with the apparent futility of appealing to the British government for reform. In the context of the oppositionist petitioning of the previous generation, however, the failure of the Rebellion is understandable. The petitioning movements had familiarized Upper Canadians with peaceful forms of protest that took the monarchy and the British connection for granted; it had not conditioned them to accept republicanism and rebellion.

Indeed, in spite of tory outrage at the activities of the oppositionists, the reform program was in many ways moderate – in class terms, bourgeois. Thus although oppositionists encouraged popular participation in politics, franchise reform was not among their objectives. Their chief political goal, responsible government, meant more power for the elected Assembly. It did not imply democracy, much less the republicanism associated with the French and American revolutions. Their major social objective, religious disestablishment, lacked revolutionary potential because of the political conservatism of religious leaders. Also, oppositionists offered no serious challenge to established patterns of gender relations. Moreover, for a variety of reasons, some pragmatic and some ideological, the mainstream tradition of reform consistently rejected violence as a means of political change.

In spite of their apparent conservatism, the oppositionists did effect important changes in the political culture of Upper Canada. From Thorpe to the Durhamites, they built on a growing consensus that rejected government restrictions on political freedom such as libel laws, prohibitions of public meetings, and expulsions from the Assembly. They persistently rejected government controls on the use of public space and defied government efforts to define in the narrowest possible fashion the scope of the officially recognized political community. Their actions and their literature challenged the paternalistic cast of official political culture and their appeals for popular support subverted official notions of political hierarchy. One measure of their success was the surprising adoption of their methods by government supporters. Even the office of the lieutenant-governor was affected. It is generally overlooked that Head's famous election campaign of 1836, while achieving a signal electoral victory for the tories, did so at the cost of utterly subverting the traditional role of the lieutenant-governor as a figure above politics.

One effect of this process was the development of an expanded public sphere where the power of public opinion assumed a greatly enhanced role as the judge of the legitimacy of state action.[4] This expanded sphere was characterized by a style of government that was less secretive than before and more open to public scrutiny. In addition, by the late 1830s, oppositionist activities had contributed to securing a considerable degree of freedom of the press, of representation, and of assembly. Reformers' articulation of the importance of the rule of law as a restraint on arbitrary government was consistent with these goals. Though vestiges would remain for decades after 1840, in its essentials the old closed system of Upper Canadian politics was gone forever.

One result of the struggle to enlarge the political arena was the creation of a common sense of political awareness in Upper Canada. The time when that sense of awareness crystallized can be pinpointed with relative precision to early 1832. That development, following the expulsions of William Lyon Mackenzie from the Assembly, did not occur suddenly and without preparation. Instead, it was preceded by a long series of oppositionist efforts to mobilize public support for change. Oppositionists like Thorpe and Willcocks had tried in the first decade of the nineteenth century to stir public opinion through a variety of devices, including addressing juries and holding public meetings. Their successor, Robert Gourlay, was the first to stress that petitioning the British government was the key to achieving reform. By the end of the 1820s, Gourlay's method was widely imitated by a number of groups seeking political, constitutional, and religious reforms. These efforts culminated in 1831 with William Lyon Mackenzie's petitioning campaign, a movement that, for the first time, addressed all oppositionist grievances.

Important though these movements were, however, it was the expulsions from the Assembly of William Lyon Mackenzie in 1831–32 that prompted unprecedented popular participation in politics. For oppositionists, the repressive actions of the government placed Mackenzie squarely in the long line of Upper Canadian "martyrs" in the crusade against arbitrary government, along with Thorpe, Gourlay, and Willis. Moreover, it raised issues that had a long history in British politics, including freedom of representation and freedom of the press. The excitement generated by the expulsion crisis prompted thousands to demonstrate and to sign petitions in support of Mackenzie. Among government supporters, this popular resistance to the expulsions threatened the paternalistic basis of the social order and called into question the fundamental loyalty of the oppositionists. Accordingly, they cast aside their customary reluctance to court popular favour in their eagerness to ensure that the peppery Scot could not claim exclusive authority to speak for the people of Upper Canada. By the time Mackenzie left for Britain in April 1832, few Upper Canadians were without an opinion as to the justice of his cause. The importance of the expulsion crisis is illustrated by the fact that it was in the midst of this excitement that the terms "reformer" and "tory" first came into widespread use, at least in the reform press. The expulsion crisis had prompted the first use of clear "party" labels in Upper Canada.

The political divisions that emerged in 1832 were reinforced by subsequent events: tory suppression of the political union movement in 1833, electoral organization in 1834, the political crisis of 1836, the Rebellion of 1837, and the reaction to Lord Durham's Report in 1839. By the time Upper Canada entered the Union of the Canadas in 1841, its population had been polarized by almost a decade of near-frenetic activity in the realm of popular politics. Though leaders on both sides would have indignantly rejected any suggestion that their activities were intended to further the cause of establishing political parties, it is nevertheless true that the petitioning movements contributed in many ways to laying the foundations for the emergence of such institutions during the Union period.

As this book has indicated, the popular politics of Upper Canada also led to the emergence of a type of interest-group politics, as leaders mobilized groups affected by social and economic change behind political platforms. To some degree, the lines of polarization that emerged in the 1830s endured into the Union period, when they were reflected in notable continuities in leadership, political idiom, programs, organization, and the tradition of constitutional means of resistance.

Although petitioning was one feature of both Loyalist political activity and the opposition of the Thorpe-Willcocks faction, it was only after the War of 1812 that oppositionists, beginning with Robert Gourlay, were able to harness the grievances of religious and "national" discontents, along with those of some members of the growing professional class. We have seen that "national" conflicts were among the most serious fissures in Upper Canadian society. Secular issues like the alien question of the 1820s clearly mobilized the energies of the American-born on behalf of reform, and it is significant that those of North American origin were disproportionately represented among the rebels of 1837. In addition, oppositionists drew strength among those born in North America who believed that their interests would be overridden in favour of those of recent immigrants from the British Isles. Some Irish Catholics supported Mackenzie in reaction to what they perceived as government supporter Ogle Gowan's efforts to revive in Upper Canada the religious conflicts of Great Britain.

Correspondingly, the government appealed to the assumed deference of British immigrants and promoted the process of their settlement through emigrant societies. S.F. Wise has also speculated that many of these immigrants were attracted to the government side as a result of "the permanence of officialdom, and the squeezing out of moderate reform options in the 1830s."[5] Some of the new arrivals, most notably Gowan himself, furthered their own political ambitions by harnessing British ethnic traditions in the service of the established order. The alliance proved to be a lasting one: the Orange Order emerged as a bulwark of the conservative party after the Union of the Canadas in 1841.

Religion was another highly divisive element in Upper Canadian politics. Government supporters received significant assistance from the Anglican and Roman Catholic clergy on numerous occasions. S.F. Wise has noted that the clergy of the Anglican, Roman Catholic, and Presbyterian churches "were instinctively social and political conservatives; all believed that churches had a public role to play; and all accepted the principle that churches should support order and government through the promotion of public and private morality and the inculcation of ideas of subordination."[6] Political reformers, on the other hand, attracted support from dissenting denominations, especially the growing numbers of Methodists, who supported the cause of religious disestablishment.

An examination of the petitioning movements indicates that religious factors loomed larger than previously suspected in the oppositionist politics of the 1820s and 1830s. In early 1827, Jesse Ketchum, who had spearheaded resistance to the 1827 Alien Bill, was able to unite members of dissenting denominations to petition the British government against the clergy reserves and the proposed Anglican-dominated university. Three years later, an interdenominational group of Protestants in York formed the "Friends of Religious Liberty" to protest the Anglican establishment. These activities were important preludes to Mackenzie's campaign of 1831, a crusade that combined religious and secular grievances. Significantly, government supporters consistently maintained that Egerton Ryerson, a leading Methodist preacher, was virtually Mackenzie's equal in the orchestration of oppositional petitioning. In addition, it was widely believed that itinerant Methodist parsons were critical to the process of circulating Mackenzie's petitions for signature. Even after Ryerson withdrew his support from reform in 1833, there is evidence that many Methodists continued to support Mackenzie. Moreover, dissenters were over-represented among the rebels of 1837, and religious grievances were among those articulated at the Durham meetings of 1839.

It would be rash to conclude on the basis of this evidence, however, that religious dissent was the chief destabilizing force in Upper Canadian politics after the War of 1812.[7] From one perspective, it is clear that religious issues were at most secondary, or even absent altogether, in many of the oppositionist campaigns, including Gourlay's activities, the petitioning campaign against the 1827 Alien Bill, and the major oppositionist petitioning in 1831–32, 1833, and 1839. It may be, of course, at a more general level, that dissenting doctrines did encourage a critical attitude to authority. But so did many other forces in Upper Canadian society, including nationality, ethnicity, ideological convictions, and prudential considerations. It was the issue of nationality, for example, that produced in the petition against the 1827 Alien Bill one of the highest totals of signatures on a single anti-government document in the Upper Canadian period. Moreover, the Baldwins, who were Anglicans, were clearly acting on other than narrow sectarian grounds when they lent their support to the Friends of Religious Liberty. It is difficult, too, to attribute the striking popular response to Mackenzie's expulsions from the Assembly in 1831–32 to religious factors; instead, these seem to have struck a wellspring of support in Upper Canada's political culture for ideological issues like freedom of the press and of representation. If religious dissent was the critical foundation of opposition to the government, it is hard to explain why the government was so successful in marshalling public support in a society where the majority of the population adhered to non-Anglican denominations.[8] Religion was an important element in the mixture of factors prompting opposition to the established order, but its significance as a source of opposition to the government should not be exaggerated.

Class issues displayed unmistakable ambiguities during the Upper Canadian period. Generally, government officials, merchants, the military, and professionals were reliably tory.[9] Yet in spite of considerable anti-lawyer sentiment among opponents of the regime, many leading reformers – including Marshall Spring Bidwell, the Baldwins, and J.E. Small – belonged to this profession. Moreover, the tories were consistently able to win support in their petitioning, and at election time, from significant numbers of farmers and artisans.[10] Reformers often charged that, in the arena of popular politics, the tories sought the assistance of disadvantaged groups like canallers and clients of the soup kitchens; this support, however, was discounted as having been purchased rather than freely given, as the reformers liked to think their adherents' loyalty was. The oppositionists, meanwhile, identified themselves as representatives of the solid yeomanry of the country, yet they also attracted support from both urban labourers and, as we have seen, professionals and other leaders of society. It is little wonder, then, that historians generally have consistently agreed that class is a less reliable indicator of political preferences in Upper Canada than religion and nationality.

Some of the patterns of ethnic and religious allegiance established during the Upper Canadian period proved enduring. Ethnic alliances are difficult to track after 1841, since, as J.M.S. Careless has pointed out, in addition to ethnicity and religion, "the individual locality and those who constituted its majority and minority factions could be critically important" in determining the outcome of elections during the Union period.[11] Nevertheless, there is clear evidence of political continuity in the ongoing link between toryism and the Orange Order, which served as the tories' extraparliamentary arm well into the Union period. The Rebellion, of course, purged the reformers of their most radical leaders and programs, but it seems likely that many of American origin followed first the Baldwin Reformers[12] and later Peter Perry and other Clear Grits in the late 1840s and early 1850s. Moreover, sympathies between the oppositionists and their counterparts in Lower Canada helped pave the way for the Baldwin-LaFontaine alliance that formed the basis of the reform party for more than a decade under the Union. Correspondingly, the historic antipathy of the Upper Canadian tories towards the followers of Papineau poisoned their relations with the French-Canadians in the Assembly until the 1850s.

By the 1850s, the rise of voluntarism in Canada West and the newly aggressive Roman Catholicism of Canada East meant that to some extent these national allegiances were overridden by religious ones. It is surely no coincidence that the forces of Protestant voluntaryism, descended from the dissenters of the Upper Canadian period, mustered behind George Brown's Liberals in the 1850s in opposition to the Conservatives, whose historic alliance with Upper Canadian Roman Catholics contributed to their willingness to accommodate the Roman Catholics of Canada East. By the 1840s and 1850s, of course, the role of religion in Upper Canadian politics was changing with the lessening of the direct influence of the clergy in politics. By this time, as J.M.S. Careless has pointed out, "the stress was increasingly on the secularization of public affairs, not on the emergence of stronger clerical influence."[13]

The primarily British idiom of politics that emerged in the course of the petitioning movements in Upper Canada continued to dominate provincial discourse throughout the nineteenth century. There were exceptions, among them the "vocal minority of conservatives" who looked to the American constitution in the late 1840s and early 1850s for a solution to the alleged evils of responsible government, which they believed gave too much power to the cabinet.[14] At the other extreme, the Clear Grits owed something to the agrarian radicalism of the 1830s, but even they, as Kenneth Dewar has demonstrated, were indebted to the British tradition for many of their ideas.[15] In the centre, however, the reform political tradition was distilled in the 1840s into the slogan "Responsible Government and the Voluntary Principle,"[16] encompassing the two major aims of the

Upper Canadian oppositionists. Once these goals were achieved in the 1850s, as J.M.S. Careless has shown, Baldwin's Upper Canadian Reform Party largely assimilated itself to mid-Victorian liberalism on the British model.[17] Mainstream conservatives, meanwhile, once the storm of the Annexation crisis had passed, maintained their loyalty, as they interpreted it, to Queen and Empire. It ultimately led them, once the British government had adopted responsible government, to acceptance of the legitimacy of opposition. The tories also continued throughout the nineteenth century to harbour many of the same suspicions of American influence, as their Upper Canadian predecessors had done.[18]

The petitioning movements also contributed to forming the character of political parties in the Union period by offering an early and sometimes prominent presence in the public arena to numerous individuals who would carry the torch of political leadership into the 1840s.[19] On the reform side, they included Robert Baldwin, Francis Hincks, and W.H. Merritt. Baldwin, the Upper Canadian leader of the great Reform ministry of 1848, became the chief extraparliamentary organizer among the reformers, drawing on his contacts with "Old Reformers" like the Buells of Brockville, Peter Perry of Lennox and Addington, and a host of others who had been actively engaged in promoting popular politics before the Union. Baldwin's chief lieutenant, Francis Hincks, who had also served his political apprenticeship in the arena of popular politics, fittingly emerged in the Union period as the chief foe of antipartyism. No doubt his personal brush with tory violence gave Hincks a particularly meaningful stake in the promotion of peaceful competition among contending political forces. It was also appropriate that W.H. Merritt, who had first declared his reform allegiance at the time of the Durham meetings in 1839, should have served as a cabinet minister in the Baldwin-LaFontaine ministry of 1849. Notable among tory activists in the cause of popular politics were W.H. Draper, who served "virtually [as] prime minister of Canada"[20] between 1844 and 1847, and Allan MacNab, a prime minister during the 1850s. Like MacNab, Ogle Gowan was a leader of the tory popular resistance to the Rebellion Losses Bill of 1849; he continued to be active in politics and in the Orange Order well after 1850.[21]

At another level, the petitioning movements contributed to the creation of the machinery of extraparliamentary organization after the Union. It was during the Upper Canadian period that the township emerged as the basic unit of organization both for the petitioning movements and for electoral organization. The county nomination meeting, attended by delegates from the townships, was a particularly favoured device of reformers organizing for the general election in

1834; it would reappear as the cornerstone of both reform and tory extraparliamentary electoral organization in the 1840s. At the provincial level, the Reform Association of the 1840s assumed some of the extraparliamentary functions once undertaken by Central Committee. On the tory side, meanwhile, the British Constitutional Society gave way, in succession, to the United Empire Association (1844) and the British American League (1849).[22] Throughout the 1840s, however, it was the Orange Order that essentially served as the main arm of extraparliamentary tory organization, just as it had done in the Upper Canadian period.

Finally, the reform tradition of constitutional rather than violent opposition made a powerful contribution to the emergence of a party system promoting peaceful competition for political office. The Upper Canadian tory tradition of political violence did continue into the Union period, notably in outbursts in Toronto over the Secret Societies Act of 1843,[23] and the Rebellion Losses Bill of 1849, which tories believed actually rewarded those who had participated in the Rebellions in Lower Canada.[24] Significantly, this was the last major outburst of conservative political violence in Toronto.

The frequency of tory political violence had been diminishing during the 1840s, and by the 1850s it seems largely to have disappeared. A major reason for this was the acceptance of political opposition during the 1840s, after the British government endorsed the Reform program of responsible government – previously a major source of discord between the conservatives and reformers.[25] Moreover, acceptance of the Rebellion Losses Bill by the British government was a signal that responsible government was here to stay, and that to oppose it was not productive.[26]

Beyond the legitimization of the concept and practice of political opposition, a number of influences discouraged conservative political violence from the late 1830s on. The British government, trying to suppress Orangeism at home, embarked after 1836 on a campaign to discountenance it in Upper Canada as well, initially with mixed results.[27] At another level, the authorities and members of the middle class became increasingly concerned about threats to public order. Toronto newspapers, too, showed great concern about the perceived increase in rowdyism during the 1850s, and the police force of the city expanded by a factor of 7 between 1847 and 1856[28]; it grew even more dramatically thereafter. Gregory Kealey has argued that by the 1850s the bourgeois elements of Toronto society had rethought their attitude to political violence in response to the threat to public order posed by the rise of an indigenous working class.[29] Peter Way, too, has noted that after Toronto's Rebellion Losses riots, the city's leading tories, perceiving the conflict between customary forms of popular protest and loyalty to Britain, opted thenceforth to support law and order and to reject a form of activity that had become associated with the labouring classes.[30] Even in areas considerably less industrialized than Toronto, the threat of "rowdyism" was an omnipresent concern for society's "respectable" elements in the 1860s and 1870s.[31] The decline of conservative political violence must also be related to a long-term decline in violence in Toronto and elsewhere between the mid and the late nineteenth century (measured by the rate of offences against the person), a phenomenon which was part of a much larger long-run decline in violence in Western society.[32] Nevertheless, the attitude that the law should sometimes be broken in the interests of preserving the established form of government has never entirely disappeared in this country, reappearing in times of acute political strife like the Winnipeg General Strike and the rise of Quebec separatism in the late 1960s and early 1970s.[33]

Politics, if it is a science at all, is a very inexact one. No doubt the activists of the Upper Canadian period would testify to this. For it is one of the great ironies of the period that in some ways neither side really achieved what they were fighting for. The tories, believing that they were maintaining the status quo, worked unwittingly to undermine it in their wholesale adoption of the techniques of popular politics and their endorsement of political violence. Reformers, on the other hand, had to wait until the late 1840s for the achievement of responsible government, and longer than that for the settlement of the clergy reserves and other questions of church and state. Moreover, though responsible government may have freed Upper Canadians from the interference of the Colonial Office in local affairs and from the domination of the appointed elite in Toronto over provincial politics, recent scholarship has stressed the degree of continuity with Upper Canadian government in the large scope of executive power in the 1840s and succeeding decades, and in the extent to which the educational system replaced the established church as the chief instrument of political socialization.[34] It could be argued, indeed, that one of the most significant results of their combined activities was a development that neither side had explicitly sought: the creation of a much expanded public sphere that facilitated the emergence by mid-century of a bourgeois state dominated by railway and other business interests.

Paradoxically, however, both tories and reformers received some benefits from the changes of the 1840s. For the former, their political anchors were the continuation of the connection with Great Britain and the maintenance of a system of government that was monarchical but not democratic. Neither of these fundamental values was ever seriously at risk in spite of the apparently dramatic changes of the Union period. Reformers, on the other hand, accepted the tory framework, but sought greater control of local political affairs, a goal that came by the 1840s to symbolize all their other aims. Though change may have been slow in coming and not entirely what they had hoped for, it was enough to secure their ongoing participation in the political process in the new political world after the Union of the Canadas. Though fully satisfactory to neither side, the political changes of the 1840s were sufficient to ensure that political stability would endure for that generation and, as it turned out, for many later generations as well.

APPENDIX A

Political Meetings, Spring 1832

No.	*Date (All except 1 were in 1832)*	*Place*	*Type (Reform=R Tory=T Split=S)*	*Source*
1	31 December 1831	Saltfleet (Gore)	T	CA 12/1/32
2	2 January	Whitby (Home)	R	BR 19/1/32 from CA
3	2 January	Augusta (Johnstown)	R	CA 12/1/32
4	5 January	S. Gower (Johnstown)	T	BG 26/1/32
5	9 January	Scarborough (Home)	R	CA 12/1/32 CO42/411/73
6	19 January	York (Home)	R	CO42/413/302 CO42/411/73
7	4 February	Malahide (London)	R	CA 16/2/32 BR 23/2/32
8	16 February	Fredericks-burgh (Midland)	R	CA 16/2/32 BR 1/3/32 CO42/411/143
9	18 February	Yarmouth (London)	R	CA BR 8/3/32
10	21 February	Bayham (London)	R	CA 15/3/32

No.	*Date (All except 1 were in 1832)*	*Place*	*Type (Reform=R Tory=T Split=S)*	*Source*
11	? February	Georgina (Home)	T	CA 23/2/32 BR 18/3/32 CO42/413/150
12	24 February	Amherst (Newcastle)	S	CA 1, 8, 22/3/32 BR 8/3/32
13	27 February	Township of Toronto (Gore)	T	CO42/413/150
14	27 February	Thorold (Niagara)	R	CA 15/3/32
15	2 March	Kingston (Midland)	T	CA 8, 15/3/32 CO42/411/134–8
16	3 March	Smithville	R	CO42/411/140
17	3 March	Hallowell (Midland)	T	BR 15/3/32 CO42/411/143, 201 NG 17/3/32
18	3 March	Grimsby (Niagara)	R	BR 15/3/32
19	3 March	Smithville (Niagara)	R	CO42/411/140
20	3 March	Middlesex (London)	R	CA 28/3/32
21	6 March	Otonabee (Newcastle)	R	CA 15/3/32
22	6 March	York Catholics (Home)	T	CA 8/3/32
23	8 March	Cornwall (Eastern)	T	NG 21/4/32
24	10 March	Belleville (Midland)	S	CO42/411/141 CA 12/4/32
25	12 March	York Catholics (Home)	T	CO42/411/143 NG 17/3/32
26	13 March	Otonabee (Newcastle)	T	CA 28/3/32
27	13 March	Perth (Bathurst)	T	CO42/411/139
28	14 March	Chippewa (Niagara)	T	CA 10/5/32 NG 28/4/32

No.	*Date (All except 1 were in 1832)*	*Place*	*Type (Reform=R Tory=T Split=S)*	*Source*
29	17 March	Brockville (Johnstown)	S	CA 5/4/32 BR 15, 22/3/32 CO42/411/142 CO42/413/154 NG 17/3/32
30	17 March	Vaughan (Home)	R	CA 5/4/32
31	19 March	Hamilton (Gore)	S	CO42/413/154 CA 15, 28/3/32
32	20 March	Lanark (Bathurst)	T	CO42/411/142
33	22 March	Bath (Midland)	S	CA 12/19/3/32 CO42/411/143ff
34	23 March	York (Home)	S	CO42/411/138
35	31 March	Niagara (Niagara)	S	CA 12, 19/4/32, 10/5/32 CO42/413/9, 114–22
36	31 March	Mariah Town (Eastern Dist)	R	CA 12/4/32 BR 12/4/32
37	End March	St Thomas	T	CA 5/4/32
38	31 March	Markham (Home)	T	CA 12/4/32
39	late March	Carleton Place (Bathurst)	T	BR 8/3/32 CO42/411/142
40	early April?	Williamsburgh (Eastern)	R	BR 12/4/32
41	early April?	Clinton (Niagara)	T	BR 12/4/32
42	early April	St Catharines (Niagara)	T	CO42/411/139–40 CO42/417/54
43	5 April	Vittoria (London)	T	CA 10/5/32 BR 26/4/32 CO42/413/150 NG 21/4/32
44	8 April	Cornwall (Eastern)	T	NG 21/4/32
45	9 April	St Catharines (Niagara)	R	CA 19/4/32
46	11 April	Chippewa (Niagara)	T	CA 10/5/32

No.	*Date (All except 1 were in 1832)*	*Place*	*Type (Reform=R Tory=T Split=S)*	*Source*
47	11 April	Grimsby (Niagara)	R	CA 19/4/32?
48	11 April	40-Mile Creek (Niagara)	T	CA 10/5/32
49	12 April	Frontenac (Eastern)	S	CO42/413/312
50	12 April	Sandwich (Western)	T	CA 5/7/32
51	16 April	Beamsville (Niagara)	S?	CO42/411/139–40 CO42/417/54
52	18 April	St David (Niagara)	R	CA 8/5/32
53	23 April	St Thomas (London)	T	CO42/413/150 CA 14/6/32 *St Thomas Liberal*, 29/11/32

APPENDIX B

Oppositionist Signatures on Petitions, 1831–32

District	*Number*	*Percentage*
Home district	10318	45.68
Gore	2490	11.2
Midland	2094	9.3
Niagara	1809	8
Johnstown	2332	10.3
Eastern	1454	6.4
London	260	1
Newcastle	211	1
Niagara	1615	7.1
	22583	99.98

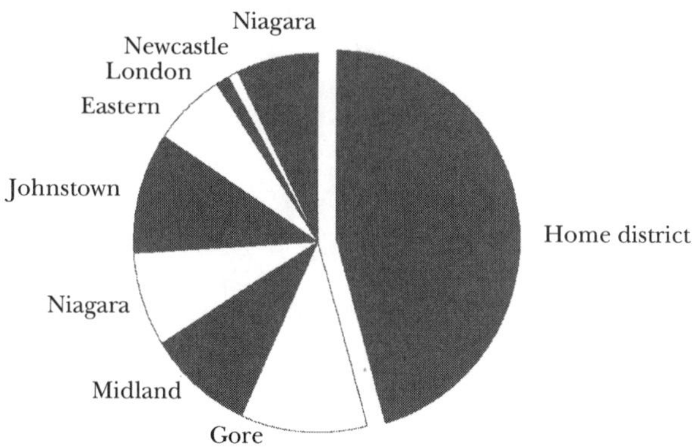

Source: CO 42/413/292

APPENDIX C

Signatures on Petitions, Government Supporters, 1832

District	*Number*	*Percentage*
Home district	3273	12.3
Gore	2340	8.8
Midland	5562	20.9
Niagara	1172	4.4
Johnstown	5147	19.3
Eastern	100	0.4
London	2400	9
Newcastle	5400	20.3
Bathurst	1178	5.2
	26572	100.6

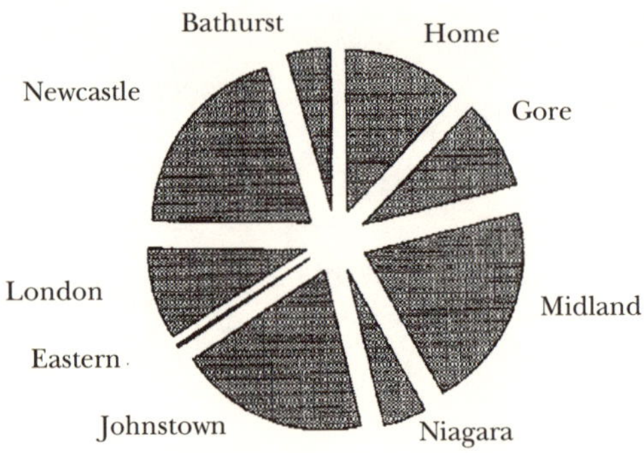

Source: CO 42/413/277–8

APPENDIX D

Tory Addresses, 1836

District	*Bathurst*	*Gore*	*Home*	*J'town*	*London*	*Midland*	*Newcastle*	*Niagara*	*Ottawa*	*P. Edward*	*Simcoe*	*Western*	*Eastern*	*Total*
Signatures	281	147	1640	46	167	716	1026	754	1090	864	70	88	973	
	465	357	114	117	183	570	351	96			80	91		
	287	485	155	53	98	43	253	192				192		
	225	361	60	129	287	388	133	112				268		
	149		73	58	81	481	3986					162		
			146	25	375	471								
			375	119	559	438								
			461	99	350									
			151	106	276									
			680	95	101									
			270	2586										
			112											
Subtotals	1407	1350	4237	3433	2477	3107	5749	1154	1090	864	150	801	973	26792

Source: Sundries, 166: 90862-4

Note: An additional 703 signatures could not be attributed to any district.

APPENDIX E

List of Durham Meetings, June – October 1839

ABBREVIATIONS

BC British Colonist
BR Brockville Recorder
BG Bytown Gazette
KC Kingston Chronicle
NC Niagara Chronicle
SCJ St Catharines Journal

1 June 1839 – Galt
Sources: *BR*, 20 June 1839; *BC*, 19 June 1839; *SCJ*, 11 July 1839
Location: township hall
Character: public meeting following militia muster

2 7 June 1839 – Town of Niagara
Sources: *BR*, 20 June 1839; *BC*, 19 June 1839
Location: British Hotel
Character: Reform gathering

3 1 July 1839 – Haldimand Township, held in Colbourne, Newcastle district
Sources: *KC*, 13 July 1839 (from *Cobourg Star*); *SCJ*, 11 July 1839
Character: a meeting of freeholders

4 8 July 1839 – Cobourg, Newcastle district
Sources: *BR*, 18 July 1839 quoting *Mirror* and *U.C. Herald*
Location: Market Square
Character: a meeting of freeholders

5 16 July 1839 – Township of Murray, Newcastle district
Source: *BR*, 1 August 1839
Location: Christopher C. Bullock's (Inn)
Advance Preparation: public requisition and handbills
Character: meeting of freeholders

6 26 July 1839 – Dundas, Halton County
Sources: *BR*, 8 August 1839; *BC*, 24 and 31 July 1839; *BG*, 31 October 1839
Location: Assembled on the green; later marched into Dundas
Advance Preparation: extensively circulated handbills; notice in the papers
Character: meeting of freeholders and other inhabitants of the county of Halton

7 26 July 1839 – Townships of Thora and Mara, in Beaverton
Source: *BR*, 15 August 1839; *BC*, 7 August 1837 (Resolutions)
Character: meeting of inhabitants

8 27 July 1839 – Gore district meeting, held in Hamilton
Source: *BR*, 8 August 1839; *BC*, 24 and 31 July, 7 August 1839; *SCJ*, 7 August, 5 September 1839; *BG*, 11 September 1839
Location: Court House Square
Advance Preparation: requisition signed by 121 freeholders and others; notice in the newspapers
Character: public meeting of the inhabitants of the district of Gore; called by the sheriff

9 29 July 1839 – Guelph
Source: *BR*, 15 August 1839
Character: public meeting of inhabitants of Guelph township and vicinity
Further particulars: addressed by participants of the Dundas and Hamilton meetings

10 2 August 1839 – Eldon, Newcastle district
Source: *BC*, 14 August 1839; *SCJ*, August 22, 1839

11 22 August 1839 – Waterloo Township, in Preston, Halton county
Sources: *SCJ*, 22 August 1839; *BC*, 14 August 1839

12 7 September 1839 – Lennox and Addington
Source: *BR*, 19 September 1839
Location: Mr Dulmage's Inn
Character: Freeholders of the counties of Lennox and Addington

13 14 September 1839 – Niagara district meeting in Thorold
Sources: *BR*, 26 September 1839; *KC*, 5 October 1839; *NC*, 19 September 1839; *BC*, 25 September 1839; *SCJ*, 22 August, 5, 14, and 28 September 1839
Advance Preparation: requisition signed by 196 freeholders; newspaper notice
Location: Thorold
Character: meeting of freeholders and inhabitants

14 21 September 1839 – Talbot district meeting, held in Simcoe
Source: *BG*, 7 November 1839; *BC*, 25 September 1839; *SCJ*, 10 October 1839
Advance Preparation: requisition; the sheriff refused to call a meeting

15 28 September 1839 – Toronto Township, held in Cooksville
Source: *BR*, 10 October 1839
Location: Scott's Tavern, Cooksville
Character: meeting of Toronto Township

16 15 October 1839 – Home district, in Richmond Hill
Sources: *BR*, 12 September 1839, 19 September, 21, 24, and 31 October 1839; *KC*, 23 October, 13, 16 November 1839; *BC*, 28 August, 11 September, 23 and 30 October, 13 November 1839
Location: Davis's late Temperance Hotel
Advance Preparation: requisition calling for a public meeting; refused by sheriff; public meeting held anyway

Notes

INTRODUCTION

1 Political unions were extraparliamentary pressure groups intended to influence the authorities through the expression of public opinion.
2 See Pross, *Group Politics and Public Policy*, 3–4.
3 The Alien Bill was unpopular with the American-born because it appeared to treat many of them as second-class citizens. See chapter 1.
4 After the Rebellions of 1837, Lord Durham was appointed governor-in-chief of the British North American colonies by the British government of Lord Melbourne. Part of his mission was to make recommendations for colonial government, a task he accomplished in his famous *Report* of 1839. On the basis of this report, Upper and Lower Canada were united as the Province of Canada in 1841. For Durham, see Fernand Ouellet, "John George Lambton," DCB 7: 476–81. For an abridged version of the report, see Craig, ed., *Lord Durham's Report*.
5 This definition has been inferred from the works of some leading British sources on popular politics, including the following: Brewer, *Party Ideology and Popular Politics*; Brewer, *The Common People and Politics 1750–1790s*; Bradley, *Popular Politics and the American Revolution in England*, 10; Gunn, "Public Spirit to Public Opinion," 260–313.
6 Cf. See, "Polling Crowds and Patronage," 128. The author comments that the electoral politics discussed there "do not lend themselves easily to a Procrustean interpretive framework constructed exclusively of economic, class, or ethnic dynamics."

7 Bowsfield, "Upper Canada in the 1820s"; Mills, *Idea of Loyalty*; and Errington, *The Lion, the Eagle, and Upper* Canada.

8 The following list is far from exhaustive, but see Cross, "The Shiners' War"; Akenson, *The Orangeman*; Akenson, *The Irish in Ontario*; Armstrong, "The York Riots of March 23, 1832"; Kealey, "Orangemen and the Corporation"; Romney, "From the Types Riot to the Rebellion."

9 Wilton, " 'Lawless Law,' " discusses this question.

10 Jackson, "The Organization of Upper Canadian Reformers, 1818–1867"; Patterson, "Elections and Public Opinion"; Bowsfield,"Upper Canada in the 1820's."

11 Bumsted, *Peoples of Canada*, 238–9; Francis and Smith, *Origins*, 235–6. Historians who have examined Gourlay's activities in more detail, including Milani, have of course appreciated the importance of petitioning in Gourlay's career.

12 Dunham, *Political Unrest in Upper Canada*, 125. Dunham also missed the fact that Mackenzie toured the province at this time collecting signatures in a series of meetings outside the Home district.

13 Craig, *Upper Canada*, 211–15.

14 Graeme Patterson's thesis, "Elections and Public Opinion," is only the most obvious example of this viewpoint.

15 S.F. Wise, "Robert Fleming Gourlay," *DCB* 9: 335.

16 This right was enshrined in the British Bill of Rights of 1689; see Johnson, " 'Claims of Equity and Justice,' " 219. This right was fully supported by the Upper Canadian courts; see *Stanton v. Andrews, 5 Upper Canada Court of King's Bench* (O.S.) 6 Wm. 4: 245. I am indebted to Dr Philip Sworden for this reference.

17 Though many women likely shared the political views of their husbands and fathers, it would be rash to conclude that the signature of one man actually also represented the political views of the household.

18 Patterson, "Enduring Canadian Myth," 485–8, considers the historiography of the term. See also, among others, Saunders, "What Was the Family Compact?"; Armstrong, "The Carfrae Family: A Study in Early Toronto Toryism"; Burns, "God's Chosen People"; Armstrong, "The Oligarchy of the Western District."

19 Noel, *Patrons, Clients, Brokers*, 61–78.

20 See, for example, Wise, "The Rise of Christopher Hagerman," and "John Macaulay: Tory for All Seasons," in Wise, ed., *God's Peculiar Peoples*, 61–90; Richards, "The Joneses of Brockville and the Family Compact," and Romney, "A Man Out of Place," 345–6.

21 Johnson, *Becoming Prominent*, 86.

22 See Wise, "Upper Canada and the Conservative Tradition," in Wise, ed., *God's Peculiar Peoples*, 31; and Mills, *Idea of Loyalty*.

23 See Fraser, " 'Like Eden in Her Summer Dress.' "

24 On paternalism generally, see Thompson, "Eighteenth-Century English Society," 133–7. Cadigan, "Paternalism and Politics," discusses it specifically in the Upper Canadian context.

25 McCalla, *Planting the Province,* 9; Careless, *Pre-Confederation Premiers,* 15.

26 Brode, *Robinson,* 143; Thomson to Lord John Russell, December 1839, in Knaplund, ed., *Letters,* 39.

27 G.M. Craig, "Marshall Spring Bidwell," DCB 10: 61–2.

28 Wise, "The Family Compact," 143.

29 Johnson, *Becoming Prominent,* 77, 79.

30 Mills, *Idea of Loyalty,* 21.

31 Hofstadter, *Idea of a Party System,* 12–13.

32 Mills, *Idea of Loyalty,* 32.

33 I am indebted to Habermas, *The Structural Transformation of the Public Sphere,* 57 ff. for this line of inquiry.

34 Francis, *Governors and Settlers,* 30–70.

35 McNairn, "Towards Deliberative Democracy." By the 1830s, the explosive growth of the Upper Canadian press and public demand for parliamentary news were among the factors that undermined this element of restricted access to the public sphere.

36 See, for example, Patterson, "Elections and Public Opinion," 68, 182, 373; Firth, ed., *Town of York,* 90–112.

37 Wright, "Sedition Proceedings," 19 ff.

38 See, for example, Bleasdale, "Class Conflict," and Wylie, "Poverty, Distress, and Disease."

39 See chapter 1.

40 Harvey Graff found that, in 1861, there was a literacy rate of ninety per cent in Hamilton, Canada West. This appears to be relatively high, but the literacy rate in rural areas was even higher. Urban centres, Graff suggested, had higher illiteracy rates than rural areas partly because of "the presence of a larger number of Irish immigrants in the city"; "Towards a Meaning of Literacy," 263–4. No figures on literacy are available for the Upper Canadian period. My unscientific impression from examining signatures on petitions of the 1830s is that the overwhelming majority of signatories could sign their own names.

41 Isaac, *Transformation of Virginia,* 261–6, offers valuable insights into the ways in which Methodism threatened social and religious conventions.

42 Wilson, *Clergy Reserves,* 75–8, 84. Most of the outstanding policy issues having apparently been resolved in the 1820s, these visits tapered off. As financial difficulties began to plague the province in the 1830s, however, Upper Canadian officials journeyed to Britain for financial assistance; Ken Cruikshank, "John Henry Dunn," DCB 8: 253–4. Prior to this time, Thomas Talbot had travelled to Britain in 1817 to lobby Colonial Office officials; Milani, *Gourlay,* 112.

43 Only about ten to twelve per cent of the population of the province enjoyed the franchise; see Jones, "The Franchise in Upper Canada," 21.
44 Craig, "The American Impact on the Upper Canadian Reform Movement"; and Clark, *Movements of Political Protest*; Rea, "William Lyon Mackenzie: Jacksonian?"
45 Mills, *Idea of Loyalty*, 5–6.
46 Wise, "Upper Canada and the Conservative Political Tradition," in Wise, ed., *God's Peculiar Peoples*, 174–8; Johnson, *Becoming Prominent*, 80–119; Noel, *Patrons, Clients, Brokers*, 61–111; Stewart, *Origins of Canadian Politics*, 9–58; Wilton, "Transformation of Upper Canadian Politics," chapter 4.
47 For this line of analysis, I am indebted to Epstein, "Cap of Liberty."
48 McNairn, "Publius of the North," 507.
49 Patterson, "Elections and Public Opinion"; Read, *Rising in Western Upper Canada*; Stagg, "The Yonge Street Rebellion"; Romney, "On the Eve of the Rebellion."
50 Fahey, *In His Name*, 6–7, 20, 37.
51 Christie, "'In These Times of Democratic Rage and Delusion,'" 36.
52 Isaac, *Transformation of Virginia*, 260–6. See also Craig, *Upper Canada*, 165–7; Semple, "The Quest for Kingdom," 100–3; and Noel, *Canada Dry*, 104–6.

CHAPTER ONE

1 Johnson, "Petitions and Petitioners," 220.
2 Potter-MacKinnon, *While the Women Only Wept*, 141.
3 Wilson, *As She Began*, 113. See also Craig, *Upper Canada*, 11.
4 Craig, *Upper Canada*, 10.
5 Potter-MacKinnon, *While the Women Only Wept*, 125, 149–51.
6 Johnson, "Petitions and Petitioners," 221.
7 Ibid., 223.
8 Rude, *Wilkes and Liberty*, 105ff.
9 Black, *Association*, 31–82.
10 Ibid., 175 ff.
11 Ibid., 279.
12 Cowherd, *Politics of English Dissent*, 22–8.
13 Black, *Association*, 233–74.
14 For example, see "Mr Gourlay's Address to the Public," *CA*, 5 January 1828.
15 Guest, "Upper Canada's First Political Party," 275–96.
16 The following paragraphs are based on Craig, *Upper Canada*, 59–63; Elwood H. Jones, "Joseph Willcocks," *DCB* 5: 854–9; G.H. Patterson, "William Weekes," ibid., 844–5; Elwood H. Jones, "Charles Burton Wyatt," *DCB* 7: 929–30; G.H. Patterson, "Robert Thorpe," ibid., 864–5.
17 Guest, "Political Party," 279.

18 Report on Canadian Archives, 1892, "Political State of Upper Canada in 1806," "Address to Lieut. Governor Gore," 52.
19 Guest, "Political Party," 291.
20 Report on Canadian Archives, 1892, Gore to Lord Castlereagh, 21 August, 107, 81, 86.
21 Guest, "Political Party," 289.
22 The full name of the riding was West York, 1st Riding of Lincoln, and Haldimand.
23 Wright, "Sedition in Upper Canada," 28.
24 Landon, *Western Ontario*, 36.
25 One historian has stated that the prewar opposition "had been disgraced by the stigma of treason." Robert Lochiel Fraser, "Robert Nichol," *DCB* 6: 543.
26 Report on Canadian Archives, 1892, "Political State of Upper Canada in 1806," Grand Jury, Western District to Judge Thorpe, 4 September 1806, 54.
27 Ibid., Petit Jury, Western District, to Judge Thorpe, 55.
28 Patterson, "Elections and Public Opinion," 18–19. I have found two references to grand juries making pronouncements on political issues in the 1830s, both in support of the status quo.
29 Report on Canadian Archives, 1892, Gore to Windham, 20 October 1806, 51.
30 Ibid., Thorpe to Edward Cooke, 1 April 1806, 47.
31 Ibid., Gore to Lord Castlereagh, 21 August 1807, 81.
32 Wilson, *Enterprises*, 156; Hamil, "The Reform Movement in Upper Canada," 10.
33 Report on Canadian Archives, 1892, 84–5. Gore appears to have been misinformed in maintaining that no such meeting took place after Thorpe was suspended as judge; ibid. 81.
34 Wilson, *Enterprises*, 160–1.
35 Jones, "Willcocks," 856.
36 Wilson, *Enterprises*, 160.
37 Jackson, *A View of the Political Situation*, 19.
38 Powell, *Letters from an American Loyalist*, 66–7.
39 Thorpe and Wyatt received the limited victory of successful libel suits against Gore, who was required to pay them damages many years after their departure from Upper Canada. Guest, "Political Party," 292; S.R. Mealing, "Francis Gore," *DCB* 8: 339.
40 CO42/350/281, J.M. Jackson, Southampton, to Joseph Willcocks, 19 July 1809, 281–2.
41 CO42/350/271, Robert Thorpe to Mr Cheniquy, 14 February 1810.
42 CO42/354/57, petition, 24 October 1811, cited in Sheppard, *Plunder, Profit, and Paroles*, 29.
43 Report on Canadian Archives, 1893, Upper Canada, Calendar of State Papers, John Mills Jackson to Joseph Willcocks, 19 July 1809.

44 See Report on Canadian Archives, 1892, "Political State of Upper Canada in 1806," 51 passim for Gore's correspondence with the British government on the grievance-mongers. See also CO42/350/5–7, Gore to Castlereagh, 1 February 1810. (Gore sent Castlereagh 150 pages refuting the charges of the group.)

45 Gourlay wrote that Thorpe had been dismissed because he had consented to carry a petition from the inhabitants of Upper Canada to the British government. Gourlay, *Statistical Account of Upper Canada* [*Account* I], 2: 335. This is not confirmed by evidence elsewhere. Gourlay's *Account* and the publications of William Lyon Mackenzie helped keep the names of Thorpe and his associates before the public.

46 Hamil, "Reform Movement," 10.

47 Milani, *Gourlay*, 71; Wise, "Gourlay," 331.

48 Gourlay had once shaken Cobbett's hand. Milani, *Gourlay*, 59.

49 Ibid., 66.

50 "Address to the Jury, at Kingston Assize, In the case of The King vs. Robert Gourlay for Libel: with a report of the trial," (1818), 3.

51 Eventually, Gourlay made good on his promise to publish the *Statistical Account*: in 1822, it appeared in Britain. However, his sour view of provincial affairs, reflected in his book, cannot have afforded much encouragement to prospective settlers. See Taylor, *Promoters, Patriots, and Partisans*, 116–33.

52 Craig, *Upper Canada*, 90–1; Robert Lochiel Fraser, "Robert Nicol," *DCB* 6: 542–3.

53 Gourlay, *Account* I, 2: 469–70. William Dickson protested the policy by "refusing to withhold the oath of allegiance from Americans ... He was consequently removed from the commission for administering the oath"; Craig, *Upper Canada*, 90–1.

54 S.R. Mealing, ed. Robert Gourlay. *Statistical Account* [Gourlay, *Account* II], 329–35.

55 Ibid., 331.

56 Ibid., 368. Italics in the original.

57 Milani, *Gourlay*, 137.

58 Gourlay, *Account* II, 374.

59 On Merritt, see J.J. Talman, "William Hamilton Merritt," *DCB* 9: 544–48.

60 Milani, *Gourlay*, 141.

61 Gourlay, *Narrative*, 10, 13.

62 Ibid., 31.

63 Gourlay, *Account* II, 364.

64 Ibid.

65 Milani, *Gourlay*, 152, 155.

66 Craig, *Upper Canada*, 94.

67 Milani, *Gourlay*, 139–40.

68 Ibid., 150–1.

69 This paragraph is based on Gourlay, *Account* II, 364 and Gourlay, *Narrative*, 3–11.
70 Milani, *Gourlay*, 153, and Gourlay, *Narrative*, 12.
71 Milani, *Gourlay*, 155 and Gourlay, *Narrative*, 27–8.
72 Gourlay, *Narrative*, 24.
73 Gourlay, *Account* I, xxix-lv, lviii, cccxxv.
74 Milani, *Gourlay*, 183.
75 In addition, after the township meetings were banned, Gourlay held a number of "purse-string" meetings in the Niagara district; ibid., 185–6.
76 See Robert S. Allen, "William Claus," *DCB* 6: 151–3.
77 Craig, *Upper Canada*, 98.
78 James Strachan, *A Visit to the Province of Upper Canada*, 184–98. On Strachan see G.M. Craig, "John Strachan," *DCB* 9: 751–66.
79 Milani, *Gourlay*, 227.
80 Wise, "Gourlay," 335.
81 Craig, *Upper Canada*, 99.
82 Perkin, *Origins of Modern English Society*, 208–13.
83 See Lillian F. Gates, "Jesse Ketchum," *DCB* 9: 422–4.
84 See Bowsfield, "Upper Canada," chapter 4, and TRL, W.W. Baldwin Papers, L11, B104, 58–62.
85 Responsible government had been proposed as a solution to Upper Canadian misgovernment as early as the first decade of the nineteenth century by Robert Thorpe; see Patterson, "Thorpe," 865. W.W. Baldwin and his son Robert, however, are considered the foremost champions of this doctrine in Upper Canada. Responsible government meant local autonomy for the colonial government in matters of provincial concern; it also involved cabinet government and party government. As such, it represented a fundamental transformation in the government of Upper Canada. Responsible government would in fact be implemented in the 1840s. For W.W. Baldwin, see Robert L. Fraser, "William Warren Baldwin," *DCB* 7: 35–44. For responsible government, see Wilton [Siegel], "The Transformation of Upper Canadian Politics."
86 Frederick H. Armstrong and Ronald J. Stagg, "William Lyon Mackenzie," *DCB* 9: 496–510.
87 Cowherd, *Politics of English Dissent*, 23.
88 For a brief overview of British politics in these years, see Beales, *From Castlereagh to Gladstone*, 21–5.
89 Mills, *Idea of Loyalty*, 23.
90 The following account of the alien issue is based on a number of sources: Craig, *Upper Canada*, 114–23; Romney, "Re-inventing Upper Canada," 78–107; Garner, *The Franchise and Politics*, 164–72; Dunham, *Political Unrest*, 73–82; Brode, *Robinson*, 41–141.
91 CO42/377/183, enclosure in Maitland to Bathurst, 6 April 1826.

92 Bowsfield, "Upper Canada," 260.
93 CO42/377/179, Maitland to Bathurst, 6 April 1826.
94 This paragraph is based on accounts in *CA*, 1 and 8 March 1827.
95 Bowsfield, "Upper Canada," 279.
96 *CA*, 15 March 1828.
97 TRL, Powell Papers, Samuel Peters Jarvis to William Dummer Powell, 3 March 1827.
98 Ibid., S.P. Jarvis to W.D. Powell, York, 3 March 1827, quoted in Quealey, "The Administration of Sir Peregrine Maitland," 545.
99 *CA*, 15 and 22 March 1827; Upper Canada *Herald* 27 March, 1 May 1827.
100 This account is based on a report in *CA*, 15 March 1827.
101 On Fothergill, see Paul Romney, "Charles Fothergill," *DCB* 7: 317–21. Almost a decade earlier, Fothergill had debated with Robert Gourlay at a November 1818 meeting in Amherst; he persuaded the crowd to pass resolutions hostile to Gourlay. See Milani, *Gourlay*, 183.
102 Upper Canada *Herald* 27 March 1827.
103 *CA*, 10 May 1827.
104 Jones, "The Franchise in Upper Canada," 14.
105 OA, Macaulay Papers, Robert Stanton to John Macaulay, York, 3 March 1828.
106 This incident and the hanging of the effigy at the crossroads near Port Hope are rare examples of expressions of public disrespect on the part of government opponents. The term "anatomized" may be a reference to the eighteenth-century practice in London, England, of surgeons dissecting the bodies of those who had been publicly hanged. See Linebaugh, "The Tyburn Riot Against the Surgeons."
107 *CA*, 6 and 27 March 1828.
108 Samuel Peters Jarvis, a lawyer and government official, for example, was appalled that the Upper Canadian bill had been "thrown aside without reference to the Prov.l Governmt," TRL, Powell Papers, Jarvis to Powell, York, 12 September 1827.
109 CO42/384/120, Maitland to Horton 20 August 1828. See also CO42/384/148–62, Maitland to Sir George Murray, 18 September 1828.
110 John Beverley Robinson, for example, observed in 1824 that William Lyon Mackenzie was "too contemptible an adventurer to notice"; quoted in Craig, *Upper Canada*, 112.
111 CO42/381/459–67, Maitland to Huskisson, 1827.
112 Upper Canada *Herald*, 18 December 1827.
113 *CA*, 3 January 1828.
114 Ibid. For the committee's first report, see *CA*, 13 and 20 December 1827.
115 See Bowsfield, "Upper Canada," 76–7; Fahey, *In His Name*, chapter 4.
116 Fahey, *In His Name*, 97; Sissons, *Ryerson*, 1: 34.
117 The Sales and Improvement Act provided for the sale of some of the clergy reserve lands, the money to be devoted to the improvement of the

remaining lands or to promote the objects for which the lands had been reserved originally. In failing to divert the proceeds from sale to secular purposes, such as education, the Imperial Parliament was refusing to bow to pressure from opponents to the pretensions of the Anglican Church. See Wilson, *Clergy Reserves*, 93–4.

118 Fahey, *In His Name*, chapter 3.

119 A select committee of the Assembly, chaired by Marshall Spring Bidwell, compiled a report whose essentials formed the basis for an address to the King from the Assembly, adopted in March 1828. The address defended the Methodists and asserted that the Anglicans made up only a small part of the provincial population. It also attacked the university charter and endorsed the secularization of the clergy reserves. Craig, *Upper Canada*, 175.

120 Semple, *The Lord's Dominion*, 75–6.

121 Craig, *Upper Canada*, 165–7; Mills, *Idea of Loyalty*, 57 ff.

122 *CG*, 9 April 1831. Strangely, Willson had been a leading Methodist in the Hamilton area some years before, though he evidently died an Anglican in 1860; Fraser, "John Willson," *DCB* 8: 945; Johnson, *Becoming Prominent*, 250. On Ryerson, see R.D. Gidney, "Egerton Ryerson," *DCB* 11: 783–95.

123 AO, Strachan Papers, Strachan to Hargreave, 7 March 1831, quoted in French, *Parsons & Politics*, 126.

124 Gates, "Ketchum," 423–4.

125 *CA*, 10 January 1828. See also the account of the County of Frontenac meeting in the same issue.

126 Ryerson, *Story of My Life*, 83.

127 TRL, Broadsides, 1478. "First Report of the Central Committee On the Petition to the Imperial Parliament, from Christians of all denominations in Upper Canada."

128 Mackenzie's participation is not recorded in the official documents of the Willis petitioners, but a hostile handbill suggested that he was involved in a subordinate capacity. See TRL, Broadsides, 1828, "Dreadful." Mackenzie later indicated that he had at least signed the petition. See NA, William Lyon Mackenzie Papers, vol. 10, William Lyon Mackenzie Collection. 21 February 1833. "To the Honorable the Commons of the United Kingdom of Great Britain and Ireland, in Parliament assembled. Petition of William L. Mackenzie, Printer."

129 Romney, *Mr Attorney*, 141 ff.

130 *Canadian Freeman*, 11 July 1828.

131 See TRL, Broadsides, "Willis, 1828," "Public Meeting."

132 This paragraph is based on the *Canadian Freeman*, 11 July 1828.

133 3 July 1828.

134 Romney, *Mr Attorney*, 145–6.

135 The text of the petition is in *Canadian Freeman*, 11 July 1828.

136 TRL, Broadsides, 1828, "Alarming Crisis," "Dreadful," and "Plain."

137 Apparently William Lyon Mackenzie had vetoed Baldwin's running for the town at a nominating meeting the previous winter. He objected on the grounds that the senior Baldwin was opposing him in the county of York. Dr Morrison ran against John Beverley Robinson in the town election of 1828 and lost the contest. According to the *Canadian Freeman*, the younger Baldwin ran in the county of York in 1828 but came last in the poll. See *Canadian Freeman*, 17 July 1828; reprinted in Firth, ed., *Town of York*, 112–17; *Canadian Freeman*, 24, 31 July 1828.

138 AO, Macaulay Papers, Robert Stanton to John Macaulay, 18 July 1828.

139 *Canadian Freeman*, 7 August 1828 contains a requisition from the electors of the county of Norfolk dated 12 July asking Dr Baldwin to stand for their county. According to the requisition, the Baldwins owned substantial property in Norfolk.

140 TRL, Powell Papers, Jarvis to Powell, 6 March 1828.

141 31 July 1828.

142 24 July, 7 August 1828.

143 Significantly, these individuals, except for Cawthra, were all involved in the York Bible Society, an interdenominational institution founded in November 1828 to promote the circulation of the Bible. The Baldwins, Ketchum, and Morrison served as vice-presidents of this society, which was under the patronage of Lieutenant-Governor Colborne. York Auxiliary Bible Society (Ontario). The Formation and Constitution of the York, U.C. Bible Society, York, 1828.

144 TRL, Broadsides, 1828 Petition, "Constitutional Meeting."

145 *Canadian Freeman*, 10 July 1828.

146 TRL, W.W. Baldwin Papers, L11, B104, Thomson to Baldwin, 14 August 1828. Thomson, editor of the very successful journal the *Upper Canada Herald*, had endorsed Gourlay's crusade and supported the Bidwells in the early 1820s. See H.P. Gundy, "Hugh Christopher Thomson," *DCB* 6: 772–4.

147 Ibid., Beardsley to Baldwin, 1 August 1828. Beardsley, however, had a long association with the cause of reform. He provided legal counsel to Bartemus Ferguson, Gourlay's publisher, and opposed the provincial government on many issues as an MPP in the Assembly of 1824–28. See H.V. Nelles, "Bartholomew Crannell Beardsley," *DCB* 8: 69–70.

148 Ibid., Rolph to Baldwin, 20 December 1828. For Rolph's career, see G.M. Craig, "John Rolph," *DCB* 9: 683–90.

149 *Canadian Freeman*, 25 June 1829.

150 TRL, W.W. Baldwin Papers, L11, B104, 28 May 1828.

151 Ibid., 20 December 1828.

152 TRL, Broadsides, "Constitutional 1829."

153 See Fairley, ed., *Selected Writings*, 255–60.

154 TRL, W.W. Baldwin Papers, L11, B103, W.W. Baldwin to Joseph Hume, York, 2 April 1830. Draft. File named "Letters from WWB."

155 First, judges were to hold office "during good behaviour" rather than "during pleasure"; second, the chief justice was not to sit on the Executive Council; see Romney, *Mr Attorney*, 141.
156 Craig, *Upper Canada*, 171–2; CG, 18 December 1830; French, *Parsons & Politics*, 117.
157 Sissons, *Ryerson*, 1: 130.
158 A characteristic Ryersonian argument; see French, *Parsons & Politics*, 114.
159 CG, 18 December 1830.
160 Ibid., 25 December 1830.
161 Ibid., letter to the editor, 9 April 1831.
162 Ibid., 15 January 1831.
163 Ibid., 5 March 1831, quoting the York *Courier*.
164 A copy of the petition is in CO42/395/466. See also Bowsfield, "Upper Canada," 81–2; Sissons, *Ryerson* 1: 129–41.
165 Sissons, *Ryerson* 1: 131.
166 Ibid.
167 Bills for secularization of the reserves were passed annually by the Assembly but rejected with equal regularity by the Legislative Council. In November 1831 Lord Goderich suggested that Colborne "seek from the legislature repeal of the reserves clauses of the Act of 1791 and the investment of existing reserves in the Crown." Nothing came, however, of this apparent modification of imperial policy. Goderich also recommended the surrender of the charter of King's College so that a new college might be established. Similarly, there was no action on this. See French, *Parsons & Politics*, 120, 12.

CHAPTER TWO

1 Rasporich, *Mackenzie*, 1.
2 Romney, *Mr Attorney* in particular, and Fraser, " 'All the Privileges,' " xxi-xcii.
3 Armstrong, "William Lyon Mackenzie."
4 See Wilton, "Transformation of Upper Canadian Politics."
5 Mackenzie also sought to capitalize on this incident by selling pamphlets on the subject, priced at 4d. each, 2s. 6d. per dozen, or $3.50 a hundred; see CA, 27 December 1827.
6 CA, 31 January 1828.
7 Ibid.
8 Lindsey, *Mackenzie*, 153–6.
9 See F.H. Armstrong and Ronald J.Stagg, "William Lyon Mackenzie," DCB 9: 496–9.
10 CA, 31 March 1831.
11 CA, 10 March 1831.
12 Beer, *MacNab*, 39–41.

13 See *BR*, 24 February 1831, report on proceedings in House of Assembly.
14 See Craig, "Rolph," *DCB* 9: 683–5.
15 TRL, W.W. Baldwin Papers, L11, Box 105–1, John Rolph, Dundas, to Baldwin, 24 March 1831 and 5 May 1829.
16 CO42/395/510 Ryerson, London, to Lord Goderich, 27 September 1831.
17 Economic factors were not responsible for the petitioning movement in 1831. There was no obvious financial crisis, as in 1836, nor was there an agricultural crisis in Upper Canada, the western frontier of settlement in British North America. (Lower Canada, of course, was suffering through a prolonged one.) There were some unsettling social changes, notably the burgeoning immigration from Great Britain, which promised future growth and prosperity, but in the meantime delivered the dreaded cholera; both immigration and the associated cholera were important issues during these years.
18 *CA*, 16 June 1831. Mackenzie's attitude was a striking contrast to that of Robert Baldwin, who once wrote: "I always have been in the strictest sense of the word *a party man.*" See TRL, Baldwin Papers, A87–1, Robert Baldwin draft letter, 2 February 1843.
19 See TRL, Broadsides, 1828, "Dreadful," "Dreadful Shipwreck."
20 Craig, *Upper Canada*, 196–7.
21 Patterson, "Elections and Public Opinion," 93 (Middlesex). Patterson's claim that the "reformers" of the Johnstown district acted in concert with "reform" organizations in other parts of the province in 1828 is not well authenticated by his evidence, pp. 191–206; he does not make this claim for the election of 1830 in the Johnstown district, nor for the Bay of Quinte region in the elections of 1828 and 1830.
22 Akenson, *The Irish in Ontario*, 173.
23 See, for example, "A Corrupt Administration," in Fairley, ed., *Selected Writings*, 286–7; *CA*, 30 June 1831. The resolutions of the election meeting in Markham of 26 January 1828 noted with disapproval that a bill to repeal "the act under which Mr Robert Gourlay was banished" (the Sedition Act of 1804) had been rejected by the Legislative Council; *CA*, 31 January 1828. See also *CA*, 26 September 1833 on Gourlay, and ibid., 26 October 1833 on Jackson.
24 "On Unheeded Petitions," in Fairley, ed., *Selected Writings*, 256–7.
25 "Corrupt Administration," in ibid., 287.
26 For example, see *CA*, 17 and 24 February, 16 March 1831.
27 Brock, *The Great Reform Act*, 78–9, 160–93.
28 *CA*, 2 June 1831.
29 Ibid.
30 Pocock, *The Machiavellian Moment*, 486.
31 *CA*, 2 June 1831.
32 *CA*, 23 and 30 June 1831.

33 CA, 14 July 1831.
34 This was probably the petition organized by the committee of Friends of Religious Liberty in December 1830 which argued that "the proceeds of the [clergy reserves] be appropriated to the purpose of general education and various internal improvements." *Report on Canadian Archives, 1899*, 27; quoted in French, *Parsons & Politics*, 118–9.
35 CA, 14 July 1831.
36 The Address and resolutions are copied from the CA in BR 28 July 1831.
37 For a discussion of popular constitutionalism and British radicalism, see Epstein, "Understanding the Cap of Liberty," 84.
38 Mackenzie later noted that the petition was drawn up chiefly by John Neilson. See Wise, ed., *Narrative*, 2.
39 CA, 28 July 1831.
40 CA, 21 July 1831.
41 Ibid.
42 "Markham July Town Meeting," CO42/395/329.
43 These included the townships of Markham, King, Whitby, Vaughan, Whitchurch, E. Gwillimbury, Etobicoke, Scarborough, Pickering, Albion, Caledon, and Toronto.
44 CA, 11 August 1831.
45 See CO42/395/310–20.
46 CA, 18 August 1831.
47 Francis, *Governors and Settlers*, chapter 2.
48 See, for example, Firth, ed., *Town of York*, 224–7.
49 CO42/395/321–2.
50 CA, 25 August, 1 September 1831.
51 See Colborne to Goderich, 21 August 1831, in CO42/394/52–62.
52 8 March 1832.
53 CA, 18 August 1831.
54 CA, 3 November 1831; see also BR, 17 November 1831.
55 CG, quoted in CA, 8 September 1831. In 1829, it was Mackenzie who had moved the amendment in the Assembly that led to MacNab's committal to jail for contempt of the Assembly, thus beginning what some have referred to as a highland feud. In return, it was MacNab who led the Assembly attack on Mackenzie for breach of privilege in 1831 on the issue of unauthorized distribution of its journals. See Beer, *MacNab*, 28–40.
56 The account used here was taken from the *Hamilton Free Press* and printed in BR, 15 September 1831.
57 See for example, CA, 19 May, 16 June 1831, 5 April 1832; BR, 10 February 1831, 17 February, 7 June 1832; NA, MG 24, D101, William Stewart and Family Papers, 240, 290. See also G. Marquis, "Anti-Lawyer Sentiment in Mid-Victorian New Brunswick," 163; Dewar, "Charles Clarke's 'Reformator,'" 224.

58 The newspaper account made no reference to the old saying that a lawyer who represents himself has a fool for a client.
59 CA, 15 September 1831.
60 Ibid.
61 Ibid.
62 In the *Constitution* for 23 August 1837, Mackenzie compared the Trafalgar meetings of 1831 and 1837: "In 1831, 30 freeholders called a political meeting in Trafalgar – 100 printed bills were published, 2 newspapers gave the tidings, and 11 persons attended the call. How different in 1837 – an unsigned notice in a radical journal brings 600 men punctually on the ground, highly excited, 20 justices inclusive, and this in the midst of the harvest!"
63 BR, 13 October 1831.
64 CA, 20 October 1831.
65 BR, 27 October 1831.
66 This connection between religion and politics evidently did not go unnoticed in high quarters. In 1832 Lieutenant-Governor Colborne told the Colonial Secretary, Lord Goderich, that Mackenzie had been allowed to hold political meetings in the Brockville chapel. CO42, (Q374–4, 783), Colborne to Goderich, 18 June 1832, cited in French, *Parsons & Politics*, 133.
67 BR, 27 October 1831.
68 For Gowan, see Hereward Senior, "Ogle Robert Gowan," DCB 10: 309–14.
69 Houston and Smyth, *The Sash Canada Wore*, 3–29; *Cobourg Star*, 18 August 1833.
70 CA, quoted in BR, 17 November 1831.
71 The amendment, however, was not put to the Chair. BR, 20 October 1831.
72 CA, 20 and 27 October, 3 November 1831. Graeme Patterson's "Elections and Public Opinion," 230, says that a riot occurred at this meeting, but I can find no evidence for this.
73 NG, 17 March 1832.
74 BR, 27 October 1831.
75 Ibid.
76 Ibid. Reform activity did not cease with the meetings. By 14 October, the day after the meeting, Andrew N. Buell of Brockville was sending out circulars around Leeds containing copies of the petition and a request for funds. A copy is in the *Brockville Gazette*, 8 March 1832.
77 CA, 20, 27 October 1831.
78 BR, 27 October 1831.
79 BR, 20 October 1831.
80 Ibid.
81 Ibid.
82 BR, 17 November 1831.

83 CA, 15 and 22 December 1831. Jones, for example, was referred to as a man whose "whose whole public life has been spent to do the people injury and fit them for slavery." The likelihood is that Mackenzie wrote the pamphlet himself. See CA, 22 December 1831.
84 CA, 22 December 1831.
85 *Brockville Gazette,* 1 December 1831, quoted in Patterson, "Elections and Public Opinion," 233.
86 CA, 22 December 1831.
87 BR, 17 November 1831.
88 CA, 3 November 1831.
89 Ibid.
90 Ibid.
91 Ibid.
92 See CA, 10 November 1831.
93 BR, 1 December 1831.
94 CA, 1st issue of January 1832 (undated).
95 CA, 3 November 1831.
96 CO42/394/52–3 in Colborne to Goderich, 25 August 1831.
97 Mackenzie to Goderich, York, 16 September 1831, quoted in CA, 8 March 1832.
98 CA, 8 March 1832. On the Marriage Act, see Craig, *Upper Canada,* 56.
99 CA, 1 and 15 December 1831. MacNab was reported as saying that "the people of Hamilton had refused to agree to the petition at the public meeting held there, and that Mr Mackenzie made his escape out of the Gore District just in time."
100 CA, 15 December 1831 and 24 November 1831.
101 Ibid.

CHAPTER THREE

1 See Patterson, "Elections and Public Opinion," 498–516.
2 CO42/411/368 Colborne to Goderich, 18 June 1832.
3 Wright, "Sedition Proceedings," 28.
4 Greenwood and Wright, "Parliamentary Privilege and the Repression of Dissent in the Canadas," 424, quoting Gourlay, *Statistical Account.*
5 Colonial Secretary Lord Goderich strongly objected to Mackenzie's expulsions, believing that "libels should be prosecuted in the courts"; Greenwood and Wright, "Parliamentary Privilege," 427.
6 Bowsfield, "Upper Canada," 282. The violent behaviour of government supporters during the 1830s, however, casts considerable doubt on the extent to which the right of free assembly had been achieved in practice.
7 See Wright, "Sedition in Upper Canada," 23.

8 CO42/411/369, Colborne to Goderich, 18 June 1832. There is a note on this document by a member of the Colonial Office staff saying "to be sure … he shd. have been treated with neglect." Colborne had been more sympathetic to the idea of prosecuting Mackenzie in February. See CO42/411/70 Colborne to Goderich, 16 February 1832.

9 *CA*, 15 December 1831.

10 Quoted in ibid.

11 See Dunham, *Political Unrest*, 125.

12 Lindsey, *Mackenzie*, 201. The issue of criticism of the government was also being agitated in Lower Canada at the same time. In January 1832, two Montreal newspaper editors, Daniel Tracey and Ludger Duvernay, attacked the Legislative Council and demanded its abolition. They were summoned before the Legislative Council, convicted of libel, and imprisoned for thirty-four days. (See Manning, *The Revolt of French Canada*, 344–6.) Fernand Ouellet notes that "there were popular demonstrations, and when the Irishman and the Canadian were released they were paraded through the streets as heroes, victims of the legislative council, and presented with gold medals." (*Lower Canada*, 225.) In an ensuing spring by-election for Montreal West, Duvernay ran under patriote auspices and won an extremely narrow victory in this, "one of the most celebrated [by-elections] in Canadian history." (Ibid., 226.) See also Greenwood and Wright, "Parliamentary Privilege," 429–35.

13 An undated clipping in CO42/411/74 Colborne to Goderich 16 February 1832 (probably from the hostile *Canadian Freeman*) expressed concern about Mackenzie's ability to ensure that his followers kept the peace and noted that disorder in York had led to notice being given of a motion to remove the seat of government from York. Such fears were somewhat hysterical, given the orderly character of Mackenzie's meetings and demonstrations.

14 *CA*, 6 January 1832.

15 These were dated 18 and 26 January respectively. See CO42/411/41 ff. for the text of these documents.

16 The Address is in CO42/411/78.

17 CO42/411/5 Colborne to Goderich, 31 January 1832.

18 CO42/411/69 Colborne to Goderich, 16 February 1832.

19 CO42/411/8 Colborne to Goderich, 31 January 1832.

20 CO42/411/251 Colborne to Goderich, 7 May 1832.

21 CO42/411/388–9 Colborne to Goderich, 5 July 1832.

22 CO42/411/68 Colborne to Goderich, 16 February 1832.

23 CO42/411/250 Colborne to Goderich, 7 May 1832.

24 Quoted in *CA*, 15 December 1831.

25 See Reid, *Concept of Liberty*, 56 ff.

26 A number of historians have written about American influences on Mackenzie and the reform movement, including Craig, "The American Impact

on the Upper Canadian Reform Movement Before 1837," and Rea, "William Lyon Mackenzie – Jacksonian?" British influences are considered in MacKay, "The Political Ideas of William Lyon Mackenzie."

27 See Rude, *Wilkes and Liberty.*

28 Not incidentally, the career of Wilkes had established the legal principle "that one house of parliament had no right to create a disability by pronouncing a member incapable of sitting"; in expelling Mackenzie, the Assembly majority was acting in defiance of the law, a fact that would come back to haunt them later. See Dunham, *Political Unrest,* 130.

29 See Romney, "Upper Canada in the 1820s," in Greenwood and Wright, *State Trials,* 505–21.

30 John Matthews was an oppositionist whose pension from the army was (temporarily) suspended following allegations of disloyal conduct that were evidently politically motivated. See Paul Romney, "John Matthews," DCB 6: 496–9.

31 "To the People of Upper Canada," CA, 12 January 1832.

32 Pocock, *The Machiavellian Moment,* 486.

33 CA, 9 February 1832.

34 Morgan, *Public Men,* 57.

35 Ibid., 79.

36 CA, 15 December 1831; copy in CO42/411/10–11 Colborne to Goderich, 31 January 1832.

37 CO42/411/7 Colborne to Goderich, 31 January 1832. Colborne was very concerned about Mackenzie's appeal to the soldiers of the 79th regiment, which seems to have consisted of no more than distributing the address to the soldiers along with everyone else.

38 See Jacob Latham to E. McMahon, 12 December 1831 in Colborne to Goderich, 31 January 1832 in CO42/411/11.

39 Lindsey, *Mackenzie,* 203.

40 CA, 15 December 1831.

41 See Brock, *The Great Reform Act,* 251–3.

42 CA, 19 January 1832.

43 Lindsey, *Mackenzie,* 203. CA, 15 December 1831.

44 For the theme of respectability, see Mills, *Idea of Loyalty,* 63–4, 68–9.

45 See CG, 21 December 1831 in CO42/413/146–7.

46 See "Report of the Select Committee to which was referred the Petition of Donald Bethune and others of Kingston, complaining of the increasing influence of a Foreign Priesthood, &c.," dated 15 February 1831, in CO42/413/158–60.

47 Colborne's remarks take on an especially offensive cast in its echoes of Strachan's famous 1825 sermon on the death of Bishop Mountain, which similarly assailed the Methodists for their alleged lack of education. This sermon was a kind of opening salvo in Strachan's aggressive

campaign to entrench the privileged position of the Anglican Church in Upper Canada.

48 See CG, 21 December 1831 in CO42/413/146–7; also Sissons, *Ryerson,* 1: 147–51.

49 See CG, 21 December 1831 in CO42/413/147–50.

50 CO42/413/144–5. This was probably the handbill that Mackenzie distributed at the hustings according to CA, 5 January 1832.

51 CA, 22 March 1832, quoting the *Christian Guardian.* See also the account of the Niagara meeting of 31 March 1832 in CO42/413/116.

52 Quoted in CA, 12 April 1832.

53 CA, 16 February 1832. See also "To the York Committee" from James Coons, CA, 5 April 1832.

54 5 January 1832.

55 Mary Ryerson, York, to Dr James Lewis, Grimsby, 3 January 1832, quoted in Sissons, *Ryerson,* 1: 159.

56 Lindsey, *Mackenzie,* 205.

57 CO42/413/144–5. Mackenzie later used his electoral victories of January 1832 in communications with the Colonial Office to bolster his argument that public opinion was in his favour.

58 CA, 5 January 1832.

59 Ibid.

60 CO42/411/7 Colborne to Goderich 31 January 1832. *BR,* 19 January 1832. The *Colonial Advocate* reported that the copies had been made for distribution to MPPs.

61 For the details, see Dunham, *Political Unrest,* 126.

62 CA, 12 January 1832; CO42/411/15 Handbill in Colborne to Goderich, 31 January 1832. According to a correspondent of the *Brockville Gazette,* 19 January 1832, a dinner was to be given to the "*glorious minority*" at Elliot's Hotel on 13 January. "This farce," said the correspondent, "is got up under the special patronage of the 'Methodist Episcopals.' "

63 It appeared in the *BR,* 19 January 1832, and probably elsewhere.

64 CO42/411/14 Enclosed in Colborne to Goderich, 31 January 1832.

65 *Canadian Freeman,* 19 January 1832 in CO42/411/74 Colborne to Goderich, 16 February 1832.

66 CA, and *BR,* 19 January 1832. See also CO42/411/15 Handbill in Colborne to Goderich, 31 January 1832.

67 CO42/411/70 Colborne to Goderich, 16 February 1832.

68 *Canadian Freeman,* in CO42/411/74 in Colborne to Goderich, 16 February 1832.

69 Ibid.

70 CA, 26 January 1832; see also *Canadian Freeman,* 19 January 1832 in CO42/411/74.

71 CA, 26 January 1832.

72 Ibid.
73 *Canadian Freeman*, CO42/411/72 in Colborne to Goderich, 16 February 1832.
74 For Draper, see George Metcalf, "William Henry Draper," *DCB* 10: 253–9.
75 *Canadian Freeman*, 26 January 1832.
76 TRL, Baldwin Room, MSS, "Political Affairs in Upper Canada." Attributed to William Lyon Mackenzie, 20.
77 On township meetings generally, see Aitchison, "Development of Local Government," chapters 10 and 11.
78 See Armstrong, "York Riots"; Lesslie, "Diary of James Lesslie, March 22–24, 1832," 193–5.
79 The *Courier* threatened that "we most assuredly would not ensure the leading revolutionary tools a whole skin ... ;" Armstrong, "York Riots," 63. *CA*, 28 March 1832 contains reproductions of certificates from individuals who testified to threats against Mackenzie and Morrison before the 23 March meeting in York.
80 *CA*, quoted in Armstrong, "York Riots," 67.
81 This was a reference to the medal which had been presented to Mackenzie on 2 January.
82 Armstrong, "York Riots," 70.
83 Ibid., 71. The account in the York *Courier* says that Mackenzie and some of his colleagues had asked the lieutenant-governor to send troops to protect their lives and property. Colborne immediately sent an officer of the militia to the police office with the message that the entire garrison would be sent if the magistrates thought it necessary. The magistrates declined the offer. Quoted in *Brockville Gazette*, 5 April 1832.
84 "Orangemen and the Corporation," 41–86.
85 AO, Macaulay Family Papers, 23 and 24 March 1832.
86 The following paragraphs are based on a document in TRL, Carfrae Papers, Scrapbook.
87 *CA*, 16 February, 1 March 1832; *BR*, 1 March 32; Patterson, "Elections and Public Opinion," 441–2.
88 William Woodruff, St David's, to Francis Hincks, 26 August 1839, in Sanderson, ed., *Arthur Papers*, 2: 372; TRL, Robert Baldwin Papers, A78, # 30, 49, 50, William Woodruff to R.B., 8 February 1849, 9 and 20 December 1847.
89 *BR*, 15 March 1832.
90 *CA*, 16 February 1832; *BR*, 1 March 1832; Patterson, "Elections and Public Opinion," 93–4.
91 *CA*, 23 February 1832.
92 The right of assembly, a hotly contested issue in Upper Canada's past, was mentioned in justification of the practice of holding public meetings.
93 *BR*, 19 January 1832 from *CA*.
94 *BR*, 19 January 1832, quoting *CA*.

95 *CA*, 10 May 1832.
96 See the letter to the editor from "Howard" in the *Brockville Recorder*, reprinted in the *Brockville Gazette*, 22 March 1832.
97 *CA*, 19 March 1832.
98 Akenson, *Irish in Ontario*, 177.
99 Patterson, "Elections and Public Opinion," 340–5.
100 Ibid., 441–2; *BR*, 1 March 1832.
101 *CA*, 10 May 1832.
102 Lord Goderich's dispatch of 8 November 1832 credited the oppositionists with a total of only 12,075 signatures on a total of forty-four petitions. A copy of the dispatch is in CO42/413/258ff. This figure was subsequently adjusted upward to 20,447 by the Colonial Office. My own calculations indicate that the real figure was 22,583.
103 CO42/413/292. The Colonial Office may subsequently have given oppositionists credit for more than this; Mackenzie later thanked Lord Goderich for acknowledging clerical errors that had led to mistakes in the calculation of reform totals; see CO42/417/42 Mackenzie to Goderich, 4 February 1833.
104 There is no way of telling whether some supporters signed both sets of petitions; the Colonial Office, however, accepted the figures of just over 20,000.
105 The list in CO42/413/292 contains no entry for petition number 15, and no figures for number 40. Number 43 is listed as "missing."
106 Nelles, "Loyalism and Local Power," 107, 113–4.
107 Read and Stagg note that at the time of the Rebellion of 1837 it was in the Gore district that there "was the greatest concentration of rebel sympathy and rebel activity outside of the two rebel areas of the province"; *Rebellion of 1837*, lxxxii.
108 Patterson, "Elections and Public Opinion," 94–5.

CHAPTER FOUR

1 On Talbot, see Alan G. Brunger, "Thomas Talbot," *DCB* 8: 857–62.
2 This account is based on CO42/413/150; *BR*, reprinted in *CA*, 14 June 1832; Hamil, *Lake Erie Baron*, 184–97.
3 There is insufficient material on the district meeting in Sandwich for its inclusion here. The Niagara District meeting of 31 March is covered in Nelles, "Loyalism and Local Power," 107–10.
4 CO42/411/138.
5 *BG*, 8 March 1832.
6 *CA*, 5 July 1832.
7 *NG*, 7 and 14 April 1832. Three of the MPPs for Lincoln, John Clark, B.C. Beardsley, and Robert Randal, were oppositionists. The whereabouts of

William Crooks on the date of the meeting is unknown. Christopher Hagerman, the other crown law officer, was not recorded as present at the meeting in his constituency of the town of Kingston.

8 CO42/413/150. According to historian Fred Coyne Hamil, the local MPP, Mahlon Burwell, played a part in encouraging Talbot to call the meeting. In contrast to tory gatherings elsewhere, the St George's day meeting was not called by a requisition signed by the leading inhabitants. Instead, Talbot issued a proclamation in his own name calling the meeting and asking the inhabitants to attend. See Hamil, *Lake Erie Baron*, 189.

9 Colborne's approval of extraparliamentary organization in support of the administration was certainly evident from his reception of the address of the township of Georgina in mid-February 1832. He said, "I receive this address with the greatest satisfaction, and request that you will express to the inhabitants of Georgina my thanks for their kind assurances, and my best wishes for their happiness and prosperity"; see CO42/413/150.

10 *CA*, 8 March 32. The chief justice of Upper Canada was expected to hold frequent dinner parties for members of the Assembly, according to McKenna, *A Life of Propriety*, 78.

11 *BR*, 19 January 1832; see also *Brockville Gazette*, 5 January 1832.

12 *CA*, 8 March 1832.

13 J.E. Rea, "Alexander McDonell," *DCB* 7: 546.

14 Quoted in Rea, *Macdonell*, 111–2.

15 Cottrell, "Political Leadership and Party Allegiance Among Irish Catholics in Victorian Toronto," argues at p. 53 that "In the 1830s, Irish Catholics were a largely disenfranchised lower class whose political involvement was limited to the 'crack of clubs on skulls' during election campaigns." This is contradicted I think by the following account of the meetings.

16 See Gary Draper and Roger Hall, "William Dunlop," *DCB* 7: 260–4.

17 See Armstrong, "Carfrae Family."

18 Francis Collins' *Canadian Freeman* referred to Catholic opponents of the meeting as "tools of the saddle-bag faction." Quoted in *The Western Mercury*, 22 March 1832 in CO42/411/140.

19 See *CA*, 5 and 25 April 1832 for other references to the "soup kitchen."

20 Mackenzie reported that this meeting would have been held in the Catholic church "had it not been for the lieutenant governor's pious remarks in his reply to the address of the methodists." *CA*, 15 March 1832.

21 Tory sources claimed that Mackenzie's supporters gathered outside beforehand and "rushed the apartment" as soon as the doors were opened. The Bishop insisted that they leave. *NG*, 17 March 1832.

22 See Frederick H. Armstrong, "George Gurnett," *DCB* 9: 345–7.

23 Barrie Dyster, "George Duggan," *DCB*, 10: 262–3.

24 Lyons has been credited with a leadership role in the Types Riot of 1826. See Raible, *Muddy York Mud*, 63.

25 CO42/412/277. The townships of Albion and Adjala, where McDonell was also said to have canvassed for signatures, contributed over three hundred signatures. Ibid.

26 *CA*, 15 March, 5 April 1832.

27 Ibid.

28 "Extracts from the Second Handbill Addressed to the Roman Catholics of Upper Canada by Daniel O'Connell Jr," *CA*, 28 March 1832.

29 See Nicholson, "William O'Grady and the Catholic Church in Toronto Prior to the Irish Famine Migration," 23–40. See also Rea, *Macdonell*, 93 ff.

30 Armstrong, "George Gurnett," *DCB* 9: 345; Armstrong, "Scottish Immigrant," in Armstrong, *City in the Making*, 164–72. Armstrong drew attention to the middle-class character of the British Constitutional Society in his doctoral thesis, "Toronto in Transition," 323.

31 Unless otherwise indicated, this paragraph is based on Armstrong, "The Carfrae Family," 169–70; *Canadian Freeman*, 15 March 1832; and TRL, Carfrae Papers, Scrapbook, 12–22.

32 CO42/413/277. The *Colonial Advocate* for 15 March 1832 identified the following individuals as the canvassers for the tories: R. Hawes, storekeeper, "a gentleman building a windmill"; A. McDonald and R. Clarke, storekeepers; Thomas Carfrae, John McDermott, Bradshaw McMurray, Hugh Maguire, Thomas Bell Junior, A. Dickson the saddler, James Taylor (Yonge Street), George Duggan, and "a gentleman who keeps a livery stable."

33 *Canadian Freeman*, 29 March, 5 April 1832.

34 The following paragraphs are based on a document in TRL, Carfrae Papers, Scrapbook.

35 Armstrong, "Toronto in Transition," 323.

36 See TRL, Baldwin Room, Broadsides, 1832 Constitutional; Armstrong, "Carfrae Family"; Wilton, "Transformation of Upper Canadian Politics," chapter 4. Not all government supporters thought the British Constitutional Society was a good idea. The *Niagara Gleaner*, for one, said "we would much rather see these underhand measures counteracted in an open constitutional manner"; 24 March 1832.

37 CO42/411/135–6, "Proceedings."

38 Akenson, *Irish in Ontario*, 166–8.

39 *Brockville Gazette*, 26 January 1832; Senior, "Ogle Gowan, Orangeism," 199.

40 *Brockville Gazette*, 8 March 1832.

41 Ibid., 22 March 1832.

42 This account is based on *Brockville Gazette*, 22 and 29 March 1832, and also on *CA*, 5 April 1832.

43 On Sherwood, see Donald Robert Beer, "Henry Sherwood," *DCB* 8: 796–801.

44 CO42/411/143.
45 See Hamil, *Lake Erie Baron,* 155 ff.
46 CO42/411/255, Talbot to Colborne, 30 April 1832.
47 CO42/411/136.
48 CA, 28 March 1832.
49 *Canadian Freeman,* 10 May 1832.
50 CO42/411/141. See also CO42/413/154.
51 *Canadian Freeman,* 10 May 1832.
52 For a different approach to this question, see Baker, "'So Elegant a Web,'" 184–205. According to Baker, Mackenzie's newspaper articles, which provoked the Types Riot in York in 1826, "challeng[ed] nothing less than providence, a divinely inspired theory of government, the gentle code, the provincial constitution, and the predestined existence of Upper Canada itself." (pp. 197–8).
53 Morgan, *Public Men,* 71–2 comments extensively on the meaning of attacks on Mackenzie's wearing of a wig.
54 *Canadian Freeman,* 9 February 1832.
55 CO42/411/72.
56 *Brockville Gazette,* 5 April 1832. See also Dundas *Weekly Post,* 1, 15 December 1835.
57 Perhaps sensitive to charges such as these, oppositionist newspapers sometimes stressed that Mackenzie was not the only leader of their movement. The *St Thomas Liberal,* for example, said "the tories are much mistaken if they suppose, for an instant, that he [Mackenzie] is the rallying point and sole dependance [*sic*] of the friends of Colonial Improvement and Reform"; 18 October 1832.
58 Indeed, the *Canadian Freeman* once suggested that the reformers should perhaps send a more fitting and proper representative such as Dr John Rolph or Robert Baldwin as an emissary to Britain in Mackenzie's stead; see CO42/411/72.
59 Government supporters considered the support of the relatively affluent and respectable Baldwins for oppositionist activities to be problematic. As Robert Stanton put it, "how Baldwin & a few others can reconcile it to themselves to act as they do, in concert with such men [as Mackenzie] is astonishing." OA, Macaulay Papers, Robert Stanton, York, to John Macaulay, 11 November 1828. A broadside of 1830 attacking the Baldwins got around this difficulty by claiming that their wealth was illegitimately obtained, putting these words in the senior Baldwin's mouth: "I'm used to treach'ry and deception, and thus/ Have prospered." TRL, Broadsides, "1830. Baldwin, W."
60 *Globe,* 24 March 1849; *Examiner,* 28 March 1849.
61 Kingston *Patriot,* 6 March 1832, quoted in Hamil, *Lake Erie Baron,* 187–8.
62 "Conservative" attacks on the Methodists are discussed in Morgan, *Public Men,* 100–109. Morgan's statement that "religious matters often were con-

strued as political affairs" (p. 101) does not do justice to the very real link in the realm of political activism between oppositionists and Methodists.

63 The *Niagara Gleaner* once referred to the Upper Canadian parliament of 1828–30 as the "saddlebag Parliament"; 17 December 1831.

64 Letter from "Erin Go Braugh" to editor of the *Brockville Gazette,* 15 March 1832.

65 Semple, *The Lord's Dominion,* 180.

66 CO42/411/138.

67 *NG,* 28 April 1832.

68 *Canadian Freeman,* 3 May 1832 from the "C. Wesleyan, Hamilton." Francis Collins, editor of the *Canadian Freeman,* had been a staunch opponent of the regime of Sir Peregrine Maitland. He became, however, an equally firm supporter of Lieutenant-Governor Colborne, and, correspondingly, an effective critic of Mackenzie in the early 1830s. See H.P. Gundy, "Francis Collins," *DCB* 6: 165.

69 This seems strange in view of the fact that the Anglican clergy also engaged in circuit-riding. When tory lawyers began to canvass the Niagara district in March/April 1832, the reform press gleefully called them "itinerant[s];" see *CA,* 10 May 1832.

70 22 March 1832.

71 CO42/411/141.

72 *CA,* 28 March 1832.

73 CO42/411/135.

74 In 1841, a select committee of the legislature of the Province of Canada made this report on Gourlay's case: "the arrest and imprisonment of [Gourlay] in 1819 was illegal, unconstitutional, and without the possibility of excuse or palliation ..." AO, Mackenzie-Lindsey Clippings, MU 1854, #1980. I am indebted to archivist Leon Warmski for this reference.

75 See Wilton, "'Lawless Law,'" 132–3.

76 Thompson, *Making of the English Working Class,* 121–3, 126–7, 746–55; Booth, "Popular loyalism and public violence," 295–313. Also of interest is Elmsley, "Repression, 'terror' and the rule of law in England," 801–25.

77 Hereward Senior, "George Strange Boulton," *DCB* 9: 68.

78 A letter from Port Hope published in the *Colonial Advocate* of 5 April 1832 involved Brown and a merchant of Cavan, Samuel Davidson, who had visited Brown's store. Brown was said to have introduced Davidson as a Methodist preacher, and said the "d – d saddlebags" were "rebels to the government and were creating a disturbance." Davidson denied this, arguing that the real disturbers of the peace were Brown and those like him, who raised an outcry in order to ingratiate themselves with the authorities. Brown suggested that Davidson should watch out, as he might be murdered. In the street, after Davidson left the store, a man who had been present during the discussion struck him on the head from behind. The assailant was soon joined by two

accomplices, but Davidson was finally rescued. Mackenzie later pursued this incident in his correspondence with the colonial secretary, noting that Davidson, "a highly influential member of the methodist connexion," had made out an affidavit certifying that this account was true. Davidson then took his case to Colborne, who referred the matter to "Mr Brown's brother magistrates," but Mackenzie was in no doubt that Brown was "perfectly safe in their hands." CO42/417/53. Mackenzie was right: see the extensive correspondence on the Brown case in CO42/416/507–23. See also Guillet, ed., *The Valley of the Trent*, 295–6. For a libel case in which Brown was involved later in 1832, see *NG*, October 1832.

79 Senior, "Ogle Gowan, Orangeism," 206.

80 Ibid., 202.

81 Letter to the editor, *CA*, 8 March 1832; *Cobourg Star*, 11 April 1832.

82 Letter to the editor, *CA*, 8 March 1832. The *Cobourg Star* later contained some correspondence on this. The *Christian Guardian* had charged that Brown had sent sleighs to the townships of Cavan and Peterborough to bring in Orangemen to the Amherst meeting. A correspondent of the *Star* argued that both John Brown and Mr Bethune had sent sleighs to an inn in Cavan. No enquiries, however, he disingenuously pointed out, were made as to the politics of those who accepted rides; *Cobourg Star*, 11 April 1832.

83 *Cobourg Star* quoted in *BR*, 8 March 1832; *CA*, 1 March 1832. The *Colonial Advocate* of 26 April 32 carried a quote from the *Old Countryman* to the effect that about fifty "low fellows" had been hired to disrupt the meeting.

84 *Cobourg Star* quoted in *BR*, 8 March 1832; *CA*, 1 March 1832.

85 The Gore *Mercury* said this was the largest meeting ever held in the country; quoted in *CA*, 22 March 1832.

86 Paul Romney, "Charles Fothergill," *DCB* 7: 317–21.

87 *Cobourg Star*, quoted in *BR*, 8 March 1832.

88 In a letter to the editor of the *Star*, Boswell vehemently denied the charge of being "an advocate of *revolutionary* principles." He had gone to the meeting, he said, after being urged by both sides to attend, though reluctant to do so because he anticipated "violent political excitement"; *BR*, 15 March 1832.

89 *BR*, 8 March 1832. The *Cobourg Star* reported that Macdonald persisted for nearly an hour in trying to obtain a hearing from the crowd; 29 February 1832. According to one eyewitness, Covert "*barked* like a *cur*" while Macdonald tried to speak.

90 *CA*, 22 March 1832.

91 Ibid., 8 March 1832

92 Other accounts say that the address was read by G.S. Boulton, and that both Boulton and Ruttan read it. See *CA*, 8 March 1832.

93 See Winstock, *Songs & Music*, 95 and McDayter, *Military Music*, 12–13. I am indebted to Carl Benn of Fort York for this information.

94 CA, 8 and 15 March 1832.
95 CA, 8 March 1832, from the *Courier.*
96 CA, 8 March 1832.
97 Ibid., 22 March 1832.
98 *Cobourg Star,* 21 August 1833 and 26 September 1832.
99 Gore *Mercury,* quoted in CA, 22 March 1832.
100 *Kingston Chronicle,* quoted in *Brockville Gazette,* 15 March 1832.
101 *Brockville Gazette,* 15 March 1832.
102 Beer, *MacNab,* 31–3.
103 On occasion, the popular politics of the district intersected with those of York, as demonstrated in the tarring and feathering of oppositionist leader John Rolph's brother George in 1826; it has been assumed that this was in fact an indirect attack on the prominent politician; see Romney, *Mr Attorney,* 109–14.
104 Beer, *MacNab,* 47.
105 NG, 31 March 1832.
106 CA, 28 March 1832.
107 Beer, *MacNab,* 48.
108 CO42/411/141 and CO42/413/154.
109 Excerpt from London (Upper Canada) *Sun,* CO42/417/51.
110 *Canadian Freeman,* 22 March 1832.
111 CO42/417/55–6. Mackenzie complained bitterly that in Kerr's trial, "the person who tried the case [Judge James Buchanan Macaulay] and the person who conducted the case for the crown [Solicitor General Christopher Hagerman] were the two counsel for the parties who destroyed my types in 1826!" Mackenzie's son-in-law believed, on the contrary, that Macaulay "showed the greatest impartiality on the trial." Lindsey, *Mackenzie,* 220.
112 CO42/411/249, Colborne to Hay, 7 May 1832.
113 Pro-government forces were also a presence in the western district, where they held a meeting in Sandwich in April; see appendix A, "Political Meetings, Spring 1832." This meeting, however, evidently failed to produce a petition that reached the Colonial Office.
114 A petition to Charles Poulett Thomson at the end of 1839 lamented that the Ottawa district "has continued to languish in comparative obscurity." NA, R.G. 5, B-3, 12: 1807.
115 CA, 15 March 1832.
116 CA, 23 April 1832.
117 CA, 5 April 1832. This is surely a revealing illustration of the pervasiveness of gender distinctions in Upper Canadian society!
118 *Cobourg Star,* quoted in BR, 8 March 1832.
119 *Cobourg Star,* 23 March 1832.
120 CA, 5 April 1832.

121 *CA*, 15 March 1832. "The Voice of a Friend to the Roman Catholics of Upper Canada. New Derrinane Abbey. York. 9 March 1832."
122 CO42/416/152.
123 "The Franchise in Upper Canada," 14.
124 Quoted in Clark, *Language of Liberty*, 304.
125 *CA*, 12 April 1832.
126 *CA*, 5 April 1832.
127 *CA*, 16 February 1832.
128 I am referring here particularly to the role of the Methodists after 1833, described in Mills, *Idea of Loyalty*, chapter 5. On the other side, there were "moderates" like the Baldwins, but their voices were silent in 1832.
129 *CA*, 28 March 1832.
130 See Patterson, "Elections and Public Opinion," 104.
131 *CA*, 28 March, 12 April 1832.
132 *BR*, 18 October 1832, from the *Colonial Advocate*.
133 *NG*, 31 March, 7 April, 5 and 12 May (from the *Brockville Gazette*) 1832.
134 *Cobourg Star*, 27 February, 23 March, 4 April 1832; *Brockville Gazette*, 9 August, 20 September 1832.

CHAPTER FIVE

1 Since the terms "tory" and "reformer" had now entered the political vocabulary in Upper Canada, these terms will be used hereafter.
2 *C&A*, 21 March 1836.
3 *Cobourg Star*, 15 August 1832
4 15 December 1832.
5 22 November 1832.
6 *BR*, 6 December 1832.
7 *Brockville Gazette*, 13 December 1832 quoting *BR*.
8 CO42/417/15, Mackenzie to Goderich, 9 January 1833.
9 *CA*, 17 January 1833.
10 See *CA*, 13 December 1832.
11 *CA*, 31 January 1833.
12 On Montgomery see Edwin C. Guillet, "John Montgomery," *DCB* 10: 529–30; on Lloyd, see Ronald J. Stagg, "Jesse Lloyd," *DCB* 7: 508–9. Montgomery's tavern on Yonge Street near Eglinton Avenue north of York was the place of rendezvous for Mackenzie's force on the eve of the Rebellion. Lloyd raised a large force from north of the city to augment Mackenzie's forces in December 1837.
13 Schrauwers, *Awaiting the Millennium*, 157–68. Opinion among members of this sect was not always unanimously in favour of Mackenzie; see McIntyre, *Children of Peace*, 161–2.

14 This was not intended as an appeal to violence, since another provision of the statement denounced the use of political violence. Moreover, this statement specifically calls for *constitutional* forms of resistance, which would not include violence.

15 The following paragraphs are based on material from the *St Thomas Liberal*, 24 January 1833.

16 *St Thomas Liberal*, 24 January 1833.

17 *The Antidote*, 23 January 1833 quoting the *St Thomas Liberal*.

18 Patterson, "Elections and Public Opinion," 113.

19 24 January 1833.

20 Quoted in Ermatinger, *The Talbot Regime*, 157–8.

21 31 January, 14 February 1833. Also in 1833, the press of the *Liberal* was wrecked by tory activists. Patterson, "Elections and Public Opinion," 110–1.

22 "Proceedings of the Annual Meeting of the Grand Orange Lodge, of British North America, assembled in the Town of Brockville on Tuesday the 5th of June 1832." *Brockville Gazette*, 21 June 1832.

23 *Brockville Gazette*, 4 October 1832. See also *Antidote*, 9 April, 14 May 1833. As Heward Senior has observed, this was an effort to revive "Independent Clubs," first proposed by Gowan two years before, and the "Patriot Clubs" of 1832. Senior observed: "These were modeled on the 'Brunswick Clubs' which had been organized around the nucleus of the Orange Order in Ireland for the purpose of rallying opposition to O'Connell's Catholic Association." See Senior, "Gowan, Orangeism," 199–206.

24 Quoted in *Brockville Gazette*, 30 November 1832.

25 It was critical of Mackenzie's methods, and dubious about the extent of his following. Goderich, moreover, believed that many of Mackenzie's complaints were best redressed through the provincial Assembly.

26 CA, 31 January 1833.

27 Craig, *Upper Canada*, 214; CO42/416/548–9 in Thompson to Goderich, 24 May 1833.

28 See the reports in BR, 28 February 1833, from the *Port Hope Telegraph*; and BR, 7 March 1833, "To the Editor of the *Cobourg Star*."

29 The following account is based on *St Thomas Liberal*, 7 March 1833, from the *Reformer*.

30 For Bethune, see Peter Ennals, "James Gray Bethune," DCB 7: 74–6.

31 *St Thomas Liberal*, 7 March 1833 from the *Reformer*.

32 This view of reform political meetings was not confined to Cobourg and vicinity. The *Toronto Patriot*, for example, applauded the conduct of Brown and his colleagues: "The view taken of public meeting generally, is correct, and we hope will be well considered all over the Province. It is quite odious to think, of the waste of time and labour, the nincumpoop *Reformers* cause in their respective neighbourhoods." *Patriot*, 8 March 1833.

33 As a result of this incident, Wainwright was charged with assaulting J.T. Williams and David Smart, another reformer, in the street. Tried in April 1833, he was convicted and fined 1 shilling – a nominal amount. AO, RG 22, ser. 31, Box 10, Wainright. I am grateful to Susan Lewthwaite for this reference.
34 Fowke was the secretary of the Port Hope meeting on 9 February 1833. A copy of the address is in *BR*, 28 February 1833. CO42/416/282–6, Fowke to Goderich, 6 April 1833.
35 Quoted in *Cobourg Star*, 20 March 1833.
36 *St Thomas Liberal*, 28 March 1833.
37 This account is taken from the *Cobourg Star*, 20 March 1833, from the *Antidote.*
38 *Correspondent*, 15 February 1834.
39 *Cobourg Star*, 20 March 1833 quoting the *Antidote.*
40 *Cobourg Star*, 15 February 1834.
41 *BR*, 28 March 1833.
42 For negative comments on tory violence in Leeds and elsewhere, see *BR*, 14 and 28 March, and 23 May 1833; *St Thomas Liberal*, 4 April 1833; CO42/416/547, Thompson to Goderich, 24 May 1833.
43 *St Thomas Liberal*, 7 March 1833, from the *Reformer.*
44 Patterson, "Elections and Public Opinion," 110–1. In 1833 the *St Thomas Liberal* carried an article arguing that the press was not just one of the targets of tory attack but the major target: 14 March 1833 quoting the *Cobourg Reformer.*
45 *Correspondent*, 13 September 1834, from the *Kingston Whig*. On Smith see Donald Swainson, "Sir Henry Smith," *DCB* 9: 725–7.
46 *St Thomas Liberal*, 21 and 28 March 1833; *Cobourg Star*, 20 and 27 March 1833.
47 CO42/416/546–52, Thompson to Goderich, 24 May 1833.
48 Joseph Hume told Mackenzie in June that he had received a petition and address to the King "to express their gratitude for the changes that have been made under Lord Goderich's orders." The documents contained 19,930 signatures. *A New Almanac for Canadian True Blues … 1834*, 7.
49 The Anglicans, meanwhile, circulated a counter-petition. *BR*, 7 March 1833.
50 CO42/416/546, Thompson to Goderich, 24 May 1833; Ryerson, "*The Story of My Life*," 221. He presented these petitions to the colonial secretary early in June 1833; Sissons, *Ryerson*, 1: 183.
51 *BR*, 7 June 1833.
52 *CA*, 29 June 1833, quoted in Clark, *Movements of Political Protest*, 358.
53 Mackenzie to Randal Wixon, 22 March 1833; *BR*, 2 May 1833.
54 Burroughs, *Canadian Crisis*, 60.

55 Hume to Dr John Duncan, Secretary to the Political Union, Aberdeen, 3 August 1833, *A New Almanac for Canadian True Blues,* 17.
56 Burroughs, *Canadian Crisis,* 43–59.
57 19 October 1833.
58 Armstrong and Stagg, "Mackenzie," 500.
59 *BR,* 10 January 1834.
60 Craig, *Upper Canada,* 216; Gidney, "Ryerson," 786.
61 United Church Archives, Egerton Ryerson Papers, Box 1, File 10, Edwy Ryerson, Stamford, to E. Ryerson, 26 November 1833.
62 Kilbourn, *Firebrand,* 102.
63 See, for example, *BR,* 1 August 1834.
64 *Cobourg Star,* 29 May, 5 June 1833.
65 In March the *Patriot* ran articles denouncing the idea of Mackenzie being the first Mayor of Toronto: "he has constantly reviled every British, and extolled every American Institution": *Patriot,* 21 and 26 March 1834. For the reaction to Hume's letter, see *Patriot,* 20 June, 15 July, 12 August 1834; see also *Patriot,* June generally. The Methodist Conference on 20 June 1834 also adopted an address to Colborne denouncing "the recent avowal of revolutionary principles and purposes."
66 *Cobourg Star,* 30 July 1834.
67 The following account is based on the *Patriot,* 29 July 1834. See also *TRL,* Broadsides, "1834 British," "British Constitutional Society of Upper Canada." For committees of vigilance, see Clark, *Movements of Political Protest,* 357–8.
68 Metcalf, "Draper," 253–9.
69 Armstrong, "Gurnett," 345–7.
70 *CA,* 19 September 1833.
71 19 October 1833.
72 *CA,* 11 July 1833.
73 *St Thomas Liberal,* 4 July 1833; Clark, *Movements of Political Protest in Canada,* 356–60.
74 *BR,* 10 January 1834.
75 Account of the township nomination meeting for the front of Yonge, Leeds, and Lansdowne, *BR,* 31 January 1834. This issues carried accounts of meetings at which similar resolutions were passed: in the township of Elmsley, and the rear of Leeds and Lansdowne. See also *BR,* 7 February 1834, Edwardsburgh and Kemptville township meetings.
76 *BR,* 10 January 1834.
77 *Correspondent,* 1 March 1834.
78 *BR,* 10 January 1834.
79 *BR,* 27 December 1833 from the *Colonial Advocate.* The resolutions of the county meeting were not published.
80 *Advocate,* 13 March 1834.

81 *Correspondent*, 1 March 1834.
82 Clark, *Movements of Political Protest*, 360–1.
83 *Advocate*, 27 February, 13 March, 16 October 1834.
84 Clark, *Movements of Political Protest*, 359–62.
85 Ibid., 360.
86 *British American Journal*, 25 April 1834.
87 Ibid., 24 June 1834.
88 *Patriot*, 25 September 1834.
89 See Wilton, "Transformation of Upper Canadian Politics," chapter 4.
90 The following account is based on the *Correspondent*, 26 April 1834, and Patterson, "Elections and Public Opinion," 468–74.
91 *Correspondent*, 26 April, 10 and 17 May, 13 September 1834.
92 Perry asked Cartwright if he had made a disparaging remark about the Methodists at a meeting in Frontenac in 1832. Though Cartwright denied it, a witness to the event testified as to the truth of Perry's report. The remark was "That the Methodist preachers neither feared God nor man, nor honored the King!"
93 Mackenzie was expelled for the third time late in 1832, again in early 1833, and lastly on 17 December 1833. Mackenzie tried to get up a petition to request the King to dissolve the Assembly because of his most recent expulsion in early 1834: *Patriot*, 11 March 1834. For public reaction, see Kilbourn, *Firebrand*, 95–7, Senior, "Gowan, Orangeism," 209.
94 Craig, *Upper Canada*, 221. C&A, 11 April 1835 says Sheriff Jarvis and the jailer "were violently opposed to the election of Mr Mackenzie, both for the City and for the second riding as member. The jailor had leave of absence to go to the country and harangue at public meetings, and distribute handbills through the west riding, of the most abusive nature, previous to the last election."
95 Akenson, *The Irish in Ontario*, 182–9.
96 The tories retook the seat at the general election of 1836. There was violence in Toronto at the time of the 1834 election, but there is no evidence that this influenced the results. See Romney, "The Ordeal of William Higgins," and "A Struggle for Authority," 29–32.
97 *Patriot*, 31 October 1834 from the *Toronto Recorder*. Duggan, a Toronto lawyer, future mayoral candidate, and judge, was also a vice-president of the British Constitutional Society: *Patriot*, 29 July 1834. He was also a prominent Orangeman who was district master by 1840. On Duggan generally, see Dyster, "Duggan," 262–3.
98 The following information is based on the *Correspondent and Advocate*, 18 and 24 December 1834.
99 C&A, 24 December 1834. See also AO, W.L. Mackenzie Papers, 963, 964.
100 C&A, 26 December 1834. The *Toronto Patriot* was incensed by these directives. The Alliance Society, it said, was attempting "to commit a breach of

the privileges of the Assembly, by an attempt to force upon them the Speaker of their choice ... and to convert the Town Meetings in January ... into riotous political assemblages." *Patriot*, 24 December 1834.

101 Jackson, "Organization of the Upper Canadian Reformers," 101–2.

102 *The Constitution*, 16 November 1836.

103 Mackenzie had given up his newspaper in late 1834; it was merged with O'Grady's *Correspondent* in Toronto to become *The Correspondent and Advocate.*

104 Buckner, *Transition to Responsible Government*, 213.

105 *Cobourg Star*, 4 March 1835 from the *Courier.*

106 *Cobourg Star*, 29 April 1835 from the *Courier.*

107 *Patriot*, 2 June and 4 August 1835. The British Constitutional Society of Leeds was very active prior to the by-election in electoral organization in that constituency in early 1836; *BR*, 29 January 1836.

108 Ibid.

109 Ibid.

CHAPTER SIX

1 See Craig, *Upper Canada*, 232–6. On Head generally, see Wise, ed., *Narrative*, xi-xxxiv; and S.F. Wise, "Sir Francis Bond Head," *DCB* 10: 342–5.

2 Cross and Fraser, "Robert Baldwin," *DCB* 8: 48.

3 Craig, *Upper Canada*, 236.

4 Wise, ed., *Narrative*, 43.

5 *C&A*, 14 March 1836.

6 *C&A*, 10, 17 and 24 March 1836.

7 Wise, ed., *Narrative*, 43–4. Head does not say which two members of the Assembly were involved. Newspaper reports of the addresses indicate that they were not worded in a similar way, though they generally mentioned the same points.

8 *C&A*, 14 March 1836. For other reports of meetings in the Home and London districts in support of the new appointments, see *C&A*, 10, 17 and 24 March 1836.

9 *C&A*, 10 March 1836.

10 *C&A*, 24 March 1836; the address is in Sundries, 164: 89244–7.

11 *C&A*, 21 March 1836.

12 Ibid.

13 *C&A*, 28 March 1836.

14 This analysis must have infuriated reformers, who habitually complained bitterly that their political opponents virtually monopolized appointive offices.

15 *C&A*, 28 March 1836.

16 Ibid.

17 See, for example, *BR*, 8 April 1836, and *C&A*, 4 April 1836.
18 The following account is based on *KC*, 13 April 1836, and *C&A*, 11 April 1836. "Strachan" was likely the Archdeacon's son.
19 *Cobourg Star*, 20 April 1836, from the *Toronto Courier.*
20 *BR*, 22 April 1836. A copy of the petition is enclosed in Sundries, 168: 91710, John McAuley, West Gwillimbury, 5 July 1836.
21 *SCJ*, 14 April 1836.
22 Sundries, 164: 89680, T. McKenna, Markham to Joseph, 30 March 1836.
23 *C&A*, 11 April 1836. In West Gwillimbury, John McAuley said he had seen the petition on 26 March.
24 Sundries, 168: 91760.
25 *C&A*, 28 March, 4, 7, 11, 14, and 27 April 1836; *BR*, 8 April 1836.
26 *C&A*, 11 April 1836.
27 *C&A*, 28 March 1836, *SCJ*, 14 April 1836.
28 *C&A*, 4 April 1836.
29 Wise, ed., *Narrative*, 46. See also *Cobourg Star*, 13 April 1836, and *SCJ*, 14 April 1836.
30 *BR*, 22 April 1836.
31 *C&A*, 11 May 1836.
32 *C&A*, 7 April 1836.
33 This total was arrived at by checking the entries under "Petitions for Relief &c.: Grievances, 1836" in the Index to the *Journals of the Legislative Assembly*, and adding together the number of signatures said to be attached: *JLAUC*, 1836, *Index, JLAUC*, 1848, 439–40. The petitions came from the following districts: Home, Niagara, London, Newcastle, London, Eastern, Johnstown, and Midland.
34 Sundries, 166: 80861–3, "List of Addresses Presented to His Excellency … up to the 25 May 1836."
35 Sundries, 165: 90186, 90331, 90321, 90378; 166: 90541, 90545,90560–1, 90582, 90628, 90657, 90652, 90678, 90701, 90762, 90762A, 90771, 90925–7; 167: 91089, 91273–4, and 91497. *Cobourg Star*, 6 April 1836, from *KC*; *SCJ*, 31 March 1836; *KC*, 13 April 1836; *BR*, 27 November 1836 quoted in Patterson, "Elections and Public Opinion," 121.
36 Sundries, 167: 91273–4, Jno. LeBreton, Brittania, Ottawa River, to J. Joseph, 10 June 1836.
37 There is some evidence that individuals in some localities undertook to obtain signatures to addresses on their own initiative. See Sundries, 165: 89543, illeg., Thornhill to Joseph, 28 March 1836; 167: 91156–7, O'Connor to Joseph, 7 June 1836.
38 Sundries, 166: 90963, Ruttan, Amherst to Joseph, 28 May 1836.
39 Sundries, 167: 91156–7, Daniel O'Connor, Bytown to Joseph, 7 June 1836.
40 CO42/430/106. On Hawke, see Wesley B. Turner, "Anthony Bewden Hawke," *DCB* 9: 377.

41 Sundries, 165: 89960, Robert E. Burns, St Catharines, to Joseph, 9 April 1836; 166: 90855–6, "Petition of the Inhabitants of Pittsburgh, County of Frontenac"; CO42/430/349–50.
42 Sundries, 166: 90929, George Hamilton to Joseph, 28 May 1836; 167: 91150, Joseph C. Lewis to Joseph, 7 June 1836.
43 Sundries, 167: 91273–4, Jno. Le Breton, Brittania, Ottawa River, to Joseph, 10 June 1836.
44 Sundries, 167: 91275–6.
45 Ibid., 91156, Daniel O'Connor to Joseph, 7 June 1836.
46 Sundries, 166: 80861–3, "List of Addresses Presented to His Excellency ... up to the 25 May 1836."
47 CO42/430/100.
48 CO42/430/43. See also the address from Pickering, ibid., 98.
49 CO42/430/99.
50 CO42/430/103.
51 CO42/430/46.
52 CO42/430/98.
53 CO42/430/97.
54 "Sir F.B. Head's Reply to an Address of Home District Electors," in Read and Stagg, eds., *Rebellion of 1837*, 9.
55 Quoted in Mills, *Idea of Loyalty* 80.
56 *Cobourg Star*, 11 May 1836 from the *Toronto Courier.*
57 Sundries, 167: 91476–9, Alex. Ross, St Thomas to Joseph, 22 June 1836; *Cobourg Star*, 15 and 22 June 1836; PAC, MGB24B7, vol. 1, Charles Jones to George Mallock, 13 June 1836; Walton, "1836 Election," 161.
58 Walton, "1836 Election," 160–1.
59 *Patriot*, 9 May 1837, 3 July 1838.
60 *C&A*, 11 May 1836.
61 *C&A*, 18 May 1836.
62 Hincks was destined for a long and useful career in politics. See William G. Ormsby, "Sir Francis Hincks," *DCB* 11: 406–16.
63 *BR*, 17 June 1836; *C&A*, 17 June 1836.
64 *C&A*, 8 June 1836.
65 Romney, "Eve of the Rebellion," 197–200.
66 Ibid., 200.
67 Kerr, "When Orange and Green United," 37–9.
68 Romney, "Eve of the Rebellion," 200.
69 Sundries, 167: 91107–10, J.B. Askin, London to Joseph, 6 June 1836; ibid., 91476–9 Alex. Ross, St Thomas to J. Joseph, 22 June 1836; Patterson, "Elections and Public Opinion," 486.
70 Sundries, 167: 91561–3, T. W. Magrath, Streetsville, 28 June 1836 (no recipient indicated).

71 TRL, W.W. Baldwin Papers, L11, B104, John Carey to W.W. Baldwin, Credit, 3 July 1836.

72 In response to an address from the Assembly, Head had announced: "The Government of this Province has neither taken nor has it determined to take any steps to prevent or discourage the formation or continuance of such Societies! I consider all *factious* combinations as hostile to the real interests of this country, but until they proceed to acts of violence or intimidation I consider that a forced remedy might prove worse than the disease." C&A, 4 May 1836. In view of the Orange record of violence since 1832, this remark must have infuriated reformers. In spite of this public support, however, Head seems to have privately encouraged Orange societies to disband. See Sundries, 166: 90605–12, correspondence between John Stewart, London, and J. Joseph. For an extended discussion of the relationship between Head and the Orange Order in 1836, see Cadigan, "Paternalism and Politics," 319–47.

73 See Wilton, " 'Lawless Law,' " 118–9. According to Graeme Patterson, the two seats in Leeds were captured by violence; "Elections and Public Opinion," 283–4.

74 *Constitution*, 9 August 1837.

75 These patents enabled those who held them to meet the property qualification for electoral purposes. See Gates, *Land Policies*, 186–8; Dawe, " '*Old Oxford*,' " 54.

76 Duncombe was a physician who represented Oxford County in the Assembly from 1830 to 1837, when he went into exile after acting as a leader in the rising in the London district. See Michael S. Cross, "Charles Duncombe," DCB 9: 228–31.

77 "Petition of Charles Duncombe," C&A, 30 November 1836.

78 C&A, 20 July 1836.

79 C&A, 7 December 1836.

80 *Upper Canada*, 239.

81 The following account is based on a report in C&A, 21 December 1836.

82 *Constitution*, 21 December 1836.

83 There were meetings of the Upper Chingacousy and Lower Caledon Political Union on 27 March and 10 May 1837, and of Lennox and Addington, probably in April; see *Constitution*, 12 April and 3 May 1837.

84 *Constitution*, 31 May 1837.

85 See Read and Stagg, eds., *Rebellion of 1837*, 55–65.

86 See Bailyn, Davis, et al. *Great Republic*, i-iii.

87 Read and Stagg, eds., *Rebellion of 1837*, xxxii.

88 *Constitution*, 26 July, 6 September 1837 .

89 *Constitution*, 23 August, 13 and 27 September, 4 and 25 October 1837.

90 This paragraph is based on Lindsey, *Mackenzie*, 335–6.

91 Read and Stagg, eds., *Rebellion of 1837*, 68.
92 Ibid., from the *Constitution*, 16 August 1837.
93 *Constitution*, 30 August 1837, letter from "D." dated 22 August 1837. See also ibid., 6 September 1837.
94 Ibid., "M.M." 24 August 1837.
95 Lindsey, *Mackenzie*, 339.
96 Read and Stagg, eds., *Rebellion of 1837*, 73, from *Constitution*, 23 August 1837.
97 Lindsey, *Mackenzie*, 339.
98 Read and Stagg, eds., *Rebellion of 1837*, 73–4, from the *Patriot*, 19 September 1837.
99 Ibid., 77–8, from *Constitution*, 4 October 1837.
100 Ibid., 79–83, quoted from London U.C. *Gazette* in *Toronto Patriot*, 13 October 1837.
101 Ibid., 68, from the *Patriot*, 15 August 1837.
102 Ibid., 74, quoting *Toronto Patriot*, 19 September 1837.
103 Ibid., 89, quoting *Hamilton Gazette*, 31 October 1837.
104 *Constitution*, 20 September 1837.
105 Read and Stagg, eds., *Rebellion of 1837*, 86, from the *Constitution*, 25 October 1837.
106 Romney, "From the Types Riot to the Rebellion," 139.
107 Economic historian Douglas McCalla argues that "the economic setback of 1837 was ... a substantial fluctuation more than a turning-point in larger growth trends in the Upper Canadian economy." He thus casts serious doubt on explanations of the Rebellion that rely heavily on material causes. See McCalla, *Planting the Province*, 187–93. Attempts to establish characteristics differentiating tories from reformers are hampered by the scattered and incomplete nature of the evidence. Historians who have attempted this, however, have discovered that it was not economic differences but those of religion (more Anglicans among the tories) and "ethnicity" (more of American origin among the rebels) that separated the two sides. See Read, *Rising in Western Upper Canada*, 164–204, and Stagg, "The Yonge Street Rebellion," chapters 6 and 8.
108 Extract from Mackenzie's speech to the electors of the Second Riding of York, June 1836; *Constitution*, 20 September 1837.
109 *Constitution*, 9 August 1837.
110 *Constitution*, 13 September 1837.
111 Those who actually resorted to arms were a relatively small group, 500–600 in Toronto and about 500 in the London district. See Read and Stagg, eds., *Rebellion of 1837*, lii, lxi.
112 Read, *Rising in Western Upper Canada*, 209.
113 Unless otherwise stated, the material in this section is based on Read and Stagg, eds., *Rebellion of 1837*, xix-c, and Craig, *Upper Canada*, 241–51.

114 Craig, *Upper Canada*, 247.
115 Read and Stagg, eds., *Rebellion of 1837*, liv.
116 See, generally, Gates, *After the Rebellion*.
117 Craig, "Marshall Spring Bidwell," DCB 10: 63; Read and Stagg, eds., *Rebellion of 1837*, xcii.
118 Ibid., lxxxiv.
119 Ibid., lxxxvii.
120 Ronald J. Stagg, "Samuel Lount," DCB 7: 518, and "Peter Matthews," ibid., 596.
121 Armstrong and Stagg, "Mackenzie," DCB 9: 505.
122 Read, *Rising in Western Upper Canada*, 148–9.
123 Boyce, *Rebels of Hastings*, 150–2.
124 Susannah Moodie, *Life in the Clearings*, 35, quoted in ibid., 168.
125 The foremost authority on the concept of a party system is Hofstadter, *Idea of a Party System*.
126 See Wilton, "The Transformation of Upper Canadian Politics."
127 Read and Stagg, eds., *Rebellion of 1837*, xciv.
128 It has been observed, for example, that the presence of a British garrison in London after 1838 did much to promote pro-British feeling in the Western district; Landon, *Western Ontario*, 184. The subject, as Read pointed out, requires further study; *Rising in Western Upper Canada*, 211.
129 *Rising in Western Upper Canada*, 211. I am also reliably informed that members of families resident in the Newmarket area north of Toronto since the days of the Rebellion still remember what political affiliations were adopted at that time; private conversation with Professor Heather MacDougall, University of Waterloo.
130 *Toronto Examiner*, 3 March 1841.

CHAPTER SEVEN

1 Sanderson, ed., *Arthur Papers*, vol. 2, [Arthur] to Colborne, 8 August 1839, 207.
2 In order to avoid excessive notes, information on the places and dates of the meetings, together with the major newspaper sources for each, has been collected in appendix E.
3 The meetings occurred in the most settled areas of the province, between Lennox and Addington in the east and the Niagara District in the southwest. The relatively remote location of many of these meetings was no doubt due, at least in part, to the toryism prevailing in so many Upper Canadian towns. The Durhamites, anxious to avoid violence at the hands of their political opponents, sensibly held most of their meetings in spots outside tory strongholds. See Wise, "Upper Canada and the Conservative Tradition," 20.

4 Estimates of the crowds were as follows: five to six hundred people at the township of Murray meeting, Newcastle District; eight hundred in Colborne, for the township of Haldimand, also in the Newcastle District; a thousand at the Gore District meeting in Hamilton; eighteen hundred in Thorold, where the Niagara District meeting occurred; and two thousand in Simcoe in the Talbot District.

5 Craig, *Upper Canada*, 264–6. See also Robinson, *Canada and the Canada Bill.*

6 New, *Lord Durham's Mission*, 189–91, 193–4, 201–4.

7 Craig, *Upper Canada*, 268.

8 Gourlay, *Neptunian No.* 2, 29.

9 Ibid., note p. 28.

10 *NC*, 19 September 1839; Milani, *Gourlay*, 255. A few days before the Thorold meeting, Gourlay, who was travelling about to promote it, was assaulted near Grimsby, the result, he maintained, of a conspiracy against him; see Gourlay, *Neptunian*, 35–6.

11 *Examiner*, 3 March 1841.

12 *BC*, 10 April 1839; William Woodruff, St David's, to Francis Hincks, 26 August 1839, in Sanderson, ed., *Arthur Papers*, 2: 372–3.

13 Although usually considered a government supporter during the 1820s and 30s, Merritt had been a strong supporter of Robert Gourlay in 1818 and offered his assistance in Gourlay's efforts at rehabilitation in 1839. See Milani, *Gourlay*, 140, 256–7.

14 See *TRL*, Robert Baldwin Papers, A57#87–99, 101–29, 132–43; A62#17–37, 39–40; A64#2–25; A75#1–22; and Wilton[-Siegel], "The Transformation of Upper Canadian Politics in the 1840s."

15 On occasion outsiders were allowed to participate; individuals who had attended the Halton and Gore meetings were permitted, for example to address the Guelph meeting. *BR*, 15 August 1839. W.H. Merritt and William Notman both addressed the Talbot meeting. Ibid., 25 September 1839. Though outsiders might attempt to influence the character of the meetings, as Hincks did in the Niagara district, they found it necessary to convince local supporters of the correctness of their position and work through them. See Woodruff to Hincks, 26 August 1839, in Sanderson, ed., *Arthur Papers*, 2: 372.

16 Resolutions have survived for twelve of the meetings; these produced nine sets of resolutions. The resolutions of the Gore and Guelph meetings were the same as those of Dundas.

17 Sir George Arthur also reported "a serious unpleasantry" at the militia muster in the Midland District on 4 June 1839: "They brought Lord Durham's flag, and an American flag and some speeches were made not very much in favor of Monarchical Institutions[.]" Arthur to Colborne, 17 June 1839, in Sanderson, ed., *Arthur Papers*, 2: 170.

18 *BR*, 20 June 1839.

19 *BR*, 1 August 1839; *BC*, 7 August 1839.
20 *SCJ*, 10 October 1839.
21 See appendix E.
22 *NC*, 19 September 1839.
23 See Sundries, 228: 124931, Sheriff K. Cameron to S.B. Harrison, 10 September 1839. Other meetings called by requisition included the Township of Murray, the Gore district, the Talbot district, and the Home district.
24 See *BR*, 12, 19 September 1839; *BC*, 28 August and 11 September 1839.
25 See Sundries, 237: 124931, Cameron to Harrison, 10 September 1839.
26 Sundries, 223: 122625, Baron de Rottenberg to Hon. John Macaulay, 26 June 1839.
27 *KC*, 13 July 1839, from the *Cobourg Star.*
28 Ibid.
29 Dr Mackenzie's Diary, 16 July 1839.
30 *BR*, 8 August 1839, from the *Examiner*, 31 July 1839.
31 *SCJ*, 1 August 1839.
32 *NC*, 19 September 1839.
33 See Epstein, "Understanding the Cap of Liberty," and Brewer, *Party Ideology*, 179. I am grateful to Professor N. Rogers of York University for drawing these sources to my attention.
34 The only exception was the Newcastle meeting, which was generally admitted to have been a gathering of the reformers of Hamilton township.
35 *BR*, 20 June 1839.
36 *NC*, 19 September 1839.
37 22 August 1839.
38 Armstrong, *Handbook*, 57.
39 *SCJ*, 14 September 1839.
40 24 July 1839.
41 This was the same Henry Ruttan who had taken the chair at the Amherst meeting in February 1832. Ruttan had evidently experienced a change of political views in the ensuing years.
42 Sundries, 222: 122230–41, Col. de Rottenberg to the Hon. John Macaulay, enclosing reports from Adam H. Meyers ... , 13 June 1839.
43 Ibid. It appears that only one man was tried as a result of these incidents. On 8 June 1830, Jeremiah Sheppard of Percy, a labourer, was convicted of assaulting Arthur Kenny, also a labourer from Percy. Sheppard was fined 5 pounds. AO, R.G. 22, Series 39, Box 1, env. 10, 1839. I am indebted to Susan Lewthwaite for this information.
44 *Cobourg Star*, 16 June 1839.
45 *BC*, 25 September 1839.
46 *NC*, 19 September 1839. The *NC* carried a report on 26 September 1839 that Mr Adams's tannery was burned in retaliation for his efforts to stop some Americans bearing a flag to the Durham meeting.

47 *BR*, 8 August 1839; *SCJ*, 5 September 1839.
48 Romney, "From the Types Riot to the Rebellion," 132. See also Romney, *Mr Attorney*, 104–57.
49 Mills, *Idea of Loyalty*. See also Baker, "So Elegant a Web"; and Romney, "Very Late Loyalist Fantasies."
50 Moderate reformers like the Baldwins had long argued to a select audience that responsible government was no more and no less than the British system of government. The argument was revived in the 1840s by reformers like Francis Hincks, editor of the *Toronto Examiner*. Thus the Durhamites provide a link connecting the pre- and post-Rebellion reform movements. See Wilton, "Transformation of Upper Canadian Politics," 83–7, 104–9.
51 Reform rhetoric, according to Jane Errington among others, was a manifestation of country-party ideology in the Pocockian sense. In 1839, however, the necessity of stressing their loyalty encouraged reformers to suppress the shriller aspects of this ideology. Moreover, their targets in the Durham resolutions were so specific that Pocock is of little analytic assistance. See Errington, *The Lion, the Eagle*, 94–5; Pocock, *The Machiavellian Moment*, 486–7.
52 For example, see Wilson, *As She Began*, 21–2.
53 See Mills, *Idea of Loyalty*, 15–18.
54 The sarcasm of this second-hand account of the speech does not warrant the inference that Eccles was endorsing the participation of women and children in politics.
55 The resolutions betrayed their elite authorship in a number of respects. In demanding the implementation of Lord Durham's Report, and in offering specific criticisms of speeches and proposed bills of the British government, the activists revealed a sophisticated attention to the minutiae of British politics as they affected Upper Canada. Similarly, the efforts to undermine the legitimacy of the House of Assembly, whose criticisms of the famous report had evidently made such an impression on British politicians, indicates a close following of politics on the part of those who drew up the resolutions. These, then, were not the spontaneous outpourings of the politically naive but carefully crafted documents produced by the politically articulate.
56 Except at the Beaverton meeting.
57 Many of these grievances had been current in Gourlay's day. See "Draft of an Address proposed for presentation to the Prince Regent ..." in Gourlay, *Account* II: 376–80.
58 Read and Stagg, eds., *Rebellion of 1837*, xxxiv.
59 This point is also made in Carol Wilton, "Administrative Reform."
60 See Brewer, *Party Ideology*, 120; Butterfield, *George III and the Historians*. For the use of analogies to the Bute situation by the Reform press in the mid-1840s, see Wilton, "British to the Core," 295–6.
61 Ibid., 296.

62 For a useful discussion of militia parades in the American context, see Davis, *Parades and Power*, chapter 3.
63 For the significance of the use of public space, see Epstein, "Understanding the Cap of Liberty," 95.
64 According to David Mills, "the Tories totally rejected the legitimacy of opposition; dissent was disloyal because it disrupted the social equilibrium and political harmony of the province. Dissent was illegitimate for several reasons: Upper Canada remained vulnerable after 1815 and unity had to be maintained; the province was still politically immature; abuses were unthinkable under the British system; and finally, oppositionists were selfish, with suspect motives. Dissent had to be crushed." Mills, *Idea of Loyalty*, 33. See also Wright, "The Ideological Dimensions of Law," 131–77; and Wright, "Sedition in Upper Canada," 7–57.
65 See the *Cobourg Star*, cited in KC, 13 July 1839, and Sanderson, ed., *Arthur Papers*, 2: 183–4, 192–3, 204–7, 211–12.
66 According to Bowsfield, "Upper Canada," 281, this right had been established in the 1820s.
67 SCJ, 11 July 1839. W.O. Mackenzie, a Scottish doctor attached to the troops, reported that "Sir Geo. Arthur had received authentic information that a great meeting, and subsequent 'rise' were to take place on the 4th [in Brighton]." Dr Mackenzie's Diary, 3 July 1839. BC, 25 September 1839.
68 SCJ, 5 September 1839; BC, 25 September 1839.
69 SCJ, 5 September 1839.
70 See CA, 15 December 1831, and CG, 21 December 1831 in CO42/413/146–7.
71 Sanderson, ed., *Arthur Papers*, vol. 2, Arthur to Thomson, 9 November 1839, 303.
72 KC, 7 September 1839.
73 Quoted in ibid., 13 July 1839.
74 BC, 30 October 1839.
75 TRL, Broadsides, "1839, Durham."
76 See Adjutant-General's Office, *Rules and Regulations*. I am indebted for this reference and the explanation of the "Vinegar Hill Croppies" to Carl Benn of Fort York.
77 In early nineteenth-century England, the cap of liberty "represented the antithesis of British constitutional 'liberty' and patriotism. The presence of the cap of liberty betrayed the real intent of plebeian radicals, exposing the constitutional guise of their proceedings as merely cover for seditious organization"; see Epstein, "Understanding the Cap of Liberty," 79.
78 Read and Stagg, eds., *Rebellion of 1837*, liv.
79 The ignorance of supporters of responsible government was a favourite target of the tory press. See, for example, BC, 11 September 1839.
80 See above, page 133.

81 Curtis Fahey, "William John O'Grady," *DCB* 7: 661–5.

82 Another popular and destructive ritual in which opponents of political change engaged was cattle-maiming. The *SCJ* for 11 July 1839 noted that a bull belonging to a reformer had been savagely attacked ["altered"] the night before the Cobourg meeting; significantly, the animal was a Durham bull.

83 *SCJ*, 11 July 1839.

84 *Toronto Mirror*, quoted in *BR*, 18 July 1839.

85 *Cobourg Star*, 10 July 1839; Kealey, "Orangeism," 50.

86 *BR*, 18 July 1839.

87 *BR*, 8 August 1839, from the *Examiner*.

88 Gibbs, ed., *Debates* 1841, 1008–10; 1843, 438–9, 442.

89 This paragraph is based on documents printed in *BC*, 28 August 1839.

90 *BC*, 2 October 1839.

91 See *BC*, 23 and 30 October 1839; *BR*, 24 and 31 October 1839; *KC*, 13 November 1839.

92 "Report on the Yonge Street Riots," *Examiner*, 27 October 1841.

93 An inquest into the death of David Leppard was held at the end of October 1839. The verdict was "Accidental death caused by the wagon wheel running over his neck." This "accident," however, occurred after the wagon in which he was travelling was stoned by a group of men leaving the meeting. *KC*, 10 November 1839.

94 *BC*, 23 October 1839.

95 Ibid., 30 October 1839.

96 Ibid.

97 By the end of the summer, efforts to suppress Durham meetings prompted the activists in Lennox and Addington to forego the prospect of a public meeting in favour of circulating a petition.

98 *SCJ*, 18 July 1839 quoting the *Toronto Guardian*.

99 10 October 1839

100 23 and 30 October 1839. OA, Mackenzie-Lindsey Papers, #448. On officially sanctioned violence, see Wilton, "'Lawless Law.'"

101 8 and 15 January 1840.

102 Ibid., 8 April 1840.

103 Careless, *Union of the Canadas*, 53–4. Many of the reformers, however, opposed Sydenham's District Councils Act because a number of key appointments were non-elective, remaining in the hands of the provincial executive.

104 Philip Buckner, "Charles Edward Poulett Thomson, 1st Baron Sydenham," *DCB* 7: 855–62.

105 Arthur had forwarded the address from the Gore district to the Colonial Office in September 1839; *PACR* 1945, 54.

106 NA, R.G. 5, B-3, 1793.

107 *Imperial Blue Book* #12, 1840, #211, 194, 196; NA, R.G. 5, B-3, 13: 1992–3. The resolutions and address were printed in handbill form.
108 An address from Prescott, for example, was clearly produced on the occasion of Thomson's visit there; *British Parliamentary Papers*, 13 and 189.
109 Ibid., 190; NA, R.G. 7, G. 18, vol. 9; R.G., 5, B-3, vol. 12, 1805–12.
110 *KC*, 9 November 1839; *BG*, 11 September 1839. One address opposing responsible government reached the Colonial Office from Guelph; see *PACR* 1945, 54.
111 Quoted in *BG*, 11 September 1839.
112 Sanderson, ed., *Arthur Papers*, vol. 2, [Arthur] to Colborne, 8 August 1839, 207.
113 10 October 1839.
114 Gowan had endorsed responsible government in seventeen columns of his journal, the *Statesman*; see *KC*, 11 September 1839.
115 *BG*, 26 September 1839. Several other lodges were of the same mind. See ibid., 3, 10 October 1839; *NC*, 19 September 1839; *KC*, 5 October 1839.
116 Members of local "compacts" had historically differed from officials in York/Toronto on matters relating to their own localities. See, for example, Richards, "The Joneses of Brockville."
117 For a fuller account of this questionnaire, see Wilton [-Siegel], "Administrative Reform."
118 *British Parliamentary Papers*, 13 and 187.
119 NA, R.G. 5, B-3, 12: 1786ff.
120 NA, R.G. 7, G. 18, vol. 9. It is unlikely that Mackenzie's old foe, Bishop Macdonell, was behind this; he had left for Britain in June 1839, never to return. See Rea, *Macdonell*, 207–11.
121 Craig, *Upper Canada*, 272.
122 Careless, *Union of the Canadas*, 38ff.
123 Hallowell, "British American League," 41–3; Careless, *Union of the Canadas*, 123 ff.
124 See NA, R.G. 7, G18, vol. 9, Addresses to Hon. C.P. Thompson [*sic*].
125 *The Addresses Presented to His Excellency.*
126 Hallowell, "British American League," 42.
127 For its drawbacks, see Thompson, *Making of the English Working Class*, 86–107.
128 See Wilton, "Transformation of Upper Canadian Politics," chapter 4.
129 Ibid.

CONCLUSION

1 See Gunn, "Public Spirit," and Houston and Prentice, *Schooling and Scholars*, 308.
2 See, for example, Chambers, *Married Women and Property Law*, 74–5; Noel, "Dry Millennium," and Stouffer, *The Light of Nature.*

3 Wise, "Upper Canada and the Conservative Tradition," 183.

4 The analysis in this paragraph owes much to Habermas, *Structural Transformation,* 16–140.

5 Wise, "Upper Canada and the Conservative Tradition," 173.

6 Ibid., 174; see also Romney, "On the Eve of the Rebellion," 211.

7 Two controversial books by J.C.D. Clark, *The Language of Liberty* and *English Society,* argue that religion was the key destabilizing force in England and the United States during this period. Among Clark's critics, see Joanna Innes, "Jonathan Clark, Social History, and England's 'Ancien Regime,'" *Past and Present,* 115, 165–200.

8 According to the 1842 census, only twenty-two per cent of Upper Canada's population was Anglican; Johnson, *Becoming Prominent,* 97.

9 Wise, "Upper Canada and the Conservative Tradition," 174.

10 Romney, "On the Eve of the Rebellion," 211.

11 Careless, "The Place, the Office, the Times, and the Men," in Careless, ed., *Pre-Confederation Premiers,* 19.

12 Francis Hincks and Robert Baldwin were the primary architects of the Upper Canadian Reform party that took shape in the 1840s. See Wilton, "Transformation of Upper Canadian Politics."

13 Careless, *Union of the Canadas,* 163.

14 McNairn, "Publius of the North."

15 Careless, *Union of the Canadas,* 167–71; Dewar, "Charles Clarke's 'Reformator.'"

16 This was the slogan on the masthead of Francis Hincks's journal, the *Examiner* newspaper.

17 Careless, *Brown of the Globe,* 2 vols.

18 Johnson, "Macdonald," in Careless, ed., *Pre-Confederation Premiers,* 233.

19 On the Union period generally, see Careless, *Union of the Canadas.* On the subject of party in the 1840s, see Wilton, "Transformation of Upper Canadian Politics," especially chapter 4.

20 Metcalfe, "Draper," 255.

21 Senior, "Gowan," 311–13.

22 Creighton, *Macdonald,* 97; Hallowell, "The Reaction of the Upper Canadian Tories."

23 The Act sought (unsuccessfully as it turned out) to suppress the Orange Order, the extraparliamentary arm of the tories.

24 On tory violence in Toronto at this time, see Kealey, "Orangemen and the Corporation," 44, 52–3, 55–60.

25 See generally Wilton, "The Transformation of Upper Canadian Politics in the 1840s," and Mills, *The Idea of Loyalty.*

26 As McNairn has shown, however, this did not discourage prominent tories from suggesting ways to enhance the conservative interest under conditions created by responsible government; "Publius of the North."

27 Conway, "Orange Order," 47–51.
28 Wilton, "Crime in Mid-Nineteenth Century Toronto," (unpublished paper, University of Toronto, 1977): 26, 34–5.
29 Kealey, "Orangemen and the Corporation."
30 Ibid., 41 passim; Way, "The Canadian Tory Rebellion of 1849," 10ff. See also Way, "Street Politics." The Rebellion Losses Bill was passed in the Assembly of the United Canadas in Montreal in 1849. Intended to meet the claims of those who had suffered losses during the 1837 Rebellion in Lower Canada, it aroused the fury of conservatives who believed that its effect would be to "compensate" many rebels. When Governor General Lord Elgin accepted the bill on 25 April 1849, his carriage was stoned. That night, an angry mob burned the Parliament buildings in Montreal. In Toronto in 1849, there were several outbursts of conservative disorder occasioned by the passage of the Rebellion Losses Bill, including a riot and effigy burnings of William Lyon Mackenzie and Lord Elgin.
31 See Anderson, "Respectability vs. Rowdyism: Non-Material Culture, Ideology and Geography in Victoria County Ontario 1860–1880" (M. A. Thesis, York University, 1984).
32 See Wilton, "Crime Rates," 32; Richardson, "Crime and the Labouring Community in Toronto, 1870–1891," 31; Gattrell and Hadden, "Criminal Statistics and Their Interpretation," in Wrigley, ed., *Nineteenth-century Society*, 336–94; Stone, "Interpersonal Violence in English Society 1300–1980," 22–33; Sharpe, "Debate: The History of Violence in England: Some Observations," 206–215.
33 See Wilton, " 'Lawless Law,' " 134–6.
34 Greer and Radforth, "Introduction," in Greer and Radforth, eds., *Colonial Leviathan*, 8–9; Curtis, *Building the Educational State.*

Bibliography

Note: newspapers are not listed here, but are referred to in the notes.

PRIMARY SOURCES

Manuscripts

ARCHIVES OF ONTARIO

Imperial Blue Book, 1840, #211.

Macaulay Papers

Mackenzie-Lindsey Clippings

Robinson Papers

Strachan Papers

R.G. 22, Cobourg General (Quarter) Sessions, convictions by Justices of the Peace, Series 31, 39.

W.L. Mackenzie Papers

BALDWIN ROOM, TORONTO REFERENCE LIBRARY, TORONTO PUBLIC LIBRARY

Broadside Collection

Carfrae Papers

[Mackenzie, William Lyon.] "Political Affairs in Upper Canada." (Manuscript.)

Robert Baldwin Papers

W.W. Baldwin Papers

Powell Papers

NATIONAL ARCHIVES

Colonial Office Records, C.O. 42.

R.G. 5, Civil Secretary's Correspondence, Upper Canada Sundries.

R.G. 5, B-3, Provincial and Civil Secretaries' Offices: Upper Canada and Canada West, Petitions and Addresses, 1792a–1841, vol. 12 and 13, "Petitions and Addresses."

R.G. 7, G18, vol. 9, Governor General's Office Miscellaneous Records. Addresses to Hon. C.P. Thompson [*sic*], 1839–40.

MG24 B7 Charles Jones Papers

MG24 B18 William Lyon Mackenzie Papers

MG24 B64 Ogle Gowan Papers

MG24 D101 William Stewart and Family Papers

MG27 I E30 Ferguson Collection

THOMAS FISHER RARE BOOK LIBRARY, UNIVERSITY OF TORONTO

"Dr Mackenzie's Canadian Diary 1839–43"

UNITED CHURCH ARCHIVES

Egerton Ryerson Papers

Printed Primary Sources

Adjutant-General's Office. *Rules and Regulations for the Manual and Platoon Exercises, Formations, Field-Exercise, and Movements of His Majesty's Forces* ... Whitehall: War Office, 1816.

5 Upper Canada Court of King's Bench (O.S.) 6 Wm. IV.

Addresses Presented to His Excellency, the Right Hon. Sir Chas. T. Metcalfe, Bart., G.C.B., Governor-General of British North America, &c., on the Occasion of the Resignation of His Late Advisers; with His Excellency's Replies. Toronto, 1844.

Gibbs, Elizabeth ed. *Debates of the Legislative Assembly of United Canada 1841-1851*, 10 vols. Montreal: Presses de l'École des Hautes Études Commerciales 1970–79: 1841, 1843.

[Gourlay, Robert.] "Address to the Jury, at Kingston Assize, In the case of The King vs. Robert Gourlay for Libel: with a report of the trial," 1818.

Gourlay, Robert. *The Banished Briton and Neptunian: being a Record of the Life, Writings, Principles and Projects of Robert Gourlay, Esquire.* Boston, 1843.

Gourlay, Robert. *General Introduction to Statistical Account of Upper Canada.* 2 vols. London, 1822; rpt. New York: Johnson Reprint Corp. 1966. [*Account* I].

Gourlay, Robert. *Narrative of a Journey through The Midland, Johnstown, Eastern and Ottawa Districts...*, 1818.

Irish University Press Series of British Parliamentary Papers. Correspondence Relative to the Affairs of Upper and Lower Canada 1840. Shannon, Ireland: Irish University Press, 1969.

Jackson, John Mills. *A View of the Political Situation of the Province of Upper Canada, in North America.* London, 1809.

Journals of Legislative Assembly of Upper Canada.

Knaplund, Paul, ed. *Letters from Lord Sydenham Governor-General of Canada 1839-1841 to Lord John Russell.* London, 1931; rpt. Clifton, New Jersey: Augustus M. Kelley Publishers, 1973.

[Mackenzie, W.L.] Patrick Swift. *A New Almanac of the Canadian True Blues; with which Is Incorporated the Constitutional Reformer's Text Book; for the Millenial and Prophetical Year of the Grand General Election for Upper Canada, and the Total Everlasting Downfall of Toryism in the British Empire, 1834.* York, 1834.

Mealing, S.R., ed., Robert Gourlay. *Statistical Account of Upper Canada*, reprint., Toronto: McClelland and Stewart, 1974. [*Account* II].

Report on Canadian Archives 1892. Ottawa, 1893.

Report on Canadian Archives 1893. Ottawa, 1894.

Report of the Department of Public Archives 1944. Ottawa, 1945.

Powell, William Dummer. *Letters from an American Loyalist in Upper-Canada, to his Friend in England, on a Pamphlet Published by John Mills Jackson, Esq., entitled, A View of the Province of Upper Canada.* Halifax, 1810.

Robinson, John Beverly [*sic*]. *Canada and the Canada Bill.* London, 1840; reprint ed. New York: Johnson Reprint Corporation, 1967.

Sanderson, Charles R., ed. *The Arthur Papers, Being the Canadian Papers Mainly Confidential, Private and Demi-Official of Sir George Arthur, K.C.H. Last Lieutenant-Governor of Upper Canada in the Manuscript Collection of The Toronto Public Libraries.* 3 vols. Toronto: Toronto Public Libraries and University of Toronto Press, 1957.

Strachan, James [John]. *A visit to the Province of Upper Canada in 1819.* Aberdeen; London, 1819.

York Auxiliary Bible Society (Ont.) The Formation and Constitution of the York, U.C. Bible Society. York, 1828.

SECONDARY SOURCES

Note: The *Dictionary of Canadian Biography* vols. 5–11 (Toronto: University of Toronto Press 1972–78) has been an invaluable resource in the preparation of this manuscript.

Aitchison, J. H. "The Development of Local Government in Upper Canada." Ph.D. thesis, University of Toronto, 1953.

Akenson, Donald Harman. *The Irish in Ontario: A Study in Rural History.* Kingston and Montreal: McGill-Queen's University Press, 1984.

Akenson, Don. *The Orangeman: The Life & Times of Ogle Gowan.* Toronto: James Lorimer & Company, 1986.

Anderson, Richard B. "Respectability vs. Rowdyism: Non-Material Culture, Ideology, and Geography in Victoria County Ontario 1860–1880." M.A. thesis, York University, 1977.

Armstrong, Frederick H. *A City in the Making: Progress, People & Perils in Victorian Toronto.* Toronto: Dundurn, 1988.

Armstrong, F.H. "The Carfrae Family: A Study in Early Toronto Toryism," *OH* 54 (1962): 205–25.

Armstrong, Frederick H. *Handbook of Upper Canadian Chronology,* rev. ed. Toronto: Dundurn, 1985.

Armstrong, F.H. "The Oligarchy of the Western District of Upper Canada, 1788-1841," *HP* (1977): 87–102, reprinted in J.K. Johnson and Bruce G. Wilson, *Historical Essays on Upper Canada: New Perspectives.* Ottawa: Carleton University Press, 1989: 513–35.

Armstrong, F.H. "Toronto in Transition: The Emergence of a City 1828–1838." Ph.D. thesis, University of Toronto, 1965.

Armstrong, F.H. "William Lyon Mackenzie: A Persistent Hero," *JCS* 6 (August 1971): 21–36.

Armstrong, F.H. "The York Riots of March 23, 1832," *OH* 55 (1963): 61–72

Bailyn, Bernard, David Brion Davis, et al. *The Great Republic: A History of the American People.* Boston: Little, Brown and Company, 1977.

Baker, G.B. "'So Elegant a Web': Providential Order and the Rule of Secular Law in Early Nineteenth-Century Upper Canada," *University of Toronto Law Journal* 38 (1988): 184–205.

Beales, Derek. *From Castlereagh to Gladstone 1815–1885.* London: Sphere Books Limited, 1969.

Beer, Donald R. *Sir Allan Napier MacNab.* Hamilton, Ontario: Dictionary of Hamilton Biography Inc., 1984.

Black, Eugene Charlton. *The Association: British Extraparliamentary Political Organization 1769–1793.* Cambridge, Mass.: Harvard University Press, 1963.

Bleasdale, Ruth. "Class Conflict on the Canals of Upper Canada in the 1840s," *Labour/le travail* 7 (Spring 1981): 9–39; reprinted in Johnson and Wilson, eds., *Historical Essays*: 261–304.

Booth, Alan. "Popular loyalism and public violence in the north-west of England 1790–1800," *Social History,* 8 (1983): 295–313.

Boyce, Betsy Dewar. *The Rebels of Hastings.* Toronto: University of Toronto Press, 1992.

Bowsfield, Hartwell. "Upper Canada in the 1820's: The Development of a Political Consciousness." Ph.D. thesis, University of Toronto, 1976.

Bradley, James E. *Popular Politics and the American Revolution in England: Petitions, the Crown, and Public Opinion.* Macon, Georgia: Mercer University Press, 1986.

Brewer, John. *Party Ideology and Popular Politics at the Accession of George III.* London: Cambridge University Press, 1976.

Brewer, John. *The Common People and Politics 1750–1790s.* Cambridge: Chadwyck-Healey Ltd, 1986.

Brock, Michael. *The Great Reform Act.* London: Hutchinson University Library, 1973.

Brode, Patrick. *Sir John Beverley Robinson: Bone and Sinew of the Compact.* Toronto: The Osgoode Society, 1984.

Buckner, Philip A. *The Transition to Responsible Government: British Policy in British North America, 1815–1850.* Westport, Conn.: Greenwood Press, 1985.

Bumsted, J.M. *The Peoples of Canada: A Pre-Confederation History.* Toronto: Oxford University Press, 1992.

Burns, R.J. "God's Chosen People: The Origins of Toronto Society, 1793–1818," *HP* (1973): 213–28.

Burroughs, Peter. *The Canadian Crisis and British Colonial Policy, 1828–1841.* London: Edward Arnold, 1972.

Butterfield, Herbert. *George III and the Historians.* London: Collins 1957 Cadigan, Sean T. "Paternalism and Politics: Sir Francis Bond Head, the Orange Order, and the Election of 1836," *CHR* 72 (1991): 319–47.

Careless, J.M.S. *Brown of the Globe.* 2 vols. Toronto: Macmillan 1959–63.

Careless, J.M.S. *The Union of the Canadas: The Growth of Canadian Institutions 1841–1857.* Toronto: McClelland and Stewart, 1967.

Chambers, Lori. *Married Women and Property Law in Victorian Ontario.* Toronto: University of Toronto Press, 1997.

Christie, Nancy. "In Times of Democratic Rage and Delusion': Popular Religion and the Challenge to the Established Order, 1760–1815," in G.A. Rawlyk, ed., *The Canadian Protestant Experience 1760 to 1990.* Burlington, Ontario: Welch Publishing Company Inc., 1990.

Clark, J.C.D. *English Society 1688–1832: Ideology, social structure and political practice during the ancien regime.* Cambridge, England: Cambridge University Press, 1985.

Clark, J.C.D. *The Language of Liberty 1660–1832: Political discourse and social dynamics in the Anglo-American world.* Cambridge, England: Cambridge University Press, 1994.

Clark, S.D. *Movements of Political Protest in Canada 1640–1840.* Toronto: University of Toronto Press, 1959.

Conway, Sean Gerard. "Upper Canadian Orangeism in the Nineteenth Century: Aspects of a Pattern of Disruption." M.A. thesis, Queen's University, 1977.

Cottrell, Michael J. "Political Leadership and Party Allegiance Among Irish Catholics in Victorian Toronto," in Mark George McGowan and Brian P. Clarke, eds. *Catholics at the "Gathering Place": Historical Essays on the Archdiocese of Toronto 1841–1991.* Toronto: The Canadian Catholic Historical Association, 1993: 53–68.

Cowherd, Raymond G. *The Politics of English Dissent: The Religious Aspects of Liberal and Humanitarian Reform Movements from 1815 to 1848.* New York: New York University Press, 1956.

Craig, G.M. "The American Impact on the Upper Canadian Reform Movement before 1837," *CHR* 29(1948): 333–52; rpt. in Johnson, ed., *Historical Essays on Upper Canada,* 317–37.

Craig, Gerald M., ed. *Lord Durham's Report.* Toronto: McClelland and Stewart, 1963.

Craig, G.M. *Upper Canada: The Formative Years 1784–1841.* Toronto: McClelland and Stewart, 1963.

Creighton, Donald. *John A. Macdonald: The Young Politician.* Toronto: Macmillan, 1965.

Cross, Michael. "The Shiners' War: Social Violence in the Ottawa Valley in the 1830s," *CHR* 54 (1973): 1–26.

Davis, Susan G. *Parades and Power: Street Theatre in Nineteenth-Century Philadelphia.* Philadelphia: Temple University Press, 1986.

Dawe, Brian. *"Old Oxford is WIDE AWAKE!": Pioneer Settlers and Politicians in Oxford County, 1793–1853.* N.p. John Deyell Company, 1980.

Dunham, Aileen. *Political Unrest in Upper Canada, 1815–1836.* 1927; reprinted Toronto: McClelland and Stewart, 1963.

Dewar, Kenneth C. "Charles Clarke's 'Reformator': Early Victorian Radicalism in Upper Canada," *OH* 78 (1986): 233–52.

Elmsley, Clive. "Repression, 'terror' and the rule of law in England during the decade of the French Revolution," *English Historical Review* 100 (1985): 801–25.

Epstein, James. "Understanding the Cap of Liberty: Symbolic Practice and Social Conflict in Early Nineteenth-Century England," *Past and Present* 122 (February 1989): 75–118.

Ermatinger, C.O. *The Talbot Regime or The First Half Century of the Talbot Settlement.* St Thomas: The Municipal World, Limited, 1904.

Errington, Jane. *The Lion, the Eagle, and Upper Canada: A Developing Colonial Ideology.* Kingston and Montreal: McGill-Queen's University Press, 1987.

Fahey, Curtis. *In His Name: The Anglican Experience in Upper Canada, 1791-1854.* Ottawa: Carleton University Press, 1991.

Fairley, Margaret, ed. *The Selected Writings of William Lyon Mackenzie 1824–1837.* Toronto: Oxford University Press, 1960.

Firth, Edith, ed. *The Town of York 1815–1834: A Further Collection of Documents of Early Toronto.* Toronto: University of Toronto Press, 1966.

Francis, Mark. *Governors and Settlers: Images of Authority in the British Colonies, 1820–60.* Houndmills, Basingstoke, Hampshire: Macmillan Academic and Professional Ltd, 1992.

Francis, R. Douglas, Richard Jones, and Donald B. Smith. *Origins: Canadian History to Confederation.* 2 ed. Toronto: Holt, Rinehart and Winston, 1992.

Fraser, Robert L. "'All the Privileges which Englishmen Possess': Order, Rights, and Constitutionalism in Upper Canada," in Robert L. Fraser, ed., *Provincial Justice: Upper Canadian Legal Portraits from the Dictionary of Canadian Biography.* Toronto: University of Toronto Press, 1992: xxi-xcii.

Fraser, Robert L. "'Like Eden in Her Summer Dress': Gentry, Economy, and Society, Upper Canada, 1812–1840." Ph.D. thesis, University of Toronto, 1979.

French, Goldwin. *Parsons & Politics: The Role of the Wesleyan Methodists in Upper Canada and the Maritimes from 1780 to 1855*. Toronto: The Ryerson Press, 1962.

Garner, John. *The Franchise and Politics in British North America, 1755–1867*. Toronto: University of Toronto Press, 1969.

Gates, Lillian F. *After the Rebellion: The Later Years of William Lyon Mackenzie*. Toronto and Oxford: Dundurn Press, 1988.

Gates, Lillian F. *Land Policies of Upper Canada*. Toronto: University of Toronto Press, 1968.

Gattrell, V.A.C. and T.B. Hadden. "Criminal Statistics and Their Interpretation," in E.A.Wrigley, ed., *Nineteenth-Century Society: Essays in the Use of Quantitative Methods for the Study of Social Data*. Cambridge, England: Cambridge University Press, 1972: 336–94.

Greenwood, F. Murray and Barry Wright, eds. *Canadian State Trials, Vol. I: Law, Politics, and Security Measures, 1608–1837*. Toronto: University of Toronto Press, 1996.

Greer, Alan and Ian Radforth. *Colonial Leviathan: State Formation in Mid-Nineteenth Century Canada*. Toronto: University of Toronto Press, 1992.

Graff, Harvey J. "Towards a Meaning of Literacy: Literacy and Social Structure in Hamilton, Ontario, 1861," in Michael B. Katz and Paul H. Mattingly, eds., *Education and Social Change: Themes from Ontario's Past*. New York: New York University Press, 1975: 246–70.

Guillet, Edwin C., ed. *The Valley of the Trent*. Toronto: University of Toronto Press, 1957.

Guest, Harry H. "Upper Canada's First Political Party," OH 54 (1962): 275–96.

Gunn, J.A.W. "Public Spirit to Public Opinion," in J.A.W. Gunn, ed. *Beyond Liberty and Property: The Process of Self-Recognition in Eighteenth-Century Political Thought*. Kingston and Montreal: McGill-Queen's University Press, 1983: 260–313.

Habermas, Jurgen. *The Structural Transformation of the Public Sphere: An Inquiry into a Category of Bourgeois Society*. Cambridge, Mass.: The MIT Press, 1987.

Hallowell, Gerald A. "The Reaction of the Upper Canadian Tories to the Adversity of 1849: Annexation and the British American League," OH 62 (1970): 41–56.

Hamil, Fred Coyne. *Lake Erie Baron: The Story of Colonel Thomas Talbot*. Toronto: The Macmillan Company of Canada Limited, 1955.

Hamil, Fred Coyne. "The Reform Movement in Upper Canada," in Edith G. Firth, ed., *Profiles of a Province: Studies in the History of Ontario*. Toronto: Ontario Historical Society, 1967: 9–19.

Hofstadter, Richard. *The Idea of a Party System: The Rise of Legitimate Opposition in the United States, 1780–1840*. Berkeley and Los Angeles: University of California Press, 1969.

Houston, Cecil J. and William J. Smyth. *The Sash Canada Wore: A Historical Geography of the Orange Order in Canada*. Toronto: University of Toronto Press, 1980.

Houston, Susan E. and Alison Prentice. *Schooling and Scholars in Nineteenth-Century Ontario.* Toronto: University of Toronto Press, 1988.

Innes, Joanna. "Jonathan Clark, Social History, and England's 'Ancien Regime,'" *Past and Present* 115: 165–200.

Isaac, Rhys. *The Transformation of Virginia 1740–1790.* Chapel Hill: University of North Carolina Press, 1982.

Jackson, Eric. "The Organization of Upper Canadian Reformers, 1818–1867," in J.K. Johnson, ed., *Historical Essays on Upper Canada*: 96–121.

Johnson, J.K. *Becoming Prominent: Regional Leadership in Upper Canada, 1791–1841.* Kingston and Montreal: McGill-Queen's University Press, 1989.

Johnson, J.K. "'Claims of Equity and Justice': Petitions and Petitioners in Upper Canada 1815–1840," *Histoire Sociale/Social History* XXVIII, No. 55 (May 1995): 219–240.

Johnson, J.K., ed. *Historical Essays on Upper Canada.* Toronto: McClelland and Stewart, 1975.

Johnson, J.K. "John A. Macdonald," in J.M.S. Careless, ed. *The Pre-Confederation Premiers: Ontario Government Leaders, 1841–1867.* Toronto: University of Toronto Press, 1980.

Johnson, J.K. and Bruce G. Wilson, eds. *Historical Essays on Upper Canada: New Perspectives.* Ottawa: Carleton University Press, 1989.

Jones, Elwood. "The Franchise in Upper Canada, 1792–1867," paper presented at the Annual Meeting of the Canadian Historical Association, Winnipeg, 7–9 June, 1986.

Kealey, Gregory S. "Orangemen and the Corporation," in Victor L. Russell, ed., *Forging a Consensus: Historical Essays on Toronto.* Toronto: University of Toronto Press, 1984: 41–86.

Keane, David and Colin Read, eds. *Old Ontario: Essays in Honour of J.M.S. Careless.* Toronto: Dundurn, 1990.

Kerr, W.B. "When Orange and Green United 1832–9: The Alliance of MacDonell and Gowan," *Ontario Historical Society Papers and Records* 34 (1942): 34–42.

Kilbourn, William. *The Firebrand: William Lyon Mackenzie and the Rebellion in Upper Canada.* Toronto: Irwin Publishing, 1956.

Landon, Fred. *Western Ontario and the American Frontier.* 1941; rpt. Toronto: McClelland and Stewart, 1967.

Lindsey, Charles. *William Lyon Mackenzie.* Toronto: Morang & Co., Limited, 1909.

Linebaugh, Peter. "The Tyburn Riot Against the Surgeons," in Douglas Hay *et al.*, eds., *Albion's Fatal Tree: Crime and Society in Eighteenth-Century England.* New York: Pantheon Books, 1975: 65–117.

MacKay, R.A. "The Political Ideas of William Lyon Mackenzie," CJEPS 3 (February 1937): 1–22.

Manning, Helen Taft. *The Revolt of French Canada 1800–1835.* Toronto: The Macmillan Company of Canada Limited, 1962.

Marquis, G. "Anti-Lawyer Sentiment in Mid-Victorian New Brunswick," *University of New Brunswick Law Journal* 36 (1987): 163–74.

McCalla, Douglas. *Planting the Province: The Economic History of Upper Canada 1784–1870.* Toronto: University of Toronto Press, 1993.

McDayter, Mark. *Military Music of the War of 1812.* Historic Fort York, Toronto Historical Board, 1993.

McGowan, Mark George and Brian P. Clarke, eds. *Catholics at the "Gathering Place": Historical Essays on The Archdiocese of Toronto 1841–1991.* Toronto: The Canadian Catholic Historical Association, 1993.

McIntyre, W. John. *Children of Peace.* Montreal & Kingston: McGill-Queen's University Press, 1994.

McKenna, Katherine M.J. *A Life of Propriety: Anne Murray Powell and Her Family 1755–1849.* Montreal and Kingston: McGill-Queen's University Press, 1994.

McNairn, Jeffrey L. "Publius of the North: Tory Republicanism and the American Constitution in Upper Canada, 1848–54," CHR 77 (1996): 504–38.

McNairn, Jeffrey L. "Towards Deliberative Democracy: Parliamentary Intelligence and the Public Sphere in Upper Canada, 1791–1840," JCS 33 (1998): 39–60.

Milani, Lois Darroch. *Robert Gourlay, Gadfly: Forerunner of the Rebellion in Upper Canada 1837.* n.p. Ampersand Press, 1971.

Mills, David. *The Idea of Loyalty in Upper Canada, 1784–1850.* Kingston and Montreal: McGill-Queen's University Press, 1988.

Moir, John. *Church and State in Canada West: Three Studies in the Relation of Denominationalism and Nationalism, 1841–1867.* Toronto: University of Toronto Press, 1959.

Morgan, Cecilia. *Public Men and Virtuous Women: The Gendered Languages of Religion and Politics in Upper Canada, 1791–1850.* Toronto: University of Toronto Press, 1996.

Nelles, H.V. "Loyalism and Local Power: The District of Niagara, 1792–1837," OH 58 (1966), 99–114.

New, Chester. *Lord Durham's Mission to Canada.* Oxford, Clarendon Press, 1929. Reprint Toronto: McClelland and Stewart, 1963.

Nicholson, Murray W. "William O'Grady and the Catholic Church in Toronto Prior to the Irish Famine Migration," in McGowan and Clarke, *Catholics at the "Gathering Place."*

Noel, Janet. *Canada Dry: Temperance Crusades before Confederation.* Toronto: University of Toronto Press, 1995.

Noel, Janet Virginia. "Dry Millennium: Temperance and a New Social Order in Mid-Nineteenth Century Canada and Red River." Ph.D. thesis, University of Toronto, 1987.

Noel, S.J.R. *Patrons, Clients, Brokers: Ontario Society and Politics 1791-1896.* Toronto: University of Toronto Press, 1990.

Ouellet, Fernand. *Lower Canada 1791–1840: Social Change and Political Nationalism.* Toronto: McClelland and Stewart, 1980.

Patterson, Graeme. "An Enduring Canadian Myth: Responsible Government and the Family Compact," *JCS* 12 (1977): 3–16, rpt. in Johnson and Wilson, eds. *Historical Essays on Upper Canada*: 485–512.

Patterson, Graeme Hazlewood. "Studies in Elections and Public Opinion in Upper Canada." Ph.D. thesis, University of Toronto, 1969.

Perkin, Harold. *The Origins of Modern English Society 1780–1880*. London: Routledge & Kegan Paul, 1969.

Pocock, J.G.A. *The Machiavellian Moment: Florentine Political Thought and the Atlantic Republican Tradition*. Princeton: Princeton University Press, 1975.

Potter-MacKinnon, Janice. *While the Women Only Wept: Loyalist Refugee Women in Eastern Ontario*. Montreal & Kingston: McGill-Queen's University Press, 1993.

Pross, A. Paul. *Group Politics and Public Policy*. 2 ed. Toronto: Oxford University Press, 1992.

Quealey, Francis Michael. "The Administration of Sir Peregrine Maitland Lieutenant Governor of Upper Canada 1818–1828." Ph.D. thesis, University of Toronto, 1968.

Raible, Chris. *Muddy York Mud: Scandal & Scurrility in Upper Canada*. Creemore, Ont.: Curiosity House Press, 1992.

Rasporich, Anthony W. *William Lyon Mackenzie*. Toronto: Holt, Rinehart and Winston, 1972.

Rea, J.E. *Bishop Alexander Macdonell and the Politics of Upper Canada*. Toronto: Ontario Historical Society, Research Publication No. 4, 1974.

Rea, J.E. "William Lyon Mackenzie – Jacksonian?" in Mid-America 50 (1968): 223–35; rpt. J.M. Bumsted, ed., *Canadian History Before Confederation*, 2 ed. Georgetown, *ON*: Irwin-Dorsey 1972: 375–86.

Read, Colin. *The Rising in Western Upper Canda 1837–8: The Duncombe Revolt and After*. Toronto: University of Toronto Press, 1982.

Read, Colin and Ronald J. Stagg, eds. *The Rebellion of 1837 in Upper Canada*. [Ottawa]: Carleton University Press, 1985.

Reid, John Phillip. *The Concept of Liberty in the Age of the American Revolution*. Chicago: The University of Chicago Press, 1988.

Richards, Elva M. "The Joneses of Brockville and the Family Compact," *OH* 60 (1968): 169–84.

Richardson, W.A. "Crime and the Labouring Community in Toronto, 1870–1891." Research paper, University of Toronto, 1976.

Romney, Paul Martin. "A Man out of Place: The Life of Charles Fothergill; Naturalist, Businessman, Journalist, Politician, 1782–1840," vol. 2, (Ph.D. thesis, University of Toronto, 1981).

Romney, Paul. "A Struggle for Authority," in Victor L. Russell, ed., *Forging a Consensus: Historical Essays on Toronto*. Toronto: University of Toronto Press, 1984: 9–40.

Romney, Paul. "From the Types Riot to the Rebellion: Elite Ideology, Anti-legal Sentiment, Political Violence, and the Rule of Law in Upper Canada." *OH* 79 (1987): 113–44.

Romney, Paul. *Mr Attorney: The Attorney General for Ontario in Court, Cabinet, and Legislature 1791–1899*. Toronto: The Osgoode Society 1986.

Romney, Paul. "On the Eve of the Rebellion: Nationality, Religion and Class in the Toronto Election of 1836," in Keane and Read, eds. *Old Ontario*: 192–216.

Romney, Paul. "The Ordeal of William Higgins," OH 67 (1975): 69–89.

Romney, Paul. "Re-inventing Upper Canada: American Immigrants, Upper Canadian History, English Law, and the Alien Question," in Roger Hall, William Westfall, *et al.* eds., *Patterns of the Past: Interpreting Ontario's History.* Toronto: Dundurn Press, 1988: 78–107.

Romney, Paul. "Upper Canada in the 1820s: Criminal Prosecution and the Case of Francis Collins," in Greenwood and Wright, eds., *Canadian State Trials*, 1: 487–504.

Romney, Paul. "Very Late Loyalist Fantasies: Nostalgic Tory History and the Rule of Law in Upper Canada," in W. Wesley Pue and Barry Wright, eds., *Canadian Perspectives on Law & Society: Issues in Legal History.* Ottawa: Carleton University Press, 1988: 119–47.

Rude, George. *Wilkes and Liberty: A Social Study of 1763 to 1774*. London: Oxford University Press, 1962.

Ryerson, Egerton. *"The Story of My Life"*. Toronto: William Briggs, 1883.

Saunders, Robert E. "What Was the Family Compact?" OH 49 (December 1957): 165- 78, rpt. in Johnson, ed., *Historical Essays on Upper Canada*: 122–39.

Schrauwers, Albert. *Awaiting the Millennium: The Children of Peace and the Village of Hope* Toronto: University of Toronto Press, 1993.

See, Scott W. "Polling Crowds and Patronage: New Brunswick's 'Fighting Elections' of 1842–3," CHR 72 (1991): 127–56.

Semple, Neil. *The Lord's Dominion: The History of Canadian Methodism.* Montreal and Kingston: McGill-Queen's University Press, 1996.

Semple, Neil. "The Quest for Kingdom: Aspects of Protestant Revivalism in Nineteenth-Century Ontario," in Keane and Read, eds. *Old Ontario*: 95–117.

Senior, Hereward, "Ogle Gowan, Orangeism, and the Immigrant Question 1830–1833," OH 66 (1974): 193–206.

Sharpe, J.A. "Debate: The History of Violence in England: Some Observations," *Past and Present* 1985: 206–15.

Sheppard, George. *Plunder, Profit, and Paroles: A Social History of the War of 1812 in Upper Canada.* Montreal & Kingston: McGill-Queen's University Press, 1994.

Sissons, C.B. *Egerton Ryerson His Life and Letters.* 2 vols. Toronto: Clarke, Irwin & Company Limited, 1937.

Stagg, Ronald John. "The Yonge Street Rebellion of 1837: An Examination of the Social Background and a Re-assessment of the Events." Ph.D. thesis, University of Toronto, 1976.

Stewart, Gordon T. *The Origins of Canadian Politics: A Comparative Approach.* Vancouver: University of British Columbia Press, 1986.

Stone, Lawrence. "Interpersonal Violence in English Society 1300–1980," *Past and Present*, 1983: 22–33.

Stouffer, Allen P. *The Light of Nature and the Law of God: Antislavery in Ontario 1833–1877*. Kingston and Montreal McGill-Queen's University Press, 1992.

Talman, James J. "The Newspapers of Upper Canada a Century Ago," CHR 19(1938): 9–23.

Taylor, M. Brook. *Promoters, Patriots, and Partisans: Historiography in Nineteenth-Century English Canada.* Toronto: University of Toronto Press, 1989.

Thompson, E.P. "Eighteenth-century English society: class struggle without class?" *Social History* 3(1978): 133–65.

Thompson, E.P. *The Making of the English Working Class* 1963; reprinted Harmondsworth, Middlesex, England: Penguin Books, 1970.

Walton, Bruce. "The 1836 Election in Lennox and Addington," OH 67(1975): 153–67.

Way, Peter. "The Canadian Tory Rebellion of 1849 and the Demise of Street Politics in Toronto," *British Journal of Canadian Studies* 10(1995): 10–30.

Way, Peter. "Street Politics: Orangemen, Tories and the 1841 Election Riot in Toronto," *British Journal of Canadian Studies* 6(1991): 275–303.

Wilson, Alan. *The Clergy Reserves of Upper Canada: A Canadian Mortmain.* Toronto: University of Toronto Press, 1968.

Wilson, Bruce. *As She Began: An Illustrated Introduction to Loyalist Ontario.* Toronto and Charlottetown: Dundurn Press, 1981.

Wilson, Bruce G. *The Enterprises of Robert Hamilton: A Study of Wealth and Influence in Early Upper Canada, 1776–1812*. Ottawa: Carleton University Press, 1983.

Wilton, Carol. "Crime in Mid-Nineteenth Century Toronto." Unpublished paper, University of Toronto, 1977.

Wilton, Carol. " 'A Firebrand amongst the People': The Durham Meetings and Popular Politics in Upper Canada," CHR 75(1994): 346–75.

Wilton[-Siegel], Carol. "Administrative Reform: A Conservative Alternative to Responsible Government," OH 68(1986): 105–26.

Wilton, Carol, ed. *Change and Continuity: A Reader on Pre-Confederation Canada.* Toronto: McGraw-Hill Ryerson Limited, 1992.

Wilton, Carol. " 'Lawless Law': Conservative Political Violence in Upper Canada, 1818–41," *Law and History Review* 13 (Spring 1995): 111–36.

Wilton[-Siegel], Carol. "The Transformation of Upper Canadian Politics in the 1840s," Ph.D. thesis, University of Toronto, 1984.

Winstock, Lewis. *Songs & Music of the Redcoats: A History of the War Music of the British Army, 1642–1902*. London: Leo Cooper, 1970.

Wise, S.F. *God's Peculiar Peoples: Essays on Political Culture in Nineteenth-Century Canada.* Ottawa: Carleton University Press, 1993.

Wise, S.F. "The Family Compact: A Negative Oligarchy," in David W.L. Earl, ed., *The Family Compact: Aristocracy or Oligarchy?* Toronto: The Copp Clark Publishing Company, 1967: 142–5.

Wise, S.F., ed. *Sir Francis Bond Head, A Narrative with notes by William Lyon Mackenzie.* Orig. pub. London, 1839; rpt. Toronto: McClelland and Stewart, 1969.

Wise, S.F. "Upper Canada and the Conservative Tradition," in Edith G. Firth, ed., *Profiles of a Province: Studies in the History of Ontario.* Toronto: Ontario Historical Society, 1967: 20–33.

Wright, Barry. "The Ideological Dimensions of Law: The Treason Proceedings of 1838," *Criminal Justice History: An International Annual* 10(1989): 131–78.

Wright, Barry. "Sedition in Upper Canada: Contested Legality," *Labour/Le Travail* 29 (Spring 1992): 7–57.

Wylie, William N.T. "Poverty, Distress, and Disease: Labour and the Construction of the Rideau Canal, 1826–32," *Labour/le travail* 11 (1983): 7–29.

Index

administration of justice, 33–4, 57, 66, 191–2. *See also* John Walpole Willis
administrative reform, 217
Alien Bill, 1827, 38–43, 49, 57, 61, 71, 228–9
American immigrants, 9, 38–9, 90, 181. *See also* immigration, American
American influence on oppositionists/reformers, 16, 184, 224, 268n26
Amherst, Newcastle district meeting 1832, 131–4
Anglican Church, support for government, 18–19, 183, 228. *See also* John Strachan
anticlericalism, 78
anti-lawyer sentiment, 74
antipartyism, 11, 199–200
Anti-Slave Trade Association, 22
Arthur, Sir George, 194, 208, 213, 216
assaults, 33, 135, 151. *See also* political violence, riots, Christopher Hagerman, William Johnson Kerr
Augusta, Grenville District, 1831 petitioning meeting, 77

Baldwin, Robert, 37, 48, 51, 127, 169, 220
Baldwin, William Warren, attitude to political violence, 202; and Constitutional Committee of York, 51; and Durham meetings, 196, 212, 215; early life, 37; in 1836 election, 180; petitioning re: constitution, 47, 51; as popular agitator, 222; president of Toronto Political Union, 1836, 183; respectability, 37, 267n59; ridiculed, 210
Bidwell, Barnabas, 39
Bidwell, Marshall Spring, 39, 49, 60, 108, 162, 165, 190
Boltontown, Home District, reform meeting 1837, 186
Boulton, George Strange, 117, 131–2
Boulton, Henry John, 131; dismissal and vindication, 1833, 153–4
Britain, extraparliamentary organization, eighteenth century, 22; nineteenth century, 22–3
British American League, 232
British Constitutional Society, in election of 1834, 156–7; in election of 1836, 179, 182; founding, 118; like political unions, 166–7; reaction to Durham's Report, 216; superseded, 232. *See also* General British Constitutional Committee
British government, criticisms of at Durham meetings, 204–5; lack of interest in Upper Canada, 155, 175; unresponsiveness to oppositionists, 188; and oppositionist petitioning 1831–32, 63, 150; and Orange Order, 232; and Up-

per Canadian politics, 14–16, 167, 184, 215, 218–19, 224, 232
British politics, 1815–20, 36; 1820s, 38; 1830s, 61–2
British Society for the Promotion of Civil and Religious Liberty, 71
Brockville, 1831 oppositionist petitioning meeting, 75–7; Orange demonstration, 1833, 152; pro-government petitioning meeting 1832, 123–4
Brown, George, 230
Brown, John, 117, 133–4, 150–1, 268n78
Buell, Andrew Norton, 76, 124
Buell, William, 152, 163
Bytown [Ottawa], tory petitioning, 1836, 177

Canadian Alliance Society, 164–5, 174–5, 179–80
Carfrae, Thomas, 105, 118, 120–2
Cartwright, John S., 123, 161–2
cattle-maiming, 286n82
Central Canadian Political Union, *see* Upper Canada Central Political Union
Central Committee, in election of 1834, 158–9; opposes clergy reserves and sectarian education, 46; origins, 40, 43. *See also* Constitutional Committee of York
Children of Peace, 146
Churchville, Home district, reform meeting 1837, 186
Clark, Thomas, 28, 30, 32, 34
class, as factor in politics, 14, 19, 73, 110, 223, 229
Clear Grits, 230
clergy reserves, defended, 76, 78, 97, 161; defined, 44; at Durham meetings, 205; Mackenzie's criticisms of, 57; Methodist petition against, 1833, 153; opposition petitioning against, 46, 51–2; reform address opposing, 1836, 172, 175
Cobourg, Durham meeting, 211, 214
Colborne, Lieutenant-Governor Sir John, criticism of Egerton Ryerson, 90; criticism of Methodists, 97–8; criticism of William Lyon Mackenzie, 89, 101–2; and expulsion crisis, 87; response to York anti-expulsion petition, 1831, 94–5; replacement, 166; role in pro-government petitioning campaign, 1832, 117
Collins, Francis, 81, 118
Constitutional Committee of York, 50–1
Constitutional Reform Society of Upper Canada, 1836, 180
conventions, political, 33, 185–9
Cornwall, burning of Gourlayite literature 1818, 32; petitioning meeting 1831, 81
country-party ideology, in Britain 64; in Upper Canada, 64, 92, 110, 284n51
Covert, Colonel John, 131, 133
Cramahe, Methodist meeting, 1827, 46

Dickson, Robert, 117
Dickson, William, 28, 30, 32, 34
disloyalty, alleged, of government, 75; of Methodists, 45, 128–9; of oppositionists 40, 77, 101–2, 135–6, 149, 172, 187, 209–10, 216, 220
Draper, William Henry, 82, 103, 156
Duncombe, Charles, 182–3
Dundas Durham meeting, 198–200
Dunlop, William "Tiger", 8, 105, 118, 121–2
Durham, Lord, 194, 216, 245n4
Durham meetings, 1839, appendix E; loyalty, 201–4; nonpartisanship, 199–200; orderliness, 200–2; organization, 196–7; publicity, 197–8; resolutions, 203–7; and respectability, 200; response to, 207–15. *See also* Cobourg (Newcastle district), Dundas (Halton county), Galt (Gore district), Haldimand (Newcastle district), Hamilton (Gore district), Niagara (Niagara district), Richmond Hill (Home district), Simcoe (Talbot district), and Thorold (Niagara district) Durham meetings, political violence, responsible government
Durham Report, 194–5

education, elementary, 81, 172; in the oppositionist petition of 1831, 66; university 45, 51–2, 57
effigies, of Egerton Ryerson, 134; of John Beverley Robinson, 43; of John Willson, 74; in Port Hope, 41; of Robert Baldwin, 127; of William Lyon Mackenzie, 106, 134
electoral organization, 10–11; election of 1834, 156–63; election of 1836, 179–83
electoral violence, election of 1836, 182; Leeds, election of 1834, 163; Simcoe county, election of 1834, 163–4

Executive Council, resignation of, 1836, 170
expulsion crisis, 1831–32, 85–90; effect of, 162; response of Legislative Council, 88–9; significance of, 139–43, 226

Family Compact, 8, 178, 205–6, 214. *See also* patronage.
Farmersville, Leeds county, reform meeting 1833, 151. *See also* riots
Ferguson, Bartemus, 34
Fergusson, Adam, 199–200
Fothergill, Charles, 40, 41, 132, 138
Fraser, Colonel Richard Duncan, 79–81
freedom of assembly, 87, 188, 208, 214
freedom of representation, 90, 92, 109–10, 133, 158, 206, 226, 229
freedom of the press, 90, 96, 109–10, 158, 226, 229
Friends of Religious Liberty, 51–3, 257n34

Galt Durham meeting, 197
gender, 6, 93, 137–8, 165, 225–6
General British Constitutional Committee, 107, 121. *See also* British Constitutional Society
General Committee on the State of the Province, 1831, 67, 70
General Convention of Delegates of the Metropolitan District of Upper Canada, 1834, 159
Glenelg, Lord, 166
Goderich, Lord, 42–3, 150
Gore, Lieutenant-Governor Sir Francis, 25–7
Gourlay, Robert, antipartyism, 11; at Durham meetings, 195; early life, 27–8; and judicial system, 32–4; petitioning experience, 2; petitioning organization, promotion, and publicity, 30–2; petitioning strategy, 29; significance to opposition movements, 35–6, 92, 221; as target of violence, 32–3
government supporters, 1832, leadership, 116–18; meetings, 1832, appendix A; petitioning, 124–9; signatures on petitions, 1832, appendix C; support, 136–9. *See also* Anglican Church, British Constitutional Society, effigies, Family Compact, Orange Order, political violence, Roman Catholic Church, tories; Ogle Gowan, Christopher Hagerman, Alan,MacNab, Bishop Alexander McDonell, John Strachan
Gowan, Ogle, Brockville demonstration, 1833, 152; Farmersville riot, 1833, 151–2; Leeds election, 1834, 163; oppositionist petitioning meetings,1831, 75–6, 79; pro-government petitioning meetings, 1832, 123–4; and responsible government, 216; ridiculed, 210; rise to power, 123, 131. *See also* Orange Order
Gurnett, George, 120–1, 157, 173

Hagerman, Christopher, 33, 101, 153–4
Haldimand Durham meeting, 198
Hamilton Durham meeting, 198–202, 211–12; oppositionist petitioning meeting,1831, 73–5; petitioning meetings 1832, 135. *See also* William Johnson Kerr, Alan MacNab
Head, Sir Francis Bond, dialogue with reformers, 1836, 171; early life, 168; and petitioning 1836, 176; Rebellion of 1837, 189; replacement, 193; response to Executive Council resignation, 1836, 169–72, 176. *See also* public sphere
Hincks, Francis, 180, 196, 209, 212, 220, 231
Hopkins, Caleb, 135, 196, 200, 203
Hume, Joseph, 43–4, 46, 53, 65, 71, 155–6

immigration, American, and Alien Bill of 1827, 38–43; and concerns of Robert Gourlay, 29; and support for oppositionists, 90, 227
immigration, British, 9, 90, 111, 119, 181, 227–8
immigration, Irish, 9, 119

Jackson, John Mills, 24, 26–7
Jarvis, William Botsford, 105, 118, 121, 170, 212–13
Johnstown, Grenville county, 1831 petitioning meeting, 79
Jones, Jonas, 32, 78

Kemptville, 1831 petitioning meeting, 78
Kerr, William Johnson, 135–6
Ketchum, Jesse, and address to Head, 1836, 170–1; early life, 37; in election of 1828, 48; exile of, 196; opposition to

Alien Bill of 1827, 40–2; opposition to clergy reserves, 46; petitioning 1830, 51–2; petitioning 1831, 67–8; petitioning re: constitution, 1828, 47; at York meeting, March 1832, 106
Kingston, meeting of government supporters, 1832, 123; public meeting 1833, 153

land granting policy, 29, 31, 66
Lennox and Addington, nomination meeting for election of 1834, 161–2; oppositionist meeting, 1832, 111
Lesslie, James, 51, 105, 164, 170–1, 190
literacy, in Upper Canada, 247n40
Lount, Samuel, 191
Lower Canada, 50, 96, 185, 189, 230, 260n12
Loyalists, late, 38–40, 118
Loyalists, Upper Canadian, 14, 21–2, 203
loyalty, as ideology of government supporters/tories, 8, 222; of oppositionists/reformers, 77, 119, 142, 201–4, 207, 220

Macaulay, J.S. 173
Mackenzie, William Lyon, in Assembly, 57, 165; assaulted, 1832, 135–6; attitude to political parties, 59–60; "baneful domination letter", 156; character, 59, 143; convention organization 1837, 185–9; criticisms of, 89, 101–2, 107,118, 126–7; demonstrations in York, 1831–32, 95–6, 98–100; early life, 37–8; election address, 1828, 56–7; effigies of, 106, 134; election of 1828, 49; exile, 190, 196; expulsion, December 1833, 156, 158; expulsion crisis, 1831–32, 85–93; expunging of expulsions from Assembly record, 165; at Hamilton meeting, 1832, 135; leadership skills, 55–6, 221; opposition to Alien Bill of 1827, 40; opposition to Head, 1836, 174; oppositional petitioning 1831, 63–8, 71–82; petitioning, late 1820s, 51, 60; petitioning 1832, 105–6; petitioning re: constitution, 1828, 47; and political unions, 145, 157; post-electoral political organization 1836, 184; Rebellion of 1837 and its aftermath, 189–93, 205; re-elections, 85, 98, 103–4, 156, 158, 275n93; renames *Colonial Advocate*, 155; response to expulsion, 90–3; return from exile, 1849, 127; role in election of 1834, 157–8, 161; trip to Britain, 1832, 136
MacNab, Alan, attempt to expel Mackenzie from Assembly 1831, 58; Durham meetings, 199, 211; petitioning 1831, 73–4; petitioning, 1832, 117, 135; and Rebellion Losses Bill, 219; Rebellion of 1837 and after, 190
Maitland, Lieutenant-Governor Sir Peregrine, 33, 39, 43, 47
Mariatown, Dundas county, 1831 petitioning meeting, 79–80
Matthews, Peter, 191
McDonell, Bishop Alexander, 8, 118–19, 138, 181, 222
McIntosh, John, 51, 101, 158
McLean, Archibald, 79–81, 170
Merrickville, Grenville county, 1831 petitioning meeting, 79; 1836 reform meeting, 175
Merritt, William Hamilton, 30, 196, 199–200, 231
Metcalfe, Sir Charles, 219
Methodists, alleged sexual transgressions of, 128; alliance with oppositionists, 46, 61, 96, 118, 150, 228; breach with reform, 155; election of 1836, 181; numbers of, 45; petitioning in 1833, 153; saddle-bag faction, 12, 126, 128, 150. as threat to established order, 19, 128–9. *See also* Sir John Colborne, Egerton Ryerson, John Willson
Middlesex Political Union, 147–8
Montgomery, John, 146
Morrison, Thomas D., 49, 51, 67, 101, 158, 170, 174, 189, 196
Mountain, Bishop, 45

newspapers, violence against, 152. *See also* Types Riot
Niagara district, Durham meeting, 197; public meetings, 1807, 26; and Robert Gourlay, 27, 30, 32, 34–5
Norton, Hiram, 77–9

O'Grady, William John, 118, 171, 210
opposition, intolerance of, 12–14, 88, 192, 285n64
oppositionist petition, 1831, 66–7; transmission of to Britain, 82–3

oppositionist petitioning, 1831, comments of Executive Council on, 70–1; organization of, 68, 73; origins of, 61–2; public support for, 68, 72; response of Assembly to, 89; significance of, 83–4. *See also* William Lyon Mackenzie
oppositionist petitioning, 1832, leadership and organization, 108; meetings, 1832, appendix A; public support, 112–14; resolutions, 109–110; signatures on petitions, 1832, appendix B. *See also* York
oppositionists, *see* Central Committee, country-party ideology, disloyalty, Durham meetings, Methodists, popular constitutionalism, freedom of assembly, freedom of the press, freedom of representation, loyalty, oppositionist petitions, oppositionist petitioning, party labels, patronage; W. W. Baldwin, Robert Gourlay, Francis Hincks, Jesse Ketchum, William Lyon Mackenzie, Robert Randal
Orange Order, history, 75; and Durham meetings, 211; and political violence, 13, 130–4, 149–52, 186–7; response to Durham's Report, 216–7; role in election of 1836, 181–3; in Union period, 230, 232. *See also* political violence, John Brown, Colonel John Covert, Ogle Gowan
Ottawa, *see* Bytown

party labels, 12, 92, 141–2, 226–7
party system, 11–12, 142, 231
paternalism, ideology of government supporters, 8–9, 76, 125–6, 141, 177, 222; resistance to, 98, 184, 226
patronage, Sir Francis Bond Head's view, 171; as an oppositionist/reform grievance, 17, 29, 172, 205. *See also* Family Compact
Perry, Peter, 108, 162, 230–1
petitioning, history, 21, 62. *See also* Alien Bill, 1827, Durham meetings government supporters (petitioning), Loyalists, oppositionist petitions, oppositionist petitioning, reform petitioning, tory petitioning, Robert Gourlay, William Lyon Mackenzie
polarization, political, 20, 192, 220, 227
political culture, province-wide, 19, 140, 223, 226
political movement, defined, 1
political parties, Upper Canadian origins, 18–20, 83, 227, 231; weakness, 1–11, 142
political unions, British, 144; definition, 245n1; in 1837, 145, 183–5; William Lyon Mackenzie's view of, 145, 157. *See also* British Constitutional Society, Middlesex Political Union, Toronto Political Union, Upper Canada Central Political Union
political violence, attitude of Francis Bond Head to, 174, 182; attitude of government supporters to, 106–7, 187; in Britain, 130; contribution to 1837 Rebellion, 187–8; decline in, 232; disruption of meetings, 105, 129–36, 147–50, 174, 186, 211–15; effects on oppositionists, 151–4; oppositionist/reform attitude to, 101, 106, 147, 150, 187, 200–2; tory attitude to in Union period, 232–3. *See also* assaults, effigies, electoral violence, Orange Order, riots, tories
popular constitutionalism, 91, 141, 206–7, 219–20, 222
popular politics, defined, 4–5; British, 16, 17, 45, 94. *See also* assaults, effigies, newspapers (violence against), Orange Order, processions, political violence
population of Upper Canada, 9
Port Hope, political meetings 1833, 151; and resistance to Alien Bill, 1827, 41
Powell, William Dummer, 26
Prescott, Gourlayite meeting 1818, 32
Price, James Hervey, 170
processions, 94–6, 98–100, 150, 152, 173, 198–9, 201
public opinion, 15–16, 62, 223–4
public sphere, and ceremonial functions, 12; oppositionists enlarge, 14, 100, 225; and petitioning meetings, 1831, 69, 72; and publication of proceedings of Assembly, 58; and Sir Francis Bond Head, 172; in Union period, 233

Randal, Robert, 40, 42
Rebellion Losses Bill, 1849, 218–19, 232
Rebellion of 1837, 189–93, 225
reformers, *see* Canadian Alliance Society, Central Committee, City of Toronto Political Union, Constitutional Committee

of York, Constitutional Reform Society of Upper Canada, country-party ideology, disloyalty, Durham meetings, freedom of assembly, freedom of representation, freedom of the press, loyalty, Methodism, popular constitutionalism, oppositionist petitioning, oppositionist petitions, party labels, patronage, reform petitions and addresses, responsible government; W. W. Baldwin, Francis Hincks, Jesse Ketchum, William Lyon Mackenzie
reform petitions and addresses, 1833, 153–4; 1836, 169, 175–6. *See also* Durham meetings, oppositionist petitions, oppositionist petitioning
religion, destabilizing force, 228–9
responsible government, and the Baldwins, 49; British government's view of, 1839, 218; at Durham meetings, 203–4, 219; and Durham's Report, 194; history, 251n85; and John Rolph, 50; and Marshall Spring Bidwell, 50; in oppositionist/reform addresses, petitions and resolutions, 67, 133, 170, 185, 216; provincial officials' view of, 217; reform address supporting, 1836, 172, 175, 185; as reform slogan in 1840s, 230; Sir Francis Bond Head's view of, 171; Sir George Arthur's view of, 208
Richmond Hill Durham meeting, 212–14
riots, 201, 211–13, 232–3. *See also* Farmersville, political violence, Types Riot
Robinson, John Beverley, effigy of, 43; and the Family Compact, 8; leadership in Assembly, 10, 60; and pro-government petitioning, 1832, 117; and Robert Gourlay, 32–3; view of Lord Durham's Report, 194
Rolph, John, 49, 58–9, 169, 189
Roman Catholic Church, alliance with government/tories of, 18, 118–20, 138, 228, 230. *See also* Bishop Alexander McDonell
Russell, Lord John, 184, 195, 215, 218
Ruttan, Henry, 132, 145, 176, 201
Ryerson, Egerton, criticisms of, 90, 128; effigy of, 134; and petitioning in 1833, 153; petitions against clergy reserves and sectarian university, 46, 52; repudiates alliance with reform, 1833, 155; response to Lieutenant-Governor Colborne's attack on Methodists, 97; ridiculed, 209. *See also* Methodists
Ryerson, George, 46, 59

Sales and Improvement Acts 1827, 45
Samson, James Hunter, 87, 117
Santa Cruz, Stormont county, 1831 petitioning meeting, 80
Scottish immigrants, 9
Secret Societies Act, 1843, 232
Sedition Act, 1804, 12, 34–5
Seditious Meetings Act, 1818, 13, 35
Sherwood, Henry, 124
Simcoe Durham meeting, 198, 201
Small, James, 170, 180
Smith, Samuel, 28, 32
Society for Constitutional Information, 22
Stanton, Robert, 48, 179
Strachan, Archdeacon John, attitude to political violence, 107, 222; conflict with voluntarists, 37, 45–6; and the Family Compact, 8; criticism of Methodists, 45; role in pro-government petitioning, 1832, 117; and Robert Gourlay, 32, 34–5

Talbot, Colonel Thomas, 8, 115, 117, 125, 148
Thomson, Governor-General Charles Poulett, 10, 215
Thorburn, David, 200, 204
Thorold Durham meeting, 195, 197–8, 200–1, 203, 205
Thorpe, Robert, 24–7, 92
Thorpe-Willcocks group, 23–7; petitioning, 26; attitude of British authorities towards, 27. *See also* John Mills Jackson, Robert Thorpe, William Weekes, Joseph Willcocks, and Charles Burton Wyatt
tories, abuse of reformers, 144–5; constitutional meeting, 1836, 172–3; criticized at Durham meetings, 205–7; electoral organization, 1834, 161–2; meetings, 1836, 172–3; response to Durham meetings, 207–18; view of reformers in 1833–34, 162–3. *See also* British Constitutional Society, electoral organization, electoral violence, Family Compact, government supporters, Orange Order, political violence, Roman Catholic Church, tory petitioning, 1836; Ogle

Gowan, Alan MacNab, John Beverley Robinson
Toronto, tory meetings, April 1836, 172–3. *See also* York.
Toronto Political Union, City of, 1836, 183–4
tory petitioning, 1836, demands, 178; signatures, appendix D; support, 176–7
tory petitioning against Rebellion Losses Bill, 219
Types Riot, 1826, 37, 56, 91, 124, 152

Union Bill, 1822, 37
United Empire Association, 232
United States, attitudes towards, 16
Upper Canada Central Political Union, 146, 153
Upper Canadian Convention of Friends to Enquiry, 33

Vankoughnet, Philip, opponent of Mackenzie, 79–81; opponent of Robert Gourlay, 32
Vaughan, reform meeting 1837, 186
Viger, Denis-Benjamin, 65
voluntarists, 44–5, 230

Weekes, William, 24
Whitby, and oppositionist petition of 1831, 69; reform meeting, 1836, 175
Wilkes, John, 22, 91
Willcocks, Joseph, 24–7, 86
Williams, J.T. 134, 151
Williamstown, Glengarry county, 1831 petitioning meeting, 81
Willis, John Walpole, 47–9, 92
Willson, John, and expulsion of Mackenzie, 1831, 87–8; opponent of Methodists, 45; petitioning 1831, 73–4; petitioning, 1832, 117, 135
Woodruff, William, 108, 196, 200
Wyatt, Charles Burton, 24
Wyvill, Christopher, 22

York (county), meetings for Robert Thorpe, 26; oppositionist petitioning meetings, 68–71
York (town), demonstration, December 1831, 94–6; demonstration, January 1832, 98–100; Gourlay convention, 33; oppositionist meeting, March 1832, 105–6; oppositionist petitioning meeting, 1831, 65; pro-government meetings, 1832, 118–22; public meeting, January 1832, 101–4; reform meeting, March 1836, 170; reform meeting April 1836, 174. *See also* Toronto
York Bible Society, 254n143